A FACTS ON FILE PUBLICATION

CZECHOSLOVAKIA:
Crisis in
World Communism

INTERIM
HISTORY

The Bridge Between Today's News and Tomorrow's History

CZECHOSLOVAKIA:
Crisis in
World Communism

INTERIM
HISTORY

CZECHOSLOVAKIA:

Crisis in

World Communism

Edited and introduced by Vojtech Mastny

Assistant Professor of History

Columbia University (New York)

FACTS ON FILE, INC.   NEW YORK

CZECHOSLOVAKIA:
Crisis in
World Communism

Copyright, 1972, by Facts on File, Inc.

Library of Congress Catalog Card Number: 70-166437

ISBN 0-87196-195-4

9 8 7 6 5 4 3 2 1

PRINTED IN THE UNITED STATES OF AMERICA

CONTENTS

Page

i

1969   179

INTRODUCTION

THE 1968 EVENTS IN CZECHOSLOVAKIA brought to a climax what may have been the most serious internal crisis in the Communist world since World War II. For the first time in history a ruling Communist party was challenged from within by reformers who questioned the very basis of its power. They attacked the authoritarian form of government considered as the model since the Soviet Union had established its domination of the international Communist movement in the early 1920s. The Czechoslovak Communists proposed an alternative that, although purported to implement the orginal tenets of Marxism, in fact incorporated some essential features of Western democracy. The proposed fusion of Marxist ideology, one-party rule, constitutional guarantees of political dissent and a state-operated but decentralized economy had never been attempted before. The presence of such apparently contradictory elements in the Czechoslovak model cast doubts on its political viability. Yet the experiment failed—before it could prove itself—not because of inner contradictions but because of foreign intervention.

The reform movement was the product of the Czech and Slovak national traditions of the past hundred years and of the specific situation in Czechoslovakia in the 1960s. The Czechs had a stronger democratic tradition than other peoples of east central Europe. Their active participation in parliamentary government dated back to the advent of Austrian constitutionalism in the 1860s. In the period between the 2 world wars, when all countries of the area gradually resorted to authoritarianism, Czechoslovakia survived longest as a parliamentary democracy.

1

Although tolerant and representative by the standards of the region, Czechoslovak democracy differed from that of most Western nations. It was more a government by consent than by participation. Its characteristic feature was the overwhelming prestige and power of the president, whose judgment was seldom questioned. Active popular participation in politics was limited, especially on the local level, where state bureaucracy and the party cliques played the decisive role.

The honesty and relative efficiency of the civil service were decisive factors in safeguarding the stability of the system, in which many political conflicts were reduced to merely administrative ones. Czechoslovakia's main problem was the lack of harmony among the different nationalities that inhabited the state. Since none of them was decisively superior in power, no severe repression could exist. Yet the preeminent position of the Czechs, who controlled the central government, fomented discontent among the other nationalities, particularly the Germans and the Slovaks, and this discontent was exploited by Nazi Germany. In 1938-9, Czechoslovakia fell victim to internal subversion and international crisis provoked by Berlin.

The occupation of the Czech parts of the country by Germany was accompanied by widespread disillusionment with democracy. The Nazis introduced a totalitarian system controlled by them but operated largely by Czech officials. Although outraged at the policies of Germanization and the police terror, the majority of the population became accustomed to regimentation in public life, particularly in the economy, and even favored its continuation in a Socialist form after the war. Intimidation combined with selective material inducement apparently generated in the occupied country feelings of impotence and acquiescence that presumably accounted for the comparatively limited resistance until the very end of the war.

In Slovakia, where the democratic traditions had always been weaker than in the Czech lands, the nominally independent pro-German authoritarian regime was initially popular because of its appeal to Slovak national pride. Its increased subservience to Berlin, however, promoted dissatisfaction during the war. The resistance movement in Slovakia was stronger than in the Czech lands, and although its attempt to liberate the country with its own forces in 1944 was unsuccessful, the Slovaks emerged from the war with increased self-confidence.

The wartime experience significantly influenced the outlook of the Communists. The Czech Communist underground was plagued by factional strife, treason and intrigue, which frustrated self-assertion. In contrast, the Slovak Communists shared in the triumph, albeit temporary, of the liberation movement in 1944, which they achieved without foreign support. After the war, tensions arose between them and the exiles returning from the Soviet Union, who were trained in subservience to Moscow and who claimed key positions in the reconstituted party.

After its liberation, Czechoslovakia was governed by a coalition of Communists, Socialists and left-wing liberals. It was neither a totalitarian nor a democratic regime. Conservative political expression was barred. Extreme nationalism, which assigned the highest priority to revenge against the Germans, seemed to absorb the political energies of the people and to hamper democratization. Lawlessness and violence, condoned by the Communists and tolerated by their coalition partners, brought new elements into Czechoslovak politics.

Czechoslovakia's voluntary subordination to Soviet leadership in foreign policy determined the country's fate once the lines of the Cold War began to harden. In order to consolidate control over its sphere of influence, the USSR backed the seizure of power by the Czechoslovak Communists in Feb. 1948. Unlike developments in other countries of eastern Europe, the establishment of the Communist regime occurred in a situation of widespread popular indifference.

Stalinism, though repressive in all countries of the eastern bloc, assumed what critics described as particularly outrageous features in Czechoslovakia. The country, culturally oriented to the West but geographically on the outskirts of the bloc, was considered particularly vulnerable to Western influences. Soviet "advisers" exaggerated and distorted these factors' influence, thus justifying intensive application of the Soviet model to counter them. The forcible collectivization of agriculture was both more rapid and more thorough in Czechoslovakia than in other countries of eastern Europe.

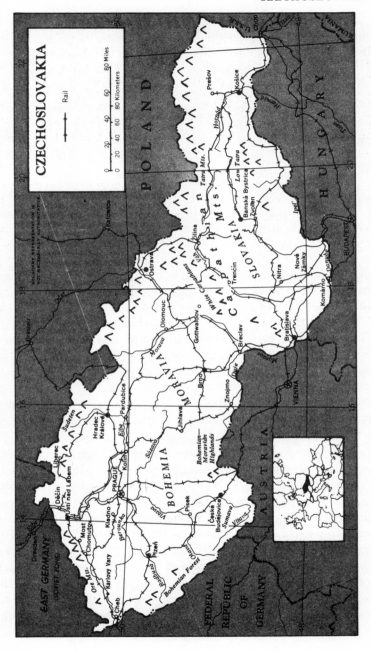

The traditional Russophilism of the Czechs, along with the considerable following of the Communist Party, prevented the growth of strong opposition. As a result, the repressive machinery was lacking in targets, and its operation, therefore, was aimed mostly at imaginary enemies. The victims were more often than not as devoted Communists as their persecutors. In Czechoslovakia, the irrationality and corruption inherent in the purges were greater than elsewhere in the Soviet bloc. Their impact on the ruling elite was therefore especially deep and demoralizing.

The regime, though unpopular, managed to secure out-wardly loyal cooperation on the part of the people. The country's considerable resources facilitated economic growth, which, despite what many considered as excessive emphasis on producer goods and despite Soviet economic exploitation, made possible at least modest improvements in the standard of living. There were setbacks, particularly the drastic currency reform in 1953 that wiped out most private savings and touched off one of the first outbreaks of rioting in eastern Europe after the death of Stalin. But on the whole, the relative prosperity in Czechoslovakia prevented such disruptions as those that upset East Germany in 1953 and Poland and Hungary in 1956. Spared the extremes of exaggerated hopes and their subsequent frustration, the population remained acquiescent. Under the leadership of Antonin Novotny, the regime curtailed Stalinist excesses in practice without, however, repudiating them in principle.

The growth of nationalism in eastern Europe in the 1960s apparently forced the Soviet Union to tolerate greater diversity among its satellites. The Novotny regime, however, was slow to adapt itself politically and economically to the specific con-ditions and traditions of Czechoslovakia. For a long time it ranked with East Germany as the most rigidly pro-Soviet regime in east central Europe. Later in the decade, manage-ment criticized as incompetent led to economic stagnation and increasingly discredited the government. The discontent of the population merged with malaise among the party elite, uncertain about both its ability to rule and the moral legitimacy of its power.

The process of political change was prompted by the revolt of intellectuals—the most privileged stratum in Czechoslovak society. Endowed with the privileges of status without its responsibilities, they were particularly well equipped to criticize the shortcomings of the regime. Their attack began at the Writers' Congress held in Prague in June 1967.

The Novotny clique responded by an attempt to discipline the writers and establish control over their most outspoken journal, the weekly *Literarni noviny*. Without sufficient backing within the party bureaucracy, however, the attempt failed—thus further undermining Novotny's position. Slovak spokesmen in the central committee exploited the situation, criticized what they viewed as excessive Czech predominance of the party and urged a greater Slovak role in the country. In Dec. 1967 the stage was set for decisive changes after the Soviet leaders pledged noninterference in the rapidly accelerating internal struggle in Czechoslovakia.

This book describes Czechoslovakia's experiment in liberalizing communism, the destruction of the experiment by the USSR and the other Warsaw Treaty powers and the events that followed. Much of the material appeared in one form or another in FACTS ON FILE. Supplementary matter came from U.S. government records and from sources in Czechoslovakia and other east European countries.

1968

Moscow's refusal to back Antonin Novotny as head of the Czechoslovak Communist Party led to his replacement at the party's helm by a Slovak, Alexander Dubcek, who became party secretary Jan. 5. Gen. Ludvik Svoboda replaced Novotny as president Mar. 30.

The official revelations of the Stalinist scandals and the abuses of the Novotny era discredited the Communist Party. But the extent of its self-criticism, promoted by intellectuals devoted to the "humanization" of Marxism, convinced the majority of the people that the new leadership wanted radical reforms. The proposals for change were embodied in a new party program published Apr. 9.

Leaders of the Soviet bloc met in Dresden Mar. 23 and issued a statement warning Czechoslovakia to proceed cautiously. (Rumania was the only bloc country not represented.) Dubcek's resistance to the Moscow-instigated efforts to slow down the democratization process earned him immense popularity. The proposed reforms were widely understood as a departure from communism—in substance, if not in theory. Such an impression was reinforced by the abolition of censorship June 26 and the drafts of laws and party statutes that would have guaranteed the right of dissent, thus breaking the ideological and power monopoly of the ruling oligarchy. The movement accelerated after Czechoslovakia's leading intellectuals June 26 issued a "2000-words" manifesto warning against a relapse into authoritarianism.

In July, the party's Central Committee rejected another critical statement, issued by the Soviet bloc leaders in Warsaw. The Dubcek regime, upholding its right to shape domestic policies without outside interference, received diplomatic support from Tito's Yugoslavia and Nicolae Ceausescu's Rumania. The leadership held firm in confrontations with the

Soviet and other Warsaw Pact representatives that took place at the end of July and in early August at Cierna and Bratislava.

During the confrontations, the Soviet Politburo apparently became convinced that the new Czechoslovak regime was unable or unwilling to control the democratization trend, which had acquired a momentum of its own. Moscow's decision to intervene by military force was a result of several factors: concern about the adverse effects of the Czechoslovak developments on the Soviet power position in Europe; fears that the Czechoslovak example might encourage anti-Soviet nationalism in other parts of eastern Europe, notably in the Ukraine; and irritation at the new ideological model that the Czechoslovak ideologists were propagating with missionary zeal.

The invasion late Aug. 20 by the armed forces of 5 Warsaw Pact powers—the Soviet Union, Poland, East Germany, Hungary and Bulgaria—encountered almost unanimous hostility on the part of the Czechoslovak population. The widespread nonviolent resistance did not prevent the invading forces from achieving their military objectives, but it forestalled the installation of a collaborationist regime that, it was evident, Moscow had planned to impose.

Despite appearances of officially sponsored resistance, the invasion had caught the Czechoslovak officials by surprise. Unwilling to admit that their country's interest was in conflict with that of the USSR, they had ruled out any appeal to the people and the armed forces that might have deterred invasion; and once the intervention came, it was too late for such actions. There was no coordination between the leaders who met at the clandestine party congress in a Prague factory and those, led by Pres. Svoboda, who consented to negotiate in Moscow. The negotiators, including Dubcek, failed to persuade the Soviets to leave the country. But the Soviet Union at least refrained from further repressive measures except for the restoration of censorship. Systematic repression, short of military rule, was hampered by the disintegration of the Czechoslovak Communist party apparatus.

Soviety Deputy Foreign Min. Vasily Kuznetsov pressed the Dubcek government to accelerate "normalization" as the alleged precondition for the withdrawal of the forces of the "Warsaw 5." Despite opposition within the party and the *resentment registered overwhelmingly against the occupiers by public opinion, the government consented to legitimize the presence of the foreign troops in a treaty agreed to Oct. 4 in Moscow.*

Popular dissatisfaction culminated in demonstrations in late October and early November. The attempts to proceed with the April reform program were frustrated by firm Soviet opposition. Against the background of mounting popular discontent, the Czechoslovak leaders met secretly with their Soviet counterparts in Kiev Dec. 7-8. Soviet demands for more stringent measures against dissent and for a purge of the reformers were linked with economic assistance that tied Czechoslovakia closer to the Soviet Union.

ADVENT OF REFORM

Novotny Ousted, Dubcek Heads Party

Alexander Dubcek, 46, was elected Jan. 5 to succeed Antonin Novotny as first secretary of the Czechoslovak Communist Party. (Novotny retained his other post as Czechoslovakia's president.) Dubcek had been first secretary of the Slovak Communist Party.

The change appeared to be the culmination of a long-rumored power struggle that was said to have developed between 2 rival factions—one reportedly led by Dubcek and composed mostly of Slovaks—within the Czechoslovak party's 10-member presidium.

The Czechoslovak party Central Committee, announcing that it had accepted Novotny's "request ... to be relieved of his position as first secretary," praised Novotny for "achievements ... accomplished in a complicated and exacting period as head of the party."

According to unofficial reports from Prague, the elevation of Dubcek, the first Slovak to fill the highest party (and most powerful) post in the country, followed growing demands by both conservative and moderate factions within and outside the party for a change in basic policies on the economy and the relationship between Czechs and Slovaks. Mounting opposition had centered on Novotny, who had been first secretary since 1953. Among complaints building up against him for years, those most often mentioned were his: (1) retention of the old Stalinist bureaucracy; (2) failure to rehabilitate fully the victims of the purges of the 1950s; (3) negative attitude toward the 4½ million Slovaks and their demand for a fairer deal; (4) failure to give full backing to the country's economic reform measures; (5) alienation of the intellectuals, especially after the stormy session of the writers' congress in June 1967.

(In his annual New Year's address Jan. 1, Novotny had asserted that "over-all development of the republic must not overshadow the important task of development of Slovakia, which does not yet equal the level of the ... [Czech] lands." In an apparent reference to artistic freedom, he said that everything "progressive," including ideas from the Western countries, would be allowed to enter Czechoslovakia.)

The Soviet Communist Party Central Committee sent "hearty congratulations" to Dubcek on the occasion of his election as first secretary.

It was disclosed Jan. 5 that these 4 new members had been elected to the Presidium: Jan Piller, deputy minister for heavy industry; Josef Spacek, secretary of the South Moravian regional party committee; Emil Rigo, a gypsy and chairman of the party works committee of the East Slovak foundries in Kosice; Josef Boruvka, chairman of the agricultural cooperative in Dolany.

Alexander Dubcek had become a leading figure behind the growing Slovak opposition to the Czech dominance in postwar years. He was born in Uhrovec, West Slovakia, Nov. 27, 1921 to working class parents with Communist leanings. After a stay in the U.S. before, during and after World War I, his father, Stefan, returned to Czechoslovakia, and, in 1925, the whole family left for the Soviet Union. While there, young Dubcek worked as a smith and an engine fitter. In 1938 the family returned to Czechoslovakia, and, a year later, young Dubcek joined the Czechoslovak Communist Party. In 1944, he joined a group of Slovak partisans operating in the Tatra mountains as part of the Slovak National Uprising against Nazi occupation. Dubcek was wounded twice in encounters with the Germans, and his brother Julius was killed Jan. 1, 1945. He began his slow rise in the party hierarchy in 1949, when he became secretary of the Trencin district party committee in West Slovakia. In 1953 Dubcek became secretary of the regional committee in Banska Bystrica, Central Slovakia. He was sent to Moscow in 1955 to study at the political college of the Soviet Communist Party Central Committee, from which he was graduated in 1958. In 1962 he became a member of the Presidium of the Czechoslovak Communist Party Central Committee as well as that of its Slovak wing. A major point of disagreement between Dubcek and Novotny was Dubcek's insistence that the Slovak National Uprising in 1944 had been "progressive" and instrumental in paving the way for the 1948 *coup d'etat* in Prague that established Communist rule in Czechoslovakia.

Novotny's teetering power stance was further undermined at the beginning of March when it was disclosed in Prague that Maj. Gen. Jan Sejna had fled the country Feb. 25 and requested permanent residence in the U.S. The U.S. State Department confirmed Mar. 6 that Sejna, accompanied by his son, Jan, 18, and Evzenia Musilova, the son's fiancee, had received visitors' visas from the U.S. embassy in Rome.

Sejna, who had been a member of the Czechoslovak general staff, the National Assembly and a party secretary in the Defense Ministry, was subsequently accused in the press of plotting to prevent Novotny's dismissal as Communist Party first secretary. (He was also wanted in connection with the alleged embezzlement of $20,000 worth of state-owned alfalfa and clover seed.) Sejna's deputy, Col. Jaroslav Moravec, had been arrested Jan. 21 in connection with the alleged plot. It was reported on Czechoslovak TV Mar. 14 that Col. Gen. Vladimir Janko, a deputy defense minister, had committed suicide while being driven to face a commission inquiry into the alleged plot and Sejna's defection. Rumors also circulated in Prague that other high officials, including Novotny himself and Defense Min. Bohumir Lomsky, had been involved in the conspiracy.

Novotny was forced to resign Mar. 22 as president of Czechoslovakia, his last post, which under the Communists was largely a ceremonial one. Some of his duties were transferred temporarily to Premier Jozef Lenart. Novotny's immediate resignation had been recommended unanimously at a committee meeting of the National Assembly Mar. 21. The Presidium (executive of the Communist Party Central Committee) was the first (Mar. 20) to suggest this course.

In his letter to the assembly's presidium, Novotny said he was resigning "after careful consideration, proceeding from the present situation in this country." The new leadership, announcing Novotny's resignation, in a communique issued by the party Presidium, warned that tendencies threatening the regime "in the guise of democracy" would not be tolerated. It also expressed continuing friendship with the Soviet Union.

Novotny's departure was viewed as marking the end of a 20-year period of Stalinism, resistance to economic reform, tight control over writers and other intellectuals, 2d-class status for the Slovaks and uncritical devotion to the Soviet Union. Novotny's ouster followed mounting popular pressure against him throughout the country. There were demands, supported by news media just freed from effective censorship, for a revival of the country's democratic traditions by a new generation of Communists, intellectuals and students and a basic reevaluation of the country's political and economic direction.

Demands for the increasing democratization of life and economic reform were believed to have been led by Dubcek. Speaking at a conference in Brno Mar. 16, Dubcek had promised the "widest possible democratization" for the country. In addition, he had promised that the new leadership would present its political and economic "action program" at the full meeting of the Central Committee, scheduled for Mar. 28. Dubcek, stressing that there would be "cadre changes" in the party to "bring in new people who can carry out the new policies," pledged greater autonomy (from the party) for the government, the courts, the trade unions and economic enterprises. Referring to foreign policy, he reaffirmed the continuation of "progressive tradition of cooperation" with the Soviet Union but hinted that with greater independence the country would be in a better position "to express its own standpoint" and play a greater role "in the center of Europe . . . as an industrialized nation."

(It had been disclosed in Prague Mar. 5 that Jiri Hendrych had been dismissed from his post as party secretary for ideological affairs. He was replaced by Josef Spacek of Brno, who had been appointed to the party Presidium after Dubcek became the Czechoslovak party first secretary Jan. 5. A close friend of Novotny's, Hendrych was regarded as a firm opponent of liberal ideas advocated by a growing number of the country's intellectuals. The decision to replace Hendrych was made at the Mar. 4 meeting of the new 15-member party Presidium, which also recommended the transfer of censorship officials from the Interior Ministry to the Culture Ministry and the denial to the censors of their customary authority to direct the ideological line of the news media.)

The party cell in the Central Publications (censorship) Board Mar. 15 (a) urged an end to the policy of secrecy, (b) asked for the abolition of "preventive [prepublication] censorship . . . at the present rate of development" and (c) recommended that censorship practices be standardized and the right of appeal be upheld and investigated.

The party Presidium announced Mar. 22 a rehabilitation
program involving about 30,000 victims of Stalinism. (The
news agency CTK reported that Novotny's last act as president
had been the granting of a pardon to Jan Benes, an author who
had been sentenced in July 1967 to 5 years in prison for
"subversion of the republic.")

At a press conference in Prague Mar. 22, Alois Polednak,
director of the state TV, confirmed that the decisive factor in
Novotny's downfall had been growing criticism (for the
failures of the previous 15 years) leveled at him at district and
factory meetings of the party activists around the country.
Polednak, who was also a member of the presidium of the
National Assembly, disclosed that a commission had been set up
to investigate the political trials, in which Novotny was said to
have played a leading part.

Informed sources in Prague said Mar. 22 that Soviet
Premier Aleksei N. Kosygin had promised that the Soviet
Union would not interfere with the ouster of Novotny. The
pledge had been made in Moscow to visiting Czechoslovak
Deputy Premier Oldrich Cernik. Cernik had been accompanied
by Maj. Gen. Egid Pepich, party secretary for political affairs
in the Defense Ministry. The Czechoslovak officials reportedly
pledged to Kosygin that the current wave of liberalization
would not prejudice continued military, political and economic
cooperation between the 2 countries.

(Novotny's son, also named Antonin, 37, was dismissed
from his job as director of a state-owned exporting agency. He
had been widely accused by the press of enriching himself by
abusing his relationship to the president. He was reported Mar.
18 to have been prevented from leaving the country on a
planned trip to West Germany.)

Svoboda Elected President

Gen. Ludvik Svoboda, 72, was elected president of
Czechoslovakia Mar. 30 by a secret vote of the National
Assembly. He had been selected by the party Central
Committee to succeed Antonin Novotny. Out of the total vote
of 288, there were 282 votes for Svoboda, and 6 ballots were
returned unmarked. The choice of Svoboda was regarded as a
necessary compromise in the face of pressures from the Soviet

Union and other Communist countries of eastern Europe, which had been following the Czechoslovak developments with growing concern.

After the oath-taking ceremony—attended by church officials for the first time in 20 years—Svoboda declared that Czechoslovakia would develop "friendly cooperation" with "states of different social systems." But he also stressed that "the Czechoslovak Republic will continue to be loyal to its alliances, which united it with the Soviet Union and other countries." (It was reported that during the ceremonies students staged a sit-in demonstration on behalf of their candidate, Dr. Cestmir Cisar, a secretary of the Central Committee.)

Svoboda, long a prominent national figure, was brought back from obscurity, to which he had been relegated by the pre-Dubcek leadership. The son of a farming family, he was born in Moravia Nov. 25, 1895. A soldier in the Austro-Hungarian army during World War I, Svoboda had deserted to the Russian side and had joined the Czechoslovak Legion. After returning from the Soviet Union in 1920, he became a lecturer at a military academy. He was the commander of an infantry company in 1936, then of a battalion during the 1938 Munich crisis. Following Czechoslovakia's occupation by Germany in Mar. 1939, he went to Poland to organize the Czechoslovak unit there. After Poland's defeat, Svoboda led his unit into the USSR, where he fought on the Ukrainian front in 1943. Svoboda returned to his native country with the advancing Red Army and helped build up the Czechoslovak army as defense minister. (His son, Mirek, 17, was captured and tortured to death by the Germans during the occupation.) He was a deputy premier until 1951, when he fell out of grace during the Stalinist purges. He was imprisoned, then allowed to work on a collective farm until 1962, when the visiting Nikita S. Khrushchev (then Soviet premier) helped his rehabilitation. Svoboda retired as head of Klement Gottwald Military Academy in 1959. Among his 50 medals were the St. George Cross (Tsarist Russia), the Order of Lenin and Hero of the Soviet Union (USSR) and the Legion of Merit (U.S.).

Cernik Heads New Cabinet

A new cabinet was formed Apr. 8. Premier Jozef Lenart
had announced the resignation of his cabinet Apr. 6. Pres.
Svoboda asked Oldrich Cernik, a deputy premier in the old
cabinet, to head a new government. Cernik presented his
cabinet to the National Assembly Apr. 8. The new government
retained 8 members of the previous cabinet.

Among the major cabinet appointments: Gen. Josef Pavel,
one of the victims of the Stalinist purges in the 1950s, became
interior minister to succeed Josef Kudrna, dismissed in mid-
March; Dr. Jiri Hajek, a former university lecturer and ex-
ambassador to Britain, replaced Vaclav David as foreign
minister; Miroslav Galuska, ex-ambassador to Great Britain,
journalist and movie writer, was named culture and informaton
minister; Prof. Ota Sik, economist responsible for the planning
of economic reform became one of the 5 deputy premiers; Lt.
Gen. Martin Dzur, a deputy defense minister in the outgoing
cabinet, become defense minister.

(Gen. Bohumir Lomsky, former defense minister and
deputy commander of the Warsaw Treaty military forces,
resigned his post during a plenary meeting of the Central
Committee Apr. 3. A loyal supporter of Novotny, Lomsky had
been subjected to growing criticism over the defection to the
U.S. of Gen. Sejna and the subsequent suicide of Col. Gen.
Vladimir Janko.)

The new cabinet (asterisk denotes old member): *Premier* —
Oldrich Cernik*. *Deputy Premiers* —Peter Colotka, Frantisek
Hamouz*, Gustav Husak, Ota Sik, Lubomir Strougal.
Agriculture —Josef Boruvka. *Defense* —Lt. Gen. Martin Dzur.
Culture & Information —Miroslav Galuska. *Foreign Affairs* —
Jiri Hajek*. *Forestry* —Julius Hanus. *Education* —Vladimir
Kadlec. *Heavy Industry* —Josef Krejci*. *Justice* —Bohuslav
Kucera. *Consumer Goods* —Bozena Machacova-Dostalova*.
Interior —Josef Pavel. *Internal Trade* —Oldrich Pavlovsky.
Mining —Frantisek Penc*. *Chemicals* —Stanislav Razl.
Transport —Frantisek Rehak. *Finance* —Bohumil Sucharda*.
Construction —Josef Trokan. *Foreign Trade* —Vaclav Vales*.
Planning —Frantisek Vlasak*. *Health* —Vladislav Vlcek.
Ministers without Portfolio —Vaclav Hula and Michal Stancel.

(Cernik had been born Oct. 27, 1926 in Ostrava, North Moravia, where he worked from 1937 to 1949 as a mechanic at what became the Klement Gottwald Vitkovice Ironworks. Since 1949 he had held a succession of posts in the apparatus of the North Moravian regional party committee and had served as chairman of the North Moravian regional national committee, the area's legislature, from 1954 to 1956. He became a secretary of the Czechoslovak party Central Committee in 1956, a Central Committee member in 1958 and, in 1960, Czechoslovak minister of fuel and power. He took over as chairman of the State Planning Commission and became a vice premier in 1963.)

The Central Committee Apr. 4 had announced major changes in the make-up of the party Presidium, whose membership was reduced from 14 to 11. Among the changes:

Ex-Forestry Min. Josef Smrkovsky was elected to the Presidium as chairman of the National Assembly. The Central Committee also named a new party secretariat to deal with the day-to-day affairs of the country. Dr. Frantisek Kriegel, a reputedly loyal follower of Dubcek, replaced Novotny in his last post as chairman of the National Front, an organization comprising all political parties. Earlier Novotny had been dropped from the Presidium. Members of the new Presidium: Frantisek Barbirek, Vasil Bilak, Alexander Dubcek, Drahomir Kolder, Frantisek Kriegel, Jan Piller, Emil Rigo, Josef Smrkovsky, Josef Spacek and Oldrich Svestka.

Alternate Presidium members: Antonin Kapek, Jozef Lenart and Martin Vaculik.

Others loyal to Novotny also lost their public posts. Miroslav Pastyrik, Bedrich Kozelka and Vaclav Pasek— respectively chairman and secretaries of the Czechoslovak trade union—resigned their posts Mar. 12. It was reported Mar. 14 that the Slovak National Council (parliament) had dismissed Michal Chudik, premier of Slovakia. The National Assembly reportedly rejected his resignation as it "did not contain a single word of self-criticism." Chudik, regarded as a close friend of Novotny's, was among the "old guard" party members who had been urged to resign or face dismissal to avoid placing the regime in danger. The Czechoslovak National Assembly Mar. 15 dismissed Dr. Jan Bartuska as prosecutor general.

Warsaw Pact Leaders Alarmed

Leaders of most east European Communist nations held a reportedly hastily convened summit meeting Mar. 23 in Dresden, where Dubcek was called on to explain the changes taking place in Czechoslovakia since Novotny's ouster from power.

Participating in the conference were East German Socialist Unity (Communist) Party First Secy. Walter Ulbricht, Polish United Workers' (Communist) Party First Secy. Wladyslaw Gomulka, Soviet Communist Party Gen. Secy. Leonid I. Brezhnev and Premier Aleksei N. Kosygin and Hungarian Socialist Workers' (Communist) Party First Secy. Janos Kadar. The Bulgarian Communist Party was represented by Stanko Todorov, member of its politburo and a secretary of its Central Committee. Rumania was not represented at the meeting, apparently because of its proclaimed policy of non-interference in the affairs of other Communist parties.

In a communique issued at the end of the conference Mar. 23, the parties' representatives expressed "confidence ... that the proletariat and all working people of Czechoslovakia, under the leadership of the Communist Party, ... would insure further progress of Socialist construction in the country." (This and other passages of the communique were not mentioned by the Czechoslovak press and TV. The omission was seen by observers as an attempt to avoid protest against the Dresden talks.)

Czechoslovak sources indicated Mar. 23 that the conference had been called by East Germany and Poland in an effort to forestall closer ties between Czechoslovakia and West Germany and to exert pressure on Dubcek to suppress demands for greater liberalization. Sources from other Communist countries said that the conferees also discussed the extension of a large credit to Czechoslovakia in an effort to discourage it from turning to West Germany.

In an interview with CTK, the official Czechoslovak news agency, Dubcek confirmed Mar. 26 that "certain worries were expressed at the meeting, mainly to the effect that anti-Socialist elements would take advantage of the democratization process." Dubcek gave the interview after 134 party writers and artists had written to the party Presidium about their concern over pressure put on Czechoslovaka by its Communist allies. The letter's signers held that "the communique of the Dresden meeting gave the impression that if we paid heed to other countries it could influence our own development."

Pravda, the official Soviet party newspaper, denied Mar. 28 what it termed Western reports that at the Dresden conference, the USSR and the other Communist countries had tried to restrain Czechoslovakia's reform program.

In an unusual development among countries of Communist eastern Europe, the Czechoslovak government Mar. 27 protested formally to East Germany over the latter's alleged interference in Czechoslovakia's internal affairs. The protest was against quasi-official East German criticism of Czechoslovak developments. The criticism was voiced by Prof. Kurt Hager, chairman of the East German party Presidium's ideological commission, at the congress of Marxist philosophers in East Berlin Mar. 25. Hager charged that events in Czechoslovakia were "in accord with West Germany's alleged policy of trying to 'isolate Czechoslovakia' from East Germany." (Hager reinforced his criticism Mar. 26 with a speech in which he attacked, by name, the then Czechoslovak Forestry Min. Josef Smrkovsky for publicly supporting democratization.)

Commenting on the charge made by Hager, *Rude pravo,* official newspaper of the Czechoslovak party, declared in a Mar. 27 editorial that there was no reason why the 2 countries should have the same foreign policy toward West Germany. The paper also complained that the Soviet Union and other Communist countries failed to give adequate coverage of Czechoslovak events to their readers. The paper assailed this treatment as "one of the old bad habits" of Communist countries.

(It had been reported from West Berlin Mar. 23 that several Czechoslovak newspapers had been confiscated in East Berlin by East German authorities and that Prague students visiting East Berlin had been prevented from participating in discussions with East German youth organizations.)

Further grounds for friction between the 2 Communist countries were provided by Czechoslovak Premier Oldrich Cernik when he declared in a speech to the National Assembly in Prague Apr. 24 that Czechoslovakia would recognize the "existing realities" of a divided Germany. "We are basing our policy on the fact of the existence of 2 German states," Cernik asserted. (*Lidova democracie,* organ of Czechoslovakia's newly revitalized [Catholic] People's Party, said Apr. 24: "The time is ripe to start with Bonn on a resumption of diplomatic relations"; "East Germany must understand that we have to follow our own interest.")

Although Cernik reaffirmed Czechoslovakia's intention to remain a Warsaw Pact member, Czechoslovak Deputy Foreign Min. Vaclav Pleskot told the UN Economic Commission for Europe in Geneva Apr. 24: "We think the objective conditions have developed to a stage when the liquidation of military blocs is becoming a historical necessity."

MOVEMENT GAINS MOMENTUM

Reform Program

The Czechoslovak Communist Party Apr. 9 published its long-awaited "action program" as a basis for reforming communism in Czechoslovakia. The program had been adopted Apr. 5, after it had been debated and amended for a week by the Central Committee. A resolution accompanying the document described the program's purpose as to purify communism of its "former aberrations" and to "build socialism in this country in a way corresponding to our conditions and traditions."

In the 60-page document, entitled "Czechoslovakia's Road to Socialism," the party pledged: (a) new guarantees of freedom of speech, press, assembly and religious observance; (b) electoral laws to provide a broader choice of candidates, greater freedom for the 4 non-Communist parties within the National Front; (c) upgrading of the parliament and the government with regard to the power of the Communist Party apparatus; (d) broad economic reforms to give enterprises greater independence, to achieve a convertible currency, to revive a limited amount of private enterprise and to increase trade with Western countries; (e) an independent judiciary; (f) federal status for Slovakia on an independent basis and a new constitution to be drafted by the end of 1969.

The document said:

> ... at the end of the 50s our society entered another stage of development. On this fact was gradually formed the political line which we want to apply in a creative way and to develop. Characteristic of the present stage are [the facts that]:

> ● antagonistic classes no longer exist and the main feature of internal development is becoming the process of bringing all socialist groupings in society closer together;

- methods of direction and organization hitherto used in the national economy are outdated and urgently demand changes, *i.e.*, an economic system of management able to enforce a turn towards intensive growth;
- it will be necessary to prepare the country for joining in the scientific-technical revolution in the world, which calls for especially intensive cooperation of [industrial] workers, [craftsmen] and agricultural workers with the technical and specialized intelligentsia, and which will place high demands upon the knowledge and qualifications of people, on the application of science;
- a broad scope for social initiative, frank exchange of views and democratization of the whole social and political system becomes virtually the condition for the dynamics of Socialist society—the condition for us being able to hold our own in competition with the world, and to honorably fulfil our obligations towards the international workers' movement.

We stand resolutely on the side of progress, democracy and socialism in the struggle of the Socialist and democratic forces against the aggressive attempts of world imperialism. It is from this point of view that we determine our attitude to the most acute international problems of the present, and our share in the worldwide struggle against the forces of imperialist reaction.

The basic orientation of Czechoslovak foreign policy was born and verified at the time of the struggle for national liberation and in the process of the Socialist reconstruction of this country—*it is in alliance and cooperation with the Soviet Union and the other Socialist states. We shall strive for friendly relations with our allies—the countries of the world Socialist community—to continue, on the basis of mutual respect, to intensify sovereignty and equality, and international solidarity.* In this sense we shall contribute more actively and with a more elaborated concept to the joint activities of the Council of Mutual Economic Assistance [or COMECON] and the Warsaw Treaty.

A full development of the international role of Socialist Czechoslovakia is inseparable from the education of citizens in the spirit of internationalism, which comprises both the grasping of common interests and aims of the world progressive forces and understanding of specific national needs. This is linked with the necessity of making prompt and detailed information on international problems and the course of our foreign policy available to the public and thus creating conditions for an active participation of Czechoslovak citizens in the shaping of foreign political attitudes.

The Communist Party of Czechoslovakia will be more active in the sphere of the international Communist and workers' movement. *We shall put special emphasis on friendly ties, mutual consultations and exchange of experiences with the Communist Party of the Soviet Union, with the Communist and workers' parties of the Socialist community, with all the other fraternal Communist parties.*

The Communist Party of Czechoslovakia will continue taking an active part in the struggle for the unity of the international communist movement, for strengthening the active cooperation of communist parties with all the progressive forces while regarding a resolute struggle against the aggressive policy of American imperialism as the most important task. The Communist Party of Czechoslovakia will take full advantage of its specific possibilities of establishing contacts with the Socialist, peaceful and democratic forces in the capitalist and developing countries. It will contribute to expanding the forms of cooperation and coordinating the work of Communist parties while attaching great importance to international party consultative meetings. From this point of view it welcomes and supports the results of the Consultative Meeting of Communists & Workers Parties [Feb. 26-Mar.5] in Budapest. With dozens of fraternal parties the Communist Party of Czechoslovakia supports the proposal for convening an international Communist consultative meeting in Moscow late in 1968.

We are not changing our fundamental orientation; in the spirit of our traditions and former decisions we want to develop to the utmost in this country an advanced Socialist society rid of class antagonisms, economically, technologically and culturally highly advanced, socially and nationally just, democratically organized, with a qualified management, by the wealth of its resources, [and] giving the possibility of dignified human life, comradely relations of mutual cooperation among people and free scope for the development of the human personality. We want to start building up a new intensely democratic model of a Socialist society, which would fully correspond to Czechoslovak conditions. But our own experiences and Marxist scientific cognition lead us jointly to the conclusion that these aims cannot be achieved along the old paths while using means which have long been obsolete and harsh methods, which are always dragging us back. We declare with full responsibility that our society has entered a difficult period when we can no longer rely on traditional schemes. We cannot squeeze life into patterns, no matter how well-intended. It is now also up to us to make our way through unknown conditions, to experiment, to give the Socialist development a new look, while leaning upon creative Marxist thinking and the experiences of the international workers' movement, relying on the true understanding of the conditions of the Socialist development of Czechoslovakia as a country which assumes responsibility to the international Communist movement for improving and taking advantage of the relatively advanced material base, unusually high standards of education and culture of the people and undeniable democratic traditions ... [for] the benefit of socialism and communism. No one could forgive us were we to waste this chance, were we to give up our opportunities.

We are not taking the outlined measures to make any concessions from our ideals—let alone to our opponents. On the contrary: we are convinced that they will help us to get rid of the burden which for years provided many advantages for the opponent by restricting, reducing and paralyzing the efficiency of the Socialist idea, the attractiveness of the Socialist example. We want to set new penetrating forces of Socialist life in motion in this country to give them the possibility of a much more efficient confrontation of the Social systems and world outlooks and allowing a fuller application of the advantages of socialism. . . .

The Central Committee also pledged a "full and just rehabilitation of all persons" who had been unjustly persecuted during 1949-54. The pledge held out "moral, personal and financial compensation" to persons affected by the rehabilitation. It asserted that "persons who took an active" part in the persecutions "must not hold any important posts in the social and political life of our society." The Central Committee postponed the scheduled May 19 elections until the fall to allow the adoption of a new electoral law.

Premier Cernik presented his government's new program to the National Assembly Apr. 24. His presentation dealt principally with Czechoslovakia's ailing economy. (Cernik had been selected by the party Presidium Apr. 6 to carry out the "action program" accepted by the Central Committee Apr.5.)

In a 3-hour speech, Cernik admitted the existence of a "number of conflicting trends in the economy that can no longer be overcome by traditional means." He attributed current economic problems to a lack of incentives and competitive spirit, a legacy of the period generally associated with the Novotny leadership.

Cernik cited shortcomings in Czechoslovakia's industry, which was "incapable of meeting the requirements of foreign trade and industrial consumption." He disclosed that Czechoslovakia had a $400 million annual trade deficit with the West and that Czechoslovakia's *per capita* income was 30% to 40% below that of the "advanced capitalistic countries." Cernik forecast that, in implementing the long-stalled economic reforms, the country would close unprofitable factories, abolish subsidies in certain sectors of the economy and even suffer temporary unemployment. The new program called for a total of 35 billion crowns (some $48.6 million at the official exchange rate) in expenditures for housing, education, health and transport, a 55% increase over 1963; investment in heavy industry, power output and mining was expected to drop by 10% below 1963.

Cernik pledged that his government would "give all political parties, social groupings and citizens without party affiliation the possibility to participate in government work." As a first step he promised the appointment of deputy ministers from among non-Communist parties "according to the new principles." Among the newly functioning non-Communist parties, which had been rapidly gaining new members, mostly from among the young, were the Socialist Party, (Catholic) People's Party and Freedom Party. He promised "full equality" for "citizens with religious convictions" and for national minorities in the creation of a "Socialist federation" of Czechs and Slovaks.

Cernik asserted that the alliance with the Soviet Union and the other Socialist countries would remain "one of those permanent and firm values that have been fully confirmed also by the critical verification of all values of our present process of revival." But he added: "We are basing our foreign policy on the fact of the existence of 2 German states. The prerequisite for the normalization of political relations is the recognition of these existing realities."

(Observers noted that despite repeated assurances of continued friendship from Czechoslovakia's new leaders, the USSR was growing increasingly apprehensive about the prospect of the resumption of diplomatic relations between Prague and Bonn. During the assembly session Marshal Ivan Yakubovsky, commander of the Warsaw Treaty Organization, consulted with Czechoslovak leaders in Prague.)

Speaking in his capacity as a deputy from Slovakia, Communist Party First Secy. Dubcek declared before the assembly Apr. 24 that he was "prepared for a wave of criticism." But, he added, "we cannot go back and we cannot go halfway." He warned that "moving along unexplored paths ... requires caution and courage."

End of Censorship

In a statement unprecedented in a Communist country, the members of the party organization in the state censorship board Mar. 14 condemned the practice of their agency.

According to the official *Ceskoslovenska tiskova kancelar* (CTK) press agency: "The Communist Party members on the board are deeply distressed that Interior Min. Josef Kudrna [who was dismissed the next day by the National Assembly], Chairman of the Publication Board Eduard Kovarik and his deputy, Jan Kovar, have not yet responded to the public criticism of censorship. During a reappraisal of the practical activities of censorship in Czechoslovakia we have come to the conclusion that preventive political censorship should be abolished." Jiri Hendrych, secretary of the Communist Party Central Committee, was responsible for the existence of censorship in Czechoslovakia. "By his political directives, decisions and public statements, he has led us astray on several occasions. Such was especially the case of judging [the Writers' Union weekly] *Literarni noviny.* The Central Publication Board and the office which preceded it—the Main Board of Press Supervision—which were established entirely without any legal basis in 1953 by a mere government decree, were headed by senior security officials who ran the boards by a system of order." This created an impossible atmosphere even for the censors.

The official relaxation of most restrictions on what could be printed or broadcast produced a spate of frank airings of old unanswered questions. One question dealt with the fate of ex-Foreign Min. Jan Masaryk. After 20 years of official silence surrounding Masaryk's death, a press campaign was initiated to reopen the case and clear up the mystery. Masaryk's body had been found in the courtyard of the Foreign Ministry in Prague Mar. 10, 1948, and he was pronounced a suicide. The foreign minister and his father, Thomas Garrigue Masaryk, the country's first president, had been revered as national heroes prior to the Communist takeover in 1948.

The demand for an investigation was initiated by the philosopher Ivan Svitak, whose letter in *Student Today,* the National Student Organization weekly, hinted Apr. 2 that Masaryk might have been the victim of a plot hatched by a Czechoslovak liaison officer with the Soviet secret police. The open letter charged that Masaryk had been "murdered as the first victim on the road to totalitarian dictatorship."

The state prosecutor's office announced Apr. 3 that an investigation had already begun and that the results would be made public.

In support of the accusation of murder, Svitak had cited eyewitness reports by Foreign Ministry employes, who had testified that there was evidence of foul play in Masaryk's death. These witnesses said they had been jailed because of their presence at the scene. It was also reported that evidence had been found implicating Maj. Franz Schramm, a former liaison officer between the Czechoslovak and Soviet security services.

Schramm was murdered in 1948. The Party newspaper *Rude pravo,* reporting the evidence Apr. 16, charged that Masaryk had been eliminated for political reasons. The charge heightened the tension already existing in relations with the USSR.

Tass, the official Soviet press agency, countered May 7 that the investigation into the Masaryk affair was designed to "stir up anti-Soviet moods among politically unstable people and to sow distrust between the 2 states." *Sovetskaya Rossiya,* published by the Central Committee of the Russian Communist Party denounced the elder Masaryk May 14 as an "absolute scoundrel" for allegedly helping to finance an anti-Bolshevik plot to murder Lenin in 1918. The Czechoslovak press promptly and unanimously condemned the accusation as "an insult without parallel."

(The Czechoslovak press Apr. 2 had reported the suicide of Dr. Josef Brestansky, 42, who had been in charge of investigation into the country's Stalinist past. Brestansky, deputy chairman of the Supreme Court, was found hanged in the woods 25 miles south of Prague. The Socialist party newspaper *Svobodne Slovo* had suggested after he disappeared from his office Mar. 28 that he might have been "eliminated because he knew too much—possibly by agents of another country." Brestansky had recently been accused of unfairly imposing severe 6 to 17-year sentences on the managers of a Bratislava chemical plant in 1955.

(Bedrich Pokorny, a former major in the Czechoslovak security police who had been involved in the 1948 investigation of Masaryk's death, was found dead in a forest near Brno Apr. 19. Although his death was termed by Czechoslovak police as suicide, some newspapers speculated that he was murdered for his role in the 1948 investigation.)

The government June 26 passed a law abolishing prepublication censorship. Availing themselves of the opportunity of free expression, leading Czechoslovak intellectuals issued an outspoken demand for the safeguarding of the newly won freedoms. The manifesto, entitled "2,000 Words to Workers, Farmers, Scientists, Artists and Everyone" and composed by Ludvik Vaculik, appeared in *Literarni listy* June 27. It read:

The life of our nation was first threatened by the war. Then followed another bad time with events which threatened the nation's spiritual health and character. The majority of the nation hopefully accepted the program of socialism. Its direction got into the hands of the wrong people, however. It would not have mattered so much that they did not have sufficient experience as statesmen, practical knowledge, or philosophical education, if they had at least possessed more common sense and decency, if they had been able to listen to the opinion of others, and if they had allowed themselves to be gradually replaced by more capable people.

The Communist Party, which after the war possessed the great trust of the people, gradually exchanged this trust for offices, until it had all the offices and nothing else. We must put it this way; those Communists among us know it to be so, and their disappointment over the results is as great as the disappointment of the others. The leadership's incorrect line turned the party from a political party and ideological alliance into a power organization which became very attractive to egotists avid for rule, calculating cowards, and people with bad consciences. Their influx into the party affected its nature and its conduct. Its internal organization was such that honest people who could have magnified it to keep up with the modern world could not wield any influence without shameful accidents. Many Communists fought this decline, but they did not succeed in preventing what happened.

The situation in the Communist Party was the pattern and cause of a similar situation in the state. Because the party became linked with the state it lost the advantage of keeping its distance from executive power. There was no criticism of the activity of the state and economic organizations. Parliament forgot how to proceed; the government forgot how to rule and the directors how to direct. Elections had no significance and the laws lost their weight. We could not trust our representatives in any committee, and even if we did, we could not ask them to do anything because they could accomplish nothing. What was still worse was that we had almost lost our trust in one another. Personal and collective honor declined. Honesty led nowhere, and there was no appreciation for ability. Therefore, most people lost interest in public affairs; they were concerned only with themselves and with money. Moreover, as a result of these bad conditions now one cannot even rely on the money. Relations among people were spoiled, joy in one's work lost. To sum up, the country reached a point where its spiritual health and character were threatened.

We are all responsible for the present state of affairs, and the Communists among us are more responsible than others. The main responsibility, however, rests with those who were component parts or instruments of uncontrolled power. It was the power of a tenacious group spread, with the help of the party apparatus, everywhere from Prague to each district and community. The apparatus decided what one might or might not do; it directed the cooperatives for the cooperative members, the factories for the workers, and the national committees for the citizens. No organization actually belonged to its members, not even the Communist organization.

The main guilt and the greatest deception perpetrated by these rulers was that they presented their arbitrary rule as the will of the workers. If we were willing to believe this deception, we would now have to blame the workers for the decline of our economy, for the crimes against innocent people, for the introduction of censorship which made it impossible for all this to be written about. The workers were to blame for the mistaken investments, for the losses in trade, for the shortage of apartments. Naturally, no sensible person believes in such guilt on the part of the workers. We all know and, in particular, each worker knows that in practice the workers did not decide anything. It was someone else who controlled the workers' representatives' vote. While many workers thought that they ruled, the rule was executed in their name by a specially educated group of officials of the party and state apparatus. In effect, they took the place of the overthrown class and themselves became the new authority.

For the sake of justice, we must say that some of them long ago realized this bad game of history. We can recognize them now by the fact that they are redressing wrongs, correcting mistakes, returning decision-making power to the membership and the citizens, and limiting the authority and numbers of *apparatchiki*. They are with us against the obsolete views in the party membership. But many officials are still opposing change, and they still carry weight! They still hold instruments of power, especially in the districts and in the communities, where they may use these instruments secretly and unimpeachably.

From the beginning of the current year, we have been taking part in a revival process of democratization. That it began in the Communist Party must be acknowledged. Even people among us outside the party who until recently expected no good to come from us recognize this fact. We must add, however, that this process could not begin elsewhere. After a full 20 years, only the Communists could live something like a political life; only Communist criticism was in a position to see things as they really were; only the opposition within the Communist party had the privilege of being in contact with the enemy. The initiative and efforts of the democratic Communists therefore is only an installment in the repayment of the debt the entire party has incurred with the people outside the party, whom it kept in a position without equal rights. Therefore, no gratitude is due the Communist Party, although it should probably be acknowledged that it is honestly striving to use this last opportunity to save its own and the nation's honor.

The revival process is not contributing any very new things. It is producing ideas and suggestions many of which are older than the errors of our socialism and others of which emerged under the surface of visible events. They should have been expressed long ago; however, they were suppressed. Let us not cherish the illusion that these ideas are now victorious because they wield the force of truth. Their victory was decided rather by the weakness of the old leadership which, obviously, first had to be weakened by a rule of 20 years in which no one hampered it. Obviously, all the defective elements hidden in the very foundations and ideology of this system had to mature before they gained their full form.

Therefore, let us not overestimate the significance of criticism from the ranks of writers and students. The source of social change is the economy. The right word carries significance only if it is spoken under conditions which have already been duly prepared. By duly prepared conditions in our country, unfortunately, we must understand our general poverty and the complete disintegration of the old system of rule, in which politicians of a certain type calmly and peacefully compromised themselves at our expense. Thus, truth is not victorious; truth simply remains when everything else goes to pot! There is no cause for a national celebration of victory; there is merely cause for new hope.

We turn to you in this moment of hope, which, however, is still threatened. It took several months for many of us to believe that we could speak out, and many still do not yet believe it. Nevertheless, we *have* spoken out, and such a great number of things have been revealed that somehow we must complete our aim of humanizing this regime. Otherwise, the revenge of the old forces will be cruel. We turn mainly to those who have so far only waited.

The time which will be decisive for many years coming is summer, with its vacations and holidays, when, according to old habit, we will want to drop everything and relax. We can be certain, however, that our dear adversaries will not indulge in summer recreation, that they will mobilize all those who are obliged to them, and that even now they are trying to arrange for calm Christmas holidays! Let us be careful, therefore, of what happens; let us try to understand it and respond to it. Let us renounce the impossible demand that someone higher up must always give us the only possible interpretation of things, one simple conclusion. Each of us will have to be responsible for drawing his own conclusions. Commonly agreed-upon conclusions can be reached only by discussion, and this requires the freedom of expression which actually is our only democratic achievement of the current year.

In the coming days we will have to display our own personal initiative and determination.

Above all, we will oppose the view, should it arise, that it is possible to conduct some sort of democratic revival without the Communists or possibly against them. This would be both unjust and unreasonable. The Communists have well-structured organizations, and we should support the progressive wing within them. They have experienced officials and, last but not least, they also have in their hands the decisive levers and buttons. Their action program has been submitted to the public; it is a program for the initial adjustment of the greatest inequalities, and no one else has any similarly concrete program. We must demand that local action programs be submitted to the public in each district and each community. By doing so, we shall have suddenly taken very ordinary and long-expected correct steps. The Czechoslovak Communist Party is preparing for the congress which will elect a new Central Committee. Let us demand that it be better than the current one. If the Communist Party now says that in the future it wants to base its leading position on the citizens' confidence and not on force, let us believe it as long as we can believe in the people whom it is now sending as delegates to the district and regional conferences.

Fears have recently been expressed that the process of democratization has stopped. This feeling is partly a manifestation of fatigue caused by troubled times and is partly due to the fact that the season of surprising revelations, resignations from high places, and intoxicating speeches of unprecedented verbal boldness is past. However, the struggle of forces has merely become less evident to a certain extent. The fight is now being waged over the content and implementation of laws, over the scope of practical steps to be taken. In addition, we must give the new people, the ministers, prosecutors, chairmen, and secretaries time to work. They have the right to this time so that they can either prove their worth or lack of it. Apart from this, one cannot presently expect more of the central political organs. They have, after all, given spontaneous evidence of admirable virtues.

The practical quality of the future democracy depends on what becomes of the enterprises and what will happen in them. After all is said and done, it is the economists who control things. One must seek out good managers and see to it that they get good positions. It is true that, compared to the well-developed countries, we are all badly paid, and some are worse off than others.

We can demand more money—but although it can be printed, its value will diminish. Let us rather demand that directors and chairmen explain to us the nature and extent of expenditures they want for production, to whom they want to sell their products and at what price, the profit they can expect, the percentage of this profit to be invested in the modernization of production and the percentage to be divided up.

Under apparently boring headlines, a very hard struggle is going on in the press relating to democracy and graft. As contractors, workers can intervene in this struggle through the people whom they elect to enterprise administrations and councils. As employes, they can do what is best for themselves by electing as their representatives to trade union organs their natural leaders, capable and honest people, regardless of party affiliation.

If at this time we cannot expect more from the present central political organs, we must achieve more in the districts and communities. Let us demand the resignation of people who have misused their power, who have damaged public property, or who have acted dishonestly or brutally. We must find ways and means to induce them to resign, for instance, through public criticism, resolutions, demonstrations, demonstration work brigades, collection drives for gifts to them when they retire, strikes, and boycotts of their doors. However, we must reject methods which are illegitimate, improper, or coarse since they might use them to influence Alexander Dubcek.

We must so generally decry the writing of insulting letters that any letter of this kind which they may yet receive could be considered a letter they had sent to themselves. Let us revive the activity of the National Front. Let us demand public meetings of the national committees. To deal with questions which no one wants to know anything about let us set up special citizens' committees and commissions. It is simple: a few people convene, they elect a chairman, keep regular minutes, publish their finding, demand a solution, and do not let themselves be intimidated.

Let us turn the district and local press, which has degenerated to a mouthpiece of official views, into a platform of all the positive political forces. Let us demand the establishment of editorial councils composed of representatives of the National Front, or let us found newspapers. Let us establish committees for the defense of the freedom of expression. Let us organize our own monitoring service at meetings. If we hear strange news, let us check on it, let us send delegations to the people concerned, and nail their replies to the gates if need be. Let us support the security organs when they prosecute genuine criminal activity. We do not mean to cause anarchy and a state of general insecurity. Let us avoid disputes among neighbors. Let us renounce spitefulness in political affairs. Let us reveal informers.

The heavy vacation traffic throughout the republic will arouse interest in the constitutional arrangement of the Czechs and Slovaks. We consider the federation a method of solving the nationality question; aside from this, it is only one of the important measures aimed at democratizing conditions. This measure alone cannot by itself ensure better living conditions for the Slovaks. The problem of the regime—in the Czech regions and in Slovakia individually—is not solved by this. The rule of the party-state bureaucracy may still survive—in Slovakia even more so, because it has "won greater freedom."

The recent great apprehension results from the possibility that foreign forces may interfere with our internal development.

Faced with all these superior forces the only thing we can do is decently hold our own and not start anything. We can assure our government that we will back it—with weapons if necessary—as long as it does what we give it the mandate to do, and we can assure our allies that we will observe our alliance, friendship, and trade agreements. Excited reproaches and ungrounded suspicions must necessarily make the position of our government more difficult and cannot be of any help to us. At any rate, we can ensure equal relations only by improving our internal conditions and by carrying the process of revival so far that one day at elections we will elect statesmen who will have sufficient courage, honor, and political wisdom to establish and maintain such relations. This, by the way, is a problem of the governments of all small countries in the world.

This spring, as after the war, a great chance has been given us. Again we have the possibility of taking into our own hands a common cause, which has the working title of socialism, and giving it a shape which will better correspond to our once good reputation and the relatively good opinion we once had of ourselves. The spring has now ended and will never return. By winter we will know everything.

With this we conclude our statement to the workers, farmers, officials, artists, scholars, scientists, technicians—everybody. It was written at the suggestion of the scholars and scientists.

The following signatures are not a complete collection of all those who agree with us. It is merely a selection from various groups of the populace and includes only those whom we were able to reach at home: National Artist Beno Blachut, member of the National Theater Opera in Prague; Doctor of Medicine and Science Jan Brod, professor and director of the Prague Institute for Blood Circulation Diseases; Marie Buzkova, sow breeder in Chotebuz; Academician Bohumil Bydzovsky, mathematician; Associate

Professor Dr. Jiri Cvekl, philosopher; Vera Caslavska, Olympic champion; Zdenek Cechrak, CKD worker; Zdenek Fiala, CKD technician; Milan Hanus, CKD worker; Engineer Jiri Hanzelka, writer; Doctor of Medicine Miroslav Holub, scientific worker of the Microbiological Institute of the Czechoslovak Academy of Science; Zdenek Holec, CKD worker; Rudolf Hrusinsky, actor and director; Dusan Hruza, CKD worker; Jan Chocena, private farmer in Chotebuz; Jaromil Jires, film director; Doctor of Medicine and Science Vilo Jurkovic, Professor and Chief of the Second Internal Polyclinic of the Medical Faculty of Charles University in Hradec Kralove; Doctor of Medicine and Science Vera Kadlecova, chief of the Ophthalmic Clinic of the Faculty Hospital of Charles University in Prague; Associate Professor A. Knop of the Pedagogical Institute in Ostrava; Karel Kosik, philosopher; Academician Jaromir Koutek, geologist; Otomar Krejca, director; Doctor of Medicine and Science Jiri Kral, professor and chief of the Prague Institute for Sports Medicine; Engineer and Candidate of Science Miroslav Kral of the Higher Political School of the Czechoslovak Communist Party Central Committee; Karel Krautgartner, conductor of the Czechoslovak Radio Dance Orchestra; Doctor of Medicine and Science Vladislav Kruta, professor and chief of the Physiological Institute of J. E. Purkyne University in Brno; Academician Vilem Laufberger, chief of the Laboratory for Graphic Research Methods in Prague; Doctor of Medicine Pavel Lukl, professor, chief of the Internal Clinic of Palacky University of Olomouc, chairman of the Cardiological Society and vice president of the European Cardiological Society; Zuzana Marysova, Chotebuz state farm; Jiri Menzel, director.

Vladmir Mostecky, CKD technician; Josef Neversil, CKD worker; Jaroslav Nemec, CKD worker; Doctor of Law Bozena Patkova, lawyer in Prague; Engineer Emil Petyrek, corresponding member of the Czechoslovak Academy of Science and director of the Mining Institute of the Czechoslovak Academy of Science; Professor and Doctor of Medicine and Science Otakar Poupa, corresponding member and chief of the third department of the Physiological Institute of the Czechoslovak Academy of Science in Prague; Doctor of Medicine and Science Jaroslav Prochazka, professor and chief of the Surgical Clinic of the Faculty Hospital in Hradec Kralove; Yvonna Prenosilova, singer; National Artist Alfred Radok, stage manager; Emil Radok, film producer; Jiri Raska, Olympic champion; National Artist Jaroslav Seifert; Doctor of Medicine B. Sekla, Professor and chief of the Biological Institute of Charles University in Prague; Academician and Doctor of Medicine and Science Zdenek Servit, director of the Physiological Institute of the Czechoslovak Academy of Science in Prague; Associate Professor Engineer Jiri Slama, Candidate of Science, Economic Research Institute of Industry and Building in Prague; Doctor of Medicine and Science Oldrich Stary, corresponding member of the Czechoslovak Academy of Science, professor and rector of Charles University in Prague; Jiri Snizek, CKD technician; Jiri Suchy, poet; Doctor of Medicine Vojmir Sevcik, associate professor and traumatologist in the North Moravian region, Ostrava; Dr. Jiri Slitr, composer.

Karel Silha, CKD worker; Vaclav Sroub, CKD worker; Jan Svankmajer, film director; Marie Tomasova, actress; Doctor of Philosophy and Science Ladislav Tondl, professor in the Department of Scientific Theory and Methodology of the Czechoslovak Academy of Science in Prague; Josef Topol, writer; National Artist Jiri Trnka, director and cartoonist; Jan Triska, actor; Ludvik Vaculik, journalist—the author of this text; Karel Vojir, CKD worker; Doctor of Medicine and Science Jan Vanysek, professor and vice rector of Purkyne University in Brno; Associate Professor and Doctor of Medicine Jiri Veleminsky, regional internist of the North Moravian Region, Ostrava; Doctor of Medicine and Science V. Vejdovsky, professor and chief of the Ophthalmic Clinic of Palacky University in Olomouc; Viktor Voros, CKD worker; Academician Otto Vichterle, director of the Institute for Macromolecular Chemistry of the Czechoslovak Academy of Science in Prague; National Artist Jaroslav Vojta, member of the National Theater; National Artist Jan Werich; Colonel Emil Zatopek, Olympic champion; Dana Zatopkova, Olympic champion; and Engineer Jindrich Zogata, agronomist in Chotebuz.

USSR Increases Pressure

The independent French daily *Le Monde* May 4 quoted Gen. Aleksei Yepishev, head of the political administration of the Soviet army, as saying in Moscow Apr. 23 that if "a group of faithful Communists" in Czechoslovakia appealed for help, the Soviet army was "ready to do its duty."

Dubcek had paid a hurried visit to Moscow May 3-5 in order to allay Soviet fears at his liberalization program and to obtain a $500 million long-term loan to bolster his country's economy. Dubcek was accompanied by Premier Cernik, National Assembly Pres. Smrkovsky and Slovak Communist Party First Secy. Vasil Bilak. A joint statement issued May 5 described the secret talks as "frank and friendly" and added that "opinions were exchanged." Such phrases were usually used in the Soviet press to signify sharp disagreements. Prior to the talks, unconfirmed reports indicated that the USSR had suspended wheat shipments to Czechoslovakia during the first quarter of 1968.

Czechoslovak Foreign Min. Jiri Hajek visited Moscow May 6 for talks with Soviet Foreign Min. Andrei Gromyko. It was Hajek's first visit to Moscow since his appointment to the cabinet.

Reports by Western military attaches stationed in Warsaw that Soviet troops had been identified May 8 as they moved west in the direction of Czechoslovakia had prompted alarmed speculations both in Czechoslovakia and in the West that a possible Soviet intervention was under way. The suspicion of an anti-Czechoslovak action was further corroborated following the barring of Western diplomats from southern Poland the same day and by the sudden arrival in Moscow May 8 of the leaders of East Germany, Poland, Hungary and Bulgaria. Commenting on the reports, Prague radio May 8 made this dramatic plea against outside interference: "For God's sake, let us not repeat the tragic experience of Yugoslavia or even the Budapest events [of 1956].... We know what we want and where we are going." The Polish government said May 15 that Warsaw Pact maneuvers, involving Polish and "Soviet forces," had taken place in regions bordering on Czechoslovakia.

It was reported in Bonn May 20 that Soviet troop shifts had taken place in East Germany, southern Poland and in the Carpathian military districts of the USSR. It was reported at the same time, however, that Hungarian CP First Secy. Janos Kadar had refused to participate in the maneuvers.

Unconfirmed reports from Prague indicated that the Warsaw Pact exercises had been decided on following the visit to Prague May 17-25 of a high-level Soviet government and military delegation headed by Premier Aleksei N. Kosygin and Defense Min. Andrei A. Grechko. Among the topics discussed by Grechko and Czechoslovak military officials was a Soviet request that Czechoslovakia allow the stationing of some 10,000 Soviet troops in Western Bohemia, near the West German border. Unofficial Czechoslovak sources said that, while the Soviet demand on troop stationing had been rejected, the Czechoslovak leaders had agreed to the advancing of the Warsaw Pact maneuvers to early June. It was reported in Prague May 19, that during Kosygin's discussions with Dubcek, an estimated 10,000 students staged an anti-Soviet rally in the city. Kosygin reportedly cut short his planned 10-day visit to Prague and returned to Moscow 3 days early.

Reports of considerable alarm in Czechoslovakia reached the West during July as Soviet troops, involving armored units, still remained in the country weeks after the Warsaw Pact maneuvers ended. Forces of the 6 active member states in the

Warsaw Treaty Organization had held joint military exercises in Czechoslovakia June 20-30. The Soviet troops, whose number was variously estimated at 6,000 to 24,000 remained in Czechoslovakia despite (a) a June 30 announcement by the Czechoslovak defense minister, Gen. Martin Dzur, that all foreign soldiers would leave the country 3 days after the war games ended and (b) repeated Soviet declarations thereafter that the troops would be removed by various deadlines.

The "final" deadline of July 20 passed with Soviet troops still there. The last Soviet troops involved in the June maneuvers did not leave Czechoslovakia until Aug. 3.

A July 11 article in *Pravda,* the Soviet party organ, had drawn what was regarded by many observers as an ominous parallel between the activities of "counterrevolutionaries" in Czechoslovakia and those in Hungary during 1956. The parallel was widely interpreted by extension as signifying a possible military intervention to halt the Czechoslovak experiment. Referring to anti-Communist elements surfacing in the uncensored Czechoslovak press, the *Pravda* article said: "There is nothing novel in these tactics. Indeed, the counter-revolutionary elements in Hungary employed similar tactics when trying to hamstring the Hungarian people's Socialist gains in 1956."

CONFRONTATION WITH MOSCOW

Warsaw Warning

The Soviet Union and its 4 more loyal east European allies—Bulgaria, East Germany, Hungary and Poland—warned Czechoslovakia July 16 that the Czechoslovak reform policy was "completely unacceptable." They demanded that Prague end the policy—reportedly within 15 days. The USSR and its 4 allies charged that liberal elements were endangering socialism in the country.

The warning was contained in a 3,000-word "common letter," addressed to the Czechoslovak party Central Committee and drafted at the conclusion of a hastily convoked 2-day summit conference held in Warsaw July 14-15. The meeting was attended by top party and government delegations from the 5 militant Warsaw Pact countries. Czechoslovakia, the focus of attention at the meeting, declined to participate. The Rumanian Communist Party also stayed away because of its previously proclaimed policy of nonintervention in the affairs of other fraternal parties.

A communique issued at the conclusion of the meeting stated that the 5 powers had "paid particular attention to the aggressive imperialist forces" in Czechoslovakia. A phrase noting that the participants had "exchanged information ... on the development of events in Czechoslovakia" was viewed as indicating differences of opinion during the discussions.

Although the Czechoslovak party, after an agitated session in the Presidium July 8, had decided not to attend the conference, it declared its willingness to hold bilateral talks with individual parties. The rejection of the invitation to Warsaw was reported in Prague to have been phoned July 8 to Soviet party Gen. Secy. Leonid I. Brezhnev by First Secy. Dubcek, who charged that the summons was an attempt to interfere in his country's internal affairs. Prague was reported to have transmitted similar rejections to the other 4 signatories of the letter. The Czechoslovak Presidium's rejection received widespread popular approval in Czechoslovakia and was believed to have strengthened the progressive faction within the leadership.

Among those attending the Warsaw conference were: Brezhnev, Soviet Premier Kosygin and Pres. Nikolai N. Podgorny; East German Party First Secy. Walter Ulbricht and Premier Willy Stoph; Hungarian Party First Secy. Janos Kadar and Premier Jeno Fock; Bulgarian party First Secy.- and-Premier Todor Zhivkov and Stanko Todorov, a Politburo member; Polish Party First Secy. Wladyslaw Gomulka and Premier Jozef Cyrankiewicz.

The letter declared that the 5 powers "do not want to interfere in ... [Czechoslovak] affairs or infringe your sovereignty," but it warned that certain forces in Czechoslovakia had "tried to take the country out of the Socialist camp." In particular, the letter singled out the "2,000 Words" manifesto, signed by 70 Czechoslovak intellectuals and supported by signatures of some 40,000 people across the country. The manifesto was denounced in the letter as a call for anarchy and counterrevolution. The letter charged that certain Czechoslovak Communist Party leaders not only failed to fight the manifesto but went so far as to defend it. The letter asserted that such manifestations were a threat to the vital interests of the whole Socialist community and that, therefore, it was "something more than only your concern." It also noted that there were within Czechoslovakia "healthy forces" capable of defending "the Socialist system and inflicting defeat on the anti-Socialist elements."

Excerpts from the joint letter:

... The development of events in your country evokes deep anxiety in us. It is our deep conviction that the offensive of the reactionary forces, backed by imperialism, against your party ... threatens to push your country off the road of socialism and that consequently it jeopardizes the interest of the entire Socialist system....

We neither had nor have any intention to interfere in [affairs that] ... are strictly the internal business of your party and your state, to violate the principles of respect, independence and equality in the relations among the Communist parties and Socialist countries....

At the same time we cannot agree to have hostile forces push your country from the road of socialism and create a threat of severing Czechoslovakia from the Socialist community. This is something more than only your concern. It is the common concern of all the Communist and workers' parties and states united by alliance, cooperation and friendship....

You are aware of the understanding with which the fraternal parties treated the January plenary meeting of the Central Committee of the Communist Party of Czechoslovakia, as they believed that your party ... would direct the entire process in the interest of socialism and not let anti-Communist reaction exploit it to grind its own axe. We shared the conviction that you would protect the Leninist principle of democratic centralism as the apple of your eye. For the flouting of any aspect of this principle, democracy or centralism, inevitably serves to weaken the party and its leading role by transforming the party into either a bureaucratic organization or debating club. We ... received from you assurances that you are aware of the dangers and are fully resolved to repulse them.

Unfortunately events have taken another course.

Capitalizing on the weakening of the party leadership, ... the forces of reaction triggered a campaign ... clearly to abolish the party's leading role, subvert the Socialist system and place Czechoslovakia in opposition to the other Socialist countries.

The political organizations and clubs that have emerged of late outside the framework of the National Front have become, in effect, headquarters of reaction.... Anti-Socialist and revisionist forces have laid hand on the press, radio and television, making of them a rostrum for attacking the Communist Party ... and undermining the friendly relations between the Czechoslovak Socialist Republic and the other Socialist countries. Some mass communications media are carrying on a systematic campaign of real oral terror against people opposing the forces of reaction or voicing anxiety over the trend of developments.

Despite the decisions of the May [29-June 1] Plenary meeting of the Central Committee of the Communist Party of Czechoslovakia, which indicated the threat emanating from rightwing and anti-Communist forces as the main danger, the increasing attacks that reaction has mounted have not met with any rebuff. This is precisely why reaction has been able to publicly address the entire country and to print its political platform, under the title of '2,000 Words,' which contains an outright call for struggle against the Communist Party and constitutional authority, for strikes and disorders. In essence, this statement is the organizational and political platform of counterrevolution....

The situation has thus arisen which is absolutely unacceptable for a Socialist country....

Don't you, comrades, see these dangers? Is it possible under such conditions to remain passive, to limit oneself to mere declarations and assurances of loyalty to the cause of socialism and allied observations? Don't you see that counterrevolution is wresting from you one position after another, that the party is losing control over the course of events and is further retreating under the pressure of anti-Communist forces?

Is it not for the purpose of sowing distrust and enmity towards the Soviet Union and other Socialist countries that the press, radio and television of your country unleashed a campaign in connection with the staff exercises of the armed forces of the Warsaw Treaty?...

The joint staff exercises of our troops with the participation of several units of the Soviet Army, customary for military cooperation, are being used for groundless accusations of violating the sovereignty of the Czechoslovak Socialist Republic. . . .

It is our conviction that a situation has arisen in which the threat to foundations of socialism in Czechoslovakia jeopardizes the common vital interest of other Socialist countries. . . .

Each of our parties is responsible not only to its working class and its people, but also to the international working class, the world Communist movement, and cannot evade the obligations following from this. . . .

That is why we believe that the decisive rebuff to the anti-Communist forces and the decisive efforts for the preservation of the Socialist system in Czechoslovakia are not only your but also our task.

The cause of defending the power of the working class and all working people, [the sake] of the Socialist gains in Czechoslovakia demands[:] a decisive and bold offensive against the rightwing and anti-Socialist forces; mobilization of all means of defense created by the Socialist state; the stopping of the activity of all political organizations coming out against socialism; the mastery by the party of the means of mass information—press, radio, television—and the use of them in the interest of the working class, all working people and socialism. . . .

We are aware that forces exist in Czechoslovakia that are capable of defending the Socialist system and inflicting defeat on the anti-Socialist elements. . . .

We express the conviction that the Communist Party of Czechoslovakia, conscious of its responsibility, will take the necessary steps to block the path of reaction. In this struggle you can count on the solidarity and all-around assistance of the fraternal Socialist countries.

Czechoslovak Response

The Presidium of the Czechoslovak party Central Committee July 18 rejected as unfounded the accusations made in the Warsaw letter and affirmed that the country's new policies were aimed at strengthening socialism.

Excerpts from the July 18 Czechoslovak reply:

. . . The May plenum of the [Czechoslovak party] Central Committee stated clearly that it is necessary to mobilize all forces to prevent a conflict situation in the country and the endangering of Socialist power in the Czechoslovak Socialist Republic. Our party has also unequivocally stated that if any such danger occurred that we should use all means to protect the Socialist system. We, therefore, ourselves saw the possibility of such danger. We understand that the fraternal parties of the Socialist countries cannot be indifferent to this. We do not, however, see any realistic reasons permitting our present situation to be called counterrevolutionary, [any reasons for] statements on the immediate endangering of the basis of the Socialist system or [for] statements that Czechoslovakia is preparing a change in the orientation of our Socialist foreign policy and that there is concrete danger of separating our country from the Socialist society. . . .

... We shall not agree to the historic achievements of socialism and the safety of the nations of our country being threatened or to imperialism either by peaceful or forceful means breaking down the Socialist system and changing the balance of power in Europe to its advantage....

The staff exercise of the allied forces of the Warsaw Treaty on the territory of Czechoslovakia is a concrete proof of our faithful fulfillment of our alliance commitments.... The obscurities and some doubts in the minds of our public occurred only after the repeated changes of the time of the departure of the allies' armies from the territory of Czechoslovakia at the end of the exercise....

In the present time it is especially essential for the party to carry out such a policy as could fully merit it the leading role in our society. We are convinced that under the present circumstances it is a condition for the Socialist development of the country.

The Communist Party depends on the voluntary support of the people. It is not implementing its leading role by ruling over the society but by faithfully serving its free, progressive Socialist development. It cannot arrogate authority to itself but must constantly acquire it by its actions. It cannot force its line by orders but by the work of its members and the veracity of its ideals....

The leading role of our party gravely suffered in the past by the distortions of the '50s and the policy of their inconsistent removal by the leadership headed by A. Novotny. He is even more responsible for the deepening of the social conflicts between the Czechs and Slovaks, between the intelligentsia and workers, between the young generation and the older generations.

The inconsistent solution of economic problems has left us in a condition in which we cannot solve a series of justified economic demands of the workers and ... the effectiveness of the entire national economy is gravely disrupted.

Under that leadership the confidence of the masses in the party dropped and there were expressions of criticism and resistance, but all this was 'solved' by interference from a position of power against justified dissatisfaction, against criticism and against attempts to solve consistently the social problems in the interests of the party and in the interests of its leading role....

... The decline in the confidence in the party was masked by external forms of directive party control. Although this regime was given out as being the firm guarantee of the interests of the entire Socialist camp, inside problems were growing, ... the real solution of which was suppressed by forceful means against those advocates of the new and creative approaches.

Any indication of a return to these methods would evoke the resistance of the overwhelming majority of party members, the resistance of the working class, the workers, cooperative farmers and intelligentsia....

Our party has laid down the following main aims and stages of political work:

1. To consistently separate the party as a whole from the distortions of the past for which specific persons of the old party leadership are responsible: These specific people are justifiably being called to task.

2. To prepare the 14th extraordinary congress of the party, which will eval-
uate the development and political situation during the January plenum and,
in accordance with the principles of democratic centralism, will lay down the
compulsory line for the entire party, will adopt an attitude towards the
federal arrangement of Czechoslovakia, will approve the new party statute
and elect a new Central Committee so that it has the full authority and confidence of the party and the entire society.

3. After the 14th congress to launch the offensive for the solution of all the
fundamental internal political questions: toward the construction of a political system based on the Socialist platform of the National Front and social
self-government, the solution of the federal constitutional arrangement, the
elections to the representative bodies of the state (federal, national and local)
and the preparation of a new constitution....

Now, too, it happens that voices and tendencies appear in the press and the
radio and in public meetings which are outside the positive endeavors of the
party, the state bodies and the National Front.

We consider the solution of these questions to be a long-term task and are
guided by the resolutions of the May plenary session of the Central Committee according to which 'political leadership cannot be imposed by the old,
administrative and power structures.' The Presidium of the Central Committee of the Communist Party of Czechoslovakia, the government and the
National Front clearly rejected the appeal of the statement of '2,000 Words,'
which urges people to engage in anarchist acts and to violate the constitutional character of our political reform. It should be noted that, after the
exposition of these negative positions, similar campaigns in fact did not occur
in our country and that the consequences of the appeal of '2,000 Words' did
not threaten the party, the National Front and the Socialist state....

We know that this situation is facilitated by the abolition of censorship in
our country and the enactment of freedom of expression and of the press.
What had been spread in the form of 'whispered propaganda,' etc. before can
now be expressed openly.

By the law of judiciary rehabilitations we basically solved the painful problem of the illegal reprisals against innocent people which took place in the
past years.

In September—immediately after the party congress—other new important
laws will be discussed: the constitutional law on the National Front, which is
to confirm the permanent existence of the system of political parties on the
ground of the National Front, and, further, a law on the right for assembly
and association which sets forth the legal regulations for the birth and activities of various voluntary organizations, associations, clubs, etc.

There is in our opinion a decisive aspect to the present situation: the rise of
the authority of the new, democratic policy of the party in the eyes of the
broadest masses of the workers and the growing participation of the overwhelming majority of the people. The overwhelming majority of the people

of all classes and sectors of our society favors the abolition of censorship and is for freedom of expression.

The Communist Party of Czechoslovakia is trying to show that it is capable of a different political leadership and management than the discredited bureaucratic-police methods, mainly by the strength of its Marxist-Leninist ideas, by the strength of its program, its just policy supported by all the people....

We, therefore, consider all pressure directed at forcing the party onto another path, that is to settle basic questions of its policy elsewhere and at another time than at the 14th congress, the principal danger to the successful consolidation of the leading role of the party in the Czechoslovak Socialist Republic.

At the present time the interest of socialism in our country can be served best by a ration of confidence in the leadership of the Communist Party of Czechoslovakia and of full support of its policy by our fraternal parties....

We discussed the proposals of the 5 parties to hold their meeting in Warsaw at the Presidium of the Central Committee of the Communist party of Czechoslovakia twice—on July 8 and 12.... Unfortunately, our meeting of July 12 was already superfluous because, notwithstanding its outcome the meeting in Warsaw had already been convened for July 14—a fact we learned only through CTK in the afternoon of July 13, at a time when the representatives of the 5 parties were already on their way to Warsaw....

We think that the common cause of socialism is not advanced by the holding of conferences at which the policy and activity of one of the fraternal parties is judged without the presence of their representatives....

We see an important task in the holding of the bilateral talks, which we proposed, in the nearest future. It would then be possible to assess the possibility of a common meeting of the socialist countries and to agree on its program and composition, and the time and place of its convening....

We do not want our relationships to become worse, and we are willing on our side to contribute to the calming of the situation in the interests of socialism and the unity of the Socialist countries. On our side, we shall do nothing which would be against this aim. We expect, however, that the other parties will aid these efforts of ours and will express understanding for our situation....

In a nationally broadcast and televised speech July 18, Dubcek further elaborated on the reasons for the Czechoslovak rejection of the arguments contained in the Warsaw letter. He said:

In the 3 weeks that have elapsed since our last meeting on the television screen, a great deal that is new has happened in our country and beyond our frontiers. ·

District and regional conferences of the Communist Party have been held. They were exciting, yet unruffled, working conferences, self-confident and full of *elan* and determination to continue further in the process of regeneration, in the building of our Socialist society. The delegates that are being sent to the [projected 14th] Congress of the party are aware of the responsibility we have towards the people of our republic, towards our Socialist Czechoslovak homeland. We are glad that the discussions of the conferences have attracted so much attention from our entire public. We consider this a pledge that the course and the decisions of our extraordinary 14th Congress will be near to them and will answer their wishes and interests.

The surface of the public has been rippled during these days by the consultation of the 5 Communist parties in Warsaw and our nonparticipation, as well as the stand taken by the 5 brother parties in regard to our Czechoslovak country. The Presidium of the Central Committee of the Communist Party of Czechoslovakia has expressed itself on this letter. Since the citizens, thanks to our television, radio and press, became acquainted with the documents published, they have sent us letters and telegrams expressing their agreement with our stand and assuring the leaders of the party of their support. I was entrusted with the task of expressing thanks for this spontaneous assent and this I do with all my heart and am very glad that the Presidium of the Central Committee has given me this task.

It is truly difficult to speak of all this. I feel the great responsibility that is lying on all of us. But we are determined and we believe we have your support in advancing in the policy which we undertook after the January plenary session of the Central Committee and which the Czech and Slovak nations support.

We have paid dearly for the practice of the past years. This is why the leaders of the party put such emphasis on the possibility of citizens to apply their creativity, to satisfy their wishes and needs, so that our country may not lag behind economically and culturally and chiefly, that in the service of the people, a policy may be followed that means socialism does not lose its human aspect.

After many years, an atmosphere has been created in our country, in which everyone can publicly and without fear, openly and with dignity, express his opinion and thus test whether the cause of this country and the cause of socialism is the cause of all of us. By an open and honest policy, by a sincere and thorough elimination of the residue of past years, our party is gradually regaining the badly shaken confidence.

Therefore we are saying openly, calmly but determinedly, [that] we realize what is now at stake: there is no other path than for the people of this country to achieve the profound, democratic and Socialist changes in our life.

We do not want to give up in the least any of the principles we expressed in the 'action program' and which were again repeated in the stand taken by the Presidium. The Communist Party is relying on the voluntary support of the people; we do not carry out our guiding role by ruling over society, but by serving their free, progressive and Socialist development in the most dedicated way. We cannot assert our authority by giving orders, but by the work of our members, by the justice of our ideals.

Since in the preceding period the masses, our people, were not satisfied with the way our policy was carried out in this country, since they were not satisfied with the practice in carrying out the policy of our party, then it is natural that if the party wants to carry out its policy, it cannot change the masses of the people, but we must change the leadership and this leadership must change its political methods to correspond truly to the interests and the desires of our nations, of our Czechoslovak homeland, our republic.

Developing socialism in a free society, on the basis of Marxism-Leninism, modern in its orientation, profoundly humane, is the great patriotic task and at the same time our truly international obligation towards the worldwide workers' and Communist movement.

Our people's land is like a wedge inserted among the Socialist countries and we shall protect this strategic position of socialism like the apple of our eye. We have not been untrue to our friends and allies, we have loyally carried out our pledges and shall continue to do so—pledges to defend the camp of the Warsaw Pact.

We consider the necessary basis for our independence in a tempestuous world, in Europe and throughout the world, to be an alliance with Socialist countries, especially with the Soviet Union, with which we are united by profound, emotionally rooted and sincere friendship. We are demonstrating actively our unswerving loyalty to proletarian internationalism. It is loyalty to these principles that compels us not to yield an inch in the path that we have entered after the January plenary session of the Central Committee of the Communist Party of Czechoslovakia. The revolutionary movement can be strong only if every individual link in this movement is strong.

The fate of socialism in our country is in good hands, for it is in the hands of our people, in the hands of our workers, farmers, our working intelligentsia to whom the cause of socialism has become their own. No one can doubt the maturity and responsibility of this people. Long years of struggle for national existence and then for the statehood of Czechoslovakia here at the crossroads of European history has armed our people with perseverance and experiences which were not broken by any previous oppression. Our [2] nations [the Czech nation and Slovakia] have a sense of justice, freedom and humanity, they are determined to defend everything which is good that they have accomplished and are loyal to their friends.

In the entire period of existence of our party we have never given any reason to doubt our loyalty to internationalism, Communist ideals, the international workers' and Communist movement. It would be an illusion to suppose that our party and people could go through this complicated period of difficulties and obstacles without making any mistake or having no possible shortcomings. We are faced with deciding fateful questions and problems which have been accumulating in the party and in our society over the past years. The May plenary session of the Central Committee of the Communist Party, and other measures taken by the party, show that we are gradually solving and overcoming these problems, in the party as a whole and under the control of the people.

Therefore, the leadership of our party, its democratically elected bodies, the membership of the party and also the public and its representatives are becoming convinced that a real turn for the better is taking place in our country and that socialism is taking on an aspect that is near and dear to all, that it is becoming stronger and is putting down new, deep roots. This is decisive for judging the real situation in Czechoslovakia and in judging the progress of our party in further building socialism. Who else and who better can comprehend and understand the interests, desires and needs of our working people than this party which is working in this country, is linked with its working people, who better than the government that was elected by the will of the people and than the representatives of our people in other elected bodies?

I believe, I am convinced that our Communist Party will pass this historic test not only before our people and [2] nations, but also before the international working class movements, of which we are and shall remain a firm part.

We are glad that along with expressions of fears about the path we have taken, we have also received from many brother parties appreciation and support. We are grateful for this. We should like to assure them [that] we do not want to set a pattern or write any recipes for others. This would deny the specific nature of the way in which the Communist Party of Czechoslovakia is working.

We are concerned only [to ensure] that socialism may be strongly rooted in the soil of our native land and in the way of thinking and feeling of our people, that—with the generally valid principles—it may correspond to our national conditions and Czechoslovak traditions. We are deciding independently and according to our own considerations, the most suitable ways of building socialism in our homeland, the most acceptable model of our Socialist life.

To proceed in any other way would mean not to proceed in harmony with our own people, would mean that our nations had lost their own Socialist conscience. Therefore, the Presidium declared that it will continue to advance along the path we took after January of this year. It relies on the confidence of our people. The people will permit no return to the period before January.

Our path will be no easy one. We need calm, united work in the common cause, which will rid us of errors and deformations, and at the same time we shall part from the narrow group of people who bear the responsibility for these errors. We call on all of you, in the name of our homeland, in the name of socialism, to cooperate in carrying out the 'action program' which was adopted by the National Front and which is supported by our entire working people.

Dear television viewers, you will surely agree with me when I say that democracy is a clash of ideas. But democracy is also a conscious civic discipline that requires statesmanlike wisdom of all citizens. It would not benefit our friendly ties, nor our further work to have needless dramatization of the misunderstandings that have risen, nor would the shortsighted kindling of passions.

We have honorably and sincerely inaugurated the process of recovery. For the benefit of our people and socialism we shall conclude it in such a way that we can at any time render accounts to the [2] nations of this country in regard to our acts, our work which we have been charged to carry out by the members of the party and the will of our people. As citizens of a sovereign Socialist country which rules its fate according to the best awareness and conscience of its people, we must in all our acts be determined, wise, aware of our great responsibility to our country, to our people, as well as to the international Communist movement.

What we need most now is the support of all of you, citizens of the Socialist Republic of Czechoslovakia, led by the party and government of this country. May your support and confidence, your prudence and determination be a dignified answer in these responsible moments, may they accord with the great democratic tradition of our common Socialist homeland. Once again, dear citizens, I am entrusted by the Presidium of the Central Committee of the Communist Party to thank you for the support we have received from you in carrying out the new policy which accords with the interests of our people and of our Czechoslovak Socialist homeland.

Crisis Approaching

Concern over the Soviet troops in Czechoslovakia was heightened July 21, when a report from Prague disclosed that the Soviet Union had renewed its demand that Czechoslovakia allow the stationing of Warsaw Pact troops on its territory along the Czechoslovak border with West Germany. The Soviet request came in the wake of a mounting anti-Czechoslovak press campaign in the USSR and other east European Communist countries, especially East Germany. It was charged that as a result of its democratization, Prague had neglected its Warsaw Pact commitments to defend its frontier with West Germany and had allowed "imperialist agents" to infiltrate the country.

The July 21 Soviet demand had been preceded by charges in the Soviet party organ *Pravda* July 19 that a cache of U.S.-made arms had been discovered by Czechoslovak security forces near Karlovy Vary, just east of the West German border. *Pravda* also charged that along with the cache had been found a secret American manual on subversion, which described methods to prepare the "liberation of East Germany and Czechoslovakia."

The Soviet Union July 22 was reported to have sent Czechoslovakia a note protesting against alleged West German influence and demanding an explanation of the arms-cache incident. Although the Czechoslovak police acknowledged that they had found an arms cache, Czechoslovak Interior Min. Josef Pavel said the incident was a "provocation intended to make the situation in Czechoslovakia more dramatic." Other sources in Czechoslovakia said East German "tourists" might have "planted" the arms to discredit the Czechoslovak reformers.

The U.S. protested July 22 against the repeated Soviet allegations about U.S. support of Prague's defiant stand against
Moscow. U.S. State Secy. Dean Rusk summoned Anatoly F.
Dobrynin, the Soviet ambassador in Washington, and
demanded an official explanation of the continuing Soviet press
campaign against the alleged U.S. involvement. State Department spokesman Robert J. McCloskey termed "ridiculous" the
Soviet charges that the reason West German Defense Min.
Gerhard Schroder was then visiting Washington was to plot
anti-Soviet activities in Czechoslovakia.

The West German Defense Ministry announced July 24
that it agreed to shift planned maneuvers away from the
Czechoslovak border to about 100-150 miles west, in the state of
Baden-Wurttemberg near France. The date of the exercises,
Sept. 15, was left unchanged. The maneuvers, to involve some
30,000 West German, U.S. and French troops, were to last for 7
days. West German Chancellor Kurt Georg Kiesinger had
asked Schroder July 22 "to examine the possibility" of altering
the time or place of the maneuvers.

The Warsaw Pact maneuvers, in which Czechoslovak
forces had been joined by units from the Soviet Union, East
Germany, Poland, Hungary and Bulgaria, had initially been
described by Marshal Ivan I. Yakubovsky, Soviet commander
of Warsaw Pact forces, as involving only small command staff,
signal and transport units, but later they were expanded into
full-scale operations. The maneuvers had ranged over the terri-
tories of Czechoslovakia, East Germany, Poland and the Soviet
Union and officially ended July 12. Yakubovsky was quoted by
diplomatic sources in Warsaw July 16 as saying that the Soviet
troops had remained in Czechoslovakia after the end of the
exercises because of the poor showing of the Czechoslovak
units. When Czechoslovak officials objected that further delay
in the troops' departure would hamper harvesting activities,
Yakubovsky was said to have replied that they would have to
remain until after the harvest season.

The timing of the exercises in Czechoslovakia prompted
widespread speculation in the censorship-free Czechoslovak
press that their real purpose was to interfere with the
democratization progress. Reports from Prague indicated that
the Czechoslovak leadership had sought to postpone the war
games but that the Soviet leaders and their hard-line allies,

especially East Germany, regarded the maneuvers as a proof of Prague's allegiance to the Warsaw alliance. Cestmir Cisar, a secretary of the Czechoslovak Central Committee, disclosed July 12 that Czechoslovak leaders had finally agreed to the maneuvers "in a complicated situation [in the country] which did not favor them—quite the contrary." But, he added, in the circumstances, the leaders had wanted to give ::firm and clear proof of our foreign-political and military-strategic attitude."

After the USSR had made an apparent concession by agreeing to hold a conference between its and the Czechoslovak party's leadership on Czechoslovak territory, the Soviet Defense Ministry had announced July 23 that it would conduct what was described in Western military circles as the biggest peacetime maneuvers in Soviet history in an area bordering on Czechoslovakia.

The announcement of the maneuvers of Soviet support and supply troops was made in the government newspaper *Izvestia* July 23. The paper said that the exercises would involve reservists and civilian motor vehicles and would continue until Aug. 10. They were to take place along the USSR's frontier from the Baltic to the Black Sea. Progressive increases in the scale of the maneuvers were made known later. Moscow disclosed July 25 that its antiaircraft forces would also participate. The purpose of the antiaircraft exercise, "Sky Shield," which included rocket units, was given as a test of these units' ability to destroy a "powerful, technically equipped and treacherous enemy." Moscow newspapers said July 27 that the Soviet air force had joined the war games, which included airborne troop movements as well. Soviet Defense Min. Andrei A. Grechko called on the Soviet forces July 27 to improve their combat readiness because of an "attempt of international imperialism to make a breach" in Communist unity.

It was reported in East Berlin July 29, the day the 2 parties' talks began, that the Soviet Union had alerted its troops in East Germany and had begun shifting major mechanized units to strategic points in border areas. The number of Soviet troops involved in the moves, mostly south to areas in Saxony bordering Czechoslovakia, was estimated by Allied officials at 75,000. (Soviet troops stationed in East Germany totaled about 307,000.) Some of the Soviet convoys used autobahns usually set aside for Western travelers to and from West Berlin.

Reports of Soviet troop movements at 2 widely separated places in eastern Poland reached the West July 29-31; scores of amphibious reconnaissance vehicles armed with machineguns had been seen 6 miles north of the Czechoslovak border. Witnesses from this area said a Soviet tank column nearly one mile long had been seen on a main highway, and there was no apparent effort to conceal its presence. More than 300 miles to the north, near Elblag (Elbing) on the coast of the North Sea, eyewitnesses reported that a column of Soviet tanks, artillery, rocket launchers and hundreds of other vehicles had "rumbled for more than 10 hours" westward. Troop concentrations were also reported in the vicinity of Poznan in western Poland. Observers generally agreed that the Soviet troops that had been seen moving westward were not from the 4 divisions usually stationed in Poland under the Warsaw Treaty. A heavy concentration of Soviet troops had been observed July 22 near Cieszyn, 3 miles north of the Polish city on the Czechoslovak border. These troops were said to have participated in the Warsaw Treaty exercises in Czechoslovakia in early June. Other Soviet troops that had taken part in the exercises were still in Czechoslovakia.

Soviet Summons

By mid-July, a mood of imminent crisis prevailed in eastern Europe. Moscow July 19 issued a summons to the Czechoslovak party Presidium, demanding that it meet July 22 or 23 with the Soviet Politburo in Moscow, Kiev or Lvov to discuss internal Czechoslovak developments. The announcement of the invitation, by the official Soviet news agency Tass July 19, was unusual since Soviet invitations were normally published only after their acceptance. (The Czechoslovak party daily, *Rude pravo,* did not publish the invitation until July 21. The *N.Y. Times* July 18 had said that Leonid Brezhnev, the Soviet Party leader, had reportedly demanded that the Czechoslovak party Presidium meet the Soviet Party Politburo in Kosiee, East Slovakia, July 19.)

In what many observers took to be a move to gain time, the Czechoslovak Presidium did not officially consider the Soviet invitation until July 22, when it announced that, although it agreed in principle to hold· bilateral talks with fraternal parties, it would not, however, agree to such a meeting outside Czechoslovakia. Unconfirmed reports said that the Prague leadership had also refused to meet with the Soviet Politburo until the Soviet troops left the country. Although the number of Soviet troops left in Czechoslovakia was not considered significant from a military point of view, their presence was thought to exert psychological pressure.

To strengthen its hand for the pending negotiations with the Soviets, the progressive faction of the Czechoslovak Presidium July 19 had convened the Central Committee. At the meeting, the Presidium had won from the Central Committee a unanimous approval of the Presidium's reply of July 18 to the "Warsaw 5's" "common letter" of July 15 and a unanimous indorsement of its plans. The convening of the Central Committee was regarded as a dangerous move because the committee's composition was thought to be divided evenly between the conservative (pro-Moscow) and progressive (pro-Dubcek) factions. In a move to assure support for its tough stand in the coming negotiations with the USSR, the Dubcek leadership invited 40 of its faithful followers, all delegates to the extraordinary (14th) party congress scheduled for Sept. 7, to take part in the proceedings as nonvoting observers. The leadership also lifted some measures of secrecy usually surrounding Central Committee meetings and permitted private citizens bringing pledges of support for the Presidium's progressive stand to enter the Spanish Hall of the Hradcany Castle, where the committee met. (An effort of the more radical members to allow live broadcast of the session was rejected.)

In his opening speech to the committee, Dubcek reiterated that the party leadership was determined to continue its liberalization program. He declared: "We paid too dearly and are still paying for the methods of the past." But he also renewed the pledge that Prague would remain loyal to communism, to the Socialist camp and, in particular, to the Soviet Union. Only Drahomir Kolder, one of 3 conservatives on the 11-man Presidium, spoke against an uncompromising stand against the Soviet's military and political pressure.

When the question came up for vote, all 88 Central Committee members approved the progressive line. There were no abstentions.

An editorial in the Moscow *Pravda* July 22 renewed a Soviet accusation that the Czechoslovak Presidium had retreated from its earlier promise to suppress anti-Communist elements in the country. The *Pravda* article, believed to reflect the position of the Soviet Politburo, claimed that the Czechoslovak Presidium had taken a "step backward" from the position the Czechoslovak Central Committee had announced at its meeting May 29-June 1, when it had declared that "anti-Socialist forces acting in Czechoslovakia were the main danger." *Pravda* charged the Czechoslovak leadership with "failure or reluctance" to meet the dangers "created by the right-wing, anti-Socialist forces."

Worse yet, by ignoring the "Warsaw 5's" appeal of July 15, the *Pravda* editorial charged, Prague had revealed "an obvious change of political appraisals." "Is there really any need to wait for the counterrevolutionary forces to become masters of the situation ... before starting to struggle against them?" *Pravda* asked. Charging that anti-Communists had "seized the mass media—the press, radio and television and [were] using them ... to fan hatred of the Soviet Union," *Pravda* insisted that Prague (a) reimpose censorship, (b) ban anti-Communist activities by suppressing right-wing forces and (c) restore Communist Party discipline and control over the country.

Josef Smrkovsky, president of the Czechoslovak National Assembly, appealed to the Soviet Union and its 4 other East European allies July 22 to respect his country's sovereignty, "which exclude[s] any kind of uncomradely interference." His appeal, made in the Czechoslovak Communist Party newspaper *Rude pravo,* was coupled with a renewed pledge that friendship and alliance with the Soviet Union would remain the cornerstone of Czechoslovak policy. "We are and will remain a country that will continue to develop socialism and to deepen Socialist truly human relations," he declared. "We therefore demand calmly, deliberately but absolutely—from our best friends too—that they respect our rights and positions...."

The surge of popular support for the Dubcek leadership was illustrated by a steady flow of spontaneous rank-and-file comment on Prague TV during interviews following the regular 7 o'clock newscast.

In what many observers regarded as a dramatic reversal of its position, the Soviet Union agreed July 22 that its entire Politburo should go to Czechoslovakia and confer with the Presidium of the Czechoslovak Communist Party. Tass announced July 22: "It has been learned here [Moscow] that the Politburo of the Soviet Communist Party's Central Committee, meeting the wishes of the Presidium of the Central Committee of the Czechoslovak Communist Party, has agreed to hold a bilateral meeting in Czechoslovakia, having in mind that it will be attended by the Politburo of the Soviet Communist Party's Central Committee and the Presidium of the Central Committee of the Czechoslovak Communist Party in a body." The Soviet Politburo comprised 11 regular and 9 alternate members, the Czechoslovak Presidium 11 members and 3 alternates.

Czechoslovak sources pointed out that the Soviet insistence that the 2 entire bodies meet was in contradiction to Czechoslovak wishes; the Prague leaders were reported to prefer a meeting between smaller delegations of the 2 ruling bodies.

The Czechoslovak Presidium July 25 removed Lt. Gen. Vaclav Prchlik as head of the Central Committee's military department. Prchlik's ouster and the simultaneous abolition of his department were regarded as a concession to Moscow, which had sharply criticized Prchlik for his outspoken anti-Soviet statements in previous months. Prchlik, however, received a top command job on Czechoslovakia's border with the USSR. *Krasnaya Zvezda,* the Soviet armed forces newspaper, had assailed Prchlik July 23 for his critical remarks about alleged Soviet domination of the Warsaw Treaty alliance. At a briefing for Czechoslovak newsmen July 15, Prchlik had called for (a) rotation of the top command of the Warsaw Pact forces among the member nations and (b) a revision of the Warsaw Treaty's structure by adopting an amendment to prevent the treaty from being used as an instrument of political goals. These demands were subsequently broadcast by Prague radio.

(Other Czechoslovak officials who had come under sharp attacks in the Soviet press included Interior Min. Josef Pavel, who had been replacing Stalinist members of the security police with those favoring Dubcek's reform program, and Ota Sik, a deputy premier, who advocated radical economic reforms.)

Dubcek vowed to the Czechoslovak people in a Radio-TV address July 27 that Czechoslovakia would continue "to the end" on the road of democratization and would "not depart by a single step" from that road. He asserted that his party's actions were "in the interest of the world Socialist cause." Dubcek also expressed confidence that "our friends [the Soviet Politburo] will understand—even if not at once—that the Czechoslovak regeneration process does not threaten the interests" of the Socialist community. "On the contrary," he declared, "it is the only possible way to make our republic a really solid part of the Socialist establishment...."

As the critical meeting neared, Czechs and Slovaks from all walks of life had collected signatures on a patriotic appeal published in a special edition of the progressive weekly *Literarni Listy* July 26. The manifesto, drafted by the writer Pavel Kohout, called on the Presidium not to yield to the Soviet Union. By July 29, more than one million signatures were collected in favor of the petition. Kohout's appeal said: "As often before in the history of mankind, a few men will decide the fate of millions.... We want to help you by expressing our support.... Tell the Soviets that we need freedom, peace and time to become better and more reliable allies than before.... To lose this one chance would be our catastrophe and your shame...."

Confrontations at Cierna & Bratislava

Czechoslovakia's leaders conferred with the leaders of the USSR and the Soviet Union's East European supporters at separate confrontations in Cierna and Bratislava in late July and early August in what at first were reported to be conferences at which the "Warsaw 5" reluctantly agreed to allow Czechoslovakia to continue with its experiment in the liberalization of communism.

9 full members of the Soviet party Politburo and the entire Czechoslovak party Presidium met July 29 in the East Slovak village of Cierna-nad-Tisou just across the border from Soviet Ruthenia.

Participating on the Soviet side in the talks were Gen. Secy. Leonid I. Brezhnev of the Soviet party Central Committee; the Politburo members Premier Aleksei N. Kosygin, Pres. Nikolai V. Podgorny, Gennady Voronov, Kirill Mazurov, Arvid Pelshe, Mikhail Suslov, Aleksandr Shelepin and Petr Shelest; the alternate members Petr Demichev and Petr Masherov; and the Central Committee secretaries Konstantin Katushev and Boris Ponomarev. Dmitri S. Polyansky and Andrei P. Kirilenko, the remaining 2 full members of the Politburo, had stayed in Moscow apparently to handle any urgent government business during the talks. They were replaced at the talks by Demichev and Masherov.

Taking part on the Czechoslovak side were First Secy. Alexander Dubcek of the party Central Committee; the Presidium members Frantisek Barbirek, Vasil Bilak, Premier Oldrich Cernik, Drahomir Kolder, Frantisek Kriegel, Jan Piller, Emil Rigo, Josef Smrkovsky, Josef Spacek and Oldrich Svestka; the Presidium alternates Antonin Kapek, ex-Premier Jozef Lenart and Bohumil Simon; Milos Jakes, chairman of the party Central Committee's central control and auditing commission; and Czechoslovak Pres. Ludvik Svoboda.

It was disclosed in Prague July 28, the day the delegation left for Cierna, that the leadership had chosen as its principal spokesmen Dubcek, Cernik, Kriegel and Simon, secretary of the Prague city party organization.

The confrontation took place July 29-Aug. 1 in the simple 2-story railwaymen's community center in Cierna, a railway-junction town on the Tisa River.

It was later reported that the Soviet group immediately scorned to recognize Kriegel as one of the 4 Czechoslovak spokesmen. Soviet Premier Kosygin was said to have cut the Czechoslovak party Presidium member short with the words "Shut your trap!" when Kriegel tried to reply to Kosygin's remark: "What is this Galician Jew doing here?"

Referring to the composition of the delegations, the conditions under which they had met and the importance of the issues, observers from both East and West viewed the talks as among the most momentous in Communist history. Although security measures barred both Czechoslovak and Western journalists from Cierna, it was reported that the conferees were in nearly continuous session for 3½ days. Both sides withdrew to their respective trains for meals and at night for rest. The green Soviet train crossed the frontier each night so that the Soviet delegation could sleep on Soviet territory.

A communique issued at the conclusion of the Cierna meeting Aug. 1 described the talks as "a broad comradely exchange of opinion ... in an atmosphere of complete frankness [and] sincerity" on matters involving the "situation" in both countries. The communique gave no details on the proceedings other than the disclosure that the participants had agreed to meet in Bratislava with representatives of Bulgaria, Hungary, East Germany and Poland. Rumania was not invited.

Several Czechoslovak concessions were reported in addition to the agreement to meet with the 4 East European critics of the Czechoslovak democratization program. The Czechoslovaks apparently also agreed to establish an "advisory council" with the aim of curbing the domestic news media. (Czechoslovak newspaper editors reportedly had received a list of 50 secret cateories and had been asked to tone down their criticism of other Communist countries.)

(It was reported from Moscow July 29 that, as the Cierna talks began, a delegation of Soviet dissidents, including artists and scientists, visited the Czechoslovak embassy in Moscow to show support for Prague's democratization program. The delegation was also said to have planned a sidewalk demonstration, but embassy officials dissuaded them. Among members of the dissident delegation were Petr G. Grigorenko, a former major general, and Ivan A. Yakhimovich, a former Latvian collective farm chairman. Both had lost their positions for their repeated demands for fair trials of accused writers in the USSR.)

Despite the tight security measures around Cierna, fragmentary reports, mostly from Czechoslovak sources in Prague, gave this account of the 3½-day proceedings:

July 29—Dubcek opened the talks with a long speech in defense of the changes that had taken place in Czechoslovakia since the ouster of ex-Czechoslovak party First Secy. Antonin Novotny in January. Dubcek described his party's Action Program and argued that it was neither incompatible with continued Communist rule in Czechoslovakia nor an obstacle to continued friendship with the Soviet Union.

In the afternoon Brezhnev charged that, as a result of loosening Communist control, counterrevolution was afoot in Czechoslovakia. To remedy the situation, Brezhnev demanded that Dubcek (a) restore censorship of all communications media, (b) abolish all "anti-Communist" political clubs that had mushroomed in the country, (c) remove "liberals" from key government positions and (d) allow the stationing of Soviet troops along the Czech-West German border.

Following Brezhnev's demands, Suslov, who was in charge of ideological matters, attacked Czechoslovakia's Action Program, line by line, as heresy. The stormy session ended late in the evening, and the Soviet delegation retired to Soviet soil across the border. (Dubcek was quoted as having told some townspeople in Cierna following the session: "We are dealing with people we call brothers but we cannot get through to them.")

July 30—Pres. Svoboda, 72, made an impassioned defense of his country's right to carry out its program of liberalization. Observers termed his address a turning point in the talks, whose atmosphere was described by Czechoslovak sources as icy until then.

July 31—The 3d day's talks were marked by persistent Soviet efforts to split the Czechoslovak delegation between the conservatives (those who had been known to oppose Dubcek's reform program) and the progressives (who favored the reforms). National Assembly chairman Josef Smrkovsky was believed to have told the conservative faction prior to the confrontation that "any Czechoslovak that doesn't back Dubcek at the talks will be known as a national traitor."

Dubcek was said to have told the Soviet delegation that he had to leave the talks to meet Yugoslav Pres. Tito, who had openly expressed his support of Dubcek and was said to have been waiting for his call to fly to Prague, on a moment's notice, in a show of solidarity. Brezhnev was said to have retorted to Dubcek: "Let Tito wait." (It was reported in Moscow July 31 that Brezhnev had been suffering from nervous exhaustion.)

A crowd of some 10,000 persons, mostly students, converged at Prague's Old Town Square Aug. 1, the day the Cierna talks ended, and demanded the "truth" about the talks. Smrkovsky told the crowd: "We explained our position [to the Soviets] and succeeded.... We told them our future must be decided by [Czechoslovaks].... In the next few days you will learn more and can then judge whether we dealt honestly." The crowd shouted back: "They [the Soviets] are not our friends!" "Long live Tito!"

Smrkovsky asserted later Aug. 1 that at Cierna "we agreed that polemics, mutual criticism, mutual accusations lead to nothing and will be ended." Referring to the July 16 5-power Warsaw summit meeting and the resulting joint letter attacking the Czechoslovak reforms, Smrkovsky added: "We will forget that there ever was any Warsaw meeting."

Dubcek told a group of workmen in Kosice, Eastern Slovakia, on his way back to Prague Aug. 1: "We have not taken a single step back. Everything today is as it was 4 days ago."

The first official statement on the outcome of the Cierna talks was made by Pres. Svoboda in a TV address from Kosice Aug. 1. Svoboda admitted that since January there may have been "faults" as a result of the democratization, but he insisted that the reform program had "great strength and [had] taken root so deeply that nobody can reverse it or deflect us from this path." Svoboda said: "Anybody who wants to abuse this [democratization] ... would have no success.... They cannot destroy our sovereignty or independence, which are so dear to us. We spoke openly and frankly to our friends and told them firmly we are determined to continue our policy and not allow anyone to destroy it."

In a nationwide TV address Aug. 3, Dubcek asserted: "We promised you that we would stand fast. We kept our promise."

The Cierna talks ended weeks of attacks by the Soviet press on Prague's reform policies and by Czechoslovak editors on the Soviet critics of Czechoslovakia. It had been reported in Prague July 31 that Smrkovsky had phoned party Secy. Cestmir Cisar from Cierna and had asked him to order the editors to tone down their polemics.

Commenting on the Cierna talks for the first time Aug. 3, the Soviet party newspaper *Pravda* called the meeting "a blow to the enemies of socialism." "The imperialist propaganda was using all means to weaken the unity [among Communist countries] and use any breach to drive a wedge between them," *Pravda* said. It asserted that Communist papers around the world were "underlining" the Cierna conference "as an example of how Socialist countries solve their problems by means of a comradely exchange of opinion in an atmosphere of sincerity and mutual understanding." Press criticism in Soviet news media had been halted Aug. 1, the day the Cierna talks ended. The East German press ended weeks of criticism Aug. 3.

Party and government leaders of Czechoslovakia and the Soviet Union met in Bratislava Aug. 3 with corresponding leaders from East Germany, Poland, Bulgaria and Hungary, and the latter group was reported to have ratified the decisions reached at the Czech-Soviet confrontation in Cierna. A joint communique issued at the conclusion of the Bratislava meeting said that Czechoslovakia's former critics would cooperate with Dubcek's regime on the basis of "equality, sovereignty and national independence."

Those attending the conference were: Bulgarian party First Secy. Todor Zhivkov and the party Politburo member Todorov P. Kubadinsky; Hungarian party First Secy. Janos Kadar, Premier Jeno Fock and the Politburo member Zoltan Komocsin; East German party First Secy. Walter Ulbricht, Premier Willy Stoph and party Politburo members Erich Honecker, Hermann Matern, Gunter Mittag and Hermann Axen; Polish party First Secy. Wladyslaw Gomulka, Premier Jozef Cyrankiewicz, the Politburo member Zenon Kliszko and Central Committee Secy. Artur Starewicz; Soviet party Gen. Secy. Brezhnev, Premier Kosygin, Pres. Podgorny, Mikhail Suslov, Petr Shelest, Konstantin F. Katushev and Boris N. Ponomarev; Czechoslovak party First Secy. Dubcek, Premier Cernik, National Assembly Chairman Smrkovsky, Slovak party First Secy. Vasil Bilak and ex-Premier Jozef Lenart, alternate member of the Presidium.

Observers, including those in Prague, described the joint communique as a routine reiteration of prior statements of the world Communist movement.

The communique stated that the representatives of the 6 nations had found it necessary to call the conference because of the "complicated situation, the subversive actions of imperialism," which had attempted to undermine the unity of the Socialist community. It said that the participants "became convinced that it is possible to advance along the road of socialism and communism only by being strictly and consistently guided by the general laws of construction of Socialist society and, primarily, by consolidating the leading role of the working class and its vanguard—the Communist parties." "In so doing," the communique added, "every

fraternal party, creatively solving the questions of further
Socialist development, takes into consideration the national
specific features and conditions." "The many-sided task of
creating a Socialist society in each of our countries," the communique said, would continue "on the basis of the principles of
equality, respect for sovereignty and national independence,
territorial integrity, fraternal mutual assistance and
solidarity."

The 6-nation communique said the participants had also
agreed: (a) "to call a top-level economic conference of the
Council of Mutual Economic Assistance (COMECON) in the
nearest future"; (b) "to rebuff any attempts to revise the results
of World War II and to break the frontiers that have taken
shape in Europe"; (c) "to insist on the invalidity of the Munich
agreements right from the beginning"; (d) "to continue to
render resolute support to the German Democratic Republic
[East Germany]" as well as to the "Communist Party of
Germany"—the communist underground in West Germany.

Observers then suggested that the communique had been
agreed on at the Cierna talks. It was regarded by Czechoslovak
sources as a face-saving device for Moscow, whose massive
military and press campaign against Czechoslovakia had
compromised the Soviet leadership.

It was reported in Prague Aug. 4 that the Soviet Union
had had difficulty in persuading its 4 allies who had taken an
open anti-Czechoslovak stand—notably East Germany and
Poland—to sign. Hungary, however, was reported to have
taken a more sympathetic view of Czechoslovak developments.
Hungary's press coverage of Czechoslovak events had been
described as balanced; the Hungarian press and broadcasts
conspicuously ignored the Soviet/Bulgarian version of the
discovery July 19 of an "arms cache" in Western Bohemia and
reported instead the Czechoslovak version, which minimized the
incident.

In a brief TV address to the Czechoslovak people Aug. 4,
Dubcek reemphasized that "the principle of sovereignty is an
indivisible part of our policy." "There is no need to fear for the
sovereignty of our country," he declared. Dubcek asserted that
the reform program "will have far-reaching significance" for
the Communist movement all over the world and that "there is
no other way, no other route."

Smrkovsky in Prague Aug. 4 called the communique a guarantee of the "sovereignty of our party, of our state and of our government." Replying to a statement that the communique had been received in Prague "without enthusiasm," he offered what he called a "translation [of the communique] into Czech": "We have succeeded not only in defending our policies and preventing a split among the Socialist countries—the double mandate assigned to us when we left—but, what is more, we have succeeded in stopping the interparty polemic. When our economists return to Moscow to continue the economic negotiations which we began in May, everything will go smoothly."

Tito & Ceausescu Visit Prague

The Czechoslovak government was visited by Yugoslav Pres. Tito Aug. 9-11 and Rumanian Pres. Nicolae Ceausescu, Aug. 15-17. Both visits were made in obvious efforts to bolster the Dubcek regime. During the 2d half of July, both Tito and Ceausescu were said to have been ready to fly to Prague at virtually a moment's notice to show their solidarity with Dubcek. Dubcek reportedly had asked for the postponement of the visits to avoid offending the USSR.

Tito was accorded a tumultuous welcome in what was generally regarded as Czechoslovak gratitude for his unconditional backing of Dubcek's strong stand against Soviet military and psychological pressures to abandon liberalization. Tito was accompanied by Mijalko Todorovic, secretary of the Executive Bureau of the Presidium of the League of Yugoslav Communists, Krste Crvenkovski, chairman of the Macedonian party, and Stane Kavcic, chairman of the Slovenian party; these 3 were considered members of the most progressive faction within the League of Yugoslav Communists. A communique issued in Prague Aug. 10 said that Tito's visit had contributed "in a significant way to further strengthening of all-round comradely cooperation between the 2 countries' Communist parties."

Tito told Czechoslovak and Yugoslav journalists Aug. 11, during a broadcast interview, that Yugoslavia believed in maintaining diplomatic relations with all countries. "No one can prevent us from granting diplomatic recognition to any country," he said. (The remark was considered a reference to the growing rapprochement between Czechoslovakia and West Germany. East Germany, in particular, vehemently opposed an accord between the 2 states.) The Yugoslav leader asserted that the "friendship between Czechoslovakia and Yugoslavia and their peoples is so great that there is no need for any formal treaties." Tito refused to answer, as too "delicate," a query on a *N.Y. Times* report of Aug. 6 that he had sent a personal message to the Soviet delegation in Cierna. He said that he did not know what factors had determined the outcome of the talks but "that the Czechoslovak people rallied around the Czechoslovak party Central Committee and that it enjoyed deep trust. This trust was not in vain, because the Central Committee defended their attitudes, and not without results."

The broadcast was Tito's only public statement during his stay in Czechoslovakia. Commenting on the 6-nation Bratislava conference, to which Tito had not been invited despite reports that Czechoslovakia had pressed for Yugoslavia's presence, Tito emphasized that the document issued at Bratislava recognized each country's sovereignty and lauded the "comradely way" as the best method to solve differences between Socialist states.

(Ex-Yugoslav Vice Pres. Milovan Djilas, who had been imprisoned by Tito for his liberal views but was later freed, said in Belgrade Aug. 12 that he "completely agree[d] with and approve[d] tito's stand on the democratization trend in Czechoslovakia.")

It was reported in Prague Aug. 11 that among the topics that ranked high on the Tito-Dubcek agenda had been the establishment of close economic ties (including mergers of enterprises) between the 2 countries. The report said that the suggestions for economic cooperation had been initiated by Yugoslavia and that negotiations were to be continued by specialists. Among the areas of cooperation under discussion were: (a) the establishment of a joint bank consortium, with the eventual creation of a joint Czechoslovak-Yugoslav bank; (b) joint investments in 3d countries; (c) Czechoslovak investment in Yugoslav tourist facilities; (d) Yugoslav aid in the form of know-how and labor to build badly needed housing in Czechoslovakia; (e) the importation of Yugoslav unskilled labor by Czechoslovakia, where the Yugoslav workers would receive specialized training; (f) the elimination of existing barriers to ease the movement of goods, labor and investment funds between the 2 nations.

Observers viewed these prospects of economic cooperation as an attempt to reduce Czechoslovakia's heavy reliance for trade on the east European trading system, the Council of Mutual Economic Assistance. (Yugoslavia, which had broken away from the Soviet-led bloc in 1948, sent only ⅓ of its exports to eastern Europe; Czechoslovakia sent ¾ of its exports to bloc countries.)

(In July Tito had publicly pledged to support Dubcek in his confrontation with the Soviet leadership. During a July 14 interview with *Al Ahram,* a Cairo daily, Tito predicted that the Soviet Union would not be so "shortsighted" as to resort to force to halt Czechoslovak liberalization. He said Yugoslavia and Czechoslovakia were strong enough to resist any danger to their political system from the West. During Tito's visit to Czechoslovakia the Soviet press agency Tass announced Aug. 10 that new joint exercises, involving Soviet, East German and Polish troops in areas bordering on Czechoslovakia, had begun in southern East Germany, Poland and Western Ukraine. The announcement said that the exercises would involve mostly communications units. The new military exercises came in the wake of earlier ones that had been scheduled to end Aug. 10.

(The League of Yugoslav Communists July 18 had issued a declaration, which was transmitted to the USSR and the signatories of the Warsaw letter, in which it gave unconditional support to the Czechoslovak reforms and denounced any threat of interference by the other parties. The declaration termed Dubcek's policy a "significant contribution to the general affirmation of the Socialist system." A July 18 article in *Politika,* a Yugoslav daily, criticized the 5-power Warsaw warning as the "Cominform 1968."

(A resolution of the League of Yugoslav Communists Central Committee, passed unanimously July 16 after Tito had received a letter of invitation from Dubcek, stated that the league "firmly believes" in Dubcek's reforms. It rejected "every outside action" against his leadership by other Communist parties.)

Ceausescu and his delegation, which included Prime Min. Ion Gheorghe Maurer, Foreign Min. Nicolae Manescu and party Executive Committee member Emil Bodnaras, received an enthusiastic welcome by thousands of Czechoslovaks Aug. 15. Before departing for Prague, Ceausescu had declared in Bucharest Aug. 15 that there could "be no justification for armed intervention in the internal affairs of any Warsaw Treaty member countries."

A 20-year accord renewing the 1947 bilateral treaty of friendship and mutual assistance was signed by Ceausescu and Pres. Ludvik Svoboda Aug. 16. Its preamble said that the 2 countries were "firmly resolved to act in keeping with the Warsaw Treaty during the time of its validity." The reference to the validity of the Warsaw Pact, due to expire in 1975, was believed to reflect Ceausescu's repeated calls for the abolition of all military blocs in Europe. Czechoslovak officials had also called for changes in the Warsaw Pact's structure to prevent the treaty from being used as an instrument of political goals within member states. The signing of the treaty was reportedly advanced to provide an occasion for Ceausescu to show support for Czechoslovakia. Rumania had not yet renewed its treaty alliances with Bulgaria, the USSR, Hungary and Poland, all of which had expired.

At a televised news conference following the signing ceremony, Ceausescu asserted Aug. 16 that he favored the continued existence of the Warsaw Pact but only as long as NATO remained in force. Referring to relations between small Communist countries and Western countries, Ceausescu stated that there was a possibility for closer ties, especially economically. (Rumania and West Germany had established diplomatic relations Jan. 31, 1967.)

Referring to the Cierna confrontation, Ceausescu declared at a Prague aircraft factory Aug. 16: "In our opinion, wherever there are differences on this or that problem, it is necessary to resolve these differences in comradely talks, with patience and understanding.... At this time so many differences have amassed between Socialist countries and in the movement that we regard it as a basic and most urgent requirement not to undertake anything that could bring new tensions or increase the present ones."

Dubcek, also speaking at the factory, pleaded with the Czechoslovak people not to drive liberalization too far and too fast. He said: "We need order in our country so that we can enjoy freedom of action in our democratization process." While he admitted that relations between Socialist countries was "not all that we would want," he stressed that "the alpha and omega of our foreign policy must be unity and alliance with the Soviet Union." Dubcek's call for order and calm was in response to increasing public demands throughout the country to dissolve the peoples' militia, an armed civilian force created during the Communist takeover in 1948.

Ulbricht at Karlovy Vary

Sandwiched in between Tito's and Ceausescu's visits was a visit by East German State Council Chairman Walter Ulbricht, 75, the East German party leader, who journeyed to Karlovy Vary for a round of talks with the Czechoslovak leaders. The public reception for Ulbricht, who arrived Aug. 12, the day Tito left Prague, was described by Reuters Aug. 13 as one of "frosty silence." About 1,000 persons at the Karlovy Vary airport chanted "Dubcek, Dubcek" as Ulbricht left his plane, but none of them cheered Ulbricht.

Ulbricht and his Czechoslovak hosts conferred for 7 hours. At a press conference later, Ulbricht did not completely mask his opposition to the Czechoslovak liberalization, although he called the reforms "historically important" and noted "significant successes in the economic development of the country." He asserted that conditions for the strengthening of European security had improved and were currently more favorable than during his last visit to the West Bohemian spa, when he attended the conference of European Communist parties in Apr. 1967.

Asked how East Germany would view an establishment of diplomatic relations between Bonn and "Czechoslovakia, Poland, Hungary and Bulgaria," Ulbricht replied that West Germany would first have to "renounce its claim of representing all of Germany and recognize the frontiers established after World War II in Europe, annul the 1938 Munich *diktat,* forswear any right to possess nuclear weapons and put its relations with East Germany on an international legal basis."

But he said there would be a time "when peace-loving, democratic forces will gain a majority in West Germany, too."

Ulbricht said his invitation to Karlovy Vary had been issued by Dubcek after the Warsaw Pact conference in Dresden Mar. 23. Ulbricht reported that he and Dubcek discussed "questions of economic cooperation which will be put for solution before a joint economic committee." He said he had offered Dubcek the benefit of the East German party's "experience with bourgeois ideology."

An East German newsman asked whether the defense of the East German and Czechoslovak borders with West Germany might be coordinated in cooperation with East Berlin. Dubcek replied: "The defense of our sector of frontier with the German Federal Republic is an exclusive affair of Czechoslovakia. We have enough forces to insure the defense of these frontiers by ourselves as the sign of our sovereignty and in the interest of the whole of Socialist society as well as in the interest of our republic."

Allgemeine Deutsche Nachrichten (ADN) the East German news agency said Aug. 13 its own version of the final communique on Ulbricht's conference with Dubcek: The talks "undoubtedly contributed to the further development of the fraternal relations between the 2 countries and the East German and Czechoslovak parties on the basis of the principles of Marxism-Leninism, Socialist Internationalism, solidarity, equality and recognition of sovereignty. The party leaders stressed that they will continue to struggle against the activization of revanchism, militarism and neonazism in West Germany and support democratic forces in that country."

Kremlin Resumes Polemics

After a lapse of 3 weeks, the Soviet Union resumed its criticism of the Czechoslovak press Aug. 16. The Soviet party newspaper *Pravda* castigated 3 Czechoslovak publications for "fierce and slanderous attacks" on neighboring Communist countries. The paper charged that the attacks had been made contrary to the 6-nation Bratislava agreement Aug. 3. The 3 publications under attack were: *Literarni listy,* a newspaper of the Czechoslovak writers' union; *Mlada fronta,* a youth newspaper; and *Reporter,* a publication of the journalists' union.

The Soviet Communist Party declared Aug. 20 that "it was a matter of urgency that imperialist intrigues against Communist rule in Czechoslovakia be nipped in the bud." The warning, appearing in *Pravda,* said that "Marxists-Leninists are not and can never be indifferent to the fate of Socialist construction in other countries and the general cause of socialism and communism on earth." *Pravda* also charged Aug. 20, in a dispatch from Prague, that Czechoslovakia was in danger from West Germany, especially from Sudeten Germans expelled from Czechoslovakia after World War II.

An emergency plenary meeting of the Soviet party Central Committee reportedly convened Aug. 20 in the Kremlin. The Soviet press made no mention of the event, however.

CZECHOSLOVAKIA INVADED

Warsaw Pact Troops Seize Country

Armed forces of the Soviet Union, East Germany, Poland, Hungary and Bulgaria invaded Czechoslovakia in a swift military action during the night of Aug. 20-21.

According to information published later in 1968 by the Institute of History of the Czechoslovak Academy of Sciences in what Americans and Englishmen called *The Czech Black Book,* Soviet KGB (state security) agents had arrived in Prague Aug. 17 and for the next 3 days worked closely with Czechoslovak STB (state security) forces in outlining the plans for the invasion and occupation.

At an afternoon meeting Aug. 20, Deputy Interior Min. Viliam Salgovic, asserting that he had the approval of the Czechoslovak party Central Committee and that he was in constant contact with First Secy. Alexander Dubcek, told certain STB members of the impending invasion and assigned them specific tasks. The STB's 2d department was instructed to guard all Western and the Rumanian and Yugoslav embassies in order to prevent Czechoslovak citizens from seeking asylum. The 7th department was instructed to intervene at Czechoslovak radio stations to prevent the Central Committee from issuing any proclamations. The 7th department later was involved in searching for the sites of the radio stations that operated clandestinely.

After midnight Aug. 21 the entire STB office was informed of the invasion. While many staff members showed surprise and opposition to the invasion, others voiced approval.

According to an anonymous eye-witness at the Czechoslovak party Presidium meeting Aug. 20-21, the following developments took place: While most of the members were shocked by the invasion, "it did not seem as if Vasil Bilak or Alois Indra were surprised, and I don't think that Oldrich Svestka was either." (All 3 were reputed conservatives.) Dubcek then read a letter that had been received Aug. 19 from Soviet party Gen. Secy. Leonid Brezhnev, who accused the

Czechoslovak leaders of not having complied with the Cierna and Bratislava agreements. Dubcek denied this allegation and "continued reading the letter in which—and I want to stress this—there was not a single remark or indication that the [Warsaw Pact] allies intended to settle the affair by means of the military occupation of Czechoslovakia. Comrade Dubcek gave his word of honor as a Communist that he had had no inkling that anyone would want to take such a step against us."

In an article Sept. 5 in *Rude pravo,* Oldrich Svestka, former editor of *Rude pravo,* denied that he had conspired with the Soviet Union to help bring about the intervention. Svestka said: "I did not betray my country, nor our Communist Party, nor my Communist convictions. Rumors claiming that I was among those who had called for the troops of the Warsaw Pact are not true.... I certainly committed mistakes, and I want to accept the responsibility for them. I cannot take the responsibility for acts that I did not commit and which many say I have committed.... I did not betray my country."

The main force of the initial invading units consisted of an estimated 200,000 troops of 5 Warsaw Pact nations who crossed the Czechoslovak borders from East Germany, Poland, Western Ukraine and Hungary about 11 p.m. Aug. 20. (The number of the invaders continued to increase during the following week and ultimately reached an estimated 650,000.)

Prague was seized in an airborne operation as military transport planes, backed by MiG jet fighters, began landing troops in great numbers beginning shortly after 1 a.m. Aug. 21. Among the first units to land at previously secured airports around Prague were detachments of the KGB and paratroopers who spearheaded the occupation of airfields, railroad stations, cable offices, broadcasting centers and buildings of the government, the Party Central Committee, the National Assembly and Hradcany Castle, the presidential palace.

The invasion was carried out by about 10 divisions of Soviet troops, supported by units from (East Germany, Poland, Hungary and Bulgaria). According to intelligence information originating from Washington Aug. 22, about 7 divisions of Soviet troops and some units of an East German division had moved toward Prague from areas around Dresden, Karl-Marx-Stadt (Chemnitz) and Plauen in East Germany.

About 2 divisions of Soviet troops, along with several Polish units, moved from the Baltic states and areas around Wroclaw, Katowice and Cracow in southern Poland to the Czech cities of Prague and Brno and the West Slovak town of Zilina. About one Soviet division moved from the Carpathian Mountain region of the Soviet Union (Western Ukraine), where it had been on maneuvers near the border, to the East Slovak municipalities of Cierna and Kosice in Czechoslovakia.

An unspecified number of Soviet troops, along with what was described as "token forces" of Hungarian troops, moved from near Budapest to Bratislava and Nitra in West Slovakia. Bulgaria also deployed in the Carpathians "token forces" that had been stationed in Hungary. Most of the troops who moved into Czechoslovakia overland had reportedly been stationed, or on maneuvers, near the Czechoslovak border. Unspecified numbers of troops were brought in on more than 200 transport planes.

In a 4-pronged pincer movement of armored and artillery divisions, the invasion forces had taken control of the whole of Czechoslovakia by early Aug. 21.

Czechoslovak Leaders Oppose Invasion

The Czechoslovak party Central Committee declared in a statement broadcast before dawn Aug. 21 that the invasion was taking place "without the knowledge" of Czechoslovakia's leaders. This is a partial text of the message (broadcast repeatedly by Radio Prague early Aug. 21 as coming directly from the party Presidium):

"To the entire people of the Czechoslovak Socialist Republic: Yesterday, on Aug. 21, around 2300 [11 p.m.], troops of the Soviet Union, Polish People's Republic, the GDR [German Democratic Republic], the Hungarian People's Republic and the Bulgarian People's Republic crossed the frontiers of the Czechoslovak Socialist Republic.

"This happened without the knowledge of the president of the republic, the chairman of the National Assembly, the premier or the first secretary of the Czechoslovak Communist Party Central Committee....

"The Czechoslovak Communist Party Central Committee Presidium appeals to all citizens of our republic to maintain calm and not to offer resistance to the troops on the march. Our army, security corps and people's militia have not received the command to defend the country.

"The Czechoslovak Communist Party Central Committee Presidium regard this act as contrary not only to the fundamental principles of relations between Socialist states but also as contrary to the principles of international law. All leading functionaries of the state, the Communist Party and the National Front: Remain in your functions as representatives of the state, elected by the laws of the Czechoslovak Socialist Republic.

"Constitutional functionaries are immediately convening a session of the National Assembly of our republic, and the Presidium at the same time is convening a plenum of the Central Committee to discuss the situation that has arisen."

Reportedly it was the absence of warning about the invasion in Brezhnev's prior message to Dubcek that prompted the Presidium, including conservative members Vasil Bilak, Drahomir Kolder and Frantisek Barbirek, to approve a protest against the occupation.

One of the first actions of the invaders was to arrest key state, party and legislative officials. Some were interned in undisclosed places. Others were put under house arrest.

According to the information published later in *The Czech Black Book,* Col. Bohumil Molnar, chief of state security for the Prague region, assigned 3 KGB agents to accompany STB members to Central Committee headquarters early Aug. 21 to arrest Dubcek, National Assembly Chairman Josef Smrkovsky and National Front Chairman Frantisek Kriegel. When someone asked whether pistols should be carried, Molnar replied, "Yes." (Molnar and Salgovic were dismissed Aug. 24 by Interior Min. Josef Pavel, a leading liberal.) The 3 Czechoslovak leaders were brought by Soviet armored carrier to the Interior Ministry, where they were searched. (Before his arrest Dubcek reportedly had sent the citizens of Prague a message in which he asked the workers of the 9th District to remain united.)

The unsuspecting party Presidiums which had been in session since the afternoon of Aug. 20 to discuss preparations for the 14th extraordinary congress scheduled for Sept. 9, had received the news of the invasion shortly before midnight. Dubcek, on learning the news, was said to have remarked with tears in his eyes: "How could they [the Soviet Union and their allies] do this to me?" "I have served the cause of the Soviet Union and communism all of my life." Premier Cernik, who had received the news by phone from Defense Min. Martin Dzur, was said to have cried: "Treason! Betrayal!"

On learning of the invasion, the Presidium called the Central Committee into emergency session and directed National Assembly Pres. Josef Smrkovsky to convene the National Assembly. Shortly thereafter 2 cars from the Soviet embassy led tanks toward the building of the Central Committee. The Soviet security forces entered the building early Aug. 21 and ordered several leading officials to stand facing the wall for several hours under the threat of a machine gun. Later, Dubcek, Cernik, Smrkovsky and Presidium members Josef Spacek and Frantisek Kriegel were handcuffed and taken to a military barrack in central Slovakia. Among the other Czechoslovak leaders seized were Interior Min. Josef Pavel and Central Committee Secy. Cestmir Cisar, also Czech National Council Chairman. Pres. Svoboda was kept under house arrest in the Hradcany Castle presidential office, which had been surrounded by Soviet armored units.

The Czechoslovak leaders were flown to Moscow Aug. 24. The KGB took control of the Central Committee building, and STB agents, with lists of employes, designated those who were "good or not."

In an article published in the Prague newspaper *Svoboda* Sept. 5, Jan Piller a member of the Czechoslovak party Presidium and reputed to be a pro-Moscow conservative, denied rumors that he had dealt "with anybody" about "entering or forming some new government in the aftermath of the Soviet invasion." He described his Aug. 21 meeting with some 50 members of the Czechoslovak Central Committee and Soviet officials at the Praha Hotel as relating solely to obtaining the release from Soviet custody of Dubcek and other party and government officials. His meeting with Pres. Svoboda, Piller added, concerned arrangements for Svoboda's subsequent trip to Moscow.

Invaders Defend Intervention

In a statement justifying the invasion, the Soviet government claimed Aug. 21 that the armed forces of 5 Warsaw Pact nations had acted after Czechoslovak "party and government leaders" had requested "urgent assistance" to repulse the threat "emanating from the counterrevolutionary forces" within Czechoslovakia. The statement, distributed by Tass, the Soviet news agency, said:

"... Party and government leaders of the Czechoslovak Socialist Republic have asked the Soviet Union and other allied states to render the fraternal Czechoslovak people urgent assistance, including assistance with armed forces. This request was brought about by the threat which has arisen to the Socialist system, existing in Czechoslovakia, and to the statehood established by the constitution, the threat emanating from the counterrevolutionary forces which have entered into a collusion with foreign forces hostile to socialism.

"The events in Czechoslovakia and around her were repeatedly the subject of exchanges of views between leaders of fraternal Socialist countries, including the leaders of Czechoslovakia. These countries are unanimous that the support, consolidation and defense of the people's Socialist gains is a common internationalist duty of all the Socialist states. This common stand of theirs was solemnly proclaimed in the Bratislava statement.

"The further aggravation of the situation in Czechoslovakia affects the vital interests of the Soviet Union and other Socialist states, the interests of the security of the states of the Socialist community. The threat to the Socialist system in Czechoslovakia constitutes at the same time a threat to the mainstays of European peace.

"The Soviet government and the governments of the allied countries—the People's Republic of Bulgaria, the Hungarian People's Republic, the German Democratic Republic, the Polish People's Republic—proceeding from the principles of inseverable friendship and cooperation and in accordance with the existing contractual commitments, have decided to meet the above-mentioned request for rendering necessary help to the fraternal Czechoslovak people.

"This decision is fully in accord with the right of states to individual and collective self-defense envisaged in treaties of alliance concluded between the fraternal Socialist countries. This decision is also in line with vital interests of our countries in safeguarding European peace against forces of militarism, aggression and revanche which have more than once plunged the peoples of Europe into wars.

"Soviet armed units together with armed units of the above-mentioned allied countries entered the territory of Czechoslovakia on 21 August.

"They will be immediately withdrawn from the Czechoslovak Socialist Republic as soon as the obtaining threat to the gains of socialism in Czechoslovakia, the threat to the security of the Socialist community countries, is eliminated and the lawful authorities find that further presence of these armed units there is no longer necessary.

"The actions which are being taken are not directed against any state and in no measure infringe state interests of anybody. They serve the purpose of peace and have been prompted by concern for its consolidation.

"The fraternal countries firmly and resolutely counterpose their unbreakable solidarity to any threat from outside. Nobody will be ever allowed to wrest a single link from the community of Socialist states."

The statement, broadcast by Moscow and other radio stations the morning of Aug. 21, also appeared in the Aug. 21 editions of the Moscow *Pravda* and the East German party organ *Neues Deutschland.* The first transmission of this statement from Moscow was at 5:20 a.m. (Czechoslovak time) Aug. 21.

The East German government version published in *Neues Deutschland* Aug. 21 declared that "personalities of the party and state of Czechoslovakia turned ... to the governments of the allied Socialist [Warsaw Pact] states" for "instantaneous help, including military aid." The statement said that the allied states had responded to the appeal "in view of the danger created by the agitation of counterrevolutionary elements and intervention efforts by imperialist powers" within Czechoslovakia.

In an article Aug. 25, *Neues Deutschland* charged that "Zionist forces have taken over the leadership [of Czechoslovakia]."

In *Trybuna Ludu,* the Polish Communist party newspaper, Maj. Gen. Jan Czapla, the first deputy political chief of the Polish army, charged Aug. 25 that "Zionist forces" were to blame for the "real threat of transition from socialism to capitalism" in Czechoslovakia.

The Hungarian CP newspaper *Nepszabadsag* asserted Aug. 22 that "hardly had the ink dried" on the Aug. 3 Bratislava declaration than "counterrevolutionary forces organized meetings in Prague ..., slandering the Soviet Union [and] taking issue with the Bratislava declaration." The article implied that the Czechoslovak regime had failed to put an end to such provocations although it had pledged secretly in Bratislava to do so.

According to East European claims, the invasion was necessitated by Dubcek's failure to carry out 5 secret pledges he allegedly had made during the July 29-Aug. 1 Cierna confrontation. In the secret agreement, ratified at the Aug. 3 conference in Bratislava, Dubcek reportedly promised: (1) to reestablish censorship of the Czechoslovak press, (2) to prevent the organization of any political groups outside the Communist-controlled "National Front," (3) to take measures to strengthen the people's militia and other security forces, (4) to assure the protection of conservative Communists opposed to the reform program, (5) to end the polemics with the Soviet Union and all other Warsaw Pact countries.

The Moscow newspaper *Pravda* Aug. 22, in a 13,000-word justification of the invasion, charged that Dubcek had led a minority faction in the 11-man Presidium that was guilty of "perfidious, treacherous activities." It said: "Even among the top party leaders there were persons who came out openly against the Leninist principles of the party system."

The Soviet government daily *Izvestia* in Moscow denounced the Czechoslovak Club of Involved Nonpartisans (or KAN, whose members, while not of any political party, nonetheless sought a voice in public affairs) and the Club of Former Political Prisoners (or K-231). *Izvestia* charged that the "ultimate aim" of the 2 groups was "the liquidation of the Czechoslovak Communist Party and of Socialist achievements

in the country and the restoration of a bourgeois republic of the
Masaryk type." It attacked Ivan Svitak, leader of the KAN, as
one of the worst "reactionaries" and a known associate of an
"agent of an international Zionist organization."

The governments of the Soviet Union and its 4 allies in the
invasion appealed to the Czechoslovak people Aug. 23 to help
them overthrow "counterrevolutionary forces." The message,
addressed to "our brothers, Czechs and Slovaks," and broadcast
over Moscow radio shortly before Pres. Svoboda's arrival in
Moscow, told Czechoslovaks that the invasion forces had been
sent to their country "so that no one can take your freedom
away from you." The statement said that "the enemies were
preparing to plunge the country into chaos, to sacrifice the
freedom and independence of their homeland to their
mercenary aims."

Resistance Starts

Reports from Czechoslovakia indicated deep, widespread
resentment of the invasion. Although there was no organized
resistance to the overwhelming occupation forces,
Czechoslovak citizens, spearheaded by students, resorted to a
wide variety of means to hamper the invaders, and several
general strikes of up to an hour's duration took place.

Starting in the early hours of the invasion Aug. 21, crowds
roamed the streets of Prague, Bratislava, Kosice and other
major towns. They shouted support for Dubcek and insults (in
Russian) at the Soviet soldiers. Some citizens, especially older
ones, wept in the streets; others, mostly students, painted
swastikas on the tanks and armored cars. In open but
nonviolent defiance, groups of students repeatedly sat in front
of tanks and raised barricades. Angry jeers of "Russians, go
home," "Dirty fascists," and "Freedom" could be heard in
various parts of Prague and Bratislava Aug. 21-26.

Stubborn, spontaneous resistance was put up in Prague
near the radio station, the National Museum and around the
statue of St. Wenceslas. Shortly before dawn Aug. 21, students
erected barricades in the streets around the radio building.
Buses and trolleys were piled up and paving stones dug up to
strengthen the defense against the tanks. Students threw stones
and garbage at soldiers on the vehicles. Prague radio

maintained its program until about 11 a.m., when tanks were able to penetrate the barricades. The broadcasts, however, were resumed later in the day from a secret studio and continued uninterruptedly by constantly switching frequency.

Before the radio building was seized, youths had charged onto the road and set tanks on fire with Molotov cocktails, burning newspapers and branches of fallen trees. Others threw mattresses, wooden crates and garbage cans onto the tanks. One tank was left in flames on the street near the radio building, and 2 flaming Soviet munitions trucks set off a series of explosions, rocking the entire area and injuring several people.

Several buildings near the radio station were burned by tank fire. Store windows were broken by explosions, but there was no report of looting. Except for food stores, nearly all business in Prague was shut; some power lines were down.

Some people during the early phase of the occupation attempted to convince the soldiers that there had been no "provocation" justifying the invasion. An estimated 20,000 peaceful demonstrators marched to St. Wenceslas Square in Prague Aug. 22 to demand the withdrawal of the occupying forces. Passing in front of the long row of Soviet tanks and soldiers with fixed bayonets beside the tanks, the demonstrators shook their fists and shouted "Russian murderers go home" and "Dubcek, Svoboda."

Wall writings denouncing the invasion quickly appeared throughout Prague and other cities. Leaflets circulating in Prague urged Czechs and Slovaks to have nothing to do with those who wanted to collaborate with the invaders.

By Aug. 23, rumors spread in Prague of arrests by the secret police. In late morning, lists suddenly went up in the city—scribbled on doorways or in shop windows—giving the license-plate numbers of the cars used by the secret police. Throughout the day, sniper fire could be heard but there were no reports of casualties. A one-hour general strike took place at noon. Later, a throng of long-haired youths, responding to instructions given through the clandestine radio, urged a crowd at St. Wenceslas Square to tear down all street signs to hamper the secret police in their hunt for leaders of the resistance movement.

3 young men were shot and killed by Soviet soldiers in Prague Aug. 24 after they had been caught distributing anti-Soviet leaflets. In defiance of a Soviet-imposed curfew, 30 youngsters Aug. 25 held a 24-hour vigil around the statue of St. Wenceslas in memory of the 3 slain men.

A train coming from the Soviet Union with radio-direction-finding equipment was derailed 60 miles outside Prague Aug. 23 by members of the resistance. The same train was halted Aug. 24 when current on the electrified rail line was cut. Soviet troops finally lifted the equipment into the capital by helicopters Aug. 25, when, for the 3d time, anti-Soviet Czechoslovaks had made it impossible to bring it by train.

By Aug. 25 the number of clandestine radio stations was estimated at 10 to 12. "Radio Free Prague," operating from a secret location outside Prague, gave continuous commentary to the country and relayed official messages from the arrested Czechoslovak leaders negotiating in Moscow. It also coordinated the other "liberation stations," which formed a network from Marianske Lazne in the west to Kosice in the east. Among stations that broadcast almost continuously were Radio Free Czechoslovakia, operating near Prague, and Radio Ceske Budejovice, broadcasting from southern Bohemia, some 30 miles from the Austrian border.

About 1,200 delegates to the Czechoslovak party 14th congress met secretly Aug. 21-22 and elected a new 160-man Central Committee, which in turn named a new 27-member Presidium. The congress was held in a large industrial plant, identified Aug. 23 by the London *Times* as the CKD factory, on the outskirts of Prague. The delegates entered the factory clad as workers, doctors, nurses or patients. According to an Aug. 24 *N.Y. Times* report, the meeting had been called less than 4 hours after the Soviet invasion had begun. The congress had been originally scheduled for Sept. 9.

A list of the secretly-elected Presidium was circulated in Prague Aug. 23. Its members: Alexander Dubcek, Oldrich Cernik, Josef Smrkovsky, Josef Spacek, Frantisek Kriegel, Cestmir Cisar, Gustav Husak, Ota Sik, Eduard Goldstuecker, Bohumil Simon, Venek Silhan, Peter Colotka, Milan Huebl, Stefan Sadovsky, Zdenek Hejzlar, Libuse Hrdinova, Vladimir Kabrna, Josef Zrak, Viktor Pavlenda, Anton Tazky, Jaromir

Litera, Vaclav Simicek, Julius Turcek, Vojtech Matejicek, Bohumil Vojacek, Zdenek Moc and Andrej Zamek.

In reaction to the Czechoslovak resistance movement, additional KGB agents were flown into Prague Aug. 25. Clandestine radio broadcasts reported that they "change into civilian clothes of Czechoslovak manufacture ... [and] carry passes of our police and the identification of our citizens, as well as a great deal of money in new banknotes."

According to preliminary reports, 22 persons died and 314 were wounded in Prague during the invasion Aug. 20-26. The Paris Bureau of the Assembly of Captive Nations in Europe reported Sept. 12 that 186 Czechoslovak citizens had been killed, 362 seriously wounded and several hundred deported to unknown destinations during the first week of the occupation.

UN Condemns Invasion

A 7-nation resolution condemning the Soviet Union and its 4 Warsaw Pact allies for invading Czechoslovakia was supported by a 10-2 vote (3 abstentions) of the UN Security Council Aug. 23 but was defeated by the USSR's 105th veto. Hungary joined the USSR in casting a negative vote. Approving the resolution were its 7 sponsors—Brazil, Canada, Denmark, France, Paraguay, Britain and the U.S.—and Nationalist China, Ethiopia and Senegal. India, Pakistan and Algeria abstained.

The resolution, introduced Aug. 22 by Otto H. Borch, representative of Denmark, expressed the Council's concern over the danger of "violence and reprisals" and the "threats to human rights" resulting from the occupation of Czechoslovakia. It called for the immediate withdrawal of all foreign forces from the country and for a halt to "all other forms of intervention in Czechoslovakia's internal affairs." *The resolution said:*

The Security Council, ...

Gravely concerned that ... troops of the Soviet Union and other members of the Warsaw Pact have entered ... [Czechoslovakia] without the knowledge and against the wishes of the Czechoslovakian government.

Considering that the action taken by the government of the Union of Soviet Socialist Republics and other members of the Warsaw Pact in invading the Czechoslovak Socialist Republic is a violation of the United Nations Charter and, in particular, of the principle that all members shall refrain in their international relations from the threat or use of force against the territorial integrity or political independence of any state, . . .

Considering that the people of the sovereign state of the Czechoslovak Socialist Republic have the right in accordance with the charter freely to exercise their own self-determination and to arrange their own affairs without external intervention,

1. Affirms that the sovereign, political independence and territorial integrity of the Czechoslovak Socialist Republic must be fully respected;

2. Condemns the armed intervention of the Union of Soviet Socialist Republics and other members of the Warsaw Pact in the internal affairs of the Czechoslovak Socialist Republic and calls upon them to take no action of violence or reprisal that could result in further suffering or loss of life, forthwith to withdraw their forces, and to cease all other forms of intervention in Czechoslovakia's internal affairs. . . .

The Council, called into emergency session Aug. 21, had voted 13-2 to include the Czechoslovak crisis on its agenda. The Soviet Union and Hungary opposed the adoption of the motion, but the veto did not apply to a procedural question.

During Council debate, Jan Muzik, Czechoslovakia's acting chief representative at the UN, delivered an address devoted largely to reading into the record 2 messages received from Czechoslovakia and circulated to the UN and to governments with which Prague had relations.

The first message, received from Foreign Min Jiri Hajek, demanded that "the illegal occupation of Czechoslovakia be stopped without delay" and that "all armed troops be withdrawn" from the country. Hajek said he had instructed the Czechoslovak ambassadors to the Soviet Union, Hungary, Poland and East Germany to file strong protests with those governments and to demand that they permit the Czechoslovak people and their "legitimate representatives" to continue their normal governmental functions "without delay."

The 2d message read by Muzik came from the presidium of Czechoslovakia's National Assembly. In a formal declaration the presidium assailed "the occupation" of the country as a violation of international law, the Warsaw Treaty and "the principles of equality between nations." It demanded the release of all government officials detained by Soviet forces in Prague, the withdrawal of all the invading troops from the country and the granting of "full respect for the sovereignty" of the Czechoslovak government. The presidium warned the Czechoslovak people not to resort to violence to justify the occupation. But it advised the workers, "if necessary," to "defend yourself by a general strike."

Delivering his own statement, Muzik declared that his government's liberalization program, which had precipitated the Soviet move against Czechoslovakia, was aimed at bringing Prague "closer to the lofty goals of real socialism" and at "retaining the human rights and liberty which are an integral part of any Socialist system."

In debate prior to the Aug. 21 vote, Yakov A. Malik, chief Soviet delegate, asserted that there was "no basis" for Council discussion of the crisis. The USSR and its allies, Malik said, had moved their forces into Czechoslovakia "at the request" of the Prague government "in view of the threats created by the external and internal reaction" against the country's "Socialist system" and "statehood." The Communist military move was "in accordance with the existing treaty obligations and on the basis of the relevant provisions of the United Nations Charter," Malik asserted. He warned that the Soviet Union would not tolerate "the attempts of the imperialist reaction to interfere" in the domestic affairs of Czechoslovakia and in "the relations between all Socialist countries."

U.S. Amb. George W. Ball, defending the Council's right to take up the crisis, called the invasion "an affront to all civilized sensibilities." The aim of the Communist incursion was "to impose by force a repressive political system which is plainly obnoxious to the people and leadership of Czechoslovakia," Ball said. The USSR's explanation of its actions was "a feeble and futile effort at self-justification." The Council, Ball asserted, must require the Soviet Union to remove its troops from Czechoslovakia and to "cease interference in that country or anywhere else."

Ball declared Aug. 22 that the 7-nation resolution introduced that day "makes 3 simple points: An inexcusable international crime has been committed"; the Czechoslovak people had the right to conduct their own affairs without external intervention, and the forces that invaded their territory must be withdrawn; the Council must demand that the Soviet Union, Poland, Bulgaria, Hungary and East Germany "refrain from further killings and tortures" that would further exacerbate the situation in Czechoslovakia.

Ball called on the 5 Communist states to adhere to the principles of the UN Charter and to abide by the "principles sanctimoniously reaffirmed at Bratislava ... in an agreement concluded between Czechoslovakia and the same 5 parties that are cynically engaged in the rape of that unhappy country." "The world is disgusted," Ball said, by the USSR's "pious assertion that this invasion and occupation ... are merely 'fraternal assistance.'" "The kind of Soviet assistance that the Soviet Union is according to Czechoslovakia is exactly the same kind that Cain gave to Abel." Ball said.

Ball scoffed at Malik's charge that "only imperialists oppose and deplore these brutal acts of your government." He then cited opposition to the Soviet actions by such "imperialists" as Indian Prime Min. Indira Gandhi, Pope Paul VI, Rumanian Pres. Nicolae Ceausescu, Yugoslav Pres. Tito, Tanzanian Pres. Julius K. Nyerere and the leaders of the Communist parties in France and Italy.

Soviet Amb. Malik, in reply, assailed the U.S. and its Western allies for "drag[ging] this question into the Security Council." Recalling that in his address Aug. 21 Czechoslovak representative Jan Muzik had not requested Council action, Malik asserted that it was NATO countries "who suddenly made a show of themselves ... and started playing the role of defenders of socialism and communism, arrogated to themselves the role of protectors of Socialist Czechoslovakia." Malik reasserted the claim that Moscow and its allies had moved their forces into Czechoslovakia "to help it protect [its] Socialist system ... from the threat of reaction and counterrevolution." Addressing himself to Ball and Lord Caradon, chief British delegate, Malik asked: "What Czechoslovakia are you defending? ... The elements which tried to make it subservient to your design or that Socialist Czechoslovakia which is truly a Socialist country." Malik said: "Relations between Czechoslovakia and other Socialist countries are determined, have been and will be determined and decided by the peoples and countries of the Socialist community themselves. And no interference from outside will be tolerated by the peoples of the Socialist countries. And against those who attempt to interfere, necessary and effective measures will be taken."

(Yugoslav Amb. Anton Vratusa told the Council Aug. 23 that "no principles of socialism whatever can be used as a screen for a gross violation of sovereignty.")

Earlier in the debate Aug. 22 Caradon had lauded Muzik and "all the leaders of his brave country who have refused to bow down before the forces of invasion and suppression." Caradon then called on Malik to tell the Council that Ludvik Svoboda, Alexander Dubcek and other Prague leaders were "free and safe" and would "be permitted to continue to speak and work for their people."

A resolution introduced by Canadian delegate George Ignatieff Aug. 23 proposed that UN Secy. Gen. U Thant send a representative to Prague "to seek the release and ensure the safety" of the detained Czechoslovak leaders. The draft was sponsored by the U.S., Britain, France, Denmark, Nationalist China, Paraguay and Brazil. Malik charged that the resolution, like the one he had vetoed in the early hours of Aug. 23, was a plot to pave the way for British and U.S. "imperialists and counterrevolutionaries" to lure Czechoslovakia away from its Communist allies. Furthermore, the resolution was an attempt to get Thant to support the Western plot of "reaction and counterrevolution" in Czechoslovakia, Malik said.

Caradon assailed Malik's reaction to the resolution as a "contemptuous personal insult" to the Council members. The resolution prompted Caradon to challenge Malik again on the whereabouts of the missing Czechoslovak leaders.

Czechoslovak Foreign Min. Hajek flew to New York Aug. 23 and reported to U Thant on the situation in his country. Hajek had arrived from Belgrade, where he was vacationing at the time of the invasion of Czechoslovakia.

In an address to the Council Aug. 24, Hajek asserted that there was no justification for the occupation of his country. Contrary to Moscow's explanations, the invasion had not been carried out "at the request of the Czechoslovak government" or any other agency of the republic, Hajek declared. Alluding to Malik's charges of counterrevolutionary activity in Czechoslovakia Hajek insisted that the Prague regime had had the situation "firmly in hand and sufficient means to repel any attack upon the foundations of socialism."

Prior to Hajek's speech, Malik had delivered a 3-hour address lauding East Germany and denouncing West Germany. Malik then introduced a proposal (in the form of a motion) requesting the participation of East Germany, which was not a UN member, in Council deliberations. The proposal was defeated by 9-2 vote (4 abstentions). Voting against the resolution—U.S., Britain, France, Paraguay, Denmark, Ethiopia, Senegal, Nationalist China and Canada; for it— USSR and Hungary; abstaining—Algeria, India, Pakistan and Brazil.

The Council recessed until Aug. 26, but decided that day to suspend meetings pending the outcome of the negotiations in Moscow between Soviet and Czechoslovak leaders. A statement issued by the Czechoslovak UN mission Aug. 25 said it had instructed its delegates not to participate in Council debate because it would not be "conducive to the solution of this significant question" in view of the Moscow talks. On the conclusion of the Moscow negotiations and the issuance of a joint Soviet-Czechoslovak communique Aug. 27, Foreign Min. Hajek formally announced at UN headquarters that day that his country's delegation would not participate in further Security Council discussion of the invasion. The Moscow communique had said that Czechoslovakia had "demanded" the removal of the subject from the Council's agenda.

(The Indian delegate's abstention on the Council's Aug. 23 vote on the resolution condemning the invasion had precipitated a sharp antigovernment outburst by opposition members in the Indian parliament later Aug. 23. Prime Min. Indira Gandhi entered parliament after the demonstration subsided and explained that India's abstention was based on its objection to the word "condemns" in the resolution; it would have preferred the word "deplores." Acceptance of the resolution would have restricted India's diplomatic maneuvering in the crisis, Mrs. Gandhi said.)

Communist Response to Intervention

The invasion aroused widespread condemnation and resentment in the Communist world. The most vehement criticism was leveled by Prague's 2 staunchest allies—Rumania and Yugoslavia—and by Communist China. Sympathy for

Czechoslovakia's plight reportedly was also voiced by private citizens in 3 of the invading countries—the USSR, Poland and East Germany. But Communist support for Moscow's move came from Cuba, North Vietnam and North Korea.

Addressing a crowd of more than 100,000 persons in Bucharest's main square, Rumanian Pres. Nicolae Ceausescu Aug. 21 denounced the invasion as "a great mistake and a grave danger to peace in Europe, to the fate of socialism in the world." Asserting that there was "no justification whatsoever" for the invasion Ceausescu warned that Rumania would use armed force to protect itself from a similar attack. A communique of the Rumanian Communist Party's Central Committee read at the rally expressed "profound anxiety" over the invasion, voiced "full solidarity" with the Czechoslovak people and urged the speedy withdrawal of the foreign Communist soldiers from the country.

The Rumanian Grand National Assembly (parliament), at a special session held Aug. 22, unanimously approved Ceausescu's reaffirmation of his program of national sovereignty coupled with strict adherence to socialism.

A Yugoslav party statement issued Aug. 22, following a meeting of the party Presidium and Pres. Tito, called the invasion an act of aggression. It said: "Involved is not only an attack on the Czechoslovak people but a significant, historical point of rupture, bearing on the relationship among Socialist countries in general, . . . as well as on peace in Europe and in the world." A rally in support of Czechoslovakia was held in Belgrade Aug. 22. Organized by the League of Yugoslav Communists, an estimated 200,000 persons marched for hours through the streets shouting "Freedom for Czechoslovakia," "Tanks Must Go" and "Tito-Dubcek." Demonstrators gathered in front of the Czechoslovak embassy and were greeted by Foreign Min. Jiri Hajek, who expressed gratitude for their display of sympathy. (Hajek had arrived in Yugoslavia with other Czechoslovak officials Aug. 21 for a vacation.)

A resolution adopted by the Yugoslav party Central Committee Aug. 25 called for an immediate end to the Soviet occupation of Czechoslovakia. It warned that Yugoslavia was ready to put up armed resistance to any threat against its territorial integrity.

Presidents Tito and Ceausescu were reported to have discussed the east European crisis Aug. 24 at Vrsac, a Yugoslav border town.

The Soviet government newspaper *Izvestia* charged Aug. 24 that Ceausescu's speeches had given aid to "the Czechoslovak counterrevolution." Ceausescu's speeches also were assailed by 2 Hungarian newspapers Aug. 24. One paper, *Magyar Nemzet,* said: "There is a strange similarity between the tone and content of Ceausescu's [Aug. 21] speech and the phrases repeated a hundred times a day by Western radio stations."

Ceausescu softened his criticism of Moscow in a speech delivered in the Transylvanian industrial city of Brasov Aug. 26. He said all Communist states must seek common cause in opposing imperialism and must try to smooth over their differences. Ceausescu reaffirmed Rumania's friendship with the USSR, Hungary, Bulgaria and Yugoslavia as well as with Czechoslovakia. The Rumanian leader's apparent retreat from his rigid position followed a meeting he had held Aug. 25 with Soviet Amb.-to-Rumania Aleksandr V. Basov.

The Albanian government Aug. 23 condemned the Soviet-led invasion but also denounced Czechoslovak party First Secy. Dubcek as a traitor "to the interests of his people."

North Vietnam Aug. 21 upheld Soviet intervention in Czechoslovakia as a "noble" act. The invasion, Hanoi said, was justified by the "increased activities against socialism" by Czechoslovakia's counterrevolutionary forces since January.

Cuban Premier Fidel Castro conceded Aug. 23 that there was no legal basis for the Communist armies' occupation of Czechoslovakia. But he supported the action as a necessary step to prevent the Czechoslovak Communist Party from "marching toward a counterrevolutionary situation, capitalism and into the embrace of imperialism."

Among statements made by west European Communist parties Aug. 21: The Italian Communist Party called the invasion "unjustified" and expressed "grave dissent." The French party Politburo voiced "surprise and reprobation" and disclosed that its leaders had cautioned Moscow against the use of military force; similar sentiments were voiced by Communist Party leaders in Britain, Austria, the Netherlands, Denmark and Belgium. Luigi Longo, Italian party first secretary, who had been in Moscow at the time of the invasion, delivered a speech in Rome Aug. 23 in which he denounced the Soviet Union's actions in Czechoslovakia.

The U.S. Communist Party was split in its attitude toward the Soviet Union. The party's general secretary, Gus Hall, said Aug. 21 that the Soviet Union and its allies had to employ force to avert a "counterrevolutionary take-over" in Czechoslovakia. The N.Y. State chairman, Gilbert Green, said he and a large number of party officers and members disagreed with Hall's views and opposed the attack on Czechoslovakia.

Communist China Aug. 23 denounced the invasion as "a shameless act." An article in the party newspaper *Jenmin Jih Pao* said the invasion pointed up the "total bankruptcy of Soviet revisionism." Deriding the Soviet contention that the invasion was designed to protect the fruits of socialism, the newspaper asked: "Who capitulated to United States imperialism and so lost the fruits of Soviet socialism? Who was it who peddled Soviet revisionism to Europe? The Chinese statement accused Soviet leaders of working "hand-in-glove" with the U.S. and said that "Czechoslovak revisionists" had hoped to work out similar cooperation with the U.S. and West Germany.

88 Soviet writers, in a letter dated Aug. 23, protested the invasion of Czechoslovakia. The letter was subsequently smuggled to the West, where it was disclosed Sept. 10 by a British author, Lord Bethell. The letter, which Bethell said had been given to him during a recent European tour, told Czechoslovak writers that "since January of this year we observed your struggle with envy, and we are delighted to see that in at least one Slavonic country there existed freedom of thought, speech and behavior." Unfortunately, the letter continued, "freedom today is being stifled not only in Czechoslovakia but in our country also." The writers said they were "ashamed of the fact that on this occasion the suppressors of freedom are men of our own country."

Several Soviet intellectuals preparing a Moscow rally to denounce the invasion of Czechoslovakia were arrested in Red Square Aug. 25. Police seized 9 persons, including Mrs. Yuli M. Daniel, wife of the imprisoned writer, and Pavel Y. Litvinov, grandson of the late ex-Foreign Min. Maxim M. Litvinov. 5 women in the dissident group, with the exception of Mrs. Daniel, were released. But one of the freed women, the poet Natalya Gorbanevskaya, was rearrested Aug. 26. The Soviet action against Czechoslovakia had been denounced earlier Aug. 25 at a meeting of the Academy of Sciences' Russian Language Institute. Similar rallies had been staged by Soviet intellectuals at other institutes, including one in Leningrad where 4 persons were arrested.

Criticism of the invasion was kept from Soviet citizens. The USSR Aug. 21 began jamming the Russian-language programs of the Voice of America and other Western stations for the first time in more than 5 years. Jamming began 2 hours after the announcement of the invasion. (The Soviet Union had stopped jamming Western stations June 19, 1963; Poland did so in 1956, Rumania in 1963, Hungary and Czechoslovakia in 1964. Bulgaria had not ceased its jamming of Western broadcasts.)

East German workers were said to have refused Aug. 23 to sign petitions "approving" the invasion of Czechoslovakia. The petitions were said to have been circulated by Socialist Unity (Communist) Party officials among factory, office and farm workers. East Berlin citizens were said to have signed a document at the Czechoslovak embassy expressing sympathy with the Prague regime.

Some Czechoslovak leaders abroad at the invasion's outset managed to confirm the doubts of many Communist allies about the self-professed idealism motivating the invaders. An appeal to the world's Communist parties was signed by 5 leading Czechoslovak officials. Released Aug. 23 by the Czechoslovak embassy in Belgrade, the statement said: "Czechoslovakia is not threatened by counterrevolution but by an attempt by a handful of dogmatists and sectarians who have betrayed party and people to set up a Stalinist type of occupation regime in Czechoslovakia and to take over the party leadership with the aid of the bayonets of foreign armies. A handful of sold souls represents a negligible minority of the progressive party leadership.... [The minority] has been deprived of its functions by the [emergency party] congress." The appeal was signed by Deputy Premier Ota Sik, Foreign Min. Jiri Hajek, Construction Min. Jozef Trokan, Economic Planning Min. Frantisek Vlasak and Stefan Gasparik, president of the State Control Commission.

Other World Reaction

U.S. Pres. Lyndon B. Johnson summoned the National Security Council in Washington into emergency session Aug. 20 to discuss the invasion. The meeting was called immediately after the President had received an aide-memoire in which Soviet Amb.-to-U.S. Anatoly Dobrynin informed him of the Communists' action. (Johnson was said to have received the message before Prague Radio had broadcast the news of the invasion.) Following the National Security Council meeting, Dobrynin held a separate meeting with State Secy. Dean Rusk.

In his first public comment on the crisis, Johnson said in a brief TV address Aug. 21: "The Soviet Union and its allies have invaded a defenseless country to stamp out a resurgence of ordinary human freedom. It is a sad commentary on the Communist mind that a sign of liberty is deemed a fundamental threat to the security of the Soviet system." The invasion was a violation of the UN Charter and the Soviet Union's justification for the action was "patently contrived."

Johnson appealed to Moscow and its allies to withdraw their troops from the country. He said he had instructed U.S. Amb.-to-UN George W. Ball "to join with others in the Security Council to insist upon the charter rights of Czechoslovakia and its people." (It was reported in Washington Aug. 22 that the U.S. and USSR had reached agreement just prior to the invasion of Czechoslovakia on the details of the opening of bilateral talks on missile disarmament. Discussion of the arrangements had been in progress for more than 6 weeks, but announcement of the agreement reportedly was being delayed because of the Czechoslovak crisis. Soviet diplomats had expressed hope to U.S. officials that U.S.-Soviet "state relations" would not be adversely affected by the invasion.)

Following a cabinet discussion of the situation Aug. 22, State Secy. Rusk confirmed that the U.S. was not planning any "retaliatory actions or sanctions" against the Soviet Union. Rusk called on the USSR and its Warsaw Pact allies "not to engage in punitive or excessive measures" against the Czechoslovaks and "to bring about a prompt withdrawal of their forces." Rusk said: The U.S. had no "direct responsibility ... in the sense that we have no bilateral commitments to Czechoslovakia"; but the U.S. had a deep concern for the interests of a UN member that were "so desperately periled as they are at the present time"; the Soviet military action "cannot help but damage East-West relations—get in the way of possible moves to more *detente....*"

Rusk took issue with the view that the U.S. had no moral right to criticize the Russians because of U.S. military intervention in Vietnam and the Dominican Republic. "There is all the difference in the world between acting to meet the common danger under a treaty of mutual security," as in the case of Vietnam, and "an attempt to prevent the people of a country from having their own government," as in the case of Czechoslovakia, Rusk explained.

Johnson's handling of the Czechoslovak crisis was backed by 27 Congressional leaders after he had briefed them in the White House Aug. 23. One member of the group, Chairman Richard B. Russell (D., Ga.) of the Senate Armed Services Committee, said that the U.S. was not called on to cope with the Soviet-led invasion through force or through NATO. He added: "I hope we'll pursue it in the UN," although "we've lost so much ground there that we can't even get a denunciation" of the Soviet Union.

A State Department statement Aug. 23 denounced reports that Soviet intervention in Czechoslovakia had been made possible through a tacit understanding on the U.S.' and USSR's respective "spheres of influence." The statement said: "The U.S. has never entered into any sphere-of-influence agreements or undertakings with anyone anywhere in the world"; suggestions to that effect were "malicious and totally without foundation."

Demonstrations in protest against the invasion were held Aug. 21 at the USSR's mission to the UN and in front of UN headquarters in New York. About 300 persons, including Dr. Benjamin Spock, gathered in front of the Soviet mission and later marched to the UN building. Their places at the UN were later taken by about 400 demonstrators representing the Conference of Americans of East European Descent, a group representing East European political refugees.

The invasion provoked virtually universal condemnation in the non-Communist world. The reactions ranged from critical statements issued by various governments to anti-Soviet demonstrations held in major capitals.

The Permanent Council of the North Atlantic Treaty Organizaton (NATO) met in Brussels Aug. 21-23 to consider the possible problems raised by the invasion. A NATO spokesman said after the Aug. 21 meeting that the Council had unanimously agreed that the Communist move constituted a "clear violation of the United Nations Charter and international law." NATO's forces, however, had taken no extraordinary military precautions. NATO diplomats reported that Soviet envoys had informed member governments that the invasion would be confined to Czechoslovak territory and would pose no menace to NATO.

The invasion spurred widespread anti-Soviet demonstrations in West German cities Aug. 21. Rallies were held in Bonn, West Berlin, Frankfurt, Hamburg, Hanover and Cologne. The Soviet embassy building near Bonn was the target of demonstrators throwing rocks and other missiles. Demonstrators also gathered before the Soviet military mission in Frankfurt.

French Pres. Charles de Gaulle Aug. 21 denounced the invasion as "an attack on the rights and destiny of a friendly nation." De Gaulle said the action was a continuation of the "policy of blocs, which was imposed on Europe by the effects" of the 1945 Yalta Conference at which the U.S., Britain and the Soviet Union had agreed on the division of responsibilities in postwar Europe.

British Prime Min. Harold Wilson Aug. 21 condemned the invasion as a "flagrant violation of the United Nations Charter and of all accepted standards of international behavior." The Soviet move was not only a tragedy for the whole world, Wilson pointed out, but it also had dealt a serious blow to future East-West relations. The British government informed the Soviet embassy in London that it rejected Moscow's explanation that the Communist armies had marched into Czechoslovakia on the invitation of the Prague regime. Wilson Aug. 26 again denounced the occupation of Czechoslovakia but affirmed that it should not deter the West from seeking a *detente* with the Communist world. He rejected any return to "the frozen immobilism of the cold war."

Violent anti-Soviet demonstrations took place Aug. 22 in London, Paris, Venice and Rome. A bomb shattered the window of the Soviet embassy in Rio de Janeiro. Government protests were voiced in Nepal, Burma, Malta and Norway.

UN Secy. Gen. U Thant Aug. 22 characterized the invasion as "another serious blow to the concepts of international order and morality" and "a grave setback to the East-West *detente* which seemed to be reemerging in recent months."

African states Aug. 22 voiced strong opposition to the invasion. The Congo (Kinshasa), which had shortly before then resumed diplomatic relations with the USSR, said in a broadcast that "Muscovite communism is degraded once again in the eyes of the world."

South Vietnamese Pres. Nguyen Van Thieu Aug. 23 deplored "the brutal repression of the budding aspirations of the Czechoslovak people for freedom, independence and human dignity."

British philosopher Bertrand Russell, 96, called on the USSR Aug. 25 to immediately end its occupation of Czechoslovakia. In a message to Moscow, Russell said: "The left cannot recognize negotiation [under] duress. The taking of hostages and occupation by hundreds of thousands of troops are entirely unacceptable." The Soviet move "strengthens reactionary factors in the West and throughout the world."

French philosopher Jean-Paul Sartre Aug. 25 called the invasion "pure aggression, such as is defined in terms of international law as a war crime." But Sartre said the invasion could not be compared with the U.S.' military intervention in Vietnam, which he labeled "ignoble genocide."

West German Chancellor Kurt Georg Kiesinger Aug. 25 called for a summit conference of heads of NATO countries to alert them to "watch over liberty and security." The purpose of such a conference, Kiesinger said, would be to determine "what one can do to fill this tired workaday operation with life." He warned West Germans to stay alert and to "make the necessary sacrifices for our defense."

About 5,000 persons demonstrated in front of the Soviet embassy in Rome Aug. 26. There were some clashes between the demonstrators and police, and at least 12 persons were reported injured.

MOSCOW AGREEMENTS

Pact Signed

Pres. Ludvik Svoboda and other Czechoslovak officials were flown to Moscow Aug. 23 to discuss with Soviet officials means of resolving the crisis. At 9:10 a.m. Aug. 23, Svoboda had announced over Radio Free Prague from Hradcany Castle in Prague that he had been unable to get satisfaction in his talks Aug. 22 with the Soviet representatives in Prague and that he had therefore decided to have "direct negotiations with the highest representatives of the Soviet Union" in Moscow. The Aug. 22 talks, according to Svoboda, had dealt with "the situation that has arisen due to the entry of Soviet and other countries' troops into Czechoslovak territory, and particularly with respect to restoration of an orderly functioning of constitutional organs" of the government.

Svoboda reported that his decision to go to Moscow had been made "in agreement with the cabinet, which met at the castle [Hradcany Castle] and is still in session here." Svoboda said he would be accompanied by Slovak Vice Premier Gustav Husak, National Defense Min. Martin Dzur, the 4 pro-Soviet members of the party Central Committee—Drahomir Kolder, Oldrich Svestka, Vasil Bilak and Alois Indra—and Justice Min. Bohuslav Kucera among others.

Svoboda said that he had informed the National Assembly and that he expected to be back in Prague that night. He appealed to his people "to continue to support my actions," and he urged them "to avoid any action or contacts that would exacerbate the atmosphere in our country and our relations with the representatives of the foreign armies."

Only half an hour earlier, Radio Ostrava had reported that when Kolder, Indra, Slovak National Council Vice Chairman Frantisek Barbirek and Bilak had urged Svoboda to sign an unspecified proclamation, Svoboda "literally threw them out and said he would not be a traitor."

93

Svoboda was received at Moscow airport with the usual ceremony by Soviet Communist Party Gen. Secy. Leonid Brezhnev, Pres. Nikolai Podgorny and Premier Aleksei Kosygin.

Still in Moscow Aug. 24 despite his previous hope of returning to Prague Aug. 23, Svoboda announced in a radio message from Moscow that his talks with the Soviet leaders were still continuing and had been joined by Dubcek, Premier Cernik and National Assembly Chairman Smrkovsky, who had been seized by the Soviets on the day of the invasion.

According to clandestine Czechoslovak radio reports Aug. 24, Dubcek, Cernik and Smrkovsky had joined the talks after Svoboda threatened to walk out of the negotiations unless they were allowed to participate. These reports said that Svoboda's action was in response to a Soviet ultimatum that he appoint a pro-Moscow government or form one himself. Among conservative Czechoslovak leaders mentioned in connection with the new government were: Alois Indra, who was said to have suffered a heart attack after other Czechoslovak leaders accused him of being a traitor; Vasil Bilak, Slovak party first secretary; and Drahomir Kolder, Presidium member.

Representatives of Poland, Bulgaria, East Germany and Hungary, whose armies had participated in the invasion, joined the parley Aug. 25.

Svoboda returned to Prague early Aug. 27 accompanied by the whole Czechoslovak delegation. A communique issued at the conclusion of the talks Aug. 27 announced an agreement. The joint statement said:

Soviet-Czechoslovak talks took place in Moscow, from 23 to 26 August 1968, in which took part:

From the Soviet side: L. I. Brezhnev, general secretary of the Central Committee of the Communist Party of the Soviet Union [CPSU]; A. N. Kosygin, chairman of the Council of Ministers of the USSR, member of the Politburo of the Central Committee of the CPSU; N. V. Podgorny, president of the Presidium of the Supreme Soviet of the USSR, member of the Politburo of the Central Committee of the CPSU; G. I. Voronov, member of the Politburo of the Central Committee of the CPSU, chairman of the Council of Ministers of the Russian Soviet Federated Socialist Republic; A. P. Kirilenko, member of the Politburo of the Central Committee of the CPSU, secretary of the Central Committee of the CPSU; D. S. Polyansky, member of the Politburo of the Central Committee of the CPSU, first vice chairman of the Council of Ministers of the USSR; M. A. Suslov, member of the Politburo of the Central Committee of the CPSU, secretary of the Central Committee of the CPSU; A. N. Shelepin, member of the Politburo of the Central Committee of the CPSU, chairman of the All-Union Central Council of Trade Unions; P. E. Shelest, member of the Politburo of the Central Committee of the CPSU, first secretary of the Central Committee of the Communist Party of the Ukraine; K. F. Katushev, secretary of the Central Committee of the CPSU; B. N. Ponomarev, secretary of the Central Committee of the CPSU; A. A. Grechko, minister of defense of the USSR; A. A. Gromyko, minister of foreign affairs of the USSR.

From the Czechoslovak side: L. Svoboda, president of the Czechoslovak Socialist Republic; A. Dubcek, first secretary of the Central Committee of the Communist Party of Czechoslovakia; J. Smrkovsky, president of the National Assembly of the Czechoslovak Socialist Republic, member of the Presidium of the Central Committee of the Communist Party of Czechoslovakia; O. Cernik, chairman of the government of the Czechoslovak Socialist Republic, member of the Presidium of the Central Committee of the Communist Party of Czechoslovakia; V. Bilak, member of the Presidium of the Central Committee of the Communist Party of Czechoslovakia, first secretary of the Central Committee of the Communist Party of Slovakia; F. Barbirek, member of the Presidium of the Central Committee of the Communist Party of Czechoslovakia, vice president of the Slovak National Council; J. Piller, member of the Presidium of the Central Committee of the Communist Party of Czechoslovakia; E. Rigo, member of the Presidium of the Central Committee of the Communist Party of Czechoslovakia; J. Spacek, member of the Presidium of the Central Committee of the Communist Party of Czechoslovakia; O. Svestka, member of the Presidium of the Central Committee of the Communist Party of Czechoslovakia; M. Jakes, chairman of the Central Control-Auditing Commission of the Communist Party of Czechoslovakia; J. Lenart, alternate member of the Presidium of the Central Committee of the Communist Party of Czechoslovakia, secretary of the Central Committee of the Communist Party of Czechoslovakia; B. Simon, alternate member of the Presidium of the Central Committee of the Communist Party of Czechoslovakia; G. Husak, vice chairman of the government of the Czechoslovak Socialist Republic; A. Indra, secretary of the Central Committee of the Communist Party of Czechoslovakia; Z. Mlynar, secretary of the Central Committee of the Communist Party of Czechoslovakia; Col. Gen. M. Dzur, minister of national defense of the Czechoslovak Socialist Republic; B. Kucera, minister of justice of the Czechoslovak Socialist Republic; V. Koucky, ambassador of the Czechoslovak Socialist Republic in the USSR.

During the talks, in a free comradely discussion, the 2 sides considered questions relating to the present development of the international situation, the activization of imperialism's machinations against the Socialist countries, the situation in Czechoslovakia in the recent period and the temporary entry of troops of 5 Socialist countries into Czechoslovak territory.

The 2 sides expressed their mutual firm belief that most important in the present situation is to carry out the mutual decisions adopted in the Cierna nad Tisou and the provisions and principles formulated by the Bratislava conference, and to implement consistently the practical steps following from the agreement reached during the talks.

The Soviet side stated its understanding of and support for the position of the leadership of the Czechoslovak Communist Party and the Czechoslovak Socialist Republic which intends to proceed from the decisions passed by the January and May plenary meetings of the Central Committee of the Czechoslovak Communist Party with a view to improving the methods of guiding society, developing Socialist democracy and strengthening the Socialist system on the basis of Marxism-Leninism.

Agreement was reached on measures aimed at the speediest normalization of the situation in the Czechoslovak Socialist Republic. Czechoslovak leaders informed the Soviet side on the planned immediate measures they are carrying out with these aims in view.

It was stated by the Czechoslovak side that all the work of party and state bodies through all media would be directed at ensuring effective measures serving the Socialist power, the guiding role of the working class and the Communist Party, the interests of developing and strengthening friendly relations with the peoples of the Soviet Union and the entire Socialist community.

Expressing the unanimous striving of the peoples of the USSR for friendship and brotherhood with the peoples of Socialist Czechoslovakia, the Soviet leaders confirmed their readiness for the broadest sincere cooperation on the basis of mutual respect, equality, territorial integrity, independence and Socialist solidarity.

The troops of the allied countries that entered temporarily the territory of Czechoslovakia will not interfere in the internal affairs of the Czechoslovak Socialist Republic. Agreement was reached on the terms of the withdrawal of these troops from its territory as the situation in Czechoslovakia normalizes.

The Czechoslovak side informed the Soviet side that the Supreme commander in chief of the Czechoslovak armed forces had given the latter appropriate orders with the aim of preventing incidents and conflicts liable to violate peace and public order. He had also instructed the military command of the Czechoslovak Socialist Republic to maintain contact with the command of the allied troops.

In connection with the discussion in the United Nations Security Council of the so-called question on the situation in Czechoslovakia, the representatives of the Czechoslovak Socialist Republic stated that the Czechoslovak side had not requested the submission of this question for consideration by the Security Council and demanded its removal from the agenda.

The leaders of the CPSU and the leaders of the Communist Party of Czechoslovakia confirmed their determination to unswervingly promote in the international arena a policy meeting the interests of strengthening the solidarity of the Socialist community, upholding the cause of peace and international security.

The Soviet Union and Czechoslovakia will, as before, resolutely rebuff the militaristic, revanchist and neonazi forces that want to revise the results of the 2d World War, to encroach on the inviolability of the existing borders in Europe. They reaffirmed their determination to fulfill unswervingly all commitments undertaken by them under multilateral and bilateral agreements between Socialist states, to strengthen the defensive might of the Socialist community, to raise the effectiveness of the defensive Warsaw Treaty Organization.

The talks were conducted in an atmosphere of frankness, comradeship and friendship.

The provisions of the agreement concluded in Moscow Aug. 26 became known in the West Sept. 8 when the *N.Y. Times* published, in unofficial translation, stenographic notes that had been taken by Czechoslovak Communists during a closed-door briefing on the accord the week of Sept. 1. The *Times* did not disclose how it obtained the notes. The text:

Information for the workers of the regional and district party committees on the basic 14 points of the Moscow agreement:

(1) The characteristics of the political development here. It was agreed that the course will be changed in accordance with the Soviet type of socialism.

(2) The declarations of the 14th party congress are not valid.

(3) The strengthening of socialism through press censorship.

(4) The Soviet side requested our side to declare that there was a counterrevolution. As the result of our protest, the word "counterrevolution" was left out and it was not repeated again in the declaration [published Aug. 27 at the end of the Soviet-Czechoslovak talks].

(5) The mass communications media may not speak or write against the allies.

(6) We submitted a request that together with the withdrawal of the troops, the Soviet security organs also be removed. The Soviet Union did agree and changed the declaration so that together with the withdrawal of troops the other groups will also be removed.

(7) The Minister of Interior, Gen. Josef Pavel, asked to be relieved from his functions because he was not ready to cooperate with the Soviet security organs.

(8) Our request for reparations for damages caused by the invasion was finally couched in such a way that a commission will probably be formed consisting of representatives of the 5 states and us to decide what can be approved as reparations and what cannot.

(9) The international situations must be adjusted in accordance with the agreement in Bratislava.

(10) The issuing of a declaration that our government did not request the United Nations and will not request the United Nations to discuss our subject.

(11) The questions of ministers. The release from their functions of Ota Sik [economic planner and deputy premier] and of Jiri Hajek [foreign minister].

(12) A declaration that our border with West Germany is not prepared for defense and must, therefore, be secured by the allies.

(13) The results of the Moscow negotiations are strictly secret and will not be published.

(14) The further strengthening of friendship and alliance with the Soviet Union and with the states of the Socialist camp.

The following additional points were discussed:

(a) The Soviet Union requested a declaration that the persons who worked for the Soviet Union [in connection with Paragraph 4] will not be persecuted.

(b) Our side requested an extra provision in the declaration that the statement that the 14th congress is not valid will be made when the foreign troops
have left the country.

National Assembly Chairman Josef Smrkovsky, in a
speech delivered in Prague Sept. 9, said that the Moscow agreement actually had contained 15 points, the 15th consisting of
assurances that Czechoslovakia could continue with the democratization policies begun in January. "Our socialism will be
democratic and will have a humane face," Smrkovsky said.

In a speech made Sept. 13 and reported Sept. 26, Zdenek
Mlynar, a member of the Czechoslovak party Presidium, had
disclosed these terms of the secret Aug. 26 Moscow protocol: (1)
The Czechoslovak Communist Party and government would
honor all existing treaties and agreements and would refrain
from seeking neutrality; (2) the 14th Party Congress, held
secretly Aug. 22, would be regarded as invalid; (3) the party
would endeavor to strengthen its leading role in the direction of
state and economy; (4) the party would strengthen its control of
the Interior Ministry; (5) the government would review the
activities of those of its members who were abroad Aug. 22; (6)
censorship would be reimposed on the mass media (but apparently not on art and culture); (7) no one cooperating with the
occupation authorities would be persecuted; (8) the UN
Security Council would be asked to drop the Czechoslovak question from its agenda; (9) economic ties between the USSR and
Czechoslovakia would be expanded; (10) Czechoslovak authorities would retain responsibility for law and order and the
normal development of the economy; (11) no new political
parties would be allowed; (12) all anti-Socialist clubs and
organizations not affiliated with the National Front would be
banned; (13) Czechoslovak foreign policy would remain within
the framework of the Socialist alliance; (14) all future negotiations and talks between the Soviet and Czechoslovak parties
would be kept secret; (15) friendship between the 2 countries
would be strengthened and expanded.

Czechoslovak Leaders Explain Treaty

Pres. Svoboda and Dubcek, in separate countrywide
broadcasts Aug. 27, reported on the Moscow meetings. The 2
leaders spoke while thousands of persons turned out in the
streets of Prague to protest as the harsh terms of the Moscow

agreement leaked out. One group, marching on the parliament building, shouted: "We want to know the truth."

In their broadcasts, Dubcek and Svoboda appealed for public calm in the face of Soviet demands for a reversal of the government's democratization program. Dubcek urged his countrymen "not to permit provocations" that would precipitate punitive measures by the occupation forces "and to try to prevent panic from entering our ranks."

Svoboda said he had returned from Moscow with other government leaders who were "also without delay taking up their offices to which they have been democratically appointed and in which you have fully supported them with your confidence." "It is the first ... step for the normalization of life in our country," he declared.

Svoboda and Dubcek pledged to continue to pursue the "original aim of expressing humanistic socialistic principles." Statements by both men appeared to contradict particulars of the Moscow accord. Svoboda promised that Prague would "not budge even one step" from the liberalization program outlined at the Central Committee meetings of January, April and May. The Moscow communique had made no mention of the April meeting, which had adopted "the action program" defining the aims of the reform program.

Svoboda and Dubcek alluded to the influence that the presence of Communist military force in Czechoslovakia exerted on Prague's future political course. Svoboda said that although in the Moscow talks "we have achieved a basic agreement on the full gradual withdrawal of the troops," their presence remained "a political reality." Dubcek conceded that political activity in the country "will proceed under a situation that is not wholly dependent on our wishes."

The published Moscow communique was vague on the disposition of the Communist occupation forces. The joint Soviet-Czechoslovak statement had referred to the occupation as "temporary" and had said the troops would be withdrawn "as the situation in Czechoslovakia normalizes." Dubcek said "the armies would be transferred to restricted areas from the towns and villages." Svoboda referred only to a "full gradual withdrawal." (Reuters quoted Czechoslovak sources as saying that the occupation troops would be pulled out in 3 stages: [1]

out of towns and villages; [2] into their barracks inside the country; [3] back to their own countries.)

In an address to his cabinet Aug. 28, Svoboda confirmed that the withdrawal of the occupation forces would take "several months and stages." He said at least 2 Soviet divisions would remain permanently stationed in Bohemia, on the West German border. Svoboda described the Moscow agreement as a moral victory for his country. He disclosed that he had rejected, on the first day of the invasion, Soviet demands to sign a cabinet list of a "workers' and peasants'" government, which he had been asked to head.

Col. Gen. Martin Dzur, defense minister, reportedly had said at the cabinet meeting that occupation troops in Czechoslovakia totaled 650,000 men. The size of this force led Dzur to speculate that Moscow must have made preparations for the invasion as long ago as January when the Czechoslovak party had deposed Antonin Novotny.

The National Assembly Aug. 28 adopted an 8-point resolution declaring the occupation of the country "illegal" and calling for a specific date for the withdrawal of the occupation troops. Premier Cernik said in a countrywide broadcast the same day that the cabinet had drafted a proposal to the USSR, Bulgaria, East Germany, Hungary and Poland to enter early talks to deal with the removal of their armies.

National Assembly Pres. Josef Smrkovsky, one of the participants in the Moscow talks, provided Czechoslovaks Aug. 29 with the first detailed account of the conditions accepted by his country's negotiators in their meetings with the Soviet leaders. Smrkovsky, speaking on the Czechoslovak radio to a countrywide audience, said:

Dear fellow citizens of the Czechoslovak fatherland, dear friends: In the past I have spoken many times to you, perhaps even too many times. Sometimes I said things that were on your minds, and I always knew it. This made it easier for me to speak. Now, I would like to tell you that never before has it been so difficult for me to speak as today. The only thing which gave me strength in these days were you, our people, the Czechs and Slovaks, and all others who in this hard and perhaps most difficult trial behaved so well that I am at a loss to find words to express my gratitude and my respect to you all. . . . I do not wish to repeat what has already been said in the statements of the president, Comrade Ludvik Svoboda, of Comrade Dubcek, first secretary of our Communist Party Central Committee, and of the premier, Comrade Engineer Cernik. Therefore, allow me to speak for myself and to say what I feel.

I am almost 60 years old, and there are quite a few things I have been through in my life.... My life has not been easy. However, I have never thought that something even more difficult and even more difficult decisions were in store for me. The past days were the most difficult I have ever lived through in my life, and I also know that the days to come will not be easier either. I know that the main subject of your thoughts and also the subject of our thoughts, not only just today but also during the whole time of our stay in Moscow, is how it will all turn out for us and for our republic.

This is neither the time nor the place to draw a balance of our post-January development. As the events of the past few days have further shown, we underrated several factors in our previous efforts, factors that have substantially influenced our development, primarily external and international factors that subsequently produced the greatest and most difficult complication in our efforts. You know that our party policy gradually became the subject of criticism and pressure by the neighboring Socialist countries, pressure which on 21 August, or more accurately during the night of 20 to 21 August, grew into formidable proportions. Our country was suddenly occupied by an enormous military force which it was absolutely hopeless and impossible to resist in the same manner.

... This has happened more than once in Czech and Slovak history, and in fact it has now happened twice in the 20th century. Therein lies the tragedy of small nations, whose fatherland lies in a particularly sensitive place of this continent. Therein lies the tragedy of the efforts for new Socialist achievements, the tragedy of those who are trying to march in front, the tragedy of the attempts by peoples who are setting for themselves great noble aims. Such an effort is never easy and it is twice as difficult with little peoples and involves twice as much risk of failure, frustration and misunderstanding. I think we were aware of this risk. I think we anticipated that we would have to pay for all this. However, and I should like to stress this, we did not expect such a force which the night of 20 to 21 August brought on us. Since that moment not only all our post-January efforts but literally the most fundamental, truly basic values of all of us—the state and its sovereignty and freedom, the management of our internal affairs, nay even the existence and security of every citizen—found themselves in mortal danger.

Our talks in Moscow were of an unusual nature. You know that we did not arrive there at the same time and you also know the circumstances under which some of us got there and negotiated. I think that I do not have to go into detail today. It is for me just as for Comrade Dubcek and the other people too difficult and painful a topic. As everyone may easily imagine for himself, to take decisions in this situation was extremely difficult. The occupation of our country by the troops of the Warsaw Treaty was a stern reality. Our contacts with home were limited, we possessed extremely little information or almost none, and more than once we had to depend ... more on our faith in the firm attitude of our peoples than on actual knowledge of the situation. But the attitude of our partners [i.e., the Soviet leaders] was communicated to us rather accurately, and we also anticipated certain difficulties in which the external military intervention had become involved politically. We knew that the world sympathized with us but that the great powers would accept a compromise solution rather than anything else. Under these circumstances, we were confronted with a dilemma from which we could not escape. We could have rejected any type of compromise and let matters develop to the point of the institution of a long-term occupation administration with all the consequences that would ensue from this for the sovereignty of the state, the political rights, the economy, and for eventual new human sacrifices that such a conflicting development would most likely have caused.

I may add that we also considered the fact that at times there is nothing left to do but reject any appeasing settlements, that in the interest of the honor and character of a people it is better to expose one's breast to the bayonets. At the same time, however, we were of the opinion that such an extreme moment had not yet come, and that despite all that had happened another possibility was left which we must not leave unexploited as politicians responsible for the destiny of the state. Therefore we tried subsequently once more to search for a way out based on an acceptable compromise. In this case, too, we were aware of the consequences, particularly of the moral ones, and of the historical consequences which such a settlement could entail.

I beg you to believe that our personal destinies—although as normal people this consideration was naturally not negligible to us—were of secondary importance at that moment. The decision for us was whether there had appeared some possibility to extricate the Czechoslovak state and socialism from a crisis into which they had slipped by no fault of our own. Such a possibility began to emerge when the clear and united attitude of the Czech and Slovak peoples towards the occupation fully manifested itself and influenced the attitude of our partners [the Soviet side] and our personal situation. In this situation we then decided to embark on the 2d road, that of a compromise, which offered hope for a continuation of the path begun in January. This was recognized by the other negotiating side as the basis for a possible settlement, but our deliberations were not easy even then. They went on virtually for a day and a night, and we realized that the decision could be regarded by the people of our country and by history as acceptable but also as a betrayal. We were also aware of the problematical and limited nature of our mandate. I beg you to believe that we did not keep silent, that we clashed sharply and repeatedly, both with our partners and among ourselves, and that we used every available argument accessible to us. All of this finally crystallized into a settlement which you know roughly, mainly from the speeches of the president, the first secretary of the Party Central Committee and the premier, who, unlike the official communique, spoke in a language which is more closely and easily understandable to all of us.

As most of you already know, the main points of the agreement are roughly as follows: First, our internal life, the transformation of Czechoslovak socialism in the spirit expressed by the Central Committee plenum of our Communist Party after January, will continue. 2d, all this political life will not be directed by a government that has been imposed but by all the existing duly elected bodies of the state. It is in this sense, too, that the National Assembly, of which I am the chairman, will exercise the functions with which it is charged by the constitution and other laws. It is further certain that Czechoslovakia's foreign policy will keep to its present course. The troops of the Warsaw Treaty powers are in temporary occupation of Czechoslovakia's territory—as the communique declares—and these troops and other bodies of these countries will not interfere in our country's internal affairs. They will leave our country as soon as conditions here have been normalized. Furthermore, our Communist Party will continue to exercise its political function in the spirit of the 'action program' in our national communities. All reasonable people will agree that precisely in the crisis of these past few days our party has proved its capabilities, that it was the sole real force able to lead our nations. We are all convinced that it will continue to give proof of these capabilities in the future also and that, united around Dubcek's leadership, with a cool head and reason, it will also solve, for the good of the January line, all its internal problems.

These are the fundamental points of the agreement reached in the Moscow negotiations. The question is bound to be asked by all: what guarantees are there now. I tell you frankly that, despite all the help we have had from our friends—of whom we now have many, and whom I thank from the bottom of my heart—our country, in the situation that now obtains in the world, our country has no other real guarantee, no hope, other than its own good sense and, above all, its unity. Let us make the best of these qualities of ours, which have so often before in our history helped to put us back on our feet. Let us brace our willpower and grit our teeth and continue marching along our road for the ideals which we inscribed on our banner after January.

I beg of you—after the first wave of pain and bitterness has passed—to view the results of the negotiations with a cool head and, if I may so put it, to use our people's well proven good sense. The point is this: the troops of the Warsaw Treaty are to remain here for some time—as the premier has said—even though the government is entering into negotiations regarding their withdrawal in stages. We shall be forced to take exceptional measures in the sphere of the press, broadcasting and television, in order to prevent anything being written or said in these media which might run counter to the foreign political needs and interests of the republic. Regarding the law of association and assembly, the measures required of us will result in the dissolution of the political clubs and will prevent additional political parties from being formed. The government will have to be granted, temporarily, certain special full powers. All these measures will be taken on the basis of laws which will be debated by the National Assembly during the next few days.

We all realize that these are steps which slow down and render more difficult the process of creating democratic socialism. We believe that you will understand why this has to happen and that you will not impute evil motives to the leadership of the party and state. We believe that you will look upon all this as indispensable with a view to the normalization of the situation, the departure of the foreign troops and a renewed acceleration of the rate of our Socialist democratization.

I am speaking to you about the results of the Moscow negotiations in the full knowledge of the immense responsibility which today burdens the shoulders of the supreme constitutional authority of our republic, the National Assembly, at whose head I stand at this time by your will. The National Assembly has honorably acquitted itself of the task which confronted it during the last few historic days. The overwhelming majority of our [Assembly] deputies have shown themselves to be courageous, sovereign, free representatives of their people who, even in the presence of foreign troops in our territory have proved themselves capable of protecting the legitimate character and sovereign exercise of the prerogatives of our constitutional authorities. It is with the same sense of responsibility that this National Assembly intends to approach its tasks in the new situation as it exists following our return from Moscow.

The National Assembly has already issued its statement with regard to that situation, a statement with which you are familiar, and it has requested the government of the republic to submit to the Assembly within the next few days a report on the Moscow negotiations, together with an account of its attitude regarding their results and its suggestions regarding the measures to be taken with a view to the comprehensive normalization of life in our country. It goes without saying that the National Assembly will debate this government statement with a full sense of awareness of its own prerogatives, its responsibility and co-responsibility as the authority which, according to the constitution of the Czechoslovak Socialist Republic, must approve any agreements whatsoever touching upon the sovereignty and territorial integrity of the republic and any changes in the internal political institutions of the country.

I have already indicated the way our thoughts went during the talks in Moscow. We knew that we would have to face our people with our views, that we would have to face the constitutional bodies of the republic. Finally, we realized that in the end we would have to submit ourselves to the relentless tribunal of time and history. For, during these past few days, we really stood at a true crossroads of history. In such a situation, one's thoughts must turn to the fundamental values that have to be protected unconditionally if our nations [the Czech lands and Slovakia] are to get their 2d breath and resume their forward march along their true road, the road which is in harmony with the sense of their history and the sense of their existence.

Your bearing, dear fellow citizens, during the past few historic days, bore witness to your loyalty to the underlying sense of our history in a manner which found an echo, a recognition and admiration throughout the world. This was our greatest source of strength in the immensely trying task that faced us over there, beyond the borders of our land. I thank you with all my heart, comrades, workers, and members of the People's Militia, who have changed our factories into bastions of strength and resolution and who have proved once again how great an historic role and how great a responsibility for society as a whole rests on your shoulders in this country. My gratitude also goes out to you farmers, who have had to garner the fruits of your year's work this summer and safeguard for us our daily bread in the shadow of tanks and aircraft. Thanks be to you, representatives of science and culture, and above all to the representatives of the press, radio and television, and to all members of our intelligentsia for your conduct, which was true to the finest traditions of Czechoslovak science and culture. Special thanks to you, our dear youth, for the sake of the future of this country—thanks to you, boys and girls, for your dash, courage and prudence. We owe gratitude too, to you comrades in the army and the security service, who remained on the side of your people. Our thanks and respect are due to our women, our mothers, who had to live through days of anxiety, suffering and grief but who remained a firm support for us.

I should especially like to thank today, the [24th] anniversary of the Slovak National Rising, the Slovak nation for their support for the unity of our Socialist republic and to assure it that we shall do everything to ensure that the legal decision concerning the federalization of the state is adopted within the time limit foreseen, that is by 28 October of this year.

I believe that we shall achieve a complete settlement of our mutual relations, both on the state and party level, and that there is sufficient goodwill present on both sides for this to be achieved. I beg of you not to allow yourselves to be confused in this regard by any temporary or secondary elements in the situation and to concentrate calmly and with confidence on the attainment of a favorable solution of our fundamental problems. And, to end with, just like Comrade Cernik, I should like, on behalf of the National Assembly and on my own behalf, to give thanks to the president of the Republic, Army Gen. Ludvik Svoboda, for his intervention at the moment which was the worst for our state and for ourselves personally.

At the same time, dear fellow citizens, I beg of you to show understanding also for us, on whose shoulders rested the heavy burden of negotiating and of making decisions. We, too, had to act and decide in the shadow of tanks and aircraft stationed on our territory. I assure you that we acted and made our decisions as patriots and soldiers, as men who were not thinking of themselves, nor of their own lives, but of the life and future of our nations. For the sake of that life and of that future of the Czechs and Slovaks—and of all the people of our country as a whole—these men now turn to you with the appeal and request which lent us so much strength during the past few days: "We are with you, be with us."

Let us bear in mind Svatopluk's 3 legendary rods.* Let us not allow our ranks to be divided, for if this were to happen that would be a real disaster and a real defeat for our cause, a defeat for socialism, for our free Czechoslovak Socialist Republic; that must not be allowed to happen.

USSR Attacks 'Counterrevolution'

Despite the accord reached in Moscow, the Soviet Union continued to attack alleged counterrevolutionaries in Czechoslovakia.

The Soviet party organ *Pravda* Aug. 28 complained of clandestine broadcasts in Czechoslovakia in which the Moscow agreement had been attacked. The newspaper expressed hope that "the country's working people, led by their Communist Party, will be able fully to grasp the complex situation in which the country now finds itself and deliver a crushing rebuff to its inveterate enemies."

---

* Svatopluk, 9th century monarch of Greater Moravia, on his deathbed, called his 3 sons and told each to try to break a bundle of 3 sticks that he gave them— so the legend goes. When they could not, Svatopluk told them to take the bundle apart and deal with each stick separately. The moral was that the brothers would be strongest so long as they remained together.

The Soviet government paper *Izvestia* Aug. 28 cited "the difficulties created by the activation of anti-Socialist forces and their reluctance to accept a loss of their position." "Counter-revolution in Czechoslovakia," the newspaper said, "is not a myth and it still makes its presence known, striving to exacerbate the situation,... incite provocations and turn unstable people against fraternal countries."

The Soviet press agency Tass charged Aug. 28 that counterrevolutionaries were trying "to stir up nationalistic hysteria and sow anarchy and disorder." Tass charged Aug. 29 that "counterrevolutionary forces in Czechoslovakia" were attempting to block implementation of the Soviet-Czechoslovak accord. Tass also accused Western radio stations, which it did not identify, of jamming pro-Soviet stations in Czechoslovakia while assisting clandestine radio transmitters in the country.

Izvestia Sept. 3 denounced Czechoslovak Foreign Min. Jiri Hajek as "a henchman of the dark forces of reaction and counterrevolution." Hajek had been abroad at the time of the invasion and was still out of the country. *Izvestia* charged that Hajek, while serving in prison camps during the 1939-45 Nazi occupation of his country, had collaborated with the Nazis to save his life. *Izvestia* alleged that Hajek "changed his name from Karpeles [a frequently found Czech Jewish surname] to Hajek" to cover up this reported wartime collaboration. The Soviet propagandists had apparently mistaken Hajek, a Social Democrat until 1948, for Bedrich Hajek (born Karpeles), a Communist who happened to have spent the war years running a Czechoslovak soldiers' club in London and who later acted under duress as a state witness in the Nov. 1952 purge trial of Rudolf Slansky. *Izvestia* also accused Hajek of favoring a resumption of diplomatic relations with Israel. The newspaper assailed Hajek for having "entered a plot" with Deputy Premier Ota Sik, "known for his rightwing views," to bring the question of the invasion before the UN Security Council.

In a situation report on Czechoslovakia, Tass Sept. 3 denounced several Czechoslovak publications for publishing "anti-Socialist and anti-Soviet" articles. Tass singled out the Slovak writers' weekly *Kulturny Zivot* of Bratislava and *Mlady Svet,* a youth magazine. 2 other Czechoslovak officials who had come under sharp attack by the Soviet press were reported Sept. 3 to have returned to Prague from Belgrade, where they had been at the time of the invasion. They were Planning Min. Frantisek Vlasak and State Control Commission Pres. Stefan Gasparik.

Plans to reimpose press censorship and disband non-Communist political clubs, announced Aug. 29 by Smrkovsky, were implemented Sept. 4.

The press censorship rules, issued by the Culture Ministry's new Press Control Office, banned discussion of the Moscow agreement and the use of the word "occupation" in referring to the presence of Warsaw Pact troops in Czechoslovakia. 3 other prohibitions were not disclosed. Under the press control law, government censors were to meet twice a week with newspaper editors; during the 20 years prior to the lifting of press censorship in January, government censors had been stationed at newspaper offices.

Moscow's *Pravda* had complained Sept. 1 that Czechoslovak newspapers were not adapting quickly enough to the new censorship rules. *Pravda* singled out *Literarni listy,* the liberal weekly of the Writer's Union, which had been published clandestinely since the occupation. *Pravda* assailed the publication as a "wasps' nest" that "continues to exist somewhere in a backyard and continues to play its abject role as one of the main ideological centers of counterrevolution." *Literarni listy* had announced in a one-page issue Aug. 29 that it would cease publication if censorship were reimposed.

Prague radio reported Sept. 2 that 3 journals considered "counterrevolutionary" by the Soviet Union would be barred from further publication. They were *Literarni listy, Reporter,* the bi-weekly organ of the Journalists' Union, and *Student,* the weekly of the Students' Union. All 3 had been in the forefront of the democratization movement. It was reported Sept. 3 that the Journalists' Union had agreed to the censorship program dictated by the Moscow agreement, but only for a 3-month period. The report quoted a Prague radio broadcast.

Josef Vohnout, newly appointed head of the Office for Press & Information, described the major aspects of the new censorship law in a televised address Sept. 8. Vohnout said there were 2 guiding principles: (1) a prohibition on "negative information" and commentary about the 5 Warsaw Pact powers that had occupied the country and (2) a ban on publishing anything that detracted from the leading role of the Communist

Party and the working class and a ban on criticism of the police, army, Ministry of the Interior or the Workers' Militia.

In a closed-door session Sept. 13, the National Assembly approved by 275-2 vote a government bill that reimposed "preventive censorship" on the press, radio and TV and provided for the implementation of certain unspecified police measures designed "to strengthen public order."

Under the terms of the new law, which revoked the earlier law abolishing censorship, a Committee for Press & Information was to be created under Deputy Premier Peter Colotka. The committee's other members: Josef Vohnout, the first director of the newly-established (post-invasion) Office for Press & Information; the director of the Czechoslovak press agency CTK; the chairman of the Slovak Committee for Press & Information; and 2 delegates from the National Front. The law empowered the committee, either directly or through commissioners appointed jointly with the editors of newspapers and magazines, "to insure that the periodic press and other mass information in disagreement with the vital interests of Czechoslovakia's domestic and foreign policy."

Party Leadership Revised

The party Central Committee Sept. 1 elected a new 21-member ruling Presidium at the end of a 2-day session in Prague called to reorganize leadership along lines demanded by the USSR. The meeting also proposed 87 new members for the 100-member Central Committee, which was to be enlarged to about 190 members when the party congress ratified the nominations at a session scheduled for later in 1968.

The Presidium and Central Committee superseded the Presidium and Central Committee that had been elected at the clandestine party congress in Prague Aug. 23. The Soviet Union had subsequently declared that congress illegal and refused to recognize its 160-member Central Committee and its 27-member Presidium.

Although the USSR had demanded the removal of liberal elements in the Prague government, the new Presidium and Central Committee were dominated by liberals. The Presidium had only 2 members considered pro-Soviet: Vasil Bilak, removed the previous week as first secretary of the Slovak party, and Jan Piller, who had sought to persuade Pres. Svoboda, after the invasion, to head a pro-Soviet government. Bilak and Piller had been members of a Presidium chosen in April. The new Presidium included 7 members who had been selected at the clandestine Aug. 23 party meeting. 87 members proposed for the new Central Committee were considered liberals. Svoboda was elected to the Central Committee and was named honorary member of the Presidium.

The new Presidium members: Dubcek; Bilak; Premier Cernik; Evzen Erban; Libuse Hrdinova, the first woman to serve on the Presidium; Jarolim Hettes; Gustav Husak, who had succeeded Bilak as first secretary of the Slovak CP; Vladimir Kabrna; Zdenek Mlynar; Vaclav Neubert, president of the National Council of Moravia; Jan Piller; Josef Pinkava; Stefan Sadovsky; Vaclav Slavik; National Assembly Pres. Josef Smrkovsky; Pres. Svoboda; Vaclav Simecek; Bohumil Simon; Josef Spacek; Anton Tazky; Josef Zrak. Frantisek Barbirek, a former Presidium member, was demoted to alternate. 2 other alternates were ex-Premier Jozef Lenart, who had held the same Presidium post before the invasion, and the Czechoslovak labor leader Karel Polacek.

In his meeting with Soviet officials in Moscow Aug. 23-26, Dubcek was said to have agreed to dismiss several officials regarded as objectionable by the USSR. Among the officials who were either ousted or forced to resign: Col. Gen. Josef Pavel resigned Aug. 31 as interior minister and was replaced by Jan Pelnar, a moderate who was head of the West Bohemian Regional Party Committee; Frantisek Kriegel was ousted from the Presidium, and Cestmir Cisar was removed as a Central Committee secretary. Ota Sik handed in his resignation Sept. 3 as deputy premier. Jiri Pelikan resigned as head of the national TV, and Zdenek Hejzlar quit as the chief of the radio network.

In a display on independence, Premier Cernik Aug. 28 had dismissed Miroslav Sulek as director General of CTK, the press agency, for having collaborated with the occupying troops. He was replaced by Jindrich Suk. Oldrich Svestka, the ultra-conservative editor of *Rude pravo,* the Czechoslovak party journal, was replaced by a moderate.

Prague sources reported Sept. 2 that all East German troops that had participated in the invasion had been withdrawn within 3 days. The USSR was said to have called for the pullout on the ground that the presence of East German troops on foreign soil could be construed as a violation of the 1945 Potsdam agreement, which forbade German rearmament.

It was reported Sept. 3 that the first phase of the troop withdrawal process—the removal of soldiers from key buildings in Prague and in other cities—was virtually completed. (The 2d phase—the troop exit from cities and towns—started later.) The Troja area, a northern suburb of Prague, was being turned into a principal Soviet base for Prague and Central Bohemia. 2 Soviet armored divisions and thousands of airborne and motorized infantry troops were concentrated there. Negotiations to end the occupation were scheduled for later.

In conformity with the Moscow agreement, Czechoslovakia Sept. 6 outlawed 2 quasi-political clubs, the Club of Involved Nonpartisans (KAN) and the Club of Former Political Prisoners (K-231). Both organizations had formed preparatory committees but had not yet been sanctioned legally. A statement issued by the Interior Ministry said that K-231, named after the law under which persons were imprisoned for crimes against the state, was "superfluous" since new legislation provided for the rehabilitation of persons unjustly imprisoned during the Novotny regime. As for KAN, the ministry said it represented a political organization with an independent program and as such could not be allowed. The ministry held that there were enough political parties and social organizations under law.

Further Advance of Red Army Feared

According to rumors circulating in the West late in August, the Soviet Union was planning to follow up the invasion of Czechoslovakia with a similar drive into Rumania. The speculation arose out of reports that the Soviet Union and Bulgaria were building up their forces along the Soviet and Bulgarian borders with Rumania and that Moscow had demanded that Bucharest permit Warsaw Pact maneuvers in Rumania.

U.S. State Undersecy. Nicholas deB. Katzenbach visited Belgrade Oct. 17-18 to demonstrate U.S. concern over the increasing Soviet pressure on Yugoslavia. Observers agreed that the talks centered largely around Yugoslavia's economic and security position in the wake of the Czechoslovak invasion. The official Yugoslav news agency, Tanyug, described a 90-minute conference of Tito with Katzenbach Oct. 18 as a "prolonged and friendly meeting." Yugoslav officials regarded Katzenbach's visit as a follow-up to an Oct. 15 White House statement in which Pres. Johnson had declared his "very clear and continuing interest in Yugoslavia's independence, sovereignty and economic development." (Yugoslavia was seeking aid for its economic reforms, designed to make its products more competitive on world markets. Yugoslav Foreign Min. Marko Nikezic conferred with French Premier Maurice Couve de Murville and Foreign Min. Michel Debre in Paris Oct. 15. It was rumored that Yugoslavia might try to get arms from France if the USSR cut off military aid.)

It was reported in Belgrade Oct. 18 that prior to his arrival there, Katzenbach had urged Common Market officials in Brussels to give Yugoslavia trade preferences. Speaking at a session of the Western European Union in Paris Oct. 16, Katzenbach had urged west European nations to assume a greater role in world affairs. Katzenbach warned Western Europe that in view of American domestic problems, the U.S. would have to readjust its foreign commitments. Referring to the recurring fear of western Europe over U.S. and Soviet supremacy, Katzenbach suggested that the solution was in a "unified and powerful western Europe whose voice cannot be ignored by the super powers." He said that one of the most important U.S. foreign policy goals of the next decade would be to create a U.S.-European association in which Europe would be an equal partner sharing world responsibilities that it was unfair for the U.S. to bear alone. Commenting on the invasion of Czechoslovakia, he declared: "We must maintain defensive forces at the level which will impel the Soviets to conclude that no political objective could possibly be worth the risk of an armed clash with the West."

A statement issued Aug. 29 by the Executive Committee of the Rumanian Communist Party Central Committee declared that "it is imperative that absolutely nothing should be undertaken that might worsen ... [Communist bloc] relations or deepen the divergencies and breed fresh sources of tension." The statement, issued in response to the Soviet-Czechoslovak agreement concluded in Moscow Aug. 26, added: "The Executive Committee expresses to the Communists of Czechoslovakia, to the Czech and Slovak people, its feelings of warm sympathy, of support and full internationalist solidarity.... The Executive Committee considers of utmost importance the carrying into effect of the complete withdrawal, in the shortest time, of the armed forces of the 5 Socialist countries from Czechoslovakia."

The Polish party organ *Trybuna Ludu* Aug. 29 assailed what it dubbed Rumania's "blind alley of nationalism." The paper charged that Rumanian support for Czechoslovakia "indicates that the objective was not 'defense of democracy and sovereignty' but disintegration of the Socialist commonwealth." For the first time since the invasion of Czechoslovakia, the paper attacked Rumanian Pres. Nicolae Ceausescu by name, charging that he was too "eager to give advice." The paper also criticized Rumania for having established relations with West Germany in 1967 and for failing to break relations with Israel following the 1967 Arab-Israeli war.

The Czechoslovak news agency CTK reported Aug. 29 that the Soviet Union had requested Rumanian approval for the staging of Warsaw Pact maneuvers in Rumania. Travelers returning from the USSR reported Aug. 29 that they had seen (a) long columns of Soviet armor and artillery near the Prut River and (b) a concentration of Soviet tanks, personnel carriers and artillery near the Ukrainian town of Kotovoskoe. Bulgarian troops were reported to be moving into the Russe area, opposite the Rumanian port of Giurgiu on the Danube River.

In a speech delivered at Cluj Aug. 29, Ceausescu repeated his call for the earliest possible withdrawal of Warsaw Pact troops from Czechoslovakia. He added: "The word freedom can be said in many languages, but it has the same meaning. What is understood is that people must be fully equal, have the right to express their opinion, be able to take part in the guiding of society in accordance with their capability and knowledge."

Dutch Foreign Min. Joseph M. A. H. Luns disclosed Aug. 29 that he had received reports of the massing of Soviet and Bulgarian troops near Rumania. Luns, who was in London to confer with British Foreign Secy. Michael Stewart, warned that the North Atlantic Alliance would "have to reassess its defense arrangements" if Soviet forces took up permanent positions along the Czechoslovak-West German border.

In a speech delivered in San Antonio Aug. 30, U.S. Pres. Lyndon B. Johnson noted that the Soviet Union had "applied the full measure of military power in Czechoslovakia" and that there were "even rumors late this evening that this action might be repeated elsewhere in the days ahead in Eastern Europe." The President warned any "would-be aggressor" not to "misjudge American policy during this Administration." Johnson added: "We cannot and we must not in the year 1968 return to a world of unbridled aggression.... Let no one unleash the dogs of war. Let no one even in this period of highly charged domestic debate in our country even doubt what the true views of the American people are on these matters." *Trybuna Ludu,* the Polish CP daily, accused Johnson Sept. 1 of spreading "idiotic and slanderous rumors."

Thousands of Rumanian citizens underwent para-military training Aug. 31-Sept. 1 amid new reports of Soviet troop movements behind the Prut River in Soviet Moldavia and Bessarabia.

The Associated Press reported Aug. 31 that Ceausescu had circulated to the Soviet Union and other Warsaw Pact members a memo offering the following concessions in exchange for a guarantee of nonintervention in Rumanian affairs: (1) renewal of the Rumanian-Soviet defense pact, which had expired earlier in 1968, (2) participation of Rumanian forces in Warsaw Pact maneuvers (but not on Rumanian soil for the time being), (3) submission of a formal declaration of loyalty to the Warsaw Pact, (4) an increase in trade with the Communist-bloc countries and (5) assumption of a greater share of the cost of the Communist bloc's program of foreign aid to the underdeveloped countries.

In speeches printed in Rumanian newspapers Sept. 1, both Ceausescu and Rumanian Premier Ion Gheorghe Maurer upheld the right of national independence. Ceausescu noted that "we have never thought that force could ever be used among Communists, among Socialist countries, to impose a certain point of view." Maurer declared that Rumania was "building socialism in such a way that it could never be said that we have deviated from it." Maurer added that "the Rumanian people cannot conceive of and would not accept living otherwise than as free, sovereign and masters of their destiny."

A U.S. State Department spokesman disclosed Sept. 3 that Soviet Amb.-to-U.S. Anatoly F. Dobrynin had assured State Secy. Dean Rusk that "rumors about possible Soviet moves against Rumania were without foundation." Dobrynin had conferred with Rusk the evening of Aug. 30.

The Warsaw *Trybuna Ludu* Aug. 31 attacked Yugoslavia for opposing the Warsaw Pact action in Czechoslovakia. The Polish United Workers' (Communist) Party daily charged that Pres. Tito's concept of national sovereignty and independence was "detached from the conditions, place, time and reality of the present world."

The Polish armed forces newspaper *Zolnierz Wolnosci (Soldier of Freedom)* Sept. 6 assailed both Yugoslavia and Rumania for their "abstract comprehension of the slogan of sovereignty" and for "slipping away from positions of proletarian internationalism."

A statement issued by the U.S. State Department Aug. 31 asserted that the East-West balance-of-power system had been upset by the movement of Warsaw Treaty forces into Czechoslovakia. As a consequence, the statement said, the U.S. and its NATO allies were reviewing their military posture in Western Europe. The USSR reacted to the U.S. assessment Sept. 3 by asserting that it was the West, not the Communist bloc, that was seeking to alter the balance of power. *The State Department statement said:*

> The movement of Warsaw Pact forces into Czechoslovakia and their continuing occupation of that country has obviously affected the military situation in Europe.

> The *status quo* has been changed. There are larger Soviet forces now present in Central Europe than at any time since the early postwar period.

The military occupation of Czechoslovakia puts Soviet forces in a country where they have not been since World War II. There is no assurance as yet that the Warsaw Pact forces will soon return to their deployments as they existed 6 months ago.

The changed East-West military situation in Europe is of significance to the security of the United States and its allies.

In the light of these events we are reviewing with our allies what the implications may be for existing arrangements to provide for our common security.

Deutsche Presse-Agentur (DPA), the West German news agency, reported Sept. 3 that Soviet Amb.-to-West Germany Semyon K. Tsarapkin had presented a toughly-worded memo to West German Chancellor Kurt Georg Kiesinger during a meeting in Bonn Sept. 2. According to DPA, the memo (1) warned Bonn that it would have to "face the consequences" if it did not end its "hostile" attitude toward the Soviet Union, (2) asserted that Bonn's "influences in the Eastern [Communist] bloc must cease" and (3) demanded that the Kiesinger government support "all steps toward international *detente* and exercise care for internal order" (the latter point was apparently a reference to the activities of the West German National Democratic Party, described as neo-Fascist).

The Bonn government Aug. 28 had issued a statement calling on the USSR to withdraw its forces from Czechoslovakia and restore complete sovereignty to the Czechoslovak nation. The statement, issued after a 2-hour cabinet meeting, also assured the West German people that "the safety of the Federal Republic is guaranteed by the North Atlantic Treaty powers, who are in a position to defend the freedom and security of all its members." The statement affirmed that Bonn was considering new proposals for bolstering the strength of the NATO alliance.

Kiesinger conferred with U.S. Amb.-to-West Germany Henry Cabot Lodge Sept. 4 and reportedly told him that Bonn was dissatisfied with the nature of the Western Allied response to the invasion of Czechoslovakia and to the buildup of Soviet forces in western Czechoslovakia across the frontier from Bavaria. Kiesinger was also reported to be concerned over the possibility of a Soviet move against Rumania.

A statement issued Sept. 4 after a meeting of NATO's Defense Planning Committee asserted that, as a result of the invasion of Czechoslovakia, "the prospects for progress in the field of balanced mutual force reductions have suffered a severe setback." The statement added that the developments "cannot fail to be of great concern, and NATO has initiated a thorough assessment of their implications for allied defense policy, particularly for force postures."

It was reported Sept. 5 that NATO members had agreed not to withdraw any of their troops from the joint command structure in the immediate future. The agreement primarily affected U.S. and British contingents.

Pravda charged Sept. 5 that NATO had planned a "military-political operation" to take over Czechoslovakia. The article cited an alleged "Secret Plan 100-1" under which "U.S. armed forces would actively interfere in case of internal disorders" in Czechoslovakia in order to effect a "revision of existing boundaries in Europe, ... tearing Czechoslovakia from the Warsaw Pact and turning it into a corridor for the [West Germany] Bundeswehr on the road to the Soviet frontier." NATO had been prevented from "carrying through its subversive actions" because of the initiative taken by the Warsaw Pact forces, the article said. It added that NATO had "not given up its plans and is hastening to adjust to the new situation." NATO officials and the U.S. State Department Sept. 5 rejected the charges as unfounded.

It was reported Sept. 8 that as a result of the Czechoslovak developments, the U.S. was seeking to bolster the military capability of NATO through these measures: (1) bringing all NATO divisions up to full strength (several were currently understrength by as much as a brigade, or over 4,000 men); (2) accelerating the refitting of West German air force planes to carry conventional armament (according to the *N.Y. Times* Sept. 9, West German combat aircraft currently were outfitted only to carry nuclear weapons); and (3) improving contingency plans for a rapid call-up of European reserve units. Administration officials said the U.S. was emphasizing these approaches to help reduce European reliance on U.S. forces.

The official Bulgarian news agency (BTA) announced Sept. 7 that Bulgarian troops had concluded "operative and tactical maneuvers" begun Aug. 26 "in eastern Bulgaria and in the Black Sea area." The maneuvers, directed by Defense Min. Dobri Dzhurov, demonstrated the "high degree of training and fighting readiness of the units and staffs of the Bulgarian people's army," BTA said. There had been some speculation in the West that the Bulgarian troops had been poised for a Soviet-led strike into Rumania.

British Foreign Secy. Michael Stewart conferred with Rumanian party and government leaders in Bucharest Sept. 9-10. A joint communique issued Sept. 11 noted that both sides had discussed "current international issues" and had "restated their convictions regarding the necessity of continuing efforts to ensure *detente* and cooperation in the spirit of the UN Charter...." *Pravda* Sept. 9 attacked Stewart's visit as an "impermissible interference in the internal affairs of East Europe." Stewart earlier had cancelled scheduled visits to Bulgaria and Hungary, both of whose armies had participated in the invasion of Czechoslovakia.

Rumanian Pres. Ceausescu said at a Bucharest rally Sept. 9 that "nothing in the world can sway the Rumanian people from the path of socialism and communism.... The Socialist countries must know that we are their friends and that we will never betray the cause of Communist unity."

Austria Sept. 10 extended for one month the military service of 11,000 draftees scheduled to complete their 9-month tour of duty Sept. 15. The move was decided on in the light of the developments in Czechoslovakia, officials of the Defense Ministry said. Chancellor Josef Klaus, speaking at a one-day special session of the National Council (lower house of parliament) Sept. 18, described the European situation as "serious" and pledged that his government would defend Austria's position of permanent neutrality.

U.S. officials disclosed Sept. 16 that Washington was prepared, in conjunction with the actions planned by other NATO members, to send 4 squadrons of F-4 fighter-bombers to West Germany in November or December, as well as 2 brigades of mechanized infantry early in 1969. Equivalent units had been withdrawn earlier in the year as part of a U.S. effort to cut down the foreign exchange cost of stationing troops in West Germany.

NATO began 2 major training maneuvers Sept. 16. A land exercise, Black Lion, involving 42,000 soldiers (mainly West Germans), was begun near Ulm, Bavaria, about 100 miles from the West German-Czechoslovak border. The other exercise, Silver Tower, was being conducted in the North Atlantic by

more than 100 ships of the U.S., Britain and the Netherlands
and aircraft of 9 countries.

A Yugoslav military commander had said in a Navy Day
speech Sept. 10 that the combat readiness of the Yugoslav navy
had been raised to the point where it could fulfill "all necessary
tasks." The commander noted that the need for such readiness
was greater than before.

Yugoslav Pres. Tito called on all nonaligned and small and
medium-sized countries Sept. 23 to close ranks against
tendencies that, he indicated, carried the seeds of a world conflict. Speaking at a banquet in honor of Emperor Haile Selassie
of Ethiopia, who was visiting Yugoslavia, Tito said: "Some big
powers are striving to impose by force upon other peoples what
is contrary to their aspirations, independence and own roads to
a better future." Some countries interfered in the affairs of
"African, Asian and now, unfortunately, European countries,
too," so it was "again necessary to unite to avert a catastrophe
which could envelop the entire world."

Tito told an audience of about 100,000 Oct. 20 that any
attack on Yugoslavia from any source would be "sharply
received." Tito issued the warning in Leskovac, southern
Serbia, at a rally marking the 25th anniversary of the formation of a wartime partisan brigade. (It was reported in
Belgrade Oct. 20 that Tito Oct. 19 had received a letter in
which the Soviet party Central Committee had attacked him
for his condemnation of the invasion of Czechoslovakia.)
Rejecting Soviet assertions that sovereignty was not too important to small Communist countries, Tito assailed what he
termed a Soviet theory of conditional sovereignty. Tito
declared: "We said 'no' in 1948 [the year Tito broke with Stalin]
to all pressures against our sovereignty and freedom, and we
have done so again, this time in connection with
Czechoslovakia." "We shall stick to this position forever."

Deriding Soviet and East European attacks on Yugoslav
economic policy, Tito said: "The very ones who criticize us
come here to do their shopping and charge into our stores like
bees after honey." Answering attacks from Bulgaria, widely
regarded as Moscow's spokesman on Balkan issues, Tito said:
Any unsolicited help from Socialist countries would be
rebuffed; "if you are not invited, it means that you are not
wanted ... and that we alone will take care of our own affairs."

Speaking to the Federal Assembly, Sept. 24, Yugoslav Premier Mika Spiljak had said that intensification of Yugoslav military readiness had become imperative as a result of the Czechoslovak invasion. He asserted that a big-power intervention in a small country "made more acute the question of security of small- and medium-sized countries." Spiljak also denounced an anti-Yugoslav press campaign waged "particularly in the Soviet Union, Bulgaria and Poland." Spiljak said that he attached "great significance" to relations with the U.S. and that "these relations can be further widened on the basis of mutual interest and mutual respect."

Ex-Yugoslav Vice Pres. Milovan Djilas said in London while en route to the U.S. Oct. 4 that if the USSR invaded Yugoslavia, the West should give his country all possible help, "including military power."

According to Western reports Sept. 11, Italy and Greece had assured Yugoslavia that they would not rekindle old disagreements in the face of the current Soviet pressure. As a result of these unofficial guarantees, Yugoslavia regrouped its armed forces, deployed mostly along the Greek and Italian frontiers, to reinforce borders with Hungary and Bulgaria.

Austrian Pres. Franz Jonas visited Belgrade Sept. 30-Oct. 5 to discuss closer Yugoslav-Austrian cooperation in the aftermath of the Czechoslovak invasion. Jonas was accompanied by Foreign Min. Kurt Waldheim. Prior to leaving for Belgrade Sept. 30, Jonas reasserted Austria's neutrality but declared that the invasion of Czechoslovakia had added significance to his visit.

Communists Differ on Moscow Agreement

Reactions varied markedly in eastern Europe to the compromise arrived at Aug. 26 between the Czechoslovak leadership and their Soviet hosts in Moscow. Rumania made no direct public comment, but Yugoslavia roundly denounced the agreement and continued military occupation. Albania, a Warsaw Treaty member in name only for 6 years, formally severed its remaining links with the alliance over the matter. The rest of the Soviet bloc supported the Kremlin.

A resolution adopted Sept. 4 at a joint meeting of the presidium and executive committee of the Yugoslav Workers' Socialist Alliance expressed "profound indignation" over the occupation of Czechoslovakia and affirmed the right of each nation to independent development. With respect to the Yugoslav nation, the resolution declared: "It has always been clear that there can be no compromise or bargaining over the independent internal development of our country or of its sovereignty with anyone or at any price. The defense of the country is a sacred thing for every citizen of Socialist Yugoslavia, in the constitution of which it has been stated that nobody has the right to sign or to recognize capitulation or occupation of the country." The resolution affirmed the intention of the Yugoslav leadership to do everything in its power to strengthen the defensive capability of the country.

Pres. Tito Sept. 5 reiterated his demand for an "urgent withdrawal" of Warsaw Pact forces from Czechoslovakia so as to "create conditions for establishing the indispensable trust for development of equal cooperation among Socialist countries and Communist parties." "We believe that the fraternal peoples of Czechoslovakia should alone be in charge and that they themselves could have solved their problems," Tito said.

Krasnaya Zvezda, the Soviet army newspaper, referred Sept. 6 to anti-Soviet attacks in the Western press as being "facilitate[d] by the actions of the Chinese splitters, headed by Mao Tse-tung, and of the Yugoslav revisionists, whose anti-Soviet themes are taken up by imperialist propaganda." The attack, with its use of the word "revisionists," reportedly was the sharpest leveled against Yugoslavia since the partial reconciliation between Moscow and Belgrade 6 years previously.

Representatives of the Yugoslav and Italian Communist parties conferred in Belgrade Sept. 7 on the Czechoslovak situation. Both sides reportedly agreed to boycott a planned Soviet-sponsored conference of the world's Communist parties if Moscow insisted on holding the meeting while Czechoslovakia was still occupied.

Albania Aug. 28 assailed the Aug. 26 Moscow-Prague agreement as a "foul compromise" between the "revisionist Czechoslovak capitulators ... to salvage their positions to the detriment of the Czechoslovak people and socialism." The official Agence Telegraphique Albanaise news agency charged that the accord had placed the Prague leadership in the "shameful role of a puppet government."

Tirana radio announced Sept. 13 that Albania had formally cancelled its membership in the Warsaw Pact. The broadcast said that the withdrawal, the first by any member of the treaty alliance, had been approved that day by a unanimous vote of the Albanian People's Assembly. Albanian Premier Mehmet Shehu had called on the assembly Sept. 12 to approve the withdrawal since Albania had "long been excluded" from the treaty and Moscow had changed the alliance from one of "defense against imperialist aggression" into one that was "aggressive ... against the Socialist countries themselves." In an Albanian language broadcast by Moscow radio Sept. 14, the Soviet government asserted that Tirana's withdrawal from the pact was the "price which Albania paid to its masters in Peking." Albania had been excluded from Warsaw Treaty meetings since 1962 because it supported Communist China.

The Bulgarian Defense Ministry newspaper asserted Sept. 6 that an early withdrawal of Warsaw Pact troops from Czechoslovakia was "unrealistic." The paper charged that the "reactionaries and counterrevolutionaries" in Czechoslovakia were seeking a rapid withdrawal so that they could "have another go at it."

Polish Premier Jozef Cyrankiewicz referred to Czechoslovakia Aug. 31 as a "convalescent" that in time would "see and understand who saved him and who wanted to drag him down to the depths." "There is no place here for enthusiasm or for fanfares," Cyrankiewicz said. "There is a place for care, as in a family which keeps watch at the bed of a sick man in order that he may stand on his own feet." Cyrankiewicz added: "We did not go there to take a single square meter of Czechoslovak soil. We went there to defend our common security jointly."

Polish TV Sept. 1 again publicized the contention that "Zionists" had been responsible for the counterrevolution" in Czechoslovakia. "The Zionist forces were the most active of those who attacked Poland in March and allowed themselves ... to designate the future Communist leaders of Czechoslovakia," the broadcast said. Polish newspapers charged Sept. 5 that "revisionist and Zionist forces" in Czechoslovakia were purposely seeking to normalize the situation within the country so as to speed the withdrawal of the occupation troops and resume the preinvasion "counterrevolution." In reality, the press asserted, normalization of Czechoslovak life was "not so easy at all and will not take place so fast."

Polish party First Secy. Wladyslaw Gomulka, in his first public statement on Czechoslovakia since the invasion, warned Sept. 8 that a "difficult and perhaps long road" lay ahead before Czechoslovakia could be expected to recover from "counterrevolutionary and anti-Socialist damage" and achieve "normalization." Implementation of the Aug. 26 Prague-Moscow agreement "depends mainly on the Czechoslovak Communist Party," Gomulka asserted. He added: Czechoslovakia had been on a "downhill" path "out of the Warsaw Pact and toward neutrality," and for this reason the Warsaw Treaty countries "sent their troops ... to protect their state and national interests and the interests of Socialist Czechoslovakia."

Hungary seemed the most reticent as well as the most reluctant of Moscow's supporters. It took the Hungarian party and government leadership longer than those of the other "Warsaw 5" countries to express to the public at large any conclusions about the Moscow compromise and Hungary's role in the invasion.

It was not until Aug. 30, a day after the Hungarian cabinet held a long session, that the party daily *Nepszabadsag* printed a comprehensive account of the matter. *Nepszabadsag* used a State Information Office communique on the cabinet's debate on invasion problems. *Nepszabadsag* asserted that Hungarian troops did not participate in any military actions and that, in districts where Hungarian units were stationed, civilians suffered no "individual or institutional financial losses." According to the communique the Hungarian troops in Czechoslovakia were being fully supplied from Hungary by rail.

Hungarian Premier Jeno Fock's long public silence gave increasing weight to rumors that he was embarrassed by the invasion. He finally discussed the matter publicly Sept. 20 at a meeting of the Federation of Technical & Scientific Societies in Budapest. He held that the Hungarian party had warned Czechoslovak party leader Alexander Dubcek and Czechoslovak Premier Oldrich Cernik repeatedly of the dangers of exaggerated nationalism and of ignoring a resurgent "right wing." Fock advised the Czechoslovaks to fully implement the

Aug. 26 Moscow agreement as the only possible basis for a return to normality. He said his government and party would do their best to ensure that "this consolidation takes place as soon as possible."

Fock returned to the subject Sept. 20 at the Budapest Military Academy's graduation exercises, where his listeners included Soviet Gen. Sergei Shtemenko, chief of staff of Warsaw Treaty forces. Fock justified the invasion as "necessary," praised Soviet-Hungarian friendship in arms, attacked NATO, and declared it a "sacred duty to increase the defensive potential of Hungary and maintain and strengthen the military organization of the Warsaw Treaty. He insisted again that the party and government had done everything in their power to effect a political solution to the crisis before taking part in the military intervention. But "Hungary did not hesitate for a moment to join the Soviet Union and other fraternal Socialist countries" when the time for decision finally came, Fock said.

Fock again demanded that the Moscow agreement should be respected "under all circumstances" but added that "speedy, spectacular results are not to be expected." He asserted that Hungary must also prepare for "a long period of struggle and slow, laborious progress" in bilateral state and party relations, while standing ever ready to "help and support those forces fighting to strengthen proletarian dictatorship and socialism in Czechoslovakia." He said several unspecified Czechoslovak leaders had "recognized that they had committed serious errors" in letting the political situation pass out of their control and thereby forcing their neighbors to act.

Hungarian party leader Janos Kadar ended 80 days of semiseclusion and silence by appearing at the Obuda Hosiery Mill in Budapest Oct. 24 to talk to workers. He assured his listeners that Hungary's course had not been changed by the Czechoslovak crisis. There had been several signs that Kadar knew about the Aug. 20 invasion timetable in advance. He had told a Radio Budapest interviewer on his return from the 5-nation conference Aug. 4 that "it is not certain that everyone will understand at this moment the meaning of the Bratislava declaration, but thinking men already understand it—and others will do so after a week, a month or longer."

Western sources had reported that Kadar had held 3 secret conferences with Dubcek prior to these major developments of the final 6 weeks of the preinvasion crisis—the Warsaw meeting of the 5 invading allies July 14-15, the Cierna nad Tisou conference of the Czechoslovak party Presidium with Soviet party Politburo members July 29-Aug. 1 and the invasion itself. In an 11th-hour attempt to convince Dubcek of the need to retreat, Kadar was said to have met Dubcek near Bratislava Aug. 17 but "to have said not a single word about the impending invasion," the Bavarian State Radio reported Aug. 21. Agence France-Presse's Moscow correspondent said this meeting took place Aug. 18 in Bratislava. The meeting was confirmed a year later—Aug. 19, 1969—by Gustav Husak, a fellow Slovak and Dubcek's successor as Czechoslovak party leader, and later still—Sept. 25, 1969—by Dubcek himself, who told the party Central Committee that he and Kadar had met again at Komarno, some 60 miles east-southeast of Bratislava, Aug. 17, 1968. It had been rumored elsewhere that the 2 met at night and that both had been seen next day in Bratislava. The *Washington Post* reported Aug. 27 that informed sources believed that Kadar had gone on to Moscow after that meeting with Dubcek.

Kadar afterwards had explained the invasion and Hungary's part in it. He did so in an unpublished speech at a joint session of the government and party Central Committee Aug. 23. Radio Budapest described Kadar's speech as a party Politburo report on the events in Czechoslovakia and on "topical questions of domestic and foreign policy." According to the broadcast, those at the joint session unanimously approved "proposals for further action," and the Central Committee received orders to inform the party rank and file of what had taken place.

Kadar then left for a long rest in the Soviet Union. He reappeared in public at the autumn session of parliament in Budapest Oct. 16, the day that the Soviet and Czechoslovak premiers signed a treaty in Prague legalizing and indefinitely extending the Soviet occupation. He turned up next at the hosiery mill Oct. 24. Kadar, analyzing the "grave events in Czechoslovakia, which took the [Hungarian] people by surprise," insisted that the basis of Hungary's foreign policy was "to go along with the Soviet Union." "Despite different standpoints," he continued, Hungary strove "for comradely relations, friendship and cooperation with every Socialist country and all Communist and workers' parties without any exceptions." Kadar indorsed a broad international meeting of Communist and workers' parties at a suitable time, and he voiced the standard Communist indictment of U.S. and West German policies.

Kadar insisted that the principles of "Marxism-Leninism, the spirit of proletarian internationalism and sentiments of friendship guided Hungary's conduct through all stages of the [Czechoslovak] crisis." He asserted that "the invasion was unavoidable and necessary because the danger of counter-revolution in Czechoslovakia grew more menacing day by day, imperiling the heart of Europe as a new field open to the imperialists." Kadar conceded, however, that "there have been, still are and will continue to be debates" about this evaluation.

Hungarian troops had begun leaving Czechoslovakia Oct. 21, Kadar reported, and were scheduled to complete their departure before Nov. 1. He said: Hungary had no "intention of taking over the Czechoslovak party or the Czechoslovak state." Hungary affirmed its bilateral friendship treaty of June 14 with Czechoslovakia. It strove for cooperation with Czechoslovakia and hoped that "the Czechoslovak party and working people will resolve the pending big, important problems of their party and society in a Socialist way." "This is what we desire, and in this we are interested parties—but we are not interested in any other respect. In those August days, somewhere in Czechoslovakia, even Hungarian tourists were greeted as 'occupiers' and 'invaders.' What sort of invaders are we? We have not brought back a single potato; normally, invaders are those who loot."

Other International Reaction

The U.S. State Department announced Aug. 30 that the entire U.S. cultural and educational exchange program with the USSR had been placed "under review" because of the occupation of Czechoslovakia. The State Department subsequently announced the cancellation of these East-West projects: a tour of the Soviet Union by the University of Minnesota symphonic band (Sept. 5), the 2d westward flight of

the USSR Aeroflot air line, which had begun regular service
July 15 from Moscow to New York (Sept. 5), the U.S.-Polish
semiofficial cultural exchange program (Sept. 6) and the
American exhibit at the September trade fair in Bulgaria (Sept.
10). (The U.S. did not have cultural exchanges planned with
Hungary and East Germany, the other Warsaw Pact countries
that participated in the invasion.) The State Department
affirmed Sept. 6 that pending U.S.-Rumanian projects would
be continued, and it announced Sept. 10 that the U.S. still
planned to participate in the Czechoslovak trade fair, scheduled
for Sept. 15-24 in Brno.

Pope Paul VI Sept. 1 deplored the invasion as an event that
had "spread uneasiness and fear throughout the free and
civilized world." "What we believed no longer possible has,
instead, happened," the pope said. "The foundations of international order have been shaken. Once again the oppression of
arms and of intimidation has been readmitted to determine by
force the relations between nations; independence and national
dignity have been gravely offended. The security of other
nations has been threatened; an extraneous will has been
imposed upon the civil life of a people; a police-like incubus
increases the psychological tension of the population."

The first official reaction of the United Arab Republic
came Sept. 4 when Mohammed H. el-Zayyat, government
spokesman, said that "no people should be coerced or victimized
by aggression." El-Zayyat said Cairo had "sympathy for people
who have stood with us against aggression, among them the
Czechs."

French Foreign Min. Michel Debre met with Soviet Amb.-
to-France Valerian A. Zorin Sept. 2 and demanded that the
USSR immediately withdraw its forces from Czechoslovakia.
Following a meeting Sept. 7 with West German Foreign Min.
Willy Brandt, Debre said: "The chances of a return to
normality in Europe are directly linked to a *detente,* and it is up
to the Soviet Union to show by her decisions that she has not
renounced such a *detente.*"

French Pres. Charles de Gaulle Sept. 9 condemned the
occupation of Czechoslovakia, but said that it would not deter
his efforts to continue to seek a political detente with the
USSR. *De Gaulle said:*

The division into 2 blocs ... that was imposed on Europe while it was torn is a misfortune for it which follows other misfortunes. Indeed, that division constitutes, for the people of our continent, a permanent encroachment on their right to independence.... Moreover, to distribute the nations of Europe into 2 camps, dominated by 2 rivals, is to prevent them from normally establishing between them the economic, cultural and human relations that are consistent with their nature and tendencies of 1,000 years.... Finally, the political and military tension maintained between them constantly puts peace in question.... France has condemned that situation since its origin....

Since 1958 we French have not stopped working to end the system of the 2 blocs. Thus, while maintaining close relations with the countries of Western Europe, ... we have gradually detached ourselves from the military organization of NATO which subordinates the Europeans to the Americans. Thus, while participating in the Common Market, we have never agreed to the so-called 'supranational' system for the 6 which would engulf France in a state-less entity....

At the same time, while we were making the advent of a Communist regime at home impossible, we have renewed with the countries of the East, and first with Russia, growing practical relations....

That is why we feel that the events of which Czechoslovakia has just been the scene and the victim within the Communist bloc are to be condemned, notably because they are absurd when viewed in the perspective of European *detente*. We had considered as a sign of an evolution favorable to the whole of Europe, the fact that [Czechoslovakia] ... who, in 1948, having barely emerged from Nazi tyranny, found itself incorporated in the Soviet bloc by a Communist *coup de force*—was showing its intention of recovering possession of itself to some degree and of opening itself a little toward the West. On the contrary, the return to submission demanded and obtained of the Prague leaders through armed intervention under cover of what those concerned call 'Socialist solidarity'—which is nothing but the expression of Soviet hegemony—reveals to us the persistence of the Eastern bloc and consequently of the Western bloc in what is furthest removed from what Europe deserves....

It is, indeed, too late for foreign domination to win the support of nations anywhere, even when it has conquered their territory. As for converting them, it is too late for any ideology, notably communism, to prevail over national sentiment.... It is too late to succeed in dividing Europe forever into 2 opposed blocs.... France, ... come what may, will continue to work everywhere, ... for the independence of peoples and the freedom of men ... for detente, entente and cooperation, in other words, for peace.

The French Communist Party Sept. 3 announced its support of the Moscow agreement and affirmed its determination to work for the "reinforcement of the unity of the international Communist movement and for friendly relations with all brother parties." The French Socialist Party served notice Sept. 5 that if the French Communist Party indorsed the occupation of Czechoslovakia, "this would put an end to the hopes of achieving unity of the French left."

128

The Italian Communist Party newspaper *L'Unita,* reacting to Soviet charges that the Italian party had been "misled" by "imperialists," declared Sept. 2 that "not only the imperialist propagandists, but also many important Communist parties consider the unrequested and unjustified military intervention ... in Czechoslovakia as a violation of the principles of equality, sovereignty and noninterference." Italian leader Luigi Longo Sept. 12 called on the 5 Warsaw Treaty nations to restore "full sovereignty" to Czechoslovakia by withdrawing their troops. Longo said that as long as Warsaw Pact troops remained in Czechoslovakia and the situation was thus "not normalized," it "would be neither useful nor opportune, and perhaps not even possible, to bring to an end the preparatory work for a world conference of Communist and workers' parties, seen for the end of November in Moscow."

A 3-day extraordinary session of the U.S. Communist Party ended Sept. 2 with the issuance of a statement indorsing both the Czechoslovak liberal reforms and the Warsaw Pact invasion. Arnold Johnson, the party's public relations director, claimed that the 2 positions were not contradictory since "the reforms themselves were never disputed; it was the revanchists and outsiders—the CIA and forces from West Germany—who exploited the reforms" and made intervention mandatory. The statement called for the "curbing of all counterrevolutionary forces" in Czechoslovakia as well as "immediate steps to continue the processes of Socialist democratization and economic reforms" begun in January.

STRUGGLE OVER 'NORMALIZATION'

Kuznetsov Mission

Soviet First Deputy Foreign Min. Vasily V. Kuznetsov made a surprise trip to Prague Sept. 6 and conferred with the Czechoslovak leaders during the following 5 days. The visit came amid reports that the Soviet Union was seeking to conciliate the differences between Prague and Moscow over the implementation of the Aug. 26 Moscow agreement.

Kuznetsov, accompanied by Soviet Amb.-to-Czechoslovakia Stefan V. Chervonenko, conferred with Pres. Svoboda Sept. 6, Czechoslovak party First Secy. Dubcek and Premier Cernik Sept. 7, Slovak party First Secy. Gustav Husak Sept. 8-9 and again with Dubcek Sept. 11. The Czechoslovak state TV network Sept. 6 described the talks between Kuznetsov and Svoboda as "open and comradely." In reference to the Kuznetsov-Dubcek meeting Sept. 7, Prague radio said that the 2 officials had "informed each other and presented opinions about current questions concerning relations between the 2 countries and parties." CTK reported Sept. 9 that Kuznetsov and Husak had held a "cordial and friendly talk" and had "discussed certain tactical problems with a view also to the current situation in Slovakia."

As Kuznetsov began his talks, the Czechoslovak party Presidium met with Dubcek Sept. 6 and issued a statement calling for "completely open and direct negotiations about all the questions that make difficult the fulfillment of the Moscow agreement." The statement noted that "conditions have been created for concrete and responsible negotiations by plenipotentiaries of both sides" in order to remove "all the obstacles to the normalization that may be put from any side." "Conditions must be created so that the affairs of our country can be fully administered by our own organs," the statement said.

It was reported Sept. 9 that, in his talks with the Czechoslovak leadership, Kuznetsov had proposed a number of Soviet
measures aimed at facilitating implementation of the Moscow
agreement. According to the *Washington Post,* which quoted
"Czechoslovak sources," the measures were: (1) a fixed timetable for phased withdrawal of most of the 650,000 Warsaw
Treaty troops currently on Czechoslovak soil, (2) a pledge that
Soviet secret police and intelligence officials currently in
Czechoslovakia, variously estimated at from 800 to 2,000,
would be removed, (3) a pledge that personal security, safety
and protection from arrest would be guaranteed to all Czechoslovak citizens and (4) the establishment of facilities providing
for direct and improved consultation between Prague and
Moscow.

Pravda in Moscow Sept. 6 defined for the first time what
the USSR meant by the term "normalization," the presumable
prerequisite for the withdrawal of Warsaw Pact forces from
Czechoslovakia. *Pravda* wrote: "The process of normalization
means, first of all, the complete exposure and stamping out of
the subversive activities of the right-wing, anti-Socialist forces;
the elimination of their influence on a part of the population,
and especially youth; the resolute strengthening of the leading
role of the Communist Party in the activities of the state
agencies, in the ideological and public spheres, in the whole life
of the country."

Pravda asserted that the cleaning of walls "blotted with
enemy slogans" constituted only the "outward aspects" of normalization; furthermore, while there had been some progress
toward normalization in the economic sphere, only a beginning
had been made in the "political" and "public" spheres. The
paper denounced "right-wing forces" and some of the news
media that "would like to reduce this vitally important project
of strengthening socialism and consolidating Czechoslovakia's
statehood merely to the withdrawal of the allied troops and
after that, it is alleged, life can be normalized." It accused
"counterrevolutionaries" of terrorism, subversion and seeking
to undermine the Prague leadership.

Efforts to Salvage Reform

A proclamation issued in Prague Sept. 10 assured Czecho-slovak citizens that their "personal security and freedom" would be guaranteed. The proclamation was signed by Pres. Svoboda, Premier Cernik, National Assembly Chairman Smrkovsky, Czechoslovak party First Secy. Dubcek and Slovak party First Secy. Husak.

The proclamation affirmed that the leaders were "fully conscious" of their "obligation to insure the personal freedom and safety of all our fellow citizens—workers, farmers, artists, scientists—young and old." It proclaimed that "every citizen of this state who does not trespass the valid legal norms enjoys to the full the protection of our valid legal code.... No one can be prosecuted criminally otherwise than for lawful reasons and in a manner as stipulated by the law. No one may be taken into custody other than in cases stipulated by the laws and on the basis of the decisions by the court or the prosecutor." In an allu-sion to the police-state rule of ex-Pres. Antonin Novotny, the signers stressed that they would "never allow deformations or violations of our legal code such as we had witnessed—and even more—in past years."

The proclamation also appealed to Czechoslovak citizens currently outside the country to return home. Noting that "staying abroad multiplies mistrust and foreign propaganda and the impossibility of first-hand knowledge of the state of affairs here amplifies helplessness [and] confusion," the proclamation said: "Your place is here. The republic needs your knowledge and education, your creative work. Your fellow citizens are waiting for you and are resolutely and selflessly continuing to build up their homeland for themselves and their children." The proclamation also noted that "the guarantee of the strict adherence of the state bodies of the Czechoslovak republic to legality also requires that every citizen of the republic without exception observe the law—whether at home or abroad."

The proclamation pledged that Czechoslovakia's leaders would "continue along the road which we entered in January to strengthen the Socialist order, to expand its democratic and humanistic character." The signers affirmed that they would "build up our economy in a determined and purposeful manner so that it would be a reliable foundation for a better, richer and fuller life for the workers, farmers and the intelligentsia."

Premier Cernik conferred with top Soviet officials in Moscow Sept. 10 and signed 2 trade protocols before returning to Prague the same day. He was accompanied by Frantisek Hamouz, deputy premier in charge of economic relations with the Communist bloc, and Foreign Trade Min. Vaclav Vales, both of whom remained in Moscow to hold further talks. The major participants on the Soviet side were party Gen. Secy. Brezhnev, Premier Kosygin and Pres. Podgorny.

A communique issued at the conclusion of the Soviet-Czechoslovak talks said that the 2 sides had signed a protocol that provided for the USSR to build a natural gas pipeline from Kiev to Czechoslovakia and to supply Czechoslovakia with natural gas "for many years," in addition to oil, iron and other raw materials, in return for Czechoslovak steel pipe, heavy trucks, industrial equipment, knitted goods, footwear and other products. A 2d protocol dealt with "other economic issues," which the communique did not disclose. Both trade agreements were reported to have been prepared during high-level negotiations earlier in the year.

The communique said that the negotiators had conducted political discussions dealing with an "elaboration" of the talks held in Moscow Aug. 23-26. Both sides "expressed firm mutual conviction that the main thing in the present situation is to bring consistently into life the practical steps" resulting from the Aug. 26 Moscow agreement.

The Soviet Union had announced Sept. 3 that it would ꞁuild a subway system in Prague totaling 4½ miles initially and ꞁventually exceeding 37 miles.

A report that had been issued Aug. 29 by the Economics Institute of the Czechoslovak Academy of Sciences described the economic effects of the Warsaw Pact invasion and occupations as "catastrophic" and said that the "prospect of a positive turn for the better which had begun to make itself felt has now been destroyed." The report estimated that production losses during the first week of the occupation totaled about $500 million. The institute said it was impossible to estimate the overall damage to the economy but that it was in the billions of Czech crowns (7½ crowns per U.S. dollar). (Figures reported by the *Washington Post* Sept. 11 put economic construction losses at $70 million and damage to transportation facilities and crops at $600 million.) The report concluded that it would take Czechoslovakia 2 years to recover from the economic effects of the invasion, "meaning that Czechoslovakia will not be in a position before the 1970s to eradicate the economic difficulties resulting from the policy of [former party First Secy.] Novotny."

Many Soviet tanks and military units were withdrawn from the center of Prague Sept. 11 to bases in the surrounding countryside. Other sections of the city, including the international airport, remained occupied by Soviet tank units, armored cars and troops. The partial withdrawal of Soviet forces from Prague apparently was the 2d stage in the pullback of Warsaw Pact troops from conspicuous occupation tasks; the first stage had been completed in the previous 10 days with the removal of troops from public buildings in Prague and other cities. The withdrawal of major Soviet armored units from Prague was linked to Premier Oldrich Cernik's talks with Soviet leaders Sept. 10 and to the meetings Soviet First Deputy Foreign Min. Kuznetsov had conducted in Prague Sept. 6-11.

The Czechoslovak Interior Ministry announced Sept. 10 that Deputy Interior Min. Frantisek Vasek had been appointed head of state security services. Vasek replaced Viliam Salgovic, the pro-Soviet secret police chief, who had been dismissed by the Prague government Sept. 1. The Interior Ministry Sept. 10 confirmed the suicide of Jan Zaruba, another deputy interior minister. Zaruba reportedly had killed himself in his office the previous week rather than turn over ministry papers to the Soviet secret police.

In an address to the National Assembly Sept. 13 prior to the vote on the censorship reimposition law, Premier Cernik said that the revival of "preventive censorship" was necessary since "in the past, our intentions were often falsely misinterpreted in the press and radio." Cernik asserted, however, that the revocation of the law abolishing censorship was only for a "provisional period." In a TV interview taped Sept. 13 and broadcast Sept. 15, Cernik assured the Czechoslovaks that, under the new censorship law, "there will be room for criticism." "There will be enough room for the expression of journalists, editors and the creative forces of the nation," he said.

In his Sept. 13 address, Cernik also outlined the major commitments that Prague had undertaken in the Aug. 26 Moscow agreement, and he cited various measures that would be taken in the economic and social fields. *Excerpts from his remarks:*
The government will do everything to [ensure that Pres. Svoboda can] proclaim on Oct. 28 the federalization of the Czech lands and Slovakia.

The government, facing the realities of the accepted conclusions of the Moscow agreement, in which the principles of equality and sovereignty were likewise concerned, is fully aware of its responsibilities to the people of this country and wishes to inform the National Assembly of the indispensable and urgent measures which the government is and will be carrying out in important segments of social life.

The present situation compels the government to concentrate on the solution of the most timely questions. The government, facing the hard situation, comes to the National Assembly with the measures it will adopt in the near future and without great promises, for which, under the present situation, there is no room.

The army has to review its fighting capacity to defend the frontiers against foreign enemies. The government also hopes that the army will find capabilities to repair the damages to the economy, especially helping with the harvests, the repairs of transportation and the like.

The minister of national defense and the minister of the interior will keep peace and order with the help of the armed forces.

The minister of national defense and the Ministry of Foreign Affairs will soon begin government-level negotiations for the gradual withdrawal of the foreign armies as the consolidation progresses. Under the "normalization" is included the further strengthening of socialism and the limitation of rightist elements.

For the purpose of strengthening the Warsaw Pact and the command of the army, a State Defense Council will be established.

In the field of foreign policy, the president has taken over many duties. The basic orientation of our foreign policy will not be changed.

The debate in the United Nations Security Council was not at our initiative, and the Czechoslovak Socialist Republic is of the opinion that this question is to be solved by direct negotiations, although foreign armies have entered our territory.

Our policy will be directed toward the maintenance of peace and security. We ask for security in Europe, and this policy will be pursued in cooperation with the European Socialists.

In the economic field, the recent events have caused many delays in deliveries, the interruption of production [and] the disruption of ties of cooperation between the industries and factories.

The recent events have weakened the sources of our future development. Can we, then, continue our programs? We foresee the following realistic way:

(1) The production shortcomings at this extraordinary time can be remedied by improved organization of work, extra production shifts and increased efforts.

(2) The economic goals for 1969 remain unchanged and the government will ask the National Assembly to authorize extraordinary measures in case of economic need.

(3) Profits will be taxed, and new taxes will be introduced, and the social and economic equalization with Slovakia will continue, although the pace will be slower.

(4) The rise in living standards will be maintained, especially by preserving the progress of the building program. Industry and agriculture will maintain their pace.

(5) The growth of the purchasing power of the currency is decisive for the growth of the living standard. All agreements made with the trade unions will be implemented. Some unions will have to wait, but those [agreements] earmarked for enforcement in 1969 will be fulfilled.

(6) The planned decrease of the working time—5 days a week—will be carried out in accordance with the existing laws.

(7) In the social field, the government will make no changes. In 1969, the increase of all old-age pensions will be carried out as well as the payment to members of the Czechoslovak army abroad during World War II.

(8) We shall establish proper relations between wholesale and retail prices. We shall introduce a new system of taxation, as well as various subsidies, and establish prices, especially in the service industries. Some prices will have to go up, but severe measures will be taken against speculation.

(9) The new situation is highly sensitive for our economic relations.

Our relations with the Soviet Union have produced certain objective facts. Our far-reaching orientation toward Comecon in the field of raw materials' delivery and of the sale of goods remains the basis of our economic life, while we shall develop relations with other countries on the basis of mutually advantageous conditions.

We have already signed an agreement to receive improved iron ore [from the Soviet Union] under acceptable conditions.

(10) In the investment field, the investments for construction will be maintained, but some projects will not be started until others are finished.

(11) We shall maintain the present economic reforms and will revise the structural and institutional organization of the economy.

We shall also carry out the planned reorganization. The industrial plan has to operate on an economically sound basis and will be economically independent.

We shall introduce, as an experiment, Workers' Councils and shall make the final decisions after the results are known.

We must end the alienation between workers and peasants and the means of production.

We have decided to continue in the new way on which we embarked after January and which went through heavy tests in recent days. Our country will continue the development begun after January, but there must be several changes.

The government will take measures in the sphere of control and direction of the press, radio and television to safeguard against any threat to the interest of the Republic.

Proceeding from the extraordinary conditions in which our country has found itself and following the interest of the speediest possible consolidation of political conditions, the government has been impelled for a provisional period to abrogate the provision of the press law on the abolition of censorship.

We are a part of the Socialist states as before. The only way out is that provided by the Moscow negotiations, and I can say that all the citizens will maintain their rights and freedoms.

Our future is in the unity of the party and the people and in the use of all our capabilities in the coming days and all the strength of our production.

Czechoslovak party First Secy. Dubcek addressed the country over TV Sept. 14 and appealed to all Czechoslovaks to refrain from provoking clashes and incidents with the occupying Warsaw Treaty troops. "I beg you again and again," Dubcek implored, "not to let anyone misuse you." If Czechoslovakia "strictly fulfilled" the Aug. 26 Moscow agreement, Dubcek said, then "we shall be able to request the justified fulfillment of the obligations by the other side." "We must do our best in the spirit of the Moscow agreement, but without any compromises, to remove all that had caused this mistrust.... We must be able to convince these 5 countries [the occupiers] of our pro-Socialist line."

At another point in his address Dubcek noted: "I know it was not easy for you to accept our words about the solution we have accepted in Moscow, but it was the only possible solution." Dubcek asserted, however, that the fulfillment of the Moscow agreement would "open possibilities" for the continuation of the democratization policies begun in January. "We are not ready to abandon them," he declared.

In a speech televised Sept. 13 and reported Sept. 15 Zdenek Mlynar, a member of the party Presidium and one of the participants in the talks that led to the Moscow agreement, disclosed that one of the provisions of that accord had been that the clandestine party congress held the night of Aug. 21-22 was to be nullified. Mlynar said that the 14th congress "will not be valid" and that a new 14th congress would be called at a later date. This statement was the first official confirmation that the congress had been nullified.

A communique issued Sept. 17 at the conclusion of a meeting of the party Presidium noted that the Presidium was preparing for "further 2-way political negotiations in the near future" between Prague and Moscow. The Presidium discussed "several internal state matters in the realm of economic policy, ideology and international relations," the communique said.

Slovak party First Secy. Gustav Husak asserted in a speech to the Slovak National Council Sept. 17 that "normalization" had almost been achieved in Czechoslovak-Soviet relations. The main current problem, Husak maintained, was to consolidate relations with "the rest of the world, especially our neighbors."

The Czechoslovak press Sept. 25 launched a counterattack on the East German press for its repeated attacks on Dubcek. This was the first direct response by Prague to attacks by one of the 5 occupying powers since press censorship had been reimposed following the invasion. The Czechoslovak counterattack was apparently made with official approval. (The Aug. 26 Moscow protocol forbade Czechoslovakia to criticize the occupying powers—the USSR, Poland, East Germany, Hungary and Bulgaria.) *Rude pravo* Sept. 25 called the attacks on Dubcek, made by the East German party newspaper *Neues Deutschland* "improper both journalistically and politically." The Socialist party paper *Svobodne slovo* Sept. 25 termed the attacks on Dubcek as "obviously ... a campaign."

A survey, conducted in northern Bohemia and disclosed Sept. 20, stated that out of 864 persons, 671 believed that the policy of "democratic socialism," which had begun in January, would still have a chance to continue, despite the country's occupation. 783 of the respondents expressed full confidence in the Dubcek-Svoboda leadership.

Another poll, conducted by *Reporter* magazine, appearing legally Sept. 20 for the first time in 4 weeks, stressed the overwhelming popularity of Dubcek and Svoboda over all other Czechoslovak leaders. The poll was based on a sampling of 208 persons over 18 in Prague; 99% regarded Dubcek as "the leading personality of our times."

Rude pravo Sept. 24 had published a letter in which 50 Czechoslovak economists lauded the government for upholding its plans for a new system of economic management. *Excerpts from the letter:*

> The events of the past few weeks have created a new political situation in our country that has important implications for our economy. In this situation, it is necessary to define clearly and unambiguously the ideas and principles that are to guide our economic policies.

In its statement before the National Assembly Sept. 13, the government declared unequivocally that it considered it essential, in the present situation, to adhere to the program of economic reform. We welcome the government's standpoint because we believe this economic policy to be the only possible one.

The economic reform in this country was not the work of a small group of men, nor a recently conceived short-term program. The ideas of economic reform were not born after Jan. 1968. Rather, they resulted from the long experience of Socialist enterprises and from the creative endeavors of economists engaged in theoretical and practical work. The entire development of economic thought and of the economy itself resulted in the ideas of economic reform. As early as the mid-50s it became obvious that bureaucratic, centralized management methods were inadequate in a highly developed industrial society. During the next decade, the efforts to change the system of management of the economy continued to grow. The first steps [toward economic reform] were taken after 1956; then at the beginning of the '60s there was a period of economic stagnation. It was in the light of this experience that the 13th Congress of the Communist Party of Czechoslovakia adopted certain fundamental conclusions.

If we wish to avoid stagnation and decline of the economy, if, instead, we wish to develop the economy in keeping with the present scientific-technical revolution, then it is essential that we change radically the system of management of the economy.

... The Czechoslovak economists considered it their duty to their country and to the entire Socialist movement to devise a system of management in keeping with the existing level of the national economy. This was not an easy task, and it is hardly surprising that its gradual execution was accompanied by exploration of various alternatives and by differences of opinion. However, the sifting of opinions that continued for many years clearly demonstrated that the overwhelming majority of Czechoslovak economists was convinced that the fundamental direction and the aims and methods of this reform were scientifically justified. Therefore, although the new situation must be taken into consideration, we must pursue this reform with the greatest possible determination.

Criticism of bureaucratic methods of economic management was, and continues to be, guided by a Socialist viewpoint, and in fact seeks to strengthen the Socialist character of the economy, ridding it of distortions which weakened it. Under no circumstances can we agree with the charge that implementation of the new system of management indicates a return to capitalism.

The question arises whether the present economic situation, with its stoppages and losses in production [and] with the breakdowns in cooperative relationships, requires the reintroduction of some central directive methods.

In our opinion, the present economic problems must not be solved by bureaucratic centralism, but by the initiative of the people and by cooperation between state and economic agencies. The state agencies will have to be more skillful and consistent; they will have to gain the cooperation of the enterprises by consultation with the people concerned and by encouraging the initiative of employees.

Special difficulties require special efforts. This is impossible without initiative, and initiative requires the independence of the enterprises and trust in the people. In our opinion, therefore, the solution to our present economic problems depends on development of the economic reform measures formulated in the "action program" of this party and in the government program announced last April.

We regard the implementation of the following reforms as basic for our future economic policies:

● Clear definition of the independence and responsibilites of the enterprises and of their associations. They should be subject to daily control by customers and consumers and should have a clear interest in the results of their work. The enterprises must be divorced from the state administration. Efforts should be made to form enterprise workers' councils. ...

● In view of the vital importance of foreign economic relations to our state, contacts between our enterprises and foreign partners should be increased. Bureaucratic obstacles interfering with export trade should be eliminated. We should seek more effective forms of economic cooperation in COMECON.

● We should succeed in applying the categories of market value; production and trade decisions should be determined on an economic basis. To achieve this, prices, credit and financial policies should be freed from subjective distortions and conditions should be established to make the currency convertible.

● Every economic unit and every workers' collective should be encouraged by concrete economic measures to show initiative and competitive spirit.

These progressive economic policies will certainly attract the support of all economists in both the theoretical and practical fields, as they did in the past. The economists have discussed and argued about all kinds of questions concerning our economic development and the principles of economic reform, its course and its implementation—and they will continue to do so. However, it is precisely because of this discussion that they are able to unite today in declaring that if our country is to participate in the modern economic development of the world, and if it is to contribute to the fulfillment of the historical role of world socialism, the basic principles of economic reform must guide our economic policies.

Soviet Pressure Increases

Czechoslovak Foreign Min. Jiri Hajek was officially relieved of his post Sept. 19 after intense Soviet pressure to effect his dismissal. Hajek's portfolio was temporarily taken over by Premier Cernik.

Dr. Hajek had reportedly submitted his letter of resignation Sept. 14, but Pres. Svoboda held out for 5 days before accepting it. Hajek, who was in Yugoslavia at the time of the invasion and returned to Prague Sept. 8, had gone from Yugoslavia on his own initiative to put the Czechoslovak case against the occupation before the UN Security Council.

Among the charges leveled against Hajek in the Soviet and East German press was a repetition of the Soviet accusation that he was a Jew who had changed his name and assisted the Nazis during Czechoslovakia's wartime occupation. (The existence of another Hajek, formerly prominent as editor-in-chief of the Czechoslovak Writers' Union monthly *Plamen* before his removal as a Novotny supporter, apparently was a source of the confused charges against the former foreign minister. According to reports from Prague, Soviet First Deputy Foreign Min. Vasily Kuznetsov, assigned to Prague to oversee the execution of the Aug. 26 Moscow protocol, subsequently apologized to the Czechoslovak government for the allegation that ex-Foreign Min. Hajek had been a Nazi agent.)

The acceptance of Hajek's resignation was seen by some observers in Prague as a conciliatory Czechoslovak gesture before a planned trip for a 2d round of talks in Moscow by a top-level Czechoslovak delegation. Other sources believed that Hajek's ouster was in exchange for the dismissal Sept. 19 of Karel Hoffmann, head of the central board of communications and a presumed Moscow favorite. Hoffmann was widely regarded in Prague as a collaborationist during and in the hours before the Aug. 20-21 invasion.

It was reported in Prague Sept. 20 that Kuznetsov had delivered to Svoboda Sept. 19 a Kremlin note suggesting that the Prague leadership consider replacing Dubcek and demanding the immediate purging of "unreliables" from the ranks of the government and news media. Svoboda was reported to have countered with a threat of his own resignation if Dubcek were forced out.

Cernik announced Sept. 21 that the occupying troops would begin a "gradual departure from Czechoslovakia within a few days." Cernik confirmed, however, that "certain contingents of foreign troops will remain among us." The number of the troops to remain would be revealed "in due time," he said.

Cernik made the disclosure, released by CTK and Prague radio, in a speech at the regional meeting of party officials in Ostrava in northern Moravia. In his speech he denied the Soviet claim that the Czechoslovak leadership had made commitments to Moscow during the Cierna confrontation in late July. "I declare quite responsibly that we concluded no agreements at Cierna," Cernik said. "We only informed the Soviet representatives what course we would take in the future to prevent both leftist and rightist excesses." (Governments of the 5 invading countries had repeatedly justified their step by charging the Dubcek leadership with violation of its Cierna promises to slow the pace of liberalization.)

Observers both in and outside Czechoslovakia received the announcement of the impending withdrawal with surprise, since the Soviet press remained strongly critical of the slow pace of "normalization." The Soviet press had charged that the "normalization" process was continually hampered by "counterrevolutionary" and "anti-Socialist" elements.

Commenting on the announcement, National Assembly chairman Josef Smrkovsky said in Brno Sept. 21 that he was "mildly optimistic" about the future. "The greatest danger to the country," he said, "would arise if national unity were broken or interrupted."

In his speech delivered in Dubcek's presence in Ostrava, Cernik insisted that the government would not "punish anybody for his political opinions." "Only those will be punished who transgress our valid laws," he declared. Cernik also asserted that there would be no return to the "methods of the '50s." "We took a bold road in January," he said. "We wanted to build socialism with a human face, as envisaged by the teaching of Marxism-Leninism." Referring to Soviet demands for the punishment of "rightist forces," Cernik countered: "It depends on what people understand by the term 'punishment.'" He said that the Aug. 26 Moscow protocol consisted not only of "the 16 points" but of the "whole concept" of liberalization policies. (His mention of 16 points marked the first time that a Czechoslovak leader disclosed that the secret Moscow agreement was made up of such a number of points.)

Czechoslovak-Soviet governmental relations remained in stalemate following the announced cancellation Sept. 24 of a trip to Moscow by a top-level delegation to be headed by Dubcek. The new round of negotiations had been authorized by the Czechoslovak party Presidium Sept. 17 amid rising disagreement over the interpretation of the Aug. 26 Moscow protocol. (It was reported in Prague Sept. 17 that, following the Presidium session, Prague had sent notes to the 5 occupying powers protesting their press attacks on Czechoslovakia. The notes specifically singled out attacks on then-Foreign Min. Hajek.)

The trip, already twice postponed, was canceled following a meeting Sept. 23 between Dubcek and Kuznetsov. A statement on the Dubcek-Kuznetsov meeting described their talks as "frank" and "comradely," terms used in Communist circles to describe sharp disagreements.

Sources in Prague said that Dubcek and Kuznetsov had failed to agree on an agenda for the Moscow talks. These sources also said that Dubcek had demanded that Moscow fulfill its part of the Aug. 26 agreement by pulling out most of the occupying troops, while Kuznetsov expressed Moscow's displeasure at the slow pace of "normalization" in Czechoslovakia.

It was reported in Prague that hundreds of Soviet civilian personnel had been seen moving into Prague Sept. 22, the day after Cernik's announcement of an imminent troop pullout. The advisory corps members and their families were reported to have taken up residence in Prague to await assignment to various Czechoslovak ministries. Some sources said that more than 600 houses and apartments had been requested by Moscow for the special personnel.

It was reported in Prague Sept. 23 that one of the points on Moscow's proposed agenda for the talks included a demand for a broad purge of the Czechoslovak press and mass media. Among the names said to appear on the Soviet list of undesirable "counterrevolutionaries" were: Prof. Eduard Goldstuecker, chairman of the Writers' Union; Prof. Karel Kosik, a noted Czechoslovak philosopher; Stanislav Budin, editor of the weekly satirical magazine *Reporter;* Czech National Council Chairman Cestmir Cisar, entrusted with preparing the federalization of the country's Czech and Slovak regions, an action opposed by the USSR; Education Min. Vaclav Kadlec, who had pressed for educational reforms, among them the ending of required Russian language studies and the toleration of religious instruction.

The Tass news agency Sept. 25 issued a statement charging that Czechoslovak leaders' actions "directly contradict" the stipulations of the Aug. 26 Moscow protocol. The statement charged that despite Prague's reimposition of censorship, "some organs of the Czechoslovak mass media have not only failed to stop anti-Socialist propaganda but are even trying to intensify it." "Recent statements by some Czechoslovak leaders contained ... praise for those who led the mass media along the antipopular road, and even attempted to win the favor of those who must bear direct responsibility for the ideological preparation of the counterrevolutionary coup," Tass said. The Soviet statement named those allegedly responsible for "subversive activities on behalf of the counterrevolution": Pavel Kohout, playwright and author of a patriotic appeal signed by more than a million Czechoslovaks; Ladislav Mnacko, novelist; Ivan Svitak, philosopher; Ludvik Vesely, literary editor; Milan Kundera, writer; Kamil Winter, former TV news director.

Although the Tass statement did not identify the Czechoslovak leaders said to sanction the subversives, the targets of the attacks were believed to be National Assembly Chairman Josef Smrkovsky and party Central Committee Secy. Zdenek Mlynar. Smrkovsky had declared Sept. 21 that the Czechoslovak press and news media had "rendered magnificent service in the critical days" during and after the Aug. 20-21 invasion. Mlynar was reported Sept. 25 to have spoken in praise of the role the press played during the invasion. The legal commission of the National Assembly was reported Sept. 25 to have upheld the activity of the underground press and radio in the days after the invasion.

USSR Asserts Doctrine of Limited Sovereignty

Abandoning its earlier justification for the invasion—the assertion that the Warsaw Treaty forces had been invited by Czechoslovakia's leaders—the Soviet Communist Party organ *Pravda* Sept. 26 advanced another ideological argument. The new thesis held, in effect, that the world Socialist community had the right to intervene when socialism was under attack in a fraternal Socialist country. It denied that the occupation had violated Czechoslovakia's "real sovereignty."

"World socialism ... is indivisible, and its defense is the common cause of all Communists," the article said. Since "right-wing anti-Socialist forces" had attacked the very basis of socialism in Czecholsovakia, the article asserted,

Czechoslovakia's "real sovereignty" required that "fraternal countries" defend it from this threat to the "very foundations of the country's independence and sovereignty."

The *Pravda* article, written by the paper's specialist on ideological matters, Sergei Kovalev, said that, although each Communist party was free to apply, independently, the principles of socialism in its country, "it cannot depart from these principles." *Kovalev wrote:*

● "The weakening of any of the links in the world system of socialism directly affects all the Socialist countries, which cannot look indifferently upon this. Each Communist party is responsible not only to its own people, but also to all the Socialist countries, to the entire Communist movement."

● "The sovereignty of each Socialist country cannot be opposed to the interests of the world of socialism, of the world revolutionary movement. Lenin demanded that all Communists fight against small-nation narrow-mindedness, seclusion and isolation, consider the whole and the general, subordinate the particular to the general interest." The Socialist countries reject not only "the leftist, adventurist conception of 'exporting revolution'" but also "the exporting and importing of counter-revolution."

● "The anti-Socialist elements in Czechoslovakia actually covered up the demand for so-called neutrality and Czechoslovakia's withdrawal from the Socialist community with talk about the right of nations to self-determination.... Such self-determination, as a result of which NATO troops would have been able to come up to the Soviet border, while the community of European Socialist countries would have been split, in effect encroaches upon the vital interests of the peoples of these countries and conflicts, as the very root of it, with the right of these people to Socialist self-determination. Discharging their internationalist duty toward the fraternal peoples of Czechoslovakia and defending their own Socialist gains, the USSR and the other Socialist states had to act decisively, and they did act against the anti-Socialist forces in Czechoslovakia."

● "People who disapprove of the actions of the allied Socialist states are ignoring the decisive fact that these countries are defending the interests of all of world socialism, of the entire world revolutionary movement. The Bratislava statement of

the Communist and workers' parties says of Socialist gains that
support, consolidation and defense of these gains, won at the
price of heroic effort and the self-sacrifice of each people,
represents a common international duty and obligation for all
the Socialist countries.... The help to the working people of
Czechoslovakia by other Socialist countries, which prevented
the export of counterrevolution from abroad, constitutes the
real sovereignty of the Czechoslovak Socialist Republic against
those who would like to deprive it of its sovereignty and give up
the country to imperialism."

● The occupation troops "do not interfere in the internal
affairs of the country, are fighting for the principle of self-
determination of the peoples of Czechoslovakia not in words
but in deeds, are fighting for their inalienable right to think out
profoundly and decide their fate themselves, without
intimidation on the part of counterrevolutionaries, without
revisionists and nationalist demagogy."

Democratization Program Surrendered

　　　After 44 days of occupation, Czechoslovakia's leaders went
to Moscow and yielded Oct. 3-4 to Soviet pressure (a) to
abandon the remnants of the democratization program and (b)
to allow the stationing in their country of foreign troops for an
indefinite period. The new Moscow talks, which had been twice
postponed and then officially canceled, were designed to resolve
the deadlock that had developed between the 2 countries over
implementing the Aug. 26 Moscow protocol.

　　　A communique announcing the Czechoslovak pledges was
signed in Moscow Oct. 4 following 2 days of secret talks. *The
communique said:*

　　Soviet-Czechoslovak negotiations were held in Moscow Oct. 3-4, 1968.

　　Taking part in the negotiations on the Soviet side were L. I. Brezhnev,
general secretary of the CPSU Central Committee; A. N. Kosygin, member
of the Politburo of the CPSU Central Committee and chairman of the USSR
Council of Ministers; N. V. Podgorny, member of the Politburo of the CPSU
Central Committee and president of the Presidium of the USSR Supreme
Soviet.

　　On the Czechoslovak side: A. Dubcek, first secretary of the Central
Committee of the Communist Party of Czechoslovakia; O. Cernik, chairman
of the Czechoslovak government and member of the Presidium of the Central
Committee of the Communist Party of Czechoslovakia; G. Husak, first
secretary of the Central Committee of the Communist Party of Slovakia and

member of the Presidium of the Central Committee of the Communist Party of Czechoslovakia.

The 2 sides studied questions on developing relations between the USSR and Czechoslovakia. Special attention was given to the fulfillment of agreements and undertakings drafted by the delegations of the USSR and Czechoslovakia in Moscow from Aug. 23 to 26 this year, proceeding from the principles recorded in the final documents of the meeting in Cierna nad Tisou and the conference in Bratislava. It was reaffirmed that these undertakings are the basis for achieving a normalization of socio-political life in Czechoslovakia and for developing Czechoslovakia's friendly relations with the Soviet Union and other countries of the Socialist community.

The Czechoslovak delegation informed the delegation of the CPSU Central Committee on the concrete measures carried out in Czechoslovakia to fulfill the indicated agreement and also about its views on further work in this direction.

The Czechoslovak delegation stated that the Central Committee of the Communist Party of Czechoslovakia and the government of the Czechoslovak Socialist Republic would take every measure to ensure the fulfillment of the Moscow agreement. They will step up efforts to raise the leading role of the Communist Party, will intensify the struggle against the anti-Socialist forces, will take the necessary measures to place all the mass information media at the service of socialism [and] will reinforce the party and state organs with people firmly adhering to positions of Marxism-Leninism and proletarian internationalism.

The delegation of the CPSU Central Committee confirmed its readiness to give the Czechoslovak comrades every assistance in the implementation of their plans directed at normalizing the situation in the country and in the party, in the spirit of the agreement reached in Moscow.

The question of the presence of allied troops on the territory of Czechoslovakia was discussed in the course of the talks. The 2 sides agreed that the governments would consider and sign a treaty on the temporary stationing of allied troops in Czechoslovakia. In accordance with the documents of the Aug. 23-26 talks in Moscow the withdrawal of the other troops will be carried out by stages.

The delegations of the Soviet Union and Czechoslovakia discussed the tasks of strengthening the fraternal alliance and inviolable friendship between the peoples of the 2 countries, the development between them of all-round fruitful cooperation in the economic, political, cultural and other spheres, and also the strengthening of relations between towns and regions which maintain traditional friendly contacts.

The most important problems of ensuring international peace and security were also discussed. The 2 sides confirmed their determination to follow unswervingly the jointly drafted foreign political course in the interests of strengthening the Socialist community and successful struggle against the policy of imperialist powers. In this the delegations recognize as the prime task the implementation of measures to create a reliable barrier in the way of the mounting revanchist strivings of West German militaristic forces, the rendering of effective aid to the people of struggling Vietnam, and the curbing of the imperialist aggression in the Middle East area.

The talks proceeded in a spirit of comradeship, businesslike cooperation and frankness.

Rumors from Prague and Moscow said the talks had taken place under less than normal circumstances. Prague sources reported Oct. 3 that the Czechoslovak party Presidium had yielded to a Soviet demand to exclude from the delegation Smrkovsky and Pres. Svoboda.

According to reports from Prague Oct. 8, the Czechoslovak leaders had not been consulted about the terms of the communique during the talks. These sources said that Dubcek, head of the delegation, had not signed the communique. Because of the conditions, the sources said, the Czechoslovak party Presidium Oct. 8, after hearing Dubcek's report on the talks, had merely "approved the procedure of the Czechoslovak delegation." During the conference, the sources said, Dubcek twice collapsed. After complaining of his country's inability to accommodate the occupying troops in winter quarters, he was said to have collapsed when told by Brezhnev that the problem could be solved by sending the Czechoslovak army to the Soviet frontier bordering on China.

The Soviet newspapers *Pravda* and *Izvestia* attacked Czechoslovakia Oct. 3, the day the Czechoslovak delegation arrived in Moscow, for poor fulfillment of the terms of the Moscow agreement. *Pravda* asserted that "normalization" called for "practical actions and not mere declarations." The paper denounced the Czechoslovak news media for its failure to suppress "anti-Socialist, anti-Soviet and right-wing revisionist forces." *Pravda* said it was "high time to curb the foes of our friendship who, either openly or in Aesopian language, still continue attacking ... friendship" between the 2 countries. *Izvestia* agreed that "normalization" had been proceeding "too slowly."

Reflecting on the mood of the country on the eve of the Moscow talks Oct. 3, Martin Vaculik, a member of the Czechoslovak Central Committee, had declared in an interview with *Rude pravo* that Czechoslovaks would have to show more "voluntary submission and discipline" toward the political realities created by the occupation. "There cannot be any tactical maneuvering" around the Moscow agreements, he said.

Speaking at Prague airport following the return of the delegation from Moscow Oct. 5, Cernik confirmed that "within the next few days" a treaty legalizing the presence of the occupation troops would be signed. (A Czechoslovak delegation led by Deputy Premier Frantisek Hamouz and Karel Rusov, army chief of staff, arrived in Moscow Oct. 8 to negotiate the treaty legalizing the stationing of the troops.)

Krasnaya Zvezda (Red Star), the Soviet Defense Ministry newspaper, declared Oct. 4 that particular conditions in certain countries could not take precedence over the needs of the larger Socialist community. The article reasserted the doctrine of limited sovereignty and denounced the Czechoslovak idea of a "new model of socialism" as against Lenin's call for "struggle against petit-bourgeois narrowness." "The entire spirit of the so-called new model is impregnated with the poison of the old social democratic model," the article declared. "The present and the future of the Socialist countries is indivisible from the fate of the world socialism, of friendship and cooperation with the great Soviet Union."

Czechoslovak newspapers Oct. 5 carried articles denouncing the Soviet news media for spreading "lies" about developments in Czechoslovakia and about leading personalities.

A communique of the Czechoslovak Writers' Union, published Oct. 5 by *Rude pravo,* accused the Soviet press of hurling "lies" and "insults" at Eduard Goldstuecker to discredit his "work and honor." Prof. Goldstuecker, president of the union and a deputy rector of Prague's Charles University, had been among the most articulate spokesmen of the Czechoslovak liberalization movement. (Goldstuecker was reported Oct. 3 to have been appointed a visiting professor for the current year at England's Sussex University.) *Literaturnaya Gazeta,* the organ of the Soviet Writers' Union, had charged Oct. 2 that Goldstuecker had been, in his youth, "an active member of Zionist youth organizations" and that he had openly advocated pro-Israeli policies since January. He was also attacked for being elected to the party Presidium at the extraordinary 14th congress, held secretly 2 days after the invasion and later declared invalid as a result of Moscow pressure.

Prace, the organ of the Czechoslovak trade unions, printed conspicuously Oct. 5 a letter in which workers of a Prague shipyard denounced Soviet and other Warsaw Treaty journalists for "twisting facts" and "spreading untruths and gossip." The letter referred to the Aug. 26 Moscow protocol, which had pledged "noninterference in the internal affairs of the Czechoslovak Socialist Republic." The letter also warned against attempts to replace either Pres. Svoboda or Dubcek.

Red Army Presence Sanctioned

Soviet Premier Kosygin flew to Prague Oct. 16 to sign a treaty authorizing the "temporary stay" of Soviet troops in Czechoslovakia and legalizing the presence of Soviet-bloc forces that had invaded the country Aug. 20-21.

Observers noted that in the treaty the USSR had won a major policy objective regarding Czechoslovakia; through similar treaties the USSR had already acquired rights to station troops "temporarily" in Poland, Hungary and East Germany. Prior to the invasion, Czechoslovak governments had resisted efforts by Moscow to get similar privileges.

The negotiation and drafting of the treaty had taken place in Moscow during visits of the Czechoslovak party delegation headed by Dubcek Oct. 3-4 and of the government delegation led by Cernik Oct. 14-15. (Cernik and his delegation returned from Moscow less than 4 hours before Kosygin's arrival in Czechoslovakia.)

Excerpts from the treaty (Tass translation):

The government of the Union of Soviet Socialist Republics and the government of the Czechoslovak Socialist Republic ... [have] agreed on the following:

Article 1. ... [The Soviet government], acting with the consent of the governments of the People's Republic of Bulgaria, the People's Republic of Hungary, the German Democratic Republic, the People's Republic of Poland and the government of the Czechoslovak Socialist Republic, have agreed that part of the Soviet troops ... [in Czechoslovakia] will remain temporarily [in Czechoslovakia] ... in order to ensure the security of the countries of the Socialist community against the increasing revanchist strivings of the West German militarist forces. The rest of the [Soviet] troops ... [and those of Bulgaria, Hungary, East Germany, and Poland] shall be withdrawn from Czechoslovak territory in accordance with the documents of the Moscow talks of Aug. 23-26 and Oct. 3-4, 1968. The withdrawal of these troops shall be started after the ratification of this treaty by both sides and shall be carried out by stages within 2 months. The number and places of dis[position] of Soviet troops which remain temporarily [in Czechoslovakia] ... shall be determined by agreement between the [Czechoslovak and Soviet] governments.... The Soviet troops ... shall remain subordinated to the Soviet military command.

Article 2. (1) The temporary presence of Soviet troops does not violate [Czechoslovak sovereignty].... Soviet troops do not interfere in [Czechoslovak] ... internal affairs. (2) Soviet troops, their personnel and members of their families shall observe the legislation operating in Czechoslovakia.

Article 3. (1) The Soviet side shall bear the maintenance costs of Soviet troops.... (2) The Czechoslovak government ... shall provide Soviet troops, persons serving with Soviet troops and members of their families ... with barrack accommodation and housing in garrison settlements, service, warehouse and other premises, airfields with stationary structures and equipment, state-owned means of communication and transport, electric power and other services....

Article 4. Soviet troops, persons serving with Soviet troops and members of their families may travel ... to the places of dis[position] of Soviet troops and back in through trains and carriages belonging to the Soviet Union or change from the carriages of one country to the carriages of the other country as well as by motor car or by air. Persons serving with the Soviet troops and members of their families are exempted from passport or visa control....

Article 6. (1) Trade and other services for the [Soviet] personnel ... will be provided through Soviet trade and service establishments. (2) The Czechoslovak side shall supply Soviet trade and service establishments with goods within amounts agreed upon between competent trade organizations.... (3) ... The Czechoslovak side shall deliver agreed-upon quantities of foodstuffs and manufactures, including fuel (coal, coke, firewood) for a planned supply of Soviet troops....

Article 9. Questions of jurisdiction ... shall be regulated as follows: (1) In cases of crimes and offenses committed by persons serving with the Soviet troops, or members of their families in [Czechoslovak] territory ..., the Czechoslovak legislation shall be applied, and the cases shall be handled by Czechoslovak courts ... [and] Czechoslovak organs competent in prosecuting for punishable offenses. Cases of crimes committed by Soviet servicemen shall be investigated by the military prosecutors' office and examined by [Czechoslovak] military judicial bodies.... (2) Provisions of Point 1 of the present article are [in]applicable: (a) In the event of [the commission] by persons serving with the Soviet troops or by members of their families of crimes or misdemeanors only against the Soviet Union, and also against persons serving with the Soviet troops or members of their families; (b) In the event of [the commission] by persons serving with the Soviet troops of crimes or misdemeanors when discharging their duties in areas where the military units are deployed. Cases, indicated in Subpoints (a) and (b) are within the competence of Soviet courts, prosecuting and other bodies, acting on the basis of Soviet legislation. (3) In case of [the commission] of punishable actions against Soviet troops ... [or] persons serving with them, the persons guilty ... will bear the same responsibility as for punishable actions against the [Czechoslovak] armed forces ... and persons serving with them....

Article 10. (1) The [Soviet] government ... agrees to compensate the [Czechoslovak] government ... for material damage which might be inflicted upon the Czechoslovak state by actions or negligence of Soviet armed units or persons serving with them, and also for damage which might be inflicted by Soviet armed units or persons serving with them during the discharge of their duties to Czechoslovak citizens, establishments, or to citizens of 3d states.... (2) The [Soviet] government agrees also to compensate the [Czechoslovak] government ... for damage which might be inflicted upon Czechoslovak establishments or citizens, and also citizens of 3d states ... as a result of actions or negligence by persons serving with the Soviet forces, caused not during the discharge of their duties, and also as a result of actions or negligence by members of the families of persons serving with the Soviet troops....

Article 11. (1) The [Czechoslovak] government ... agrees to compensate the [Soviet] government ... for damage which might be inflicted upon the property of Soviet military units ... or upon persons serving with the Soviet troops by actions or negligence of Czechoslovak state institutions.... (2) The [Czechoslovak] government agrees also to compensate the [Soviet] government ... [for] damage which might be inflicted upon Soviet armed units ... or persons serving with the Soviet troops and members of their families by actions or negligence of Czechoslovak citizens....

Kosygin was accompanied to Prague by Soviet Foreign Min. Andrei A. Gromyko, Defense Min. Marshal Andrei A. Grechko and First Deputy Foreign Min. Vasily V. Kuznetsov, who had been acting as emissary to Prague to oversee the execution of the Aug. 23-26 Moscow protocol.

Speaking at the treaty-signing ceremony, attended by Dubcek and Pres. Svoboda, Kosygin asserted that the purpose of the treaty was to "provide guarantees for ensuring Czechoslovak security [and] its Socialist achievements." "The agreement is based on the mutual confidence of the Communist parties, governments and people of the Soviet Union and Czechoslovakia," Kosygin said. Kosygin announced that the troops would be "gradually withdrawn in the [next few] months ... in the conviction that the process of normalizing the situation in Czechoslovakia which has now started will continue and that the Czechoslovak people will not give an opportunity to anti-Socialist forces to stop this process." Kosygin said that the treaty was also "dictated" by the "growing revanchist efforts of West German militarists [who] are threatening the peaceful life of nations and [who dwell] where war preparations of the aggressive bloc of NATO are being intensified."

In his speech, Cernik echoed Kosygin's sentiments on the threat of West Germany and NATO, and he appealed to the Czechoslovak people for understanding. He said: "In this divided world, our security can be ensured only in the family of Socialist countries, in strong alliance with the Soviet Union."

According to reports from Prague Oct. 17, Svoboda had charged the Russians Oct. 16 with having reneged on promises of the total withdrawal of the occupation troops. He was reported to have reminded Kosygin of his understanding of the Aug. 23-26 Moscow talks, according to which the invading troops were to have evacuated Czechoslovakia in 3 stages, the last one being a total pull-out after normalization had been achieved. (It was reported Oct. 17 that neither Dubcek nor Svoboda had met Kosygin and his delegation at the Prague airport nor had seen them off, as required by protocol.)

The treaty authorizing the stationing of Soviet troops was passed by the 300-member Czechoslovak National Assembly Oct. 18 by a vote of 228 to 4, with 10 abstentions; 58 deputies did not attend. The Presidium of the USSR Supreme Soviet ratified the treaty unanimously the same day.

In presenting the document, Premier Cernik appealed to the assembly delegates to approve it as part of a "new reality." He said Czechoslovakia was "not an isolated island separated from the outside world." "The basic platform for evaluating our activity from the international aspect must be full respecting of the existence of 2 world systems and the fact that Czechoslovakia belongs to the Socialist community," he declared. Given the growing danger to world peace from "imperialist circles of the United States" and the "revanchist elements of West Germany," and war in Vietnam and the "dangerous situation created in the Middle East, there can be no such thing for a small country like Czechoslovakia as an absolute sovereignty," Cernik declared.

Cernik disclosed that while the bulk of the occupation forces would leave the country in the near future, an undetermined number of Soviet troops—estimated at 65,000 to 100,000—would remain. But he insisted that the treaty would "fully respect the sovereign execution of [Czechoslovakia's] state power and administration."

It was reported in Prague that during the treaty negotiations Moscow had demanded that the treaty contain (a) a declaration that, in effect, would have legalized the country's occupation, as well as (b) an acknowledgement that the occupation had taken place at the request of the Czechoslovak constitutional organs to help combat the threat of a counter-revolution. After the Czechoslovak leaders had rejected these demands, the impasse was said to have been resolved only by Kosygin's acceptance of the Czechoslovak stand in opposition to a reputedly conservative faction in the Soviet party Politburo.

A statement issued by the 21-member Presidium of the Czechoslovak party Oct. 9, after a 12-hour session, had assured the Czechoslovak people that, despite the Soviet occupation, guarantees to preserve the legal rights of the citizens would be maintained. But the statement also stressed the necessity for tighter press censorship to strengthen the "unity of the Socialist countries." The communique said that those "who do not violate our legal norms" should not fear reprisals. But it categorically denied that there would be a return to the pre-January policy of repression.

(Before the communique was issued, Deputy Interior Min. Frantisek Vasek and Dr. Karel Pesta, an official in the general prosecutor's office, had gone on TV and denied rumors of mass arrests and political trials of alleged counterrevolutionaries. Pesta said that, to ensure against the misuse of authority, the general prosecutor's office would sever its link with the Justice Ministry and become an independent body, responsible directly to the National Assembly.)

Occupation Troops Withdraw

The withdrawal of Hungarian, Polish and Bulgarian troops began after mid-October. This had been negotiated in Moscow by Soviet and Czechoslovak leaders. Hungarian troops that had participated in the invasion began their gradual withdrawal from central Slovakia Oct. 21. (Hungary and Poland had each contributed an estimated 2 divisions, about 25,000 men; Poland had also sent one air division of 150 MIG jet fighters.)

The Hungarian press gave detailed coverage to the withdrawal of Hungarian troops from Slovakia. Radio Budapest confirmed Oct. 31 that all the troops had left. Defense Min. Lajos Czinege read an order of the day praising the troops' behavior in Czechoslovakia. He stressed Hungary's desire to restore "mutual trust, friendly relations and the emergence of political and economic cooperation" with Czechoslovakia.

An unsigned article in the Hungarian government political weekly *Magyarorszag* Oct. 27 had asserted that the Czechoslovak party's current leadership was quite capable of handling the problems of "normalization" and "consolidation." It provided the first acknowledgement in any of the 5 invaders' publications or broadcast outlets that the Czechoslovak government and National Assembly disputed the invaders' claim that a military intervention had been needed to neutralize "the nationalistic propaganda of anti-Socialist forces."

Bulgaria hailed the occupation treaty signed Oct. 16 in Prague as the death knell of alleged Western schemes involving Czechoslovakia. Sofia began immediately to pull out the Bulgarian occupying troops from Banska Bystrica, capital of Central Slovakia, and then ordered the departure of its troops in Prague. The troops were airlifted to the Soviet Union, and they sailed home from the Crimean port of Odessa in succeeding weeks.

Radio Warsaw reported Oct. 25: "Units of the Polish people's army are returning today from beyond the southern frontier.... There is general agreement that the presence of Warsaw Pact armed forces on the territory of Czechoslovakia was justified and purposeful."

Czechoslovak Deputy Defense Min. Josef Dvorak said Nov. 9 that Soviet occupation troops scheduled to return to the USSR would complete their withdrawal by Dec. 15 but that, under the Oct. 16 agreement, an estimated 65,000 to 100,000 troops would "temporarily" remain in western Bohemia. Soviet troops had begin withdrawing Oct. 24, and the Prague government announced Nov. 8 that 86% of the occupation forces had left.

Soviet newspapers reported Oct. 24 that Soviet soldiers had been given a heroes' welcome on their return to the USSR. Roads were lined with banners proclaiming "You have fulfilled your international duty" and "The Motherland is proud of you." At welcoming ceremonies the solders were told: "We were sure that the Soviet soldiers would help the fraternal people of Czechoslovakia frustrate the plots of reactionaries. You have justified our confidence."

TENSION CONTINUES

Federalization Approved

The Czechoslovak National Assembly Oct. 27 unanimously passed a bill creating the basis for a federated country of 2 nation-states. One state would comprise the Czech people of Bohemia and Moravia in the west; the other would be made up of the Slovaks in the southern and eastern part of the country. The law, long desired by the Slovaks, would give them home rule with veto power over matters affecting their interests. The law was one of the major goals of the democratization movement. Although the law legally took effect after its signing by Pres. Svoboda in Bratislava Oct. 30, it was not to become really operative until new state and federal administrative organs were created.

According to the law, each state was to have its own departments of justice, interior, agriculture, health and communications but there were to be common portfolios for foreign affairs, foreign trade, defense, finance and planning as parts of a national government. The parliament also passed a nationalities law granting linguistic privileges and the right to form social and cultural associations to the Hungarian, German and Ukrainian national minorities, numbering about 2 million. But it was not intended that the minorities would get direct political representation in the new federal assembly (which was to replace the current National Assembly through elections later).

The bill's passage had been strongly recommended in the nationally televised session of the National Assembly in Hradcany Castle in Prague by National Assembly Chairman Josef Smrkovsky, Premier Oldrich Cernik and leaders of the Czech and Slovak National Councils.

An estimated 10,000 persons, who had gathered to greet Pres. Ludvik Svoboda, party leader Alexander Dubcek and other Czechoslovak leaders when they arrived in Bratislava Oct. 30 for the signing of the federation law, demonstrated Oct. 29 against the Soviet-led occupation of the country. The demonstrators, mostly youths, surged through the city shouting anti-Soviet slogans.

Intraparty Struggle

The first known major step toward the creation of a pro-Soviet opposition to the Dubcek regime apparently took place in a Prague factory district Oct. 9, when a large group hostile to his program held a 3-hour secret meeting. Among those attending the meeting were reported to be 8 uniformed Soviet army officers, who pledged Soviet aid to consolidate the group's power.

As reported by Radio Moscow Oct. 11, 600 "old Communists" had met in the Prague working-class district of Liben and demanded that the Communist Party of Czechoslovakia act to suppress those "who spread untruths about the Soviet Union and other Socialist countries." The broadcast, a home service transmission, reported that the participants in the meeting had adopted a resolution demanding that "the Central Committee of the Communist Party take a resolute stand against all who spread fabrications against the Soviet Union, about other Socialist countries and their soldiers."

According to the Moscow broadcast the meeting's participants had asked the Soviet party newspaper *Pravda* to print a resolution demanding that the Czechoslovak Communist Party publicly declare its "friendship, comradely feelings and attitude to the Soviet party, the Russian people and those in all Socialist countries." *The resolution said:*

"To this day, the Central Committee has not condemned the press, radio, television and newsreels, which, entirely at the service of the counter-revolution, have waged a struggle against all that was sacred, and for which whole generations fought."

The participants in the Liben meeting criticized the Czechoslovak leadership for "ideological softness, weakness and incompetence" since January and hailed the Warsaw Treaty invasion as preventing "white terror." They repudiated the current members of the party Central Committee, which, they charged, had co-opted members in an atmosphere of "moral terror," and they demanded the rehabilitation of party members accused of collaboration with the occupation forces.

Despite Radio Moscow's claim that 600 persons attended the meeting, the Swedish Liberal daily *Dagens Nyheter* of Stockholm Oct. 13 cited participants as estimating the attendance at about 300. The meeting was presided over by Antonin Kapek, an ousted alternate member of the party Presidium, protege of ex-Pres. Antonin Novotny and ex-director of the CKD auto works who had resigned after the workers had denounced him for alleged collaboration with the occupation forces; ex-Agriculture Min. Karel Mestek, a Central Committee member also criticized for alleged involvement with the occupation authorities; Emanuel Famira, ex-director of the Prague art school and an outspoken opponent of the liberalization; Kvetoslav Innemann, ex-director of the Svoboda publishing house; Josef Jodas, who in March had published a condemnation of Ota Sik's economic reforms; and Vilem Novy, ex-rector of the party college in Prague, who had also been criticized as an alleged collaborator with the occupation authorities. *Dagens Nyheter* reported that the meeting was attended by 8 Soviet officers.

According to Prague reports Oct. 12, Kapek was the major speaker and organizer at the meeting Kapek echoed the Soviet charge that there had been a "counterrevolution," "waged not with guns but with pencil and microphone..., the most subtle counterrevolution in history." Kapek charged the Presidium, composed mostly of pro-Dubcek members, with misusing power and with allowing the information media to wage a campaign of "hysterical national chauvinism." In particular, he attacked Dubcek and Smrkovsky for allegedly having secret talks with "intellectuals" before taking major actions. He deplored attacks against what he termed "true Communists." Kapek demanded "drastic action" against (a) non-Communist organizations and (b) censors who had not lived up to the stipulations of the Moscow agreement. A resolution passed at the meeting demanded that transgressors of the press law (which had reimposed press censorship Sept. 4) be tried. "There are plenty of people in this room who could take their place," Kapek declared.

According to the London *Times,* the Liben meeting had been spurred by the creation, by an ultraconservative group in South Bohemia, of a Gottwald party (named after the late Pres. Klement Gottwald). The Slovak party daily *Pravda* of

Bratislava reported Nov. 2 that Jodas was the leader of the Gottwald party. *Pravda* Nov. 2 also reported that a pro-Moscow group in Kladno had distributed an "illegal" mimeographed newspaper, *Kladenska svoboda,* which "ridicules the present leadership of our party as 'Dubcek and company.'"

According to Prague reports Oct. 19, the Czechoslovak party had come under intense pressure from the USSR to reduce its membership by purging its progressive wing. These sources quoted a remark made by Brezhnev to Dubcek during their conversation in Moscow in early October. Brezhnev was said to have told Dubcek that a party of 1.7 million was too large for a country like Czechoslovakia, with a population of 14.3 million. Brezhnev reportedly had suggested as more appropriate a party of 350,000-400,000.

Emerging after 2 weeks of public silence, Dubcek asserted Oct. 25 that the party would have to move faster toward meeting Soviet demands on "normalization." "The sooner we realize what must be done, the faster we shall create conditions for the further advance, creative activity and upsurge of the life of our [Czech and Slovak] nations," Dubcek told party functionaries in the factory town of Pardubice, eastern Bohemia. Dubcek also said that (a) the Czechoslovak party would not hold its long-planned 14th congress "this year"; (b) there was a need to improve relations with East Germany, whose "existence is an important factor of the overall struggle against the revenge-seeking course of militaristic West German forces."

(The Czechoslovak government, acting apparently under Soviet pressure, announced Oct. 24 that it had decided not to implement its worker-management plan. The plan, first introduced by Yugoslavia and later denounced as a heresy by Moscow, had been a key feature of the reform program prior to the invasion. Designed under the guidance of then-Deputy Premier Ota Sik, the plan had called for the creation through free elections of workers' councils in factories.)

Conservatives & Reformers Debate Policy

The Czechoslovak Communist Party Central Committee met in closed session in Hradcany Castle in Prague Nov. 14-17.

The discussions were marked by sharp debates between conservatives and reformers on party policies and by an attempt by Dubcek to balance his policy of "humanistic socialism" with the "harsh realities" of the Soviet occupation.

At the meeting, which had originally been scheduled for Nov. 7 and which the Russians had reportedly attempted to delay until after an international meeting of Communist parties in Budapest Nov. 18, the Central Committee adopted several measures that reflected compromise. These included the approval of Dubcek's proposal to organize a separate Czech party, the creation of an inner Presidium executive committee and a Central Committee resolution entitled "Principal Tasks of the Party in the Immediate Future," which discussed at great length the post-January developments and the current situation. Several changes in personnel were also announced.

At the opening session Nov. 14, Dubcek, in a report entitled "The Main Tasks of the Party in the Forthcoming Period," emphasized that his new policies were designed to develop "positive features" of the liberalization policies. After allegedly admitting that he was responsible for not curbing press "excesses" following the Aug. 21 invasion, Dubcek stated that in the future the press would be subjected to "unconditionally strengthened" government control. He criticized excessive liberalism and insisted on maintaining the alliance with the Soviet Union. He warned that "the biggest stumbling block in the consolidation process is the attitudes of those who directly accuse the political leadership of capitulation and treason and create an anti-Soviet psychosis."

Dubcek balanced these remarks, however, with an insistence that Moscow and its Warsaw Pact allies fulfill their promises to Czechoslovakia. Dubcek also refused to reduce the size of the 192-member Central Committee by dropping the 80 new members added after the invasion or to purge the party. (According to the Sept. 28 N.Y. Times, 7,199 persons had joined the party after Aug. 21. Since 63.8% of these reportedly were under 30 years old, the move to join was regarded as an attempt to strengthen the reform movement from within.)

Dubcek pledged that the party would try "to guarantee fundamental civil rights and freedoms, observe Socialist legality and rehabilitate all the citizens of our country who were unjustly persecuted in the past." He added that "in no case" would punitive measures be taken against persons opposing socialism except if laws were violated. Dubcek also pledged to seek ways to expand economic reforms and improve the standard of living. He said that his regime would make every effort to increase the actual participation of workers in administration ... and to make our young generation participate in public life."

The conservatives initially levelled their attack not at Dubcek but at Smrkovsky. They accused him of giving the West German news magazine *Der Spiegel* of Hamburg a tape-recorded interview between himself and Soviet Deputy Foreign Min. Vasily Kuznetsov. The conservatives also attacked several "liberal" Czechoslovak magazines for publishing "articles of anti-Socialist tendencies." At a later meeting, the conservatives charged that the Dubcek reforms were contrary to Marxism and that the admission of the 80 new Central Committee members Aug. 31 was illegal.

Dubcek failed to win from the Soviets approval for the formation of a separate Czech party, to be organized along the lines of the existing Slovak party under the aegis of the countrywide Czechoslovak party. A special Czech lands party bureau was created instead in the Czechoslovak party Central Committee to organize the new party, and Deputy Premier Lubomir Strougal, 44, a conservative, was appointed chairman. (Of the 10 bureau members, it was reported that 5 were progressives, 2 centrists and 3 pro-Soviet.)

Personnel changes and the creation of an 8-man executive committee of the Presidium were announced Nov. 17. Zdenek Mlynar, a progressive Central Committee secretary and Presidium member, resigned his posts in the Presidium and Central Committee secretariat and as chairman of the Central Committee's legal commission. He was replaced on the Presidium by Strougal, who was also appointed a Central Committee secretary. Vasil Bilak, another conservative, was named a Central Committee secretary, as were the progressive Jarolim Hettes and Josef Kempny.

Although the Czechoslovak party Presidium membership remained 21, contrary to Moscow's demand for a reduction in number, the creation of the 8-man executive committee introduced an element of collective leadership, thereby undermining Dubcek's power. The executive committee's functions were to "permit evaluation of the urgent political problems . . . , inform the Presidium of its work and place before it all its significant decisions for approval."

The executive committee, however, was said to have the power to make final decisions without consulting the full Presidium. The committee was composed of Dubcek as chairman, Premier Cernik, Pres. Svoboda, National Front Chairman Evzen Erban, Slovak party leader Gustav Husak, Smrkovsky, the Presidium member Stefan Sadovsky and Strougal. Smrkovsky was regarded as the only certain ally of Dubcek's on the committee; Strougal was a conservative, and Husak was Dubcek's most powerful rival in Slovakia.

In his closing speech Nov. 17, Dubcek again urged a compromise between Soviet demands and his progressive program. He asserted that "we are united in that we shall further develop the basic positive aspects and decisive parts of the post-January policies, cleaned of the errors and the deficiencies that occurred in that period." He added that party members were united "on the strategic questions of our policy, our alliance with the Soviet Union" and on the demand to "face resolutely the anti-Socialist provocations and the extremist opinion that fail to comprehend the new tasks, the needs and the search for new methods."

The Central Committee resolution, which was not announced until Nov. 18, had been passed at the meeting by a show of hands on each paragraph. (Only excerpts were given by the official Czechoslovak news agency, but the full text was printed in *Izvestia* Nov. 21.) The first part of the resolution gave a general assessment of developments since January. Concentrating on the "errors" and negative aspects of the reform program, the resolution asserted that the "Socialist development of Czechoslovakia has had a number of serious weak sides and mistakes of a subjective and objective nature" and that the "authority of the party and confidence in its policy have been weakened." The resolution declared that the lack of firm determination by the Central Committee and the government had "introduced substantial elements of spontaneity in the development process, with which we did not always cope correctly in the course of further development," and that neither body "had a well-conceived system of guiding the press, radio and television. Censorship was abolished ... and the mass information media were gradually turned into an uncontrolled force."

Stressing that party policy was grounded in the principles of Marxist-Leninist thought and proletarian nationalism, the resolution called for strengthening the role of the party in all aspects of "Socialist development." It asserted that "the press, radio and television are, above all, an instrument for the implementation of the party and state policy." The resolution called for "the strong alliance and all-round cooperation of our country with the Soviet Union and other Socialist countries" and warned against the "militarist and revanchist circles of West Germany."

The document concluded with strong support for the "principles expressed in the Moscow agreements of Aug. 26 [and] the communique ... of Oct. 3-4, as well as the principles of the Declaration of 6 Parties of Aug. 4 in Bratislava."

(The *N.Y. Times* reported Nov. 26 that Dubcek, Cernik and Husak had made a secret trip to Warsaw Nov. 15 to confer with Brezhnev on the text of the Central Committee resolution. The *Times* said Dubcek had won Brezhnev's approval for the omission from the final resolution of a specific assertion that "counterrevolution" had existed in Czechoslovakia prior to the Aug. 21 invasion and for the deletion of an explicit condemnation of the Czechoslovak press for protecting "anti-Socialist forces.")

In a public speech Dec. 5, Dubcek disclosed that Soviet leaders had been consulted on "certain parts" of the Nov. 18 resolution. He reported that "Soviet comrades" had been advised of the resolution so that its conclusions would not become "a new target for polemics but a platform for unification in international relations as well."

Anti-Soviet Demonstrations

Despite pleas by party and government leaders that citizens refrain from demonstrations, thousands of

Czechoslovaks marched in anti-Soviet protests in Prague Oct. 28, the 50th anniversary of the founding of the first Czechoslovak republic. This was the first major public protest against Soviet occupation in Prague since August.

Celebrating the anniversary for the first time since the Communist *coup d'etat* in 1948, thousands of angry persons, mostly youths, surged through various parts of Prague as the country's leaders were celebrating the 1918 founding of the republic. Beginning late in the morning and continuing late into the night, demonstrators held rallies at the National Theater, Wenceslas Square, near the Soviet embassy and at Hradcany Castle. Throughout the day they carried signs and shouted slogans of: "Down with Brezhnev," "Tito yes, Brezhnev no," "Russians go home," "Away with Russian censorship, We don't want Asiatic culture" and "Masaryk, Svoboda, Dubcek." Portraits of Thomas G. Masaryk, the republic's founder—and for 2 decades a target of official oblivion—had appeared all over the country, along with portraits of Svoboda and Dubcek. The revival of admiration for Masaryk as part of the anniversary celebration was in defiance of a Soviet-waged press campaign. Before the invasion, the Soviet press had denounced Masaryk as a "bourgeois reactionary" who had been acting as a paymaster in a plot to murder Lenin.

Later in the afternoon, thousands of youths marched to the Soviet military headquarters where they burned copies of *Pravda,* the Soviet party newspaper, in front of Soviet soldiers guarding the building. The soldiers looked but did not interfere. Other protesters had attempted to march to the Soviet embassy but were stopped by Czechoslovak police within 500 yards of the building. The group, numbering about 3,000, then sat in the road. This was the only occasion in which demonstrators were opposed by the Czechoslovak police, who remained sympathetic to them throughout the day. (On one occasion, in front of the embassy, Czechoslovak policemen pulled a West German tourist from the arms of the Soviet soldiers who had seized him. The West German youth was later released by the police.)

Speaking to party and government leaders in Hradcany Castle, Dubcek was quoted as saying: "We shall preserve the continuity of the policy of the Communist Party of Czechoslovakia upon which we embarked after January."

New anti-Soviet demonstrations erupted in Prague Nov. 6 on the eve of the 51st anniversary of the Russian revolution. Several hundred persons demonstrated outside the National Theater, which was presenting a commemorative performance of *Swan Lake.* Later, Soviet flags were torn from buildings and burned. Students and young workers, chanting "Russians go home" and other anti-Soviet slogans, demanded Nov. 7 that all Soviet flags be removed from government buildings. Soviet flags were again burned. Later Nov. 7 the police, using clubs and tear gas, broke up a demonstration by 2,000 people in Wenceslas Square. At least 8 persons were reported arrested there. The demonstrations and the subsequent police action were said to have exceeded the intensity and scope of the Oct. 28 demonstrations.

Earlier Nov. 7, at wreath-laying ceremonies commemorating Russian and Czechoslovak war dead, about 1,000 "old-guard Communists," loyal to Moscow, shouted at Dubcek and Cernik: "Long Live the Soviet Army! Long Live the Soviet Union!" Outside the Soviet embassy other pro-Moscow Communists shouted similar slogans.

Students also took to the streets of Brno, Bratislava, and Ceske Budejovice Nov. 7. Leaflets described the demonstrations as part of a campaign of protest against the occupation, which was compared with that of the Nazis. The police dispersed the demonstrators, 167 of whom were arrested (the majority were later released). The pro-Soviet Radio Vltava criticized the police for being too lenient in breaking up the demonstration; it asserted that the students had been encouraged by the presence of Western correspondents in Prague.

The Prague government Nov. 8 announced several measures allegedly designed to curb anti-Soviet activity. These included: the suspension of the Czech Journalists' Union's *Reporter* and the party Central Committee's *Politika,* 2 weekly magazines that reportedly had published anti-Soviet articles and cartoons; the assignment of a deputy premier to oversee press activities; the expulsion of Western journalists who wrote articles contrary to government policies; orders to the Education Ministry to halt student demonstrations.

Another anti-Soviet demonstration took place in Prague Nov. 10 when a crowd of some 300 to 500 Dubcek supporters jeered at 3,000 to 5,000 pro-Moscow Communists emerging from a Czechoslovak-Soviet Friendship Union meeting in Lucerna Hall. They chanted "collaborators" and "the whole nation is against you." Members of the crowds were reported to have thrown garbage at Soviet army vehicles and to have spat at Soviet army officers. As the demonstrators began to attack the pro-Moscow "old Communists" and fist fights developed, police began to escort people to safety.

Vaclav David, Central Committee member and National Assembly deputy who had been foreign minister under Novotny, said at the meeting of conservatives in Lucerna Hall in Prague Nov. 10 that there would have been no need for Warsaw Pact troops to enter Czechoslovakia if anti-Socialist forces had been opposed from the start. He complained that Dubcek had unleashed these anti-Socialist forces by his policies and that the invasion had been necessary to block "rightist and openly counterrevolutionary forces." The meeting, called by the Czechoslovak-Soviet Friendship League to commemorate the October Revolution, was by invitation only and was closed to liberal Czechoslovak and foreign journalists. Radio Prague reported Nov. 10 that some 3,000 persons were present, but the East German party daily *Neues Deutschland* Nov. 11 put the number at 5,000. The friendship league's presidium consisted of David; Emanuel Famira; Jan Nemec, secretary general of the league and a Central Committee member; Bedrich Svestka, dean of the Prague Faculty of Medical Hygiene; Jaromir Lang, ex-dean of the Philosophy Faculty in Olomouc; Bozena Fabianova, a former Health Ministry press spokesman; and Miroslav Kliver, a former lecturer in dialectical materialism at the Prague Higher School of Art.

After David's keynote address, the participants heard the reading of greetings from: (a) the 90 Soviet Praga automobile plant workers whose criticism of the Dubcek regime had been published in *Pravda,* the Soviet party daily, before the invasion; (b) Jaromir Hrbek, ex-rector of the Palacky University in Olomouc; and (c) Gusta Fucikova, the widow of Julius Fucik, a Communist dogmatist killed by the Nazis. The group then adopted 2 documents: (1) a missive to the Central Committee affirming that it was a "national and patriotic duty" to cooperate with the invasion forces, and (2) a letter to Pres. Svoboda pledging the assembly's support for him.

Similar meetings of conservatives were held in other parts of Prague and in several towns throughout the country.

More than 1,000 journalists met in Lucerna Hall in Prague Nov. 18 and adopted a resolution calling for a meeting with government leaders to discuss "how to face together the efforts to liquidate Socialist freedom of the press, which is the right of every citizen." The resolution protested the Soviet attacks on the media, and the banning of *Reporter* and *Politika*. It charged that the attacks on journalists were being conducted by reactionary forces that wanted to revert to the conditions existing in the 1950's.

Massive nationwide demonstrations by university and high school students took place Nov. 16-21. Students throughout Czechoslovakia staged sit-in strikes at their schools and were joined in most instances by their professors. The students issued a 10-point proclamation that demanded the implementation of the "action program" and called for the preservation of the freedoms of the press, assembly and association as "indisputable human rights."

The sit-ins, which began at Prague's Charles University Nov. 16, were timed to coincide with the 29th anniversary of the closing of the Czechoslovak universities. The students originally had planned a march to commemorate the 29th anniversary Nov. 17 of the closing of all Czechoslovak universities and the slaying of students and workers by the Nazi occupation forces. But the Prague government, fearing another outbreak of anti-Soviet demonstrations, refused to allow the march. Premier Cernik had said Nov. 11 that the government would use "strength and determination" to prevent anti-Soviet activity because it could result in "chaos and tragedy." Cernik added that "we can enter into the thoughts of the young people, but ... the outstanding principle of our policy ... is that we have to deal with political problems by political means." Dubcek issued a similar appeal Nov. 12. Slovak party leader Gustav Husak, in a stronger warning to students Nov. 13, threatened that "any demonstration will be declared subversive, and we will take steps against them."

Czechoslovak police were ordered on first-degree alert Nov. 15, and Soviet infantry units were reported placed in Czechoslovak police stations to support security forces. Police headquarters appealed to citizens to avoid any "rash or provocative" actions, and mixed units of police and armed Czechoslovak soldiers patrolled Prague's streets.

Faced with strong government opposition to the march and the threat of reprisals, students began a sit-in strike at Prague University Nov. 16. Demanding a restoration of the freedoms lost as a result of the Aug. 21 invasion, the students threatened to remain on strike for a week. The official Czechoslovak news agency CTK reported Nov. 17 that the students wanted to "show their determination and ability to participate in political events," and that "the Prague secondary school council and workers' collectives from factories have also expressed their solidarity with the Prague students."

Support of the Czechoslovak students by factory workers beyond Prague was also reported. At the Skoda automobile and industrial plant in Plzen (Pilsen), workers reportedly prepared to pick a new ruling body to "implement the political and organizational democratization process." At the Kladno steel mills, 22,000 workers were said to have demanded the removal of leaders opposed to the liberalization program. TV broadcasts in Bratislava reported similar demands from plants in Slovakia. Police and soldiers continued to patrol cities, and National Council Chrmn. Cestmir Cisar appealed on TV Nov. 16 for restraint.

Students in Bohemia and Moravia began Nov. 18 "the legally permissible and peaceful way of making a public stand—a strike in the university buildings." The Union of University Students in Bohemia and Moravia submitted a list of 10 demands to the Czechoslovak party Central Committee, then in plenary session in Prague. The message protested the loss of freedom of press, the right to assembly and freedom of travel. It declared that the Central Committee had to meet demands for the restoration of these freedoms and for the return to the Dubcek reform program if the party were to retain the people's confidence.

The musicians of the Czech Philharmonic and members of the Prague Union of Journalists joined their names to those already supporting the students. The newspaper *Lidova demokracie,* daily of the Catholic People's Party, reported Nov. 19 that 40,000 miners in north Bohemia were ready to strike if the students' demands were not met. Workers at the CKD machine factories in Prague and the Kralovoppolska Zbrojovka arms factory in Brno were also reported to be supporting the student strikes.

The sit-ins, scheduled to end Nov. 20, continued in Bohemia and Moravia as students defied a government and party appeal and warning Nov. 20 that "irresponsible people were seizing the initiative and trying to channel the students' action into a much broader scope" and particularly to involve "the factories, thus dividing the working class and the unity of the workers." (600 CKD factory workers went on an all-day strike Nov. 20.)

The strikes ended quietly Nov. 21, when the students left their university and high school buildings. An estimated 100,000 students had participated in the strikes, which were described as well-organized and peaceful. (According to reports, students refused to permit foreign newsmen to enter university buildings because the demonstrators were afraid that they would be charged with inciting "anti-Socialist propaganda.") Although the students' demands had not been recognized by the end of the strike, the students viewed the strike as a success because, according to some reports, they had been able to make contact "with other strata of the population, chiefly the working class," and had demonstrated their ability to stage an "organized and disciplined protest under difficult circumstances."

Public Criticism Rises

In a declaration issued jointly by 9 cultural organizations Nov. 26, intellectuals warned that loss of freedom of the press and of expression always led to "the limitation and liquidation" of civil liberties, and they pledged never to surrender their right to exercise "free and critical thought." The intellectuals, however, did not make public demands on the Prague government but expressed their views in letters to Dubcek and Cernik. Their public declaration was thus limited to generalities. The intellectuals said they wanted to make their voices heard "after the workers and the students" and to assure the continuation of "permanent values" in order to maintain the "humanistic character of our Socialist life."

Originally the intellectuals had intended to publish an 11-point resolution adopted at a meeting of 600 members of various cultural organizations Nov. 22. The key demand of the resolution called for the establishment of a special committee to investigate and report publicly on who had invited the Warsaw Pact nations to invade Czechoslovakia. The resolution criticized the censorship of information media and the loss of freedom of travel. But Dubcek had asked the group to refrain from publishing the resolution pending a meeting held with him Nov. 25.

Other groups had spoken out in October. The Association of the Pastors of the (Hussite) Evangelical Church of the Czech Brethren, in an Oct. 31 declaration, had called for the "complete withdrawal" of Soviet troops from Czechoslovakia. The declaration, agreed to unanimously at a meeting in Pardubice, northeastern Bohemia, was not published until it was brought to the West in November by British Council of Churches officials. It declared strong support for the continuation of the reform program. The declaration said: "In the years that have passed we did not do enough to defend the humanitarian principles of T[homas] G. Masaryk. Now our conviction that the truth must finally triumph compels us to struggle bravely with our immediate and urgent problems."

The reasons given by the USSR for invading Czechoslovakia were denounced by the Czechoslovak Academy of Sciences as "lies," "inventions," "distortions of Marxist-Leninist thought" and "schoolboy logic." The academy statement, circulated Oct. 22 at the academy's annual general assembly, was a 12,000-word rebuttal to the Soviet pamphlet *On the Events in Czechoslovakia,* published in the USSR in September. The statement warned: "Inasmuch as this material [the Soviet pamphlet] contains the twisting or denial of facts that are verifiably known to all our citizens and since this material is distributed here by the Soviet forces, we are seriously worried that it will make considerably more difficult the chances for friendship between Czechoslovakia and the Soviet Union."

(39 of the 42 members of the secretariat of the Union of Soviet Writers charged certain Czechoslovak writers with having joined "anti-Socialist destructive forces" and urged them to help correct "mistakes." In an open letter in the union's *Literaturnaya Gazeta* Oct. 23, the Soviet writers defended the Aug. 21 invasion. Signers included novelist Mikhail Sholokhov and playwright Aleksander Korneichuk. The 3 non-signing members were poet Aleksander Tvardovsky, editor of the literary monthly *Novy Mir,* and novelists Konstantin Simonov and Leonid Leonov.)

A 494 -page account of the Aug. 20-21 invasion, compiled and written by the Institute of History of the Czechoslovak Academy of Sciences, revealed that Czechoslovak State Security forces had collaborated with the Soviet Union prior to and during the invasion. The book, entitled *The 7 Days of Prague* but commonly known as the "Black Book" because of the color of its cover, had been circulated among Czechoslovak intellectuals in late November-early December. Reports on the "Black Book" appeared in the *N.Y. Times* Dec. 9 and 12; excerpts from the book were reprinted in the Dec. 16 issue of *Newsweek* magazine, and the publishing firm of Frederick A. Praeger in New York later published the complete text.

A public opinion poll conducted by the Czechoslovak Academy of Sciences Nov. 28 and published in the Catholic People's Party newspaper *Lidova demokracie* reported that 85% of people polled had expressed confidence in the Dubcek party regime. (55% had supported the Dubcek regime in a poll conducted in February.) But a large segment of the population believed that the leaders were going too slowly in following the goals of the post-January reforms. The poll also showed that 75% of those polled favored a free press and the right of the press to "express opinions on current issues."

(According to a public poll conducted by the Czechoslovak National Public Opinion Institute and made public Dec. 3, a majority of Czechoslovaks regarded Yugoslavia as the nation whose culture was most similar to their own. The poll also reported that the majority of the people believed that France had contributed the most foreign influence in the development of Czechoslovak culture. Only 11% of Czechs and 19% of Slovaks thought that Russia had been the main contributor.)

Press Controversies

The Prague government announced Nov. 30 that it had asked Moscow to ban the distribution of the Soviet Czech-language newspaper *Zpravy,* which had been started shortly after the Aug. 20 invasion. Deputy Premier Peter Colotka said in a TV interview that the government had examined the problem of the newspaper and that it would work through "diplomatic channels" for its suspension. The newspaper, which was circulated by Soviet civilian and military personnel in Czechoslovakia, had continually attacked "progressive" Czechoslovak leaders and had charged that the danger of "counterrevolution" still existed in the country.

The government move reportedly was in response to a resolution, adopted by the presidium of the National Assembly Nov. 28, demanding the publication's suspension. The resolution asserted that *Zpravy,* allegedly printed in Dresden, East Germany, had not been registered under Czechoslovak law and, therefore, had been distributed illegally.

The government Nov. 27 had authorized the weekly journal of the Czech Union of Journalists, *Reporter,* which had been suspended Nov. 8, to resume publication. *Reporter's* editors, it was said, had agreed to drop a suit against the government challenging the legality of the suspension.

Central Committee Secy. Alois Indra, a pro-Moscow conservative, said Nov. 26 that he was "fully in favor of abolishing censorship" providing that press freedoms would not be "abused."

(Although the Soviet government newspaper *Izvestia* said Nov. 28 that "healthy forces" in Prague were combating "anti-Socialists," other Soviet newspapers Nov. 30 renewed their attacks against "right-wing" elements in Czechoslovakia after almost a month's silence. The newspapers charged that certain people were resisting the "normalization" process and were preventing the fulfillment of Czechoslovakia's obligations to the Warsaw Pact nations.)

Vice Premier Peter Colotka, a Bratislava law school professor, was removed from his post as chairman of the government Press & Information Office Dec. 5. The establishment, effective Jan. 1, 1969, of Czech and Slovak federal states was given Dec. 6 as the official reason for his dismissal, which came after a day-long meeting Dec. 5 of the Council of Ministers (cabinet). Colotka was replaced by Dr. Jaroslav Havelka, deputy minister of education and ex-Czechoslovak ambassador to Sweden. (Havelka announced Dec. 18 that the government intended to publish its own newspaper in 1969. In reply to press criticism over accessibility of information, Havelka said that his office was making efforts to "solve the problems that have arisen and to improve the supply of information to the press.")

Although official and journalistic sources denied that there was a connection between Colotka's dismissal and his participation in the request to Moscow for the suspension of *Zpravy,* a Czechoslovak state radio and TV broadcast Dec. 4 disclosed that he had told the nation's general prosecutor Sept. 25 that the newspaper had not been registered in Czechoslovakia and, therefore, was illegal. The general prosecutor had informed Colotka's office Nov. 1 that because of *Zpravy's* libels against certain Czechoslovak leaders, the activities of the newspaper were considered "criminal." The broadcast (later joined by the Czechoslovak press) accused the Interior Ministry of preventing an investigation of *Zpravy's* activities. The ministry asserted Dec. 5 that there was nothing to investigate.

Josef Smidmajer was appointed director of the Czechoslovak state TV Dec. 6. The director's position had been vacant since the removal Sept. 3 of Jiri Pelikan.

Czechoslovak Party First Secy. Alexander Dubcek, in a speech in Most, Bohemia, said Dec. 5 that additional stress would be placed "on an active Socialist approach of all the information media to the current problems so that our society may weather the present complicated period in an organized way, without a deeper upheaval."

In protest against the government's failure to approve the publication of a weekly Slovak Writers' Union journal, *Kulturny zivot,* 9 of 13 members of the union presidium resigned Dec. 18. The writers declared that under no circumstances would they renounce their right to exercise "free and critical thought." The writers included Ladislav Novomesky, a leading Slovak author, who had been imprisoned during the Stalinist era in Czechoslovakia.

N.Y. Times correspondent Tad Szulc was expelled from Czechoslovakia Dec. 16 on charges that he had taken "an interest in secret military questions" and had obtained classified information from the government and Communist Party. According to Szulc, he had been told only that his activities in general had not been compatible with his work as a correspondent. Szulc denied that he had acted incorrectly. *N.Y. Times* foreign news editor Seymour Topping also said that Szulc "did not engage in any improper activity." *N.Y. Times* correspondent Henry Kamm had been barred from re-entering Czechoslovakia Aug. 19, and AP newsman Peter Rehak was forced to leave in September when his residence visa expired. *Newsweek* correspondent Allan Tillier was expelled Dec. 19. Tillier, a British subject, was in Prague on a temporary journalist visa from his post in Vienna.

Kiev Meeting & Economic Pacts

The Soviet press agency Tass reported Dec. 8 that Czechoslovak and Soviet leaders had conferred secretly in Kiev Dec. 7-8. The Tass report said the talks had been held in a "cordial atmosphere and in the spirit of comradeship and friendship," but it did not give details of the discussions. Informed sources indicated that economic matters, the formation of the Czechoslovak federal state Jan. 1 and the approval of the agenda for the party Central Committee meeting Dec. 12 had been the principal topics.

The Czechoslovak leaders at the Kiev meeting included party leader Dubcek, Premier Cernik, Pres. Svoboda, Slovak Party First Secy. Gustav Husak, and the party Central Committee's Czech Bureau chairman, Lubomir Strougal. (Observers noted that the exclusion of National Assembly Chairman Josef Smrkovsky appeared to confirm reports of his alienation from major party affairs.) The USSR was represented by party leader Brezhnev, Premier Kosygin, Pres. Podgorny, the Ukrainian party leader Petr Shelest (who allegedly had been the leading protagonist of the Czechoslovak invasion), Ukrainian Premier Vladimir Shchervitsky and Soviet First Deputy Foreign Min. Vasily V. Kuznetsov. (Kuznetsov had arrived in Prague Sept. 6 and had been

Moscow's chief negotiator in Czechoslovakia. Diplomatic sources said Nov. 29 that he had left the country.)

A purported transcript of the Kiev meeting was disclosed in Vienna Feb. 16, 1969. According to the transcript, the Soviet leaders were reported to have said that "the departure of Soviet troops from Czechoslovakia is impossible and unacceptable at the present time." It also said that the Soviet leaders were dissatisfied with the Prague government's stand on emigration (the government had allowed persons to leave the country) and with the continuation of strikes and demonstrations.

Czechoslovak Foreign Trade Min. Vaclav Vales and Soviet Foreign Trade Min. Nikolai S. Patolichev in Moscow Nov. 20 had signed an agreement to increase their nations' trade by 10% in 1969. The value of the trade was estimated at 2 billion rubles ($2.22 billion). The USSR, it was reported, had disapproved of Czechoslovakia's increased trade relations with the West and had told Prague that one of the reasons for the Aug. 21 invasion was to halt this trade.

Prof. Radoslav Selucky, writing in the trade union newspaper *Prace,* warned Dec. 3 that failure of the Prague government to reinstitute the economic reforms halted by the Aug. 21 invasion could result in economic "catastrophe." Czechoslovaks had "spoken a great deal about economic reform ... and its eventual aims, but we have done very little about it," Selucky said. Selucky's strong defense of the economic reform program coincided with frenzied consumer buying that subjected the Czechoslovak crown to severe inflationary pressure and was emptying stores of consumer goods.

Details of a new Czechoslovak-Soviet economic aid agreement were revealed Dec. 22. The agreement, negotiated by Soviet Deputy Premier Nikolai K. Baibakov in Prague, provided for Soviet export of natural gas, crude oil, raw materials and foodstuffs in exchange for Czechoslovak manufactured goods, chemical equipment and gas turbine engines. Under the agreement, the 2 countries would cooperate on the development of computers.

Refugee Problem

Thousands of Czechoslovak citizens were reported to have fled the country soon after the August occupation. The majority fled to Vienna, where an estimated 12,000 to 24,000 had gathered by Sept. 2. Thousands of others, still in Czechoslovakia, obtained exit visas as insurance against a possible blocking of movement out of the country.

Some 20,000 Czechoslovaks who had been on vacation in Yugoslavia, Italy or Austria prior to the invasion were reported Sept. 2 to have passed through Vienna on their way home. There were then believed to be some 30,000 additional vacationers still abroad. It was reported Sept. 4 that, as of that date, about 750 Czechoslovaks had applied for political asylum in Austria.

On several occasions the Prague leadership appealed to citizens residing abroad to return home. Slovak Party First Secy. Gustav Husak, in a speech before the Slovak party Central Committee Sept. 6, blamed the flight of citizens on fears that the Soviet authorities were carrying out arrests in the country. Emphasizing that these fears were groundless and that the Soviet secret police had not interfered in Czechoslovak internal security matters, Husak warned that the borders might have to be closed if the flight continued.

Austrian border authorities reported Sept. 9 that Soviet officers manned at least 3 of the Czechoslovak border crossings with Austria. The authorities reported a number of shooting incidents on the Czechoslovak side of the border during previous nights.

The Czechoslovak government announced Nov. 25 that it would prohibit all trips to the West "not conforming to the interests of the state." The restrictions, described as temporary, did not apply to permanent visas for visits to Communist countries. Multiple exit visas to "capitalist states" were voided. The announcement did not state exactly which visits were included in "state interests," but travel abroad for employment or study was definitely banned. Although the restrictions were made effective retroactively as of Nov. 19, the government said it would honor existing visas until Nov. 30.

The Interior Ministry confirmed Nov. 25 that nearly 5,000 Czechoslovak citizens had asked for sanctuary in the West as of Oct. 31. The ministry also reported that 2,067,000 persons (about 15% of the entire population) had made foreign visits, mainly to the West, under liberalized regulations in 1968's first

10 months. (The Intergovernmental Committee for European Migration had reported Sept. 13 that more than 25,000 Czechoslovaks had left Czechoslovakia since the Aug. 21 invasion. 15,000-20,000 were in Austria, 5,000 in Switzerland, 4,000-5,000 in West Germany, 1,500 in Italy.)

Stanislav Budin, a protagonist of the reform movement, returned to Prague after living abroad following the invasion. Budin, whose return was disclosed Dec. 6, was one of a group of Jewish intellectuals sharply attacked by the Soviet Union; others in the criticized group included the economist Ota Sik and the literary critic Eduard Goldstuecker, chairman of the Czechoslovak Writers Union. Sik, who was living in Switzerland, and Goldstuecker, who was residing in Brighton, England, reportedly had been advised that they could safely return to Czechoslovakia. But after receiving a warning that he would be prosecuted if he returned to Czechoslovakia, Sik cancelled a planned trip to Prague Dec. 11. Sik had expected to attend the party Central Committee meeting Dec. 12, but Czechoslovak Amb.-to-Switzerland Pavel Winkler had warned him that he would be subjected to Central Committee and party Presidium charges. As a result of the warning, Sik said, "it is not possible for me to go to Prague. I am not willing to appear as the accused. . . . This is the action of the Russians. They are forcing our leaders to fire me from the Central Committee." (Despite his exile, Sik still maintained his post as director of the Czechoslovak Academy of Sciences' Economic Institute.)

A spokesman for the Nuremberg Sports Club said Dec. 6 that 2 Czechoslovak wrestlers, Jan Verecky, 25, and Jan Martinek, 27, had asked for political asylum in West Germany.

1969

The transformation of centralized Czechoslovakia into a federal union of the Czechs and Slovaks Jan. 1, 1969 was the only important part of the Czechoslovak Communist Party reform program that was realized despite the Soviet occupation. Regardless of this achievement, extreme tension persisted during the first 2 months of 1969. Under pressure from Moscow and the pro-Soviet faction within the Czechoslovak party, Josef Smrkovsky, the widely popular protagonist of the reform movement, was demoted.

Protests against the government's policy of compromise with the Soviet Union culminated in the dramatic suicides by fire of the students Jan Palach and Jan Zajic and of other youths. In the wake of Palach's death, progressives attempted to organize a coalition of intellectuals, particularly students and workers, in order to prevent further concessions to Soviet wishes. The government, threatened by the renewed activity of the conservatives, tried to steer a middle course by curbing criticism of its policies in the mass media. The relations with the Soviet occupation force were marked by an intense popular hostility that precipitated several incidents.

The 2d Czechoslovak victory over the Soviet team in the 1969 world ice hockey championship series Mar. 28 touched off anti-Soviet riots in Prague and other cities. Some of the disturbances, it was felt, might have been provoked by Russians who exploited the situation in order to put more pressure on the Prague government. The unannounced visit by Marshal Grechko, the chief of the Warsaw Treaty forces, may have been the prelude to a coup d'etat contemplated by pro-Soviet Czechoslovak military officers. After intensive maneuvering, Alexander Dubcek was replaced as Czechoslovak party leader by another Slovak, Gustav Husak.

179

Although sympathetic to the 1968 reform movement, Husak had avoided excessive involvement in it and, after the Aug. 21 invasion, had been advocating accommodation with the USSR. The new party regime tightened censorship and mastered the opposition of students and labor unions. Although the Central Committee expelled several leading progressives, it did not explicitly repudiate the main tenets of the reform movement and stopped short of indorsing the Soviet invasion as justified by the alleged danger of counterrevolution.

The Husak regime used massive force in quelling disturbances during the first anniversary of the invasion. It did so to demonstrate its determination to suppress dissent and its ability to maintain order without Soviet help. More progressives were removed from positions of influence while Husak continued to resist the ultras' demands for power and for massive purges.

THE CHALLENGE TO SOVEREIGNTY

Federation Inaugurated

The new Czechoslovak federal government was inaugurated by Pres. Ludvik Svoboda Jan. 1. Addressing the nation over TV, Svoboda reviewed the full spectrum of Czechoslovak domestic developments in 1968, but he made no mention of the Soviet-led invasion and occupation. "The historical meaning of the past year," Svoboda said, "was a sound, selfless and progressive endeavor, the endeavor to make socialism in our country really more worthy of its name." Svoboda cautioned that "the coming year will not be easy...."

After his address, Svoboda formally named the leaders of the federal state. Of the new regime's 7 federal ministers (previously there had been 23), these 5 were ministers of the old government who retained their posts: Lt. Gen. Martin Dzur, defense minister; Jan Pelnar, interior; Frantisek Vlasak, planning; Michal Stancel, labor and social welfare; Bohumil Sucharda, finance. The 2 new ministers were Jan Marko, foreign affairs, who succeeded Jiri Hajek (ousted Sept. 19, 1968), and Jan Tabacek, foreign trade, who replaced Vaclav Vales. Vales and Samuel Faltan, chairman of the Slovak National Front, were appointed deputy premiers. Prof. Peter Colotka and Frantisek Hamouz kept their posts as deputy premiers, but Gustav Husak, Slovak Communist Party secretary, and Lubomir Strougal, chairman of the Czech bureau within the Communist Party Central Committee, were relieved as deputy premiers. Oldrich Cernik was again designated premier. Alexander Dubcek maintained his position as the Czechoslovak Communist Party's first secretary.

At inauguration ceremonies in Bratislava Jan. 2, Stefan Sadovsky was sworn in as premier of the new Slovak Socialist Republic. Sadovsky, an agricultural specialist and reportedly a political moderate, vowed to work for the democratic development of the Slovak people. "The declaration of the Slovak Socialist Republic," he said, "will create favorable preconditions for the intellectual [life] and the industriousness of

181

our nation to be developed in full." Maj. Gen. Egid Pepich, 45, reportedly instrumental in thwarting preparations for a pro-Novotny coup in Dec. 1967, was named Slovak interior minister. Other appointments included the known conservative Lucan Matej, education minister; Soviet Amb.-to-France Valerian Zorin's son-in-law Miroslav Valek, culture minister; and Ladislav Dobos, minister without portfolio. Dobos was chairman of Csemadok, the association of Hungarian Czechoslovaks, and represented that minority in the Slovak cabinet.

Czechoslovak TV reported from Prague Jan. 2 that ex-Foreign Min. Vaclav David had been named ambassador to Bulgaria and ex-Deputy Premier Frantisek Krajcer ambassador to East Germany.

Stanislav Razl, ex-minister of the chemical industry, was named premier of the Czech Socialist Republic Jan. 8. Prof. Antonin Cervinka and Ladislav Adamec were appointed deputy premiers. Razl's government, sworn in Jan. 9, included these ministers: Leopold Ler, finance; Josef Groesser, interior; Vaclav Hrabal, justice; Dr. Karel Loebl, technology; Prof. Vilibald Bezdicek, education; Dr. Emanuel Bosak, youth; Dr. Vladislav Vlcek, health; Frantisek Cihak, industry; Miroslav Galuska, culture; Josef Cerny, food and agriculture; Ladislav Hruzik, forestry; Prof. Josef Stary, transport; Mrs. Ruzena Urbanovka, post and telecommunications; Miroslav Kohoutek, trade; Frantisek Jaska, minister without portfolio; Frantisek Toman, labor and social welfare.

Controversy over Smrkovsky

The Czechoslovak Communist Party Presidium Jan. 7 relieved Josef Smrkovsky, a Czech, from his post as chairman of the National Assembly and recommended the appointment of Dr. Peter Colotka, a Slovak, as chairman of the new, bicameral Federal Assembly. Smrkovsky was recommended for the post of deputy chairman and also for the chairmanship of the House of Peoples. He also retained his membership on the 8-man Executive Committee of the Presidium. Dr. Dalibor Hanes, a member of the Slovak National Council, was proposed for the chairman's post of the House of Nations. Although the final decision on the Federal Assembly positions was not taken until the party Central Committee met in mid-January, the Presidium's recommendations were accepted without exception.

In demoting Smrkovsky, the Presidium said that it had concurred with the demand of the Slovak Communist Party that since the other top government posts were held by Czechs—Svoboda as president and Cernik as premier—the chairman of the Assembly should be a Slovak. The Czech Bureau Jan. 6 had also proposed that Smrkovsky be given the 2d-ranking position in the Federal Assembly.

The Presidium's decision ended the controversy over the position to be given Smrkovsky in the federal government. Because of his liberal views, Smrkovsky had received wide support from workers and students. The 900,000-member Czech Union of Metal Workers had threatened to strike, and students to demonstrate, if Smrkovsky were not appointed Federal Assembly chairman. In response, the Presidium, in a radio broadcast Jan. 4, had warned the people to stop agitating for political and economic reforms and, by implication, had raised the possibility of further Soviet intervention. The Presidium said:

"These campaigns are driving our society into conflicts whose consequences it is possible the initiators cannot even imagine unless of course they themselves wish it. We therefore consider it necessary to warn citizens of the gravity of the situation and the consequences that could result from any unconsidered steps...." "There is no truth in speculation about attempts to remove Comrade Smrkovsky from party and state functions and to exclude him from political life."

The Presidium simultaneously defended Dr. Gustav Husak, who had been one of the leading Presidium members to urge the replacement of Smrkovsky by a Slovak in the post of Assembly chairman. Husak had been assailed Jan. 3 by Vlastimil Toman, chairman of the Metal Workers Union, for making "extremist" statements against Smrkovsky's appointment.

On a TV broadcast Jan. 5, Smrkovsky pressed his supporters not to strike on his behalf. He promised to abide by the decision taken by the party Central Committee. Smrkovsky said: "We have to wait in a disciplined manner for this solution and respect it." Since the party was attempting to find a positive solution to the problems that beset the nation, he said, "I beg you urgently to help such a positive solution, to do nothing that would threaten it. By this I have especially in mind the slogan of strike which appeared in some resolutions."

In a speech delivered to metal workers Jan. 8, Smrkovsky said he agreed with the decision of the Presidium to have a Slovak as chairman of the Federal Assembly. "Any actions against the justified Slovak demands could lead to a violation of relations between Czechs and Slovaks," Smrkovsky declared. "I will never join my name with an act that would lead to the split between Czechs and Slovaks."

The Union of Metal Workers, after a 2-day meeting, decided Jan. 9 not to strike in support of Smrkovsky. But it called for a "democratic election" in the Federal Assembly to select the assembly's chairman.

Although Smrkovsky was not appointed assembly chairman, the fact that he had been named to 2 assembly posts and had maintained his position on the Presidium's Executive Committee was cited by Communist informants in Prague Jan. 9 as a victory for progressives against Moscow pressure. The key decision to retain Smrkovsky reportedly had been taken Jan. 4: Czechoslovak party First Secy. Alexander Dubcek had phoned Soviet party Gen. Secy. Leonid I. Brezhnev and had informed him that it was not possible to remove Smrkovsky and appoint Moscow's candidate, Jozef Lenart, a Slovak and an alleged reactionary; Brezhnev agreed. The appointment of Colotka, a known liberal and close associate of Dubcek and Smrkovsky, was also seen as a victory for the progressives.

Colotka said Jan. 14 that he had accepted the position only after Smrkovsky had urged him to do so. Denying that he was a rival candidate, Colotka maintained: "I finally agreed to the candidature because Smrkovsky himself asked me not to refuse this solution as a way out of today's complicated situation."

Smrkovsky was elected chairman of the House of Peoples, one of the 2 houses of the Federal Assembly, Jan. 29. The vote was 185 to 85, with 10 abstentions. The vote indicated that the pro-Soviet element within the government leadership had gained strength. Dalibor Hanes was elected chairman of the House of Nations by a vote of 135 to 1. Colotka was elected chairman of the bicameral Federal Assembly Jan. 30. Dubcek had been elected to membership in the assembly's presidium Jan. 29, receiving 225 of the 256 votes cast.

Eduard Goldstuecker, chairman of the Czechoslovak Union of Writers, and Ota Sik, principal architect of the country's economic reform program, were elected members of the Czech National Council Jan. 23. Both men had returned to Prague earlier in the week for the first time since before the 1968 Soviet invasion. Sik returned to Basel, Switzerland Jan. 27 and told newsmen that he had the Prague government's approval to remain in Switzerland for 2 to 3 years. As a result of their election to the council, both men reportedly enjoyed parliamentary immunity.

Discontent Increases

A week-long censorship dispute between the Czechoslovak party and journalists resulted in a compromise Jan. 13 under which editors agreed to scrutinize their publications more thoroughly. The new self-censorship included these controls that the government reportedly had imposed earlier: (a) temperance in all political commentaries; (b) broadcast and publication only of "positive" resolutions by students, trade unions and other groups; (c) exclusion of any direct or indirect criticism of party leaders. The editors, members of the executive committeee of the Union of Czech Journalists, also agreed to attend weekly meetings with party officials to work out guidelines more in line with government policies.

In turn, Josef Kempny, representing the party, and Jaroslav Havelka, chairman of the government's Press & Information Office, agreed to delay placing government censors in newspaper and journal offices. (Sources in Prague had reported Jan. 9 that government censors had taken up positions in 4 Prague newspapers and 3 journals—the Czechoslovak Writers' Union weekly *Listy,* the Czech Journalists' Union weekly *Reporter* and the independent weekly *Zitrek*—in accordance with a 21-point program adopted by the government.) The government further agreed to delay the implementation of other press restrictions reported Jan. 10. (The most important of these would have rescinded the right of the press to sue for damages against government actions and to appeal decisions through the courts.) The government also delayed a hearing to discipline Jiri Hochman, an essayist on *Reporter,* but instead "invited" him to discuss his role on the

magazine with government officials. (*Reporter* appeared in
Prague Jan. 14, but a satirical article written by Hochman had
been deleted. The magazine, however, published a letter in
which Ludek Pachman, Czechoslovakia's chess champion,
declared that Col. Emil Zatopek, an Olympic runner, "had to
leave the Ministry of Defense" as a result of his criticism of the
invasion.)

In a TV address Jan. 13, Slovak Premier Stefan Sadovsky
criticized the press for deprecatory remarks about Slovak party
First Secy. Gustav Husak. Sadovsky assailed "those who
launch passions and try to complicate our relations." He lauded
"those who search for ways out and have the courage to look at
the hard truth, at the risk of their own popularity." (Sadovsky
also attacked a committee of the Prague University Student
Union that allegedly was considering a Czechoslovak "cultural
revolution.") Husak, in a speech to factory leaders Jan. 10, had
accused the press and workers who had threatened to strike of
"putting a knife at the throat" of the nation's leaders. He
declared that it was necessary to "strengthen internal
discipline" and warned against "private meetings in apartments
for inventing campaigns." Members of the Czech Printers'
Union Jan. 11 refused to print the first issue of the new
Czechoslovak party weekly *Tribuna,* a publication of the
Central Committee's Czech party affairs bureau. (The union
also named Josef Smrkovsky their honorary chairman.)
Tribuna, edited by Oldrich Svestka, appeared in Prague Jan.
14, nevertheless.

Lidova Democracie, the newspaper of the People's
(Catholic) Party, printed Jan. 11 a resolution of printers that
"recogniz[ed] the work of journalists" and proclaimed
"astonishment that millions of people in the country are seen as
pressure groups."

The Printers' Union refused to distribute in Ostrava a
brochure, entitled *2-Faced Politics,* which criticized
Smrkovsky. The brochure reportedly had been ordered by
conservatives wanting to discredit Smrkovsky.

Karel Kral, a CTK correspondent in New York,
announced Jan. 14 that he had rejected orders for his recall to
Prague and had decided to remain in the U.S. Kral said that he
could not return to an "occupied country."

Some 2,000 students and workers met in Prague Jan. 15 and adopted a "Prague Manifesto" that condemned the Soviet occupation. The manifesto declared that good relations with the 5 occupying nations (the USSR, Poland, Hungary, Bulgaria and East Germany) could be possible again only when full sovereignty was restored and the "humiliating consequences" of the invasion ended. Speakers, who included leaders of the Union of Printers and of the Metal Workers' Union, asserted that they would never relinquish their right to participate in policy-making.

In a TV address made while the protest meeting was in session, Premier Cernik told the nation that "the situation ... has now quieted down." He said: "The positions of an overwhelming majority of our intelligentsia, workers and farmers are essentially positive. But, of course, there still appear to be certain extreme opinions and moods."

The *Washington Post* reported Jan. 22 that anti-Semitic slogans had appeared on billboards in Bratislava, the capital of Slovakia. The slogans were erased by soldiers but not before they had been seen by large crowds. The slogans read: "The Jews are with the Russians" and "Slovaks united against the Jews." Since the 1968 invasion, many prominent Jews reportedly had left Slovakia. Some Slovak intellectuals allegedly were concerned over anti-Semitic remarks in speeches by Husak, who had said that extremist groups were being controlled by international groups in Vienna—a city to which many Czechoslovak Jews had fled.

Self-Immolators Spurn Occupation

Jan Palach, 21, a student at Charles University in Prague, burned himself publicly Jan. 16 in protest against the Soviet occupation of his country. He died of his burns Jan. 19 in a Prague hospital. Before his death, Palach told a friend, in a statement later broadcast by Prague radio: "My act has achieved its purpose. But it would be better if nobody repeats it. Lives should be used for other purposes. We are involved in a great struggle today...."

In a note found in his jacket, Palach had demanded the end of government censorship and a ban on distribution of the Soviet Czech-language newspaper, *Zpravy.* The note was posted in Prague's Wenceslas Square, where Palach set himself afire. It said: "With regard to the fact that our nations are at the edge of hopelessness, we decided to express our protest and awaken the people of this country in the following way: Our group is composed of volunteers who are ready to burn themselves for our cause. I had the honor to draw the first lot and I have gained the right to write the first letter and set the first torch.... Should our requirements not be fulfilled within 5 days [by Jan. 21] and if the people will not come out with sufficient support (such as a strike for an indefinite period) further torches will go up in flames." The letter was signed "Torch Number One."

Palach's burning and subsequent death touched off a wave of student and worker protests. In a statement by students at Charles University Jan. 17, Palach was described as a "deeply human, thoughtful, political thinking man." The statement went on to denounce the Soviet Union and the Prague government: "We accuse the Soviet leadership of adding by its policies yet one more victim of the 21st of August [approximate date of the Soviet invasion]. We accuse the political leadership of the Czechoslovak Communist Party of dragging, in the name of so-called political realism, the people of Czechoslovakia into this situation by the smallness of its policy and by treason of the previously proclaimed ideals." The Communist Party responded to student demands by issuing a statement that expressed sympathy and concern for students and the liberalization movement.

As news of Palach's death spread in Prague the afternoon of Jan. 19, thousands of people crowded into Wenceslas Square. Students carried the Czechoslovak flag and the black flag of mourning; others carried candles and wreaths. 4 persons set up a tent in the square and began a hunger strike. Posters compared Palach to Jan Hus, the Czech religious reformer who had been burned at the stake in 1415. Elsewhere in Prague, 1,000 Prague University students drew up a new list of demands, which included the immediate withdrawal of Soviet troops.

A telegram sent to Palach's mother by party First Secy. Alexander Dubcek and Pres. Ludvik Svoboda said: "We know well that he was led to this by his genuine and honest love of his country." In a TV broadcast later that evening Cestmir Cisar, chairman of the Czech National Council, declared: "This was not the act of an individual psychotic. The state of mind which led to this act is shared by quite a proportion of our youth. But the ideas of the youth are not very far from those of us who are not so young." Nevertheless, government officials told students and others at meetings that Palach's demands could not readily be met.

During the afternoon of Jan. 20, a crowd estimated at more than 100,000 gathered in Wenceslas Square. A march, organized by Charles University students, began at the square and proceeded to the university. The procession was led by a student carrying the flag of the first Czechoslovak Republic. Before leaving Wenceslas Square the students posted paper signs changing its name to "Jan Palach Square."

In a TV address that evening, Svoboda announced that another youth, Josef Hlavaty, 25, had burned himself in Pilsen, 50 miles southwest of Prague. Hlavaty, a brewery worker, was described as in serious condition, suffering from 2d-degree burns. Svoboda continued: "This is a tragic event. As a soldier I appreciate his personal courage and sacrifice, but as president I cannot agree.... On behalf of your parents, of all the people in the country, and myself, and in the name of humanity, I urge you to stop these terrible acts." (The Ministry of Interior reported Jan. 21 that Hlavaty had been treated several times as an alcoholic, had family problems and had told people "of his intention to commit suicide.")

More than 1,300 delegates attending the first congress of Czech region trades unions in Prague Jan. 21 expressed their support for the students' demands. Karel Polacek, chairman of the Czechoslovak Central Trades Unions Council, said: "We can assure the public that the trade union movement will do all possible for realization of the hopes of citizens. We believe working people ... will support the students and will find means of achieving solidarity which will not harm our common interests and aims.... We shall not wait with folded arms for the miracle which would fulfill our targets."

The meeting was attended by Premier Cernik, who called for moderation and an understanding of the Nov. 1968 Central Committee resolution he and Dubcek had presented to Soviet leaders in Warsaw. "Some demands and attitudes in the given circumstances cannot be fulfilled and they are creating serious situations of conflict," Cernik said.

Rudolph Pacovsky, the congress' chairman, said that unions would cooperate with the government, but workers would not give up their right to strike. "We shall not strike indiscriminately," Pacovsky declared, "but only in extreme cases, and then only if the aim of the strike is greater than the losses that would arise from it." (Pacovsky was elected Jan. 23 as the new chairman of the Czech Trades Unions Council.)

Hunger strikes in support of Palach's demands spread to several cities Jan. 22. While police were trying to quell the strike in Prague, students began hunger strikes in Brno, Bratislava, Ceske Budejovice and Karlovy Vary.

Prague Radio reported Jan. 22 that 2 more youths had attempted suicide by fire. In Brno, Miroslav Malinka, 23, a mechanic, set himself afire and received 2d-degree burns covering 12% of his body. In Leopoldov, in western Slovakia, Frantisek Bogyi, 23, who was serving a prison sentence, attempted to commit suicide by fire. His condition was described as not serious. Official reports said that the motives of the 2 men were personal rather than political.

Palach received a hero's funeral in Prague Jan. 25. At brief ceremonies in the courtyard of Charles University, Prof. Oldrich Stary, rector of the university, delivered the eulogy. He said that Palach's death was "an expression of a pure heart and the highest degree of love for country, freedom and democracy." "Jan Palach brought to the altar of his home the highest possible sacrifice which will remain in the memory of Czechs and Slovaks and millions of people elsewhere," Stary added.

After the ceremonies, the long cortege proceeded to the Old Town Square and Wenceslas Square, earlier—albeit temporarily—renamed "Jan Palach Square" by Prague students. The Czech government was represented in the procession by Emanuel Bosak, minister of youth and physical education, and Vilibald Bezdicek, minister of education. Behind Mrs. Libuse Palachova, the suicide's mother, walked 3 men closely identified with the Czechoslovak liberalization movement: Jiri Hajek, ex-foreign minister; Vladimir Kadlec, ex-education minister; and Eduard Goldstuecker, chairman of the Czechoslovak Writers' Union. A crowd estimated at 500,000 persons lined the streets and squares to watch the procession. At Wenceslas Square, the Czech national anthem was played; afterwards, Stary thanked the audience for its support and calm behavior and asked it to disperse in an orderly way. Palach's family then proceeded alone to the burial grounds at suburban Olsany Cemetery. The marshalling of the silent and restrained public was completely in the hands of students. During the day an estimated 70,000 persons had filed by the bier at Charles University. At noon, all traffic in Prague halted and the city was shrouded in silence in observance of a student slogan that "Sorrow Is Silent."

The Prague government had expected that Palach's funeral would evoke disturbances and possible violence. The government had warned Jan. 23 that "all legal means" would be taken to prevent demonstrations during the funeral ceremonies. Party First Secy. Alexander Dubcek Jan. 24 issued a statement warning citizens "not to permit spontaneous and uncontrollable actions" at Palach's funeral. He added that "attempts at provocation of the present tense situation by extremist forces ... might lead to unpredictable consequences." On Prague TV that night, Jaroslav Havelka, chairman of the Government Committee for Press & Information, said that troops would be brought into Prague to help maintain order during the funeral and that the government would take "all necessary steps" against disturbances.

Disturbances erupted in Prague Jan. 26 as students and workers clashed with police in Wenceslas Square. Defying the ban on demonstrations and posters relating to Palach's death, 1,000 persons attempted to decorate St. Wenceslas' statue with a Czechoslovak national flag and a portrait of Palach. When the crowd began shouting "Russian stooges" and "Gestapo" at the police, the police moved in, using tear gas to disperse the demonstrators. A crowd of 500 youths then attempted to march on the residence of Pres. Svoboda but were halted by the police. (In Slovakia, Interior Min. Egid Pepich prohibited all public gatherings without authorization and warned that violators would be prosecuted.)

Students and police again clashed Jan. 27 near the St. Wenceslas statue when youths tried to raise the national colors and a photo of Palach. But no attempt was made to evict the students from the area. (The police reported Jan. 27 that 199 students had been seized during the demonstrations the day before.) In the Czechoslovak Union of Youth's newspaper *Mlada fronta* Jan. 27, Michael Dymacek, described as a student leader, declared that his group had agreed to halt demonstrations but had rejected an order to remove posters and flowers from the statue. In a communique issued Jan. 27, the party Presidium warned of attempts to stir unrest "through anti-social, and even anti-Socialist, directed provocations."

Among other events related to Palach's death:

● Police officials reported Jan. 26 that 9 other Czechoslovak youths had taken or tried to take their lives. Blanka Nachazelova, 18, a student, committed suicide by gas Jan. 22; she left a note saying that her motives "were the same as Jan Palach's."

● Speaking at a gathering in St. Peter's Square Jan. 26, Pope Paul VI said that he could not approve of the suicides of the Czechoslovak youths, but he added that "we can treasure the valor that puts above all else self-sacrifice and love for others." Vatican sources had confirmed Jan. 24 that a Vatican Radio broadcast lauding the Czechoslovak youths who had burned themselves had been directed by the pope's Secretariat of State. The broadcast had compared the youths to early Christian martyrs and said that their actions "deserved the gratitude" of the world. Josef Cardinal Beran, the exiled archbishop of Prague, appealed in Rome Jan. 25 for an end to the suicides. His message, broadcast by Vatican Radio to Czechoslovakia, called on his countrymen to abstain from "consuming our spiritual energies in hate."

● An estimated 2,000 students marched through Rome Jan. 23 in protest against the occupation of Czechoslovakia and to demonstrate sympathy for the death of Palach. The demonstrations were backed by an overnight strike of public transportation workers. Similar demonstrations were held in other parts of Italy.

● The Czechoslovak trade union newspaper *Prace* Feb. 1 denied a charge by Vilem Novy, a member of the Czechoslovak Communist Party Central Committee, that Palach had been tricked into immolating himself by West German agents. Novy allegedly had said that Palach's suicide was due to "a machination installed by certain Western powers, especially our nearest western neighbor [West Germany]."

Jan Zajic, 18, committed suicide by fire in a courtyard near Wenceslas Square Feb. 25 in protest against the Soviet occupation. His death took place on the 21st anniversary of the Communist takeover of the country. Sources in Prague said that Zajic, a high school student from Sumperk, in northern Moravia, had left a note saying he was "human torch number 2" and was taking his life in support of Jan Palach's protest against Soviet censorship.

Zajic was buried in Prague Mar. 2. In contrast to Palach's immolation, which touched off large demonstrations and which subsequently led to a hero's funeral Jan. 25, Zajic's suicide reportedly aroused little public concern. Since Palach's death, about 30 Czechoslovaks had attempted to kill themselves. Prague authorities had attributed almost all of the attempts to mental disturbances and family problems.

Shortly before Zajic's death, Dubcek had said: "We have succeeded in overcoming the most acute stage of the political crisis that occurred in January." Dubcek's statement, in apparent reference to Palach's death, was made in an address to 400 delegates of the worker's militia—the party's paramilitary forces—at a ceremony at Prague Castle Feb. 25 commemorating the 1948 Communist coup.

(Based on a London *Observer* story, the *Washington Post* reported Mar. 1 that a group of pro-Soviet conservatives had planned a coup for Jan. 25, the day of Palach's funeral. The group intended to use any funeral demonstrations as an excuse for the take-over, the story said, and had informed the commander of the Soviet forces in Czechoslovakia of their plans. A new "revolutionary government of workers and peasants" was to have been proclaimed, headed by Party Central Committee Secy. Alois Indra, and the ex-Presidium member Drahomir Kolder was to have replaced Dubcek as Czechoslovak party first secretary. The orderly funeral reportedly averted the coup.)

(Ex-Maj. Gen. Petr Grigoryevich Grigorenko of the Soviet army, a leading political dissenter, circulated to Soviet citizens an appeal for the withdrawal of Soviet troops from Czechoslovakia, it was reported Mar. 7. Citing the deaths of Palach and Zajic, the appeal said: "We call upon all Soviet people, without doing anything rash or hasty and by all legal methods, to bring about the withdrawal of Soviet troops from Czechoslovakia and the renunciation of interference in her internal affairs.")

(The Soviet press agency Novosti had charged Jan. 31 that reformist Czechoslovak journalists had been responsible for the "terror" that led to the suicides of Czechoslovak youths.)

Strengthening of Controls

Speaking at the first session of the new Czechoslovak Federal Assembly, Premier Cernik revealed Jan. 30 that the government intended to remove about 120 alleged reformist journalists from their jobs. In response, a number of TV announcers threatened to boycott news programs until the decision was rescinded. (The weekly journals *Reporter, Zitrek* and *Listy* were said to be threatened with pre-publication censorship; however it was reported Feb. 3 that the government had dropped its plans to impose censorship on the journals.)

Cernik also informed the assembly Jan. 30 that the security police would be divided into 2 independent organizations: public security and state security. He added: "We want to strengthen the assurance that nobody in our state will be exposed to danger or prosecution for his political opinions."

In an interview published in the party newspaper *Rude pravo* Jan. 31, Cernik said that Czechoslovakia's political program had been disrupted by political tensions and not by foreign interference, but he did not specifically mention the press. Reports reaching Vienna, however, said that about 60 TV, radio and newspaper journalists had been disciplined, either by suspension or by transfer to foreign posts.

12 Western journalists were expelled from Czechoslovakia Jan. 25. They included Stuart Smith of the *Baltimore Sun;* William Mader of *Time* magazine; Peter Young and Enrico Sarsini of *Life* magazine; and Ian Mather of the London *Daily Mail.* Government officials said that the journalists had worked illegally after entering the country on tourist visas. (The London *Times* reported that 4 Columbia Broadcasting System newsmen were expelled Jan. 29 for making a documentary film without government permission.)

The 8-man Executive Committee of the party Presidium announced Feb. 4 that the government intended to reimpose control over the trade unions and youth movements. A communique said: (a) a number of steps had been approved "designed

195

to increase the ideological influence of Communists in the youth movement"; (b) the party planned to take action for the "political preparation of Communist Party trade union members" for the Mar. 4 Czechoslovak trade union congress.

Federal Defense Min. Martin Dzur told an all-army group in Prague Feb. 5: The federal government's "efforts in the last few weeks have been aimed at turning our army into a stabilizing force, just now realized." "We must frankly say that this will also be so in the future. This is how the recent government resolution on the army's participation in ensuring public order must be understood. This resolution is consistent with the military service act."

Interior Min. Jan Pelnar had announced Jan. 28 that security forces would be tightened "to liquidate all anarchist tendencies in the interests of society." Speaking at a news conference, Pelnar said "extremist elements" were "trying to use any occasion to create an atmosphere of fear, uneasiness, panic and street disturbances." He did not enumerate what measures would be taken, but he pledged that there was "no danger that the counterespionage center will return to old unfortunate practices."

Pelnar said in his opening speech at a meeting of employes of the Federal Interior Ministry in Prague Feb. 19: Under the new constitutional structure it was necessary to implement "the positive features of the party's post-January policy, [as] expressed in the ministry's long-term plan" and to specify "concrete tasks in keeping with present needs." "Members of the security forces welcomed Jan. 1968 and understood it as a positive and serious step towards overcoming the growing difficulties in the party and in society as a whole." Later, however, there had been "not only justified criticism of incorrect methods in the work of the security forces but also incorrect attacks on the mission and leading role of the Communist Party and its principles, as well as against the organs of the Socialist state." "The unfortunate consequences of this period will have to be overcome both inside the security forces and in public opinion. At the same time the Socialist character of our security organs and their relationship with the people must be strengthened. Since August ... [1968], no one has been restricted in any way or called to account for his political opinions, convictions, or personal beliefs. But anyone who works against the republic and violates its laws must expect to get into conflict with the law and have to answer for his unlawful activities. The enemies of the republic must bear in mind that there exists here Socialist security, faithfully serving our party, Socialist state and its working people." The security forces must "be modern,... really Socialist [and] aware of their responsibility towards the Socialist state, the party, the people and all Czechoslovakia's allies."

Addressing the Interior Ministry employes, party First Secy. Dubcek took the line that the problem had become "how to defend the November and January resolutions against opposition and hostile tendencies." Although tension in the country had somewhat abated, its basic causes had not been removed, he said. "The main danger now" came from "the anti-Socialist forces in society": although unable to change the Socialist structure, these forces were "relying on the survivals of the capitalist past and the support and inspiration of the capitalist camp." Within the party itself, the main danger lay in "right-wing tendencies," Dubcek said. He promised that the party would fight "sectarian and dogmatic attitudes" that had led to "the isolation of the party from the working masses." Speaking of the tasks of the security apparatus, Dubcek charged that enemy espionage and subversive activity were being systematically organized from abroad and that, even in Czechoslovakia, "hostile individuals" were "under the influence of imperialist circles, or even in liaison with them."

Premier Cernik, another speaker at the Interior Ministry conference, was quoted by CTK as saying that the consolidation process was not taking place smoothly. Various tendencies were constantly cropping up that hampered still further the already complicated solution of "current social problems," Cernik said.

Gustav Husak stressed to regional government and Slovak party officials in Martin, Central Slovakia Feb. 21 the need to make "a thorough Marxist analysis of the deficiencies in political life over the past 20 years in order to restore the confidence of the people, who should be proud of past achievements." He said: "The change last January was inevitable, but gradually tendencies and organized forces entered the political arena which in Feb. 1948 had lost their possibility of exercising political influence." "These anti-Socialist forces attacked the role of the party, and even within the party rightist-opportunitist forces began to form themselves, stressing only guarantees and essentially abandoning the Marxist approach to problems." Both extremes—"rightist anti-Socialist forces and the Novotny methods"—were dangerous for the political life of the country. There were also disputes with neighboring Socialist states and Communist parties. Although these states said that their action in Aug. 1968 was inevitable since the Socialist system in Czechoslovakia was directly threatened, the leadership of the "Czechoslovak Communist Party, of which I was not then a member, considered that there were sufficient forces in Czechoslovakia to deal with the situation." "The August events very much complicated political life and work, but this cannot be erased" and it would not do to think otherwise. But there was no unified approach to these questions. "There are those who thanked God that the Soviet troops came, as at least order had been restored, and there are those who even express hate towards the Socialist states." "Those who think that the August events saved socialism should realize that every major political event should be prepared so that the people know what the issue is and can approve of it; the party must not isolate itself from the masses." After the party's assessments in Nov. 1968 and Jan. 1969 of the August events, there were "anti-Socialist extremist right-wing forces" who misused the offended national feelings of the people for campaigns against the USSR and the party leadership. This was the main obstacle to more rapid progress. Some people had even become so reckless as heedlessly to endanger the federative experiment. Slovakia had been criticized for its positive consolidating role in Czechoslovak policy, and elements in the Czech press had launched an anti-Slovak campaign, claiming that pre-January conditions prevailed in Slovakia as in the Novotny era. They misused "certain undigested ideas on federalization" to stir up anti-Slovak feelings.

Intellectuals & Workers Seek Political Role

Writing in the Czechoslovak party newspaper *Rude pravo* Feb. 28, Zdenek Bradac asserted that the world Communist movement could not "return to outdated centralist forms" of unity. The article, written on the 50th anniversary of the founding of the Communist International (Comintern), recalled the relative openness of the organization under Lenin. Bradac questioned whether the forthcoming world Communist meeting scheduled for May in Moscow might not play a role similar to that of the Comintern.

In another reference to the Communist movement under Lenin, the article obliquely condemned the Soviet invasion of Czechoslovakia. "Lenin and some other Comintern functionaries," the article said, "were aware that a permanently active concentration of revolutionary forces could not be fruitful through mere military occupation." The article warned that because of variations under which Communist countries develop, "principles of democratic centralism corresponding to parties' internal structures can no longer be applied to their mutual relations.... Mechanical imitation tends to violate ties of international solidarity rather than strengthening them."

In a resolution adopted Feb. 24, the Czech union of TV and film artists had rejected the theory of "limited sovereignty" advanced by the USSR to justify the occupation. The union also stressed the "desire for democratic elections."

The Union of Czech University Students Feb. 25 published the first issue of its weekly *Studentske listy*. An editorial noted that the journal would try to provide a platform for the formulation of the students' own positive program of action, which called for participation in the administration of the country, the right of free decision about one's own future and opposition to all that was conservative and retrogressive. The paper stressed that the young intelligentsia in Czechoslovakia did not succumb to demagogy and extremes characteristic of foreign student movements and did not accept prefabricated ideas. The first issue noted, and pointed out as a remarkable political action, the establishment of student cooperation with workers, "an alliance created spontaneously, without the slightest trace of formality and without ulterior motives and maneuvering." *Studentske listy*'s first issue ran to 80,000 copies.

Reports on preparations for the 7th Trade Union Congress included a CTK account according to which many of the preparatory congresses of individual Czech and Slovak trade unions had decided that the right to strike and have a strike fund should be incorporated in their statutes. Czech scientists, in a statement reported by Prague radio in German for West

Germany Feb. 24, demanded democratic elections and freedom of thought, speech, assembly and travel.

Karel Polacek, chairman of the Czechoslovak Central Trades Union Council, declared Mar. 4 that the unions intended to become a force independent of the Communist Party. Speaking at the opening session of the 7th Congress of the Czechoslovak Revolutionary Trades Union Movement (RTUM) held Mar. 4-7 in Prague, Polacek said that the 5½ million-member union "recognized the leading role of the party," but this would not impede the unions' "independent approach, restrict their own attitudes or push them into a 2d-class position as mere executors of party decisions." Polacek stressed, however, that the unions would not become an opposition force; rather, they would refuse to accept arbitrary decisions by the party. "We shall not allow a return to the situation before January [1968] either in the trade unions or in the society," he said.

Polacek's address supported the formation of workers' councils, which in the form currently under study would have a role in election of factory managers and would negotiate work contracts with enterprises. Party First Secy. Dubcek, who attended the meeting, appealed for moderation by the unions but said that it was not his intention to "limit discussion and the possibilities to express various demands and points of view."

On the 2d day of the congress Mar. 5, Vlastimil Toman, chairman of the Metal Workers Union, rejected the idea that the trade unions should remain silently obedient to government policy. Toman warned: "We cannot tolerate at any price that uncontrolled power be established in our country." While he expressed agreement as to the country's need for calm, Toman cautioned on the adverse effects of "quiet at any price." "Such calm solves nothing," he said, "but, on the contrary, creates conditions for the activities of conservative and extremist forces."

(Without specifically mentioning Czechoslovakia, an article in the Moscow *Pravda* attacked the concept of workers' councils Mar. 4. Sergei Titarenko, the author, traced the idea of councils to "anti-Communist propaganda from the imperialist camp." He warned that "the demand to hand over enterprises entirely to complete ownership-and-management-of-production collectives is particularly dangerous" and that "anarcho-syndicalism is a step toward corporationalism and fractionalism, toward degeneration and capitalism in Socialist society." He warned that it would "undermine the authority of Communist parties." The term "anarcho-syndicalism" had long been used in the USSR to describe a situation in which the workers assumed complete responsibility without accepting trade-union or party discipline.)

Czech Premier Stanislav Razl announced Mar. 6 that a series of austerity measures would be imposed to combat inflation. Speaking at the 7th RTUM Congress, Razl implored labor leaders to support the "unpopular steps." The austerity measures, some of which were to be instituted in the next few weeks, included reductions of state subsidies to industry and of state expenditures, an increase in prices and a refusal to allow "spontaneous wage increases" above the level agreed on by trade unions and the government in 1968.

Struggle to Implement Reform Program

In order for the progressive leadership to salvage anything of the reform, they apparently accepted a policy of a retreat for every couple of advances. A "2-front" policy also came into vogue.

In a speech to 1,500 high army and political officials in Prague Feb. 5, Dubcek pledged "resolute steps" against extremists—both neo-Stalinists and liberals—who had criticized the government and political leaders. Attacking those who had accused him of capitulating to Soviet pressures and conservatives who had issued literature "slandering party and government leaders," Dubcek declared that the government's policies were "the only real solution for further development" of the reform movement, and there was "almost universal support against extremist tendencies." He praised the army for its "resolute stand" during the events following the suicide of Jan Palach.

Dubcek asserted Feb. 10 that communism in Czechoslovakia would have to follow its own course of development. Speaking in his native village of Uhrovec, in Slovakia, Dubcek affirmed: "We can really help socialism only by trying to develop [it] in theory and in practice according to our Czechoslovak traditions." Then, in an apparent attack on

conservatives in the Czechoslovak party, he added: "It will be
no help for us to defend the post-January [reformist] principles.
It is necessary to develop all values of the post-January policy
of the Communist Party Central Committee in our confrontation with the present, more complicated reality." (Dubcek's
position was upheld by *Rude pravo* Feb. 11 in an article
commenting: "There are only 2 alternatives: either to uphold
Dubcek's political leadership ... and to continue the post-
January development or to lose our security by permitting the
present leadership of the party and state to quit.")

At a news conference in Prague Feb. 7, Premier Cernik
announced that Czechoslovakia had obtained pledges of $200
million to $300 million in loans to make the nation's industries
more competitive on world markets. He said that contracts had
been signed, "mostly in the form of factory-to-factory and
bank credits." Cernik confirmed that the country was seeking
up to $500 million in loans during the "next several years."

Cernik, however, did not indicate the source of the loans.
He said only that there had been no pressure from the Soviet
Union to restrict Czechoslovak trade with the West.
(Czechoslovakia's business with the West amounted to roughly
30% of its total foreign trade.) Cernik's statement touched off
speculation on the source of the loans. American bankers
reported no knowledge of the loans; one said that since the U.S.
could not guarantee loans to Czechoslovakia, the banks
involved probably were European. Other bankers contended
that because of the size of the loans the credits would be impossible to conceal from the banking community.

Cernik's announcement was the first public mention of
loans since the Aug. 1968 invasion. In May 1968
Czechoslovakia had failed to obtain $500 million in long-term
loans from the USSR. But in November the Soviet Union and
Czechoslovakia had signed an agreement to increase their trade
by 10% during 1969, and in December the 2 countries had
signed an agreement on economic aid.

Cernik, at ceremonies Feb. 27 marking 1969 as a "Year of
Quality," criticized the quality of Czechoslovak commodities
produced in 1968. Cernik said: "We can hardly be satisfied with
a state of affairs when, in evaluating the quality of products of
the past year under a state testing scheme, it was found that out
of the entire number of products evaluated, only about 12%

would have held their own in a competition with top world products; 15% of those evaluated were obsolete and unsuitable and 73% were of average quality." Prices had to be set so that they could support good-quality products. The primary problem was disequilibrium in the economy. "We would certainly like to see a healthy economy, full of the initiative of people of enterprising spirit."

Lubomir Strougal, chairman of the Central Committee's Czech Bureau, said in Prague Feb. 19 that it was doubtful whether national parliamentary elections would be held in 1969. Strougal explained that new election laws had to be prepared and administrative problems solved. (Both parliamentary and party elections had been scheduled for the fall of 1968. Elections reportedly had been delayed since 1968 because of Soviet fear that they would result in victory for the progressives.)

The Slovak party daily *Pravda* had reported Jan. 27 that Slovak Interior Min. Egyd Pepich had told the Slovak parliament at its late January session that "We know what is possible and what is not." "For example," Pepich said, "categorical state demands for action of the following sort are absolutely unrealistic and exert pressure on the government and party leadership: Immediate elections to the representative organs; the precise determination of the date of the Soviet troops' departure from our territory; the immediate abolition of censorship and the guarantee of absolute freedom of speech and assembly; the demand for the immediate convocation of the congresses of the Czechoslovak Communist Party and the Communist Party in the Czech Lands, etc."

Rude pravo called Mar. 18 for the prompt holding of party and parliamentary elections. An editorial argued that despite the need for a number of political decisions before elections could be held, "the renewal of representative bodies can no longer be delayed." The editorial added that various government and party organizations had recognized the need for the elections, and it quoted Premier Cernik as pledging that an election date would be announced before July.

Speaking at a meeting of the Czechoslovak Union of anti-Fascist Fighters in Prague Mar. 26, Cestmir Cisar, chairman of the Czech National Council, said that the most important problem facing Czechoslovakia was the need to overcome the "negative effects" of the invasion. He said: "Aug. 21 cannot easily be forgotten, it is not easy to rectify the consequences. But our fate is irrevocably connected with the entire Socialist world, and we have no alternative but to seek an honorable solution." The holding of a party congress and national elections were the "key to determining the political program and internal conditions in our country."

Radio Prague had reported Feb. 14 that the government would assist citizens wishing to return home. The broadcast said that embassies would arrange to pay for travel tickets and help with acquiring necessary documents. Premier Cernik had said at a news conference Feb. 7 that 35,000 persons had left Czechoslovakia since the invasion.

Foreign Trade Min. Miloslav Kohoutek announced Mar. 26 that steps had been taken to eliminate restrictions on foreign tourists; the curbs had been in force since the invasion. He said visitors would be given visas at the borders rather than be required to obtain them in advance from Czechoslovak consulates abroad. He also announced plans for new consulate services in Austria and Italy and possibly West Germany.

(An article in *Rude pravo* Mar. 24 had recommended amending the tourist restrictions. The article said that Czechoslovakia had earned $61 million from tourism in 1968, less than projected. The press agency CTK reported Mar. 21 that only 6% of the USSR tours offered to Czechoslovaks by Cedok, the official travel agency, had been sold. Less than 50% of the vacancies to East Germany and Bulgaria had been sold. In contrast, CTK said, Cedok had sold 96% of its trips to Yugoslavia, 84% of its trips to Rumania and almost 80% of its trips to Western Europe, Asia and to Arab and African countries.)

A special commission of the Foreign Ministry Mar. 2 had recommended the rehabilitation of diplomats who had been purged after the Communist takeover of Czechoslovakia in 1948. Bedrich Biheller, chairman of the commission, said that many diplomats had been dismissed for disagreeing with their superiors or with Russian officials. He said that other persons had been purged for "other than professional reasons"—*e.g.,* underground resistance work during World War II, service in the Spanish Civil War and because of their "nationality of origin" (a reference to Jews and Slovaks). Among diplomats named for rehabilitation was Eduard Goldstuecker, chairman of the Czechoslovak Union of Writers, who was living in England. Some 200 of the 350 diplomats who had applied for rehabilitation had been cleared by the commission. They would receive both moral and financial compensation.

For the first time, Czechoslovakia Mar. 8 officially honored the 3,800 Czechoslovak Jews gassed by the Germans 25 years previously at the Auschwitz (Oswiecim) concentration camp in southern Poland. Memorial services were held at the 15th Century Pinkas Synagogue in Prague's Old Town and were attended by Pres. Ludvik Svoboda, Czech Premier Razl and National Front Chairman Evzen Erban.

Svoboda had established a State Defense Council Mar. 1. The purpose of the council was to prevent the armed forces from misusing political power, and to separate government functions from those of the party in defense matters. The council was made subordinate to civilian control and responsible to the Federal Assembly. (Similar councils had already been created in the Czech and Slovak Republics.) Party First Secy. Dubcek was named chairman of the nine-man council and Cernik was appointed his deputy. The others named as members were Razl, Slovak Premier Stefan Sadovsky, Slovak party First Secy. Husak, Federal Interior Min. Jan Pelnar, Defense Min. Martin Dzur, Lt. Gen. Karel Rusov, army chief-of-staff, and Lubomir Strougal, head of the Czech Party Affairs Bureau.

Both houses of Czechoslovakia's Federal Assembly had earlier approved the government draft of the constitutional act calling for the establishment of the Defense Council.

According to the trade union daily *Prace* Feb. 1, one of the act's main provisions drafted before Aug. 20, 1968 provided that "in the event of a sudden attack on Czechoslovakia by an external enemy, temporarily rendering the activity of the Federal Assembly presidium or the Czechoslovak government impossible, the State Defense Council will take the necessary and urgent measures for defense that otherwise would be within the competence of these organs. At the same time, the State

Defense Council will determine the way in which these measures shall be proclaimed."

The Slovak party daily *Pravda* had attempted Feb. 4 to assure Slovaks that they "need have no fear that the defense council will mean a militarization of the state or a limitation of the jurisdiction of constitutional organs."

Conservatives in Ascendancy

Party dogmatists had made conspicuous statements at the January plenum of the party Central Committee Jan. 16 and 17 in Prague as well as at public meetings at about this time.

Radio Moscow Jan. 23 beamed in Czech the news that in a hall in Prague's industrial district of Liben where "600 old Communists" had met Oct. 9, "workers and representatives of the intelligentsia and of the youth" had listened Jan. 22 to a pro-Soviet address by Central Committee member and Federal Assembly Deputy Vilem Novy. The speaker claimed for Lenin's teaching victory in "the cause of socialism, peace, progress and freedom." Novy hailed the USSR as "the most powerful and invincible bastion of socialism, peace and progress—champion of the ideas of Marxism-Leninism."

Presidium member Lubomir Strougal was the principal speaker at a meeting of the People's Militias of the Prague and Central Bohemian regions Jan. 24 in the Congress Hall of the Julius Fucik Park of Culture & Relaxation, a large edifice built to accommodate several thousand persons. The motto of this gathering was: "Into the struggle for the Marxist-Leninist unity of the party." Strougal discussed the issue of workers' councils in the enterprises, the leading role of the party, the state's new territorial arrangement and a date for the 14th Party Congress. "Without solving all these questions first, the congress—if it is to be a congress and is meant to fulfill its mission—cannot be contemplated," he said.

In a resolution, the Prague People's Militia demanded that "the Central Committee and those responsible Communists in state organs implement the Nov. 17 resolution and draw the appropriate conclusions in regard to those workers in the mass media who do not want to take a self-critical look at their activities." The resolution said: "If these people cannot or do not want to work in a positive Socialist spirit, let them go and work somewhere else where they will not confuse the public."

The Jan. 24 meeting was followed by other regional People's Militia meetings. In the South Bohemian regional capital of Ceske Budejovice, the regional People's Militia adopted a resolution asking "the party Central Committee, as well as responsible Communists in all state and social organizations, fully and consistently to implement the legal measures and decisions adopted" by the Central Committee.

At a meeting of the party Presidium Jan. 28, Strougal admitted that the party was "split into 2 different parts with different ideas." In order to mend the schism, Strougal said, the forces supporting the Central Committee had to be strengthened and the "extremists, particularly the right-wing forces" had to be curbed. (The meeting was not attended by Dubcek, who reportedly had been ill for 2 weeks.)

Rude pravo Jan. 21 had published excerpts of speeches at the January plenum by conservatives Drahomir Kolder, Alois Indra, Milos Jakes, Otakar Rytir, Antonin Kapek and Antonin Krcek. These 6, in their speeches, attacked party members responsible for the post-January program of political reforms. The Slovak party leader Gustav Husak criticized the behaviour of those "who make commitments abroad but try to wriggle out of them at home."

Strougal addressed Czech regional and district party first secretaries and chairmen of the Czech regional and district national committees Feb. 6 in Hradcany Castle. He said: There was a conflict between "substantially 2 platforms since April." "Some people still don't have enough understanding of the [present stand] of the party and state leadership." "Enough time has passed since August for some people to understand that a platform of defiance and radicalism cannot be a platform for the forward movement of society."

Party Central Committee Secy. Alois Indra, speaking Feb. 11 at the factory-complex town of Kurim, near Brno, attacked the trade unions. Claiming that "attempts are being made to deprive the working class of its historical role," Indra said: "Perhaps a group of officials and the intelligentsia should direct the working class. The trade unions ought to carry out a constructive policy, especially in regard to personnel. Otherwise, there is a danger that the party will lose support among the trade unions."

At a district party committee meeting Feb. 17 in Gottwaldov, Moravia, Indra told members of his constituency: He was "not a traitor and collaborator" during the invasion; as proof, he had received support from "Comrades Dubcek, Svoboda, Cernik, Strougal and Spacek after August."

The progressive journalist Jiri Hochman, writing in the magazine *Reporter,* suggested that Czech Interior Min. Josef Groesser was involved in several alleged police abuses during February. Hochman also said that a number of pro-Soviet conservatives had returned to power in the ministry and secret police.

Vasil Bilak, succeeded by Dr. Gustav Husak as Slovak party leader after losing his Slovak party functions, had received permission in February to speak in the Central Slovak city of Martin. In a speech at the Turcianske Engineering Works in Martin Feb. 12, Bilak complained that "the party's ranks are not united" and that "there are diverse views of problems that the Central Committee has already clarified." He said that "opportunistic and anti-Socialist forces are active on a rather broad scale in our society, formulating a different concept concerning the party's platform—and outside it."

Prof. Miroslav Kusy, head of the Slovak party Central Committee's ideological department, began to condemn Bilak in a series of articles in Bratislava newspapers, including the Youth Union's Slovak daily, *Smena,* Feb. 20; the Bratislava party committee's afternoon daily, *Vecernik,* Feb. 21; and the Slovak trade union daily, *Praca,* Feb. 27. The Slovak party presidium subsequently removed Kusy from his position for his attacks on Bilak.

Kusy charged Feb. 27 that pro-Soviet conservatives were attempting to gain control of the Slovak party apparatus. Kusy said in an interview in *Praca,* the Slovak trade union daily, that the forces that had been practically silent before Christmas were coming to the fore and beginning to organize. "Vasil Bilak calls meetings of the party apparatus in districts during visits in Slovakia," he said. "The so-called left wing, if we may use this term, is becoming an organized force today. At the same time it is anonymous activity. Their method of organization and their conduct indicate that they are not relying on mass support. They think it is enough if they have the party apparatus, the [People's] Militia and the security service in their hands. In the apparatus the progressive forces are on the defensive. Before Christmas they still set the tone, today the very opposite is the case. The conservative forces today are not working through the party or trade union organizations. They do not dare. The situation is such that up to August the working class as a whole behaved relatively passively but since August it is the most revolutionary and most active force. Therefore, the conservative forces are seeking other forms, for example, the militia, which can be controlled through military organization."

In the 2d part of the interview, Kusy spoke about the dangerous nationalistic wave in Slovakia, which, however, had lately been losing its edge, particularly as a consequence of the student movement. Nationalistic cliches had come into being in Slovakia around the justified Slovak demands, Kusy said. "The point is not to seek national traditions—this might be an inspirational starting-point—but we must build up a modern Slovak awareness in a European context. We must open windows onto the world and be inspired much more by Europe than only by our own national sources. The national wave was a surprise. Before August, university students behaved quite nationalistically but now they stress the idea of Czecho-Slovak cooperation. They are rather disappointed by the expressions of nationalistic tendencies and therefore turn to the Czech public or to those democratic forces which play an intensive role there. Thus, the more there is the danger of a separation, the more there appears an inclination towards Czechoslovak statehood."

The Czechoslovak Journalists' Union's weekly, *Reporter,* reported Mar. 6 that the management of the shoe factory in Bardejov, East Slovakia had refused Bilak admission after the employes threatened to strike to prevent it. It also reported that when Bilak showed up unannounced at the Chemostav enterprise in Humenne, a sugar mill town less than 40 miles to the southeast, the workers had protested so vigorously that Bilak "had to leave by the back door."

In an article published Mar. 20 by *Politika,* the journal of the Czechoslovak party's Central Committee, Kusy warned against the threat of Slovak separatism and totalitarian rule. He said: "Federalization ... contains within itself the danger

that there will develop 2 different republics in Czechoslovakia—
one more or less democratic and one more or less totalitarian;
that the policy of the tough hand will operate in the latter in the
same way as before Jan. 1968." Kusy's remarks were viewed as
a direct rebuff to Husak's rule in Slovakia. In an article in
Politika Mar. 27, Kusy charged that conservatives in the
Slovak party were waging a concerted effort to impede the
fulfillment of liberal reforms.

Slovak Party First Secy. Gustav Husak speaking at a one-
day meeting of the Slovak Communist Party Central
Committee in Bratislava Mar. 12, announced the dismissal of
Kusy as head of the party Central Committee's ideological
department. Claiming that "anti-Socialist and right-wing
forces" were the main dangers to the Slovak party, Husak said
that Kusy had "practically assumed rightist-opportunist views
on a number of important problems in the policy of our party
and engaged in public polemics with the fundamental documents of the [Party] ..., and it is necessary to dissociate ourselves publicly from his incorrect views." Husak's words were
regarded as the most virulent to be used against a party leader
since the ouster of Novotny.

Other shifts in the Slovak party leadership made at the
plenary meeting included the removal of Koloman Boda, chairman of the Federal Commission for Agriculture & Nutrition,
Stanislav Luptak, minister of industry, and Maria Sedlakova,
minister of labor and social welfare, from their posts in the
Slovak presidium. The number of presidium members was
increased from 12 to 13, and the following members were
added: Ladislav Abraham, Josef Elsik, Michael Hanko, Julius
Turcek. Slovak Premier Stefan Sadovsky and Deputy Premier
Josef Zrak were relieved of their posts in the party secretariat.
They were replaced by Ladislav Abraham and Vincent Kyslak.
The secretariat was also enlarged from 7 members to 11. The
changes reportedly were made to remove moderate progressives
from the Slovak party hierarchy.

(The Slovak newspaper *Pravda* reported Mar. 24 that 153
Slovak industrial plants had recently formed a separate "union
of Slovak industry." The alleged purpose of the union was to
safeguard Slovak interests. Other Slovak developments deemed
separatist in character reportedly included plans for a Slovak

banking system, separate investment in industrial developments, and greater control of the Slovak press.)

The *Washington Post* reported Mar. 21 that conservatives in the Czechoslovak party had established a youth group in an attempt to counter the liberals' public popularity. The group, called the Union of the Young, was sponsored by the Czech Bureau for Political Affairs to counteract the reformist Czech and Slovak National Congress of Youth Organizations. In a letter to Dubcek, the new group declared: "We want to be based on the glorious traditions of the [Soviet] Komsomol so that we can support the Marxist-Leninist policy of our Communist Party."

Czechoslovak students and most of the country's youth had generally shunned the conservative front. Organizational opposition took another form. A congress of the Czechoslovak Children & Youth Organizations, the newly formed federal youth council, adopted a resolution Mar. 12 demanding an official investigation of the actions of the rump pro-Soviet youth group.

The resolution referred to a closed-door meeting of the group Mar. 7 at the Tichy Hotel in Zizkov, a suburb of Prague. (The Slovak Renaissance Party daily *Lud* of Bratislava reported Mar. 14 that the Czechoslovak party Central Committee bureau for party affairs in the Czech lands, directed by presidium member Lubomir Strougal, had paid the congress' refreshment bill.) The resolution called for immediate action on discovery of a "misuse of official power" by the new group. The "by-invitation-only" meeting was attended by 250 to 300 young people, aged 15 to 28. The Agriculture Ministry's daily *Zemedelske noviny* Mar. 12 reported that admittance was denied to journalists and representatives of the federal youth organization, the Student Union of Charles University, the club of leftist students from the university's philosophical faculty and the party organization of the philosophical faculty.

Zemedelske noviny also reported an appeal to "the youth of the Czechoslovak Republic" to build an organization similar to the Czechoslovak Youth League (CSM), which the new federal youth organization replaced. Such a "Union of the Young" was openly supported by such pro-Soviet spokesmen as Slovak party Central Committee members Vilem Novy, Josef Jodas and Antonin Kapek. Young people reported to have attended the meeting included Z. Dedic, the former university secretary of the Czechoslovak party; Vilem Chvalovsky, former editor of *Nova praha,* the organ of the Prague National Committee; and Josef Jodas' daughter, Hana, reportedly one of the organizers of the union.

Relations with USSR

The London *Times* reported Jan. 8 that according to information reaching Bonn from Prague, the number of Soviet troops remaining in Czechoslovakia had dwindled to 45,000. (The status-of-forces treaty signed Oct. 16, 1968 had provided for the stationing of an estimated 65,000 to 100,000 Soviet troops.) In addition to the troops, about 75,000 Soviet civilians, mainly technical and administrative staff, relatives, and members of the Soviet secret police (KGB) were in Czechoslovakia.

Maj. Gen. Martin Korbela, who became Czechoslovak liaison officer with the Soviet occupation forces Jan. 10, announced Jan. 11 that the Soviet troops would conduct exercises "at various levels" in military areas in Czechoslovakia. Korbela denied that special Soviet troops had arrived in Czechoslovakia as a result of NATO military exercises being held near the Czech border during January and February. Soviet troops had been redeployed as part of "winter training," he said, and Soviet draftees were being rotated to Czechoslovakia for their military service. (In an article in the Czechoslovak trade union newspaper *Prace* Jan. 11, Cestmir Suchy suggested that the strengthening of NATO forces that winter had been forced by the Soviet-led invasion of Czechoslovakia. Prior to the invasion, NATO had undergone setbacks, he said, but currently "all these troubles are behind it now.")

In an article in the party newspaper *Rude pravo* Jan. 3, Defense Min. Martin Dzur strongly attacked West Germany as "the danger menacing our Socialist state." He said Bonn did not "recognize the invalidity of the [1938] Munich agreement from its very start, the borders resulting from the defeat of Hitlerite Germany nor the existence of the German Democratic Rupublic." He charged that West Germany was supporting neo-Nazi forces and was attempting to acquire nuclear weapons. He cited the "unity" of the Warsaw Pact armies as the key factor to restraining the "imperialist" forces of the world.

A delegation of Czechoslovak National Front leaders arrived in Moscow Feb. 2 for a 2-day visit. Evzen Erban, chairman of the front, said that the purpose of the trip was to "clarify a number of questions" impeding the "normalization" of relations between the 2 countries. In late January, Premier Cernik had pledged that the Prague government would work towards "gradual normalization and restoration" of relations with the Warsaw Pact countries. Bohumil Simon, leader of the Prague city party organization, had previously visited his Hungarian counterpart in Budapest, and a Czechoslovak deputy foreign minister had visited Poland in late January.

The USSR and Czechoslovakia Feb. 7 signed an agreement for joint prosecution of Soviet soldiers committing offenses in Czechoslovakia. The agreement stipulated that Czechoslovak citizens committing offenses against Soviet soldiers would be turned over to Czechoslovak authorities.

The Soviet military command obtained approval for the construction of 3 apartment houses in Olomouc, central Moravia, Feb. 9. The apartments would provide housing for some 300 Soviet army families. Similar approval was given Feb. 8 for the construction of 2 apartment houses for Soviet troops in Trutnov in northern Bohemia. The Soviet Union and Czechoslovakia Feb. 11 signed an agreement providing housing and services for Soviet troops wherever stationed in Czechoslovakia. Radio Prague reported that the pact, signed in Prague by Soviet Deputy Defense Min. Sergei Sokolov, covered the "conditions for the use of goods and services and means of payment for housing and services" as well as the "means of transportation for soldiers and their families and the means for checking them when crossing ... borders."

For the first time since the Aug. 1968 invasion, Radio Vltava, the pro-Soviet radio station, went off the air Feb. 13. Radio Vltava had begun operating from army vans in Prague Aug. 21 but a few days later had been moved to East Germany. The station's broadcasts had constantly justified the invasion and occupation. Prague newspapers reported Feb. 14, however, that an East German radio station was continuing to broadcast, on the same wavelength, programs critical of the Prague reform movement. (The Soviet Czech-language newspaper

Zpravy continued to be circulated in Prague. *Zpravy* Mar. 3 accused Vlado Kaspar, chairman of the Czechoslovak Journalists' Union, of having "Zionist" connections. *Zpravy* claimed that Kaspar had helped train "a special unit of young Jews from which there was formed an armed unit that was sent to the Middle East to fight the Arabs." The distributors of *Zpravy* in the Victorious February Works in Hradec Kralove, northeastern Bohemia, had promised never to distribute it there again. *Prace,* quoting the factory's magazine, *Unorovec,* reported that, as opposed to other factories, where the distributors of illegal pamphlets mostly remain anonymous, *Unorovec* had published their names.)

The supplementary agreements to the Treaty on the Temporary Stationing of Soviet Troops in Czechoslovakia were the subject of a press conference held in Prague Feb. 21 by Czechoslovak Deputy Premier Frantisek Hamouz; Vaclav Pleskot, state secretary of the Foreign Ministry, and Maj. Gen. Korbela, government commissioner for Questions Connected with the Temporary Stationing of Soviet Troops. Hamouz said that the talks on supplementary agreements derived from the intergovernmental agreement of Oct. 18, 1968 and without them the facilitation of the "temporary" stay of Soviet troops would not be possible. The talks had been held up mainly because the preparations had to be carried out very thoroughly. From the beginning the Czechoslovak side insisted on the fulfillment of its demands and views, and its goals had been fully reached, Hamouz added. Hamouz said:

The agreement concerning adherence to Czechoslovak laws fully guarantees its application: no Czechoslovak citizen can be tried for any offense or misdemeanor by anyone in any other way than according to Czechoslovak laws. If a Soviet soldier commits an offense or misdemeanor against Czechoslovak citizens, he will be prosecuted by the Czechoslovak Prosecutor's Department and tried by Czechoslovak courts.

In the supplementary economic agreement all economic, financial and payment questions are fully solved in that the expenditure incurred by the stay of the Soviet troops will be borne in full by the Soviet side according to Czechoslovak norms, regulations and prices.

As regards supplies for [the Soviet] troops, only such goods and materials for the personal consumption of soldiers will be supplied by the Czechoslovak side as the latter itself decides to supply to avoid shortages on the market. As regards footwear, knitwear and ready-made clothes, supplies were refused, and the Soviet side solved this question by leaving in Czechoslovakia, for the needs of its troops, part of such goods from Czechoslovakia's normal supplies to the Soviet Union.

The amount of financial means available to the Soviet troops is strictly limited by the agreement. On the whole, Soviet troops can buy goods worth 120 million crowns annually on the Czechoslovak market, which is merely 8/10,000 of the Czechoslovak annual retail trade turnover of 140 billion crowns—from a national point of view, therefore, a relatively small sum. But if the whole thing is seen against the conditions of a garrison town, problems will probably continue. Because in a township of several thousand people the turnover will not be increased by some ten-thousandths, but by some tens of percents. And that is an amount which could be in conflict with the possibilities of the local retail network. The over-all purchases, too, will probably exceed the sum of 120 million crowns, because Soviet servicemen acquire additional means through various ways which are difficult to control, such as illicit trading in petrol. But this is also a matter for our citizens. Services provided to Soviet troops in Czechoslovakia will be paid for by the Soviet side in goods needed for the Czechoslovak economy.

Pleskot told the newsmen that the Soviets paid rent for military areas, training grounds, airfields and water.

Korbela said that recently the number of serious incidents between Czechoslovaks and members of the Soviet forces had declined. Korbela said there had been fewer serious incidents lately but that those that occurred were also the fault of Czechoslovaks. Such conflicts, he said, were solved exclusively by the Czechoslovak security force, the prosecutor's department and the courts, whether they concerned Czechoslovak citizens or members of the Soviet forces, since only the Czechoslovak legal code was valid on Czechoslovak territory.

The Prague radio home service Feb. 22 reported an incident that had taken place one week before at a "solemn soiree" of the Czechoslovak-Soviet Friendship Association in Semily, northern Bohemia: Outside the local movie house where the soiree took place a crowd of mainly young people had gathered and had "chanted various slogans expressing disagreement with the holding of this soiree." The crowd ignored warnings from agents of the security organs, who "decided to clear the space in front of the local cinema."

Czechoslovak party Central Committee Sec. Josef Kempny, a conservative, declared in Volgograd during a late winter visit to the USSR that the stronger his country's friendship with the Soviet bloc became, the more successful would be its construction of socialism. According to Radio Moscow Mar. 6, Kempny added that the Czechoslovak people were still being guided by the slogan of the late Pres. Klement Gottwald: "With the Soviet Union forever!"

CTK announced Mar. 29 that Czechoslovak troops had joined those of Poland, East Germany and the USSR in Warsaw Pact maneuvers on Czechoslovak territory. (The maneuvers were being directed by Brig. Gen. Boleslaw Chocha, Poland's deputy defense minister and chief of general staff; Hungary and Bulgaria were not participating in the exercises.) The announcement said that Czechoslovakia would participate 'n maneuvers later in Poland and East Germany.

Foreign Economic Ties

An article in the Soviet party daily *Pravda* Feb. 26 expressed strong opposition to efforts of the Prague government to reduce its dependence on trade with the USSR. The article, written by Nikolai N. Inozemstev and Ilya I. Semyonov, high-level officials of the Soviet State Planning Commission, declared: "In the past 20 years the volume of Soviet-Czechoslovak trade increased nearly 9 times and in 1969 will exceed 2 billion rubles [$2.2 billion]."

The article assured Czechoslovaks that their country could not have realized the same trade profits if it had sold its goods on Western markets rather than to the USSR. It warned that "the purchase of raw material and food products in the capitalist market in the quantities supplied to Czechoslovakia by the Soviet Union would have required about $600 million a year." (The Prague government had attempted to obtain a $500 million long-term loan from the USSR in May 1968 but had failed.) The article asserted: "Both in Czechoslovakia and in the Soviet Union, there is a mutual desire to preserve the orientation of their foreign economic ties which have taken shape and to still further strengthen them in the future by expanding and qualitatively improving mutually advantageous cooperation."

The *Pravda* article was regarded as an implicit attack on the Czechoslovak government's hopes for credits from the West. (Premier Cernik had announced Feb. 7 that Czechoslovakia had obtained $200 million to $300 million worth of credits, possibly from the West.) The article made it clear that Moscow had no intention of allowing Czechoslovakia to shift its export markets to the West.

Cernik, Vice Premier Vaclav Vales and Planning Min. Frantisek Vlasak went to Moscow in March for a day of economic talks with Soviet party leader Leonid Brezhnev and other officials. A communique issued Mar. 13 said that they had held "detailed" discussions regarding economic cooperation. They conferred on coordinating national economic plans over the next 5 years and on Czechoslovak requirements of raw materials and industrial equipment during 1971-5. The communique asserted that Soviet deliveries of raw materials "vital" to Czechoslovakia would be increased in 1970. The communique said that the discussions were "cordial and friendly, conducted in a spirit of full and mutual understanding."

Foreign Trade Min. Jan Tabacek said at a press conference in Prague Mar. 19, after visiting Iran and Turkey, that he had signed a barter agreement under which Czechoslovakia would receive 1½ million tons of Iranian crude oil annually and extend $200 million in credits to Iran for the purchase of complete plants and machinery. He reported that Czechoslovakia was negotiating with Yugoslavia and Hungary for the construction of a pipeline to transport the oil to Czechoslovakia from Yugoslav ports. The line would make it possible to buy 6 or more million metric tons of Iranian oil a year during 1975-80. He said Czechoslovakia also expected to increase its imports of Soviet oil and natural gas soon.

DEMONSTRATIONS PROMPT
LEADERSHIP CHANGE

Rioters Sack Aeroflot Offices

A Czechoslovak team's 4-to-3 victory over a Soviet team Mar. 28 during the 1969 world championship hockey tournament in Stockholm touched off widespread anti-Soviet demonstrations in Prague and in other parts of Czechoslovakia. The Soviet team's loss was Czechoslovakia's 2d victory in 8 days over the USSR in the world ice-hockey championships.

A torchlight victory parade held late Mar. 28 in the capital's Wenceslas Square began the demonstrations. Carrying posters marked "4-3," the demonstrators shouted "Russians go home" and "Today Tarasov [the Soviet hockey coach], tomorrow Brezhnev." As jubilant crowds, chanting "Dubcek 4, Brezhnev 3," "No tanks, no victory," and even "Ussuri, ha, ha, ha" (an allusion to Sino-Soviet border incidents), exulted in Prague's Wenceslas Square, some demonstrators shattered the windows of the Prague offices of Aeroflot, the Soviet airline. Riot police finally dispersed the crowd. In the early morning hours of Mar. 29, intruders smashed the Soviet airline's office equipment, ransacked its files and burned its furniture on the square in a bonfire with pictures of Lenin, signs and travel posters.

(A correspondent of the *Baltimore Sun,* filing from Bonn, reported in the Apr. 8 editions of his newspaper that a few police had arrived in a truck, observed the vandalism in process and then had driven away without doing anything. The correspondent, citing "Czechoslovak sources," said that Czech Interior Min. Josef Groesser, "an ardent Stalinist," had ordered the police not to intervene. He cited reports that questions were being asked in the Federal Assembly as to why the police had failed to act.

.(According to Groesser, whose ministry published a report on the "hockey riots" Mar. 31: The Aeroflot office in Prague was wrecked around 10 p.m. Mar. 28 after "about 20,000 to 25,000 citizens had gathered at the lower end of the square" in defiance of the police. "Some of those assembled attacked the security patrols who were trying to intervene and prevented them from arresting the perpetrators.")

Assailing the sacking of the Aeroflot offices, the Soviet authorities lodged a formal protest, including a charge that Josef Smrkovsky, chairman of the House of Peoples in the Federal Assembly, had taken part in the demonstrations. (The Federal Assembly's press spokesman denied the allegation at once to the Czechoslovak trade union daily *Prace* of Prague.) The Soviet protest note was reported to have threatened that Soviet troops would be used to suppress any future demonstrations in Czechoslovakia. The Soviet party daily *Pravda,* which reported the protest Mar. 31, criticized the Czechoslovak leadership for also allegedly allowing demonstrations following Czechoslovakia's first hockey victory against the Soviet team by a 2-0 score in Stockholm Mar. 21. The article said: "The events of recent days have shown that the right-wing anti-Socialist forces once again seek to aggravate the situation in Czechoslovakia."

The Czechoslovak government at once offered to pay the USSR "several million Czechoslovak crowns" in damages for the losses sustained by Aeroflot and by Soviet occupation forces elsewhere in the country, the Czechoslovak party daily *Rude pravo* reported Mar. 31.

The Czech Interior Ministry Mar. 31 issued a report listing several incidents of vandalism in various towns and stating that 51 members of the police had been injured. "During the demonstrations, 39 persons were arrested, and in several cases it was recommended that they be kept in custody," the report said. It continued:

> Public order was seriously disturbed at Mlada Boleslav, 50 kilometers [about 31 miles] north of Prague, where 81 window screens were broken in the barracks and Soviet representatives were the target for abusive language. No offenders were apprehended there because the police were prevented from doing so by the demonstrators.

At Usti nad Labem, the building housing the Soviet command was severely damaged. A group of people overturned a GAZ vehicle and a truck, poured gasoline on them and set them on fire. Firemen were called, and one of them was injured with broken glass. The damage to the vehicles amounts to about 150,000 crowns. Police reinforcements took action against the offenders.

Gross violation of public order also occurred at Liberec and Plice: Soviet representatives were subjected to abusive language, a Soviet flag was burned and military vehicles were damaged. The police apprehended the main offenders and handed them over to the District Prosecutor with a recommendation to take them into custody.

Anti-Soviet hysteria and attacks occurred also in northern Moravia, for instance at Olomouc; similar provocation took place in southern Moravia. At Brno, abusive slogans were shouted at Soviet representatives, and public order was seriously disturbed. At Jaromer in Eastern Bohemia, a hospital was attacked and some of its windows were broken.

According to the Slovak Interior Ministry, the public security police took action against those who seriously disturbed public order in the Slovak towns of Bratislava and Kosice. The demonstrators threw stones, burned papers, and obstructed the police, who started to intervene only when the general joy became vandalism on the part of some groups of citizens and assumed sharp forms of anti-Soviet hysteria with a criminal action. For these reasons, members of the public security police used truncheons and chemical weapons.

Around the Aeroflot office [in Bratislava], the police took control of the situation only with great difficulty, because of obstruction by the crowds; there 10 members of the police were injured, 2 seriously, with paving stones or bars....

The report was issued by Czech Interior Min. Groesser, whose responsibility for the maintenance of public order did not officially extend beyond Bohemia and Moravia, the Czech lands. *Rude pravo* Apr. 1 published the document without comment.

A day later, however, the Slovak Interior Ministry stated—as reported by *Pravda* of Bratislava Apr. 2—that nothing beyond "expressions of jubilation," mostly by students, took place in most Slovak towns on the night of Mar. 28. Even in Bratislava, the most serious occurrence was an incident in which 8,000 to 10,000 persons "chanted derogatory slogans and shouts" outside of the Soviet army headquarters, the statement said. It asserted that nothing more serious had taken place "during the other demonstrations on the night of Mar. 21" after Czechoslovakia's 2-0 victory over the Soviet hockey team.

Further reports and statements on the disturbances of Mar. 28-29 included an Apr. 1 CTK press review, according to which the Czechoslovak papers were comparing the official denial of allegations that Smrkovsky had been present in Wenceslas Square Mar. 28 with the assertions about him in the Moscow

Pravda. The Czechoslovak Socialist Party's daily *Svobodne slovo* wrote: "All our people will take this in the light of their own experience and will leave it to the editorial board of *Pravda* to look into the truth and accuracy of their report on Czechoslovakia. But it is another matter that the article takes this occasion to besmirch the character of Josef Smrkovsky, chairman of the Chamber of the People, who has done too much during his life for the relations of our [Czech and Slovak] nations with the USSR to deserve, as a statesman enjoying the confidence of Communists and non-Communists and in his state and political functions, such a write-up as he has got from the Moscow daily."

The Youth Union's *Mlada fronta* said: "It would perhaps do no harm for the *Pravda* editorial board to think a little about the feelings such an article arouses among the Czech and Slovak people.... Every critical reader can testify that *Mlada fronta* did not stir up the passions of the general public long before the [hockey] championship started," as the Soviet paper had claimed; "neither did [*Mlada fronta*] publish insulting anti-Soviet articles. And where vandalism is concerned, its first issue after the occurrence dissociated [*Mlada fronta*] from it and condemned it," *Mlada fronta* declared.

(10 youths were found guilty Oct. 25 of having pillaged and damaged Soviet command headquarters in Prague following the Czechoslovak hockey victory over the USSR in Stockholm. The defendants received sentences ranging from 5 months to 2 years in prison.)

Grechko in Prague

Pressure on the Prague government to take resolute steps against anti-Soviet attacks had mounted Mar. 31 with the arrival in Czechoslovakia of Marshal Andrei A. Grechko, Soviet defense minister, and Vladimir S. Semyonov, Soviet deputy foreign minister. (According to a Tass statement Apr. 2, Grechko and Semyonov had gone to Prague "on the instructions of the Soviet government." There was no claim that they had been invited by the Czechoslovak government.)

Sources in Prague said that the Soviet officials met with party First Secy. Alexander Dubcek and Pres. Ludvik Svoboda Apr. 1. In a note brought by Grechko and Semyonov from Moscow, the Czechoslovak leadership was accused of being "either unable or unwilling to master the situation" that gave rise to the anti-Soviet violence. It was also charged with failing to control the mass media. The USSR then warned that if similar outbursts occurred again if the Czechoslovak government did not control them, the USSR would use Soviet troops and tanks to quell the demonstrations, with or without Prague's approval. (According to a Reuters dispatch, Czechoslovak leaders attempted to persuade the Soviet officials that the demonstrations were a spontaneous reaction to the hockey victory, but the Russians had remained adamant.)

The London *Times* reported Apr. 3 that Soviet troops in Czechoslovakia had been put on alert during the demonstrations. *Newsweek* magazine reported in its Apr. 28 issue that an additional 20,000 Soviet troops had arrived in Czechoslovakia in April and that Grechko had ordered local Soviet commanders to be prepared to occupy the 3 largest cities. It said that Grechko had warned Svoboda: "If you don't clean the bad flock out of your party, government and country, I'm going to order my troops to take over full control." Svoboda then reportedly had appealed to Semyonov, but Semyonov had replied: "Marshal Grechko told you the conditions. Nobody can change them." Commenting on reports that Dubcek was thinking of going to Moscow to appeal to Brezhnev, Semyonov reportedly said: "Nobody in Moscow will change the conditions either."

Federal Premier Oldrich Cernik Apr. 1 briefed top-ranking federal, Czech and Slovak cabinet members on the situation that had developed as a consequence of the hockey victory demonstrations Mar. 28-29. (He also discussed with, them measures aimed at consolidating Czechoslovakia's dislocated economy, setting up a state information system and defining federal administrative jurisdictions, as well as the agenda of a forthcoming extraordinary meeting of COMECON, the Soviet bloc's economic community.)

According to the *Washington Post* Apr. 4, the Czechoslovak leaders pledged mutual loyalty during the crisis. Slovak party leader Gustav Husak reportedly supported Dubcek and other party leaders at the party Presidium meeting Apr. 1-2. The article said that Svoboda, during his talks with Grechko, had firmly opposed any change in composition of the government and had refused to accede to a Soviet demand that the Oct. 18, 1968 agreement, legalizing the stationing of Soviet troops in Czechoslovakia, be amended to provide that the Soviet commander could employ his forces to protect Soviet military and civilian personnel if they were subject to an "immediate threat."

Acting on the party Presidium's instructions, the federal government took several steps Apr. 2 to "secure peace and order." It directed the federal Interior Ministry to arrest those guilty of "recent criminal offenses" and to start a "systematic" drive against "anti-Socialist" forces threatening public tranquility. It ordered increased manpower in police units, authorized calls on the Czechoslovak army for help "when the need arises" and instituted tighter censorship.

Censorship Tightened

Bowing to Soviet pressures, the Prague government Apr. 2 imposed new curbs on the press and threatened to discipline "liberal" Communist Party members.

Acting on the Czech Interior Ministry's report that anti-Soviet violence had erupted Mar. 28-29, the Presidium of the party Central Committee Apr. 2 issued a statement in which it accused the press of having played a major role "in arousing moods which in some cases grew into anti-Soviet hysteria." The statement read:

The Czechoslovak Communist Party Central Committee Presidium at an extraordinary meeting Apr. 1, 1969, discussed a report by the ministers of the interior and national defense on the events that occurred during the night of Mar. 28-29, 1969 in Prague, Brno, Bratislava and some other cities. It condemned most emphatically the fact that in the course of the events riots occurred in gross violation of public order and Czechoslovak law. It is particularly serious that these included acts of vandalism directed against facilities used by Soviet organs and institutions, gross and undignified insults to members and representatives of the Soviet Union and even defilement of the symbols of the liberation of our country by the Soviet Army. Such actions very seriously damage the good reputation, international authority and sovereign interests of our state and are at odds with the Socialist aims of our party and people.

We are compelled to state that these actions were not coincidental but occurred in an atmosphere of artificially fanned passions stirred up by some of our mass communications media, by intensive bourgeois propaganda from abroad and by direct action by other anti-Socialist forces that have behaved similarly several times since August.

The party Central Committee has repeatedly stressed that if our society is to have security and good prospects, if we arᴗ to concentrate our forces toward the practical solution of urgent economic tasks, there must be above all a normalization of relations with the Soviet Union and the Socialist countries. Attempts by anti-Socialist and right-wing opportunist forces to cause conflicts and to violate the party course must be frustrated, an atmosphere of responsibility and order necessary for calm and creative work must be established and united action under the party's leadership must be founded throughout our society on the basis of the consistent application of the principles of democratic centralism.

... Again and again opposition forces and tendencies have been at work dragging society into conflicts. Instead of guiding society toward positive tasks, they incite nationalist passions and create an atmosphere of hopelessness and defiance. These forces have not been countered with enough determination. The November resolution [of the party Central Committee, taken Nov. 17, 1969 at the close of a 3-day plenum] is being interpreted in different ways, and its conclusions are frequently distorted or openly rejected.

That those Communists who persisted in deviating from the party course were not called to account was a mistake. Anti-Socialist forces are above all spreading anti-Sovietism, wishing by this means to divide the leadership of the party and the state from the workers.

The party Presidium has affirmed with the utmost seriousness that every demonstration of anti-Sovietism is directed against the unity of the Socialist countries, is at variance with the vital interests of our people, and in fact turns into anticommunism, into an anti-Socialist attitude. We shall take consistent action against anything that might damage our close relations with the Soviet Union, which in our action program [of Apr. 5, 1968] we have outlined as the strategic course of our policy. In this connection the Presidium stressed the vital importance for our security of alliance with the countries of the Socialist system and our participation in the Warsaw Treaty.

Again and again attacks are being made on the Marxist concept of our party's leading role and on the principle of democratic centralism in the party and in society. These [attacks] weaken the effective guidance of society. Instead of a consistent implementation of the November resolution, political crises are occurring again and again. A dangerous situation bordering on catastrophe is being prolonged.

The Communist Party will strengthen its leading role, which is a historic necessity and which does not consist of ideological and political leadership alone, but also of a purposeful reshaping of society in the interest of the working class and the workers. ...

In this situation in which everything is at stake, we cannot confine ourselves to appeals and calls for prudence. We must at the same time assume a firm and decisive political attitude, ensure united action on the part of the party and state leadership, and take steps that will leave no doubt in anyone's mind that we will not allow socialism or our republic to be disrupted.

The party Presidium has therefore instructed Communists in state organs to take decisive steps to achieve full and unconditional application of the laws and norms of our legal order and consistent application of the principles of democratic centralism, to ensure the reliable functioning of state administration and the implementation of obligations arising from international agreements.

The party Presidium stressed in particular that all legal means must be used against any kind of provocative actions on the part of reactionary, anti-Socialist and anti-Soviet forces, which represent the main and most serious threat.

At the same time the Central Committee Presidium expressed its recognition of those members of units of the Interior Ministry and of the armed forces who, through their actions during the past days, contributed to the defense of public order. It stressed that it was necessary to punish those who organized the illegal actions that occurred during the events of the night of Mar. 28-29.

The Central Committee Presidium assessed and sternly criticized the information media's political and moral responsibility for the emergence of critical situations and lasting political tension in the country. It noted that their activity had a large share in stirring up an atmosphere that in some cases grew into anti-Soviet hysteria. The Presidium noted that certain periodicals are deviating very seriously from the party's line and from the National Front's action program—for example, *Listy, Reporter* and *Zitrek.* It noted that the government will adopt measures so that these and other periodicals will be able to function only if there are safeguards that their activity will be in complete harmony with the Socialist objectives of our society.

The Presidium further resolved to call to account Communist journalists who make statements in the pages of the press or on radio and television in conflict with the party's policy. The Presidium charged Communists in the federal and national governments to draft and enact at once whatever further measures are necessary to ensure that the state information media respect and assert the interests of Socialist society.

The Presidium also dealt in particular with the activity of the party press, above all *Rude pravo.* It noted that *Rude pravo* is not fulfilling the role of organ of the party Central Committee satisfactorily and is far from always taking unequivocally Communist-principled political stands. It supports party resolutions inadequately and fails to combat views alien to socialism. The Presidium resolved to suspend temporarily the publication of the weekly *Politika* because of grave political errors.

... The Presidium ... criticized the conduct of certain members of the Central Committee and of the central activists who have wrongly interpreted and actively violated the conclusions of the November resolution. [First Vice Chairman of the Federal Assembly Josef] Smrkovsky was criticized by name for certain utterances at variance with the November resolution. At the same time, the Presidium also charged all other party organs to draw their own conclusions from the violations of the principles of democratic centralism and infringements of the party's unity of action....

We must shape the conditions for a peaceful and creative life for society and for all citizens, whatever the cost....

The federal government charged Apr. 2 that "irresponsible articles, in which sports results were assigned political motives and aims, partially contributed" to the Mar. 28-29 events. It concluded, therefore, that "current measures in the field of mass communications have proved insufficiently effective." It therefore ordered the Czech and Slovak governments to cooperate in imposing "preliminary censorship on those mass communication media where there is no guarantee" that party views would be upheld.

In a TV address Apr. 3, Dubcek warned that any new demonstrations could result in further Soviet intervention. Appealing for "calm, prudence and discipline," Dubcek said: "Either we manage immediately to safeguard public order, to prevent all extremist phenomena, prevent various anti-Soviet and anti-Socialist statements, or the growing tension in the internal situation and international relations will bring us back to where we found ourselves at the end of August [1968]." Dubcek also affirmed the necessity of adhering to the Presidium's resolutions on press censorship.

(The UPI reported Apr. 4 that at the extraordinary meeting of the party Presidium Apr. 1, some of the Presidium's 21 members had demanded Dubcek's resignation. The majority, however, both backed Dubcek and defeated the conservative effort to oust Smrkovsky. The UPI reported that Soviet party leader Brezhnev had phoned Dubcek to give him his approval of the new restrictions imposed by the federal government.)

A dispatch by the Yugoslav news agency Tanyug reported Apr. 2 that the latest issues of *Zitrek* and the satirical weekly *Dikobraz* had been confiscated. The UPI reported Apr. 8 the seizure of the latest issues of the Czechoslovak Writers' Union weekly *Reporter;* it said that 8 chief editors and 8 writers had been called before the party.

The London *Times* reported Apr. 5 that government censors had been installed in all major daily newspapers. The only exception was *Rude pravo,* which was expected to exercise self-censorship; 3 known conservative correspondents were appointed deputy editors, and 2 liberal deputy editors were demoted. The journals *Listy* and *Reporter* were required to submit advance proofs of their issues to the government's Press & Information Office before publication. (*Zitrek* reportedly suspended publication rather than submit to censorship.)

The 8-man Executive Committee of the Czechoslovak party Presidium sharply attacked the Czechoslovak Union of Journalists Apr. 5 for failing to indorse fully the restoration of censorship. The committee accused journalists of defying party policy, of protecting "anti-Socialist forces" and of irresponsibility. The committee's attack was in response to a union resolution that had implied opposition to prepublication censorship and a preference for continued self-censorship. The union contended that the new curbs would "seriously weaken" relations between the mass media and the people.

The independent British news agency Reuters reported Apr. 5 that the federal government and party intended to leave press censorship in the hands of regional and district party officials until enough government censors could be appointed.

The Soviet youth newspaper *Komsomolskaya Pravda* charged Apr. 6 that Czechoslovak "reformers" were using pornographic pictures in the press to distract public attention from politics. The article said that under the guise of press freedom, Czechoslovak moral standards were in danger of being destroyed. It reported that 2 strip-tease clubs had opened in Prague and Bratislava.

The Czechoslovak party Presidium announced Apr. 8 that it intended to bring disciplinary action against writers who published articles "at variance" with party policy. Asserting that the political situation "continues to be very serious" and that "anti-Soviet and anti-Socialist tendencies and forces" were still operative, the Presidium indicated that it would impose sanctions against editors who "permitted publication" of deviant articles. Sources in Prague reported Apr. 8 that editors of *Mlada fronta,* the youth newspaper, *Prace,* the trade union newspaper, and some illustrated weeklies had been threatened with party discipline Apr. 4. The sources also said that 3 staff members of *Reporter*—Jiri Hochman, Jiri Lederer and Jiri Rouml—had been similarly threatened. The weekly *Listy* was ordered to suspend publication Apr. 8.

CTK reported Apr. 8 that the government had relieved Josef Vohnout "at his own repeated request" from his post as chairman of the Czech Press & Information Office Apr. 4. Vohnout, a known liberal, was replaced by Josef Havlin, a former deputy minister of education and member of the Communist Party's ideological commission. Havlin, a conservative, reportedly had been responsible for ordering a police attack on a student demonstration in Prague the evening of Oct. 31, 1967. (The Yugoslav press agency Tanyug reported Apr. 10 that a committee of the Czechoslovak Artistic & Creative Unions had supported the Student Union in a protest against the appointment of Havlin.)

In an article in *Rude pravo* Apr. 11, Jiri Svoboda, the newspaper's commentator, reported that many journalists disagreed with the party Presidium's censorship orders. Svoboda wrote: "I have heard from various directions that if future developments and the possibility of writing are not in keeping with the honor of a journalist, it will be better to give up."

Slovak party First Secy. Gustav Husak attacked the Prague government Apr. 11 for permitting "irresponsible elements" to use the information media to spread "anti-Socialist" views. Husak said that the party had underestimated this danger, and he added that "freedom of the press ... has its limits by the basic conceptions of the party and state leadership and of our policy." It was the first time that Husak had spoken out publicly on recent events, and sources viewed his attack as a harbinger of the conservative position at the Czechoslovak party Central Committee meeting scheduled for Apr. 17.

According to a survey of factory workers' opinion throughout Czechoslovakia, published by the trade union newspaper *Prace* Apr. 12, workers demanded the right "to express their views in the trade union press without fear that the editors might be subjected to punitive measures." Respondents also expressed opposition to the distribution of the Soviet Czech-language newspaper *Zpravy* and called for noninterference in Czechoslovak internal affairs.

Meanwhile, the central committee of the Czechoslovak Writers' Union had cancelled its 5th Writers' Congress, scheduled for Apr. 22 in Bratislava. It held that "under present political circumstances it could not fulfill its mission." The cancellation was supported by the Czech Writers' Union's executive group and the Slovak Writers' Union's executive committee, which also dropped plans for an extraordinary pre-congress conference to elect new officers.

The central committee of the Union of Czechoslovak Writers, meeting in Brno Feb. 6, had originally called a Congress of Czechoslovak Writers for the 2d half of March. The committee had said: "If technically possible the congress will be held in Bratislava. In the present cultural and political situation, the writers' supreme organ considers the capital of Slovakia to be an especially important place for enabling [the writers] to express and stress the need of mutual Czech and Slovak relations."

Soviet Troop Reinforcement Feared

Within a period of 2 hours Apr. 12, the Czechoslovak government issued and then retracted an announcement that the Soviet Union would send troop reinforcements to Czechoslovakia.

A Prague broadcast made the announcement at 3 p.m. It said: "... There will be introduced in Apr. 1969 parts of Soviet forces and technical equipment to supplement the number of soldiers as stated in the [Oct. 16, 1968] agreement. The introduction of the Soviet forces will be carried out by rail to garrisons where Soviet armies are located as determined in advance." At 5 p.m. a Prague broadcast said: "It is announced from official places that the broadcast of a communique of the government of the Czechoslovak Socialist Republic about the supplementing of Soviet forces on the territory of Czechoslovakia is, in view of the changed facts, unsubstantiated." The broadcast did not explain what the "changed facts" were.

The initial statement was broadcast only a few hours after it was announced that Marshal Andrei A. Grechko, Soviet defense minister, had returned to Czechoslovakia Apr. 11. (Grechko had left earlier in the week for a visit to East Germany.) Grechko, who had arrived in Prague Mar. 31, reportedly returned for talks with Lt. Gen. Martin Dzur, Czechoslovak defense minister.

After a meeting of the 8-man Executive Committee of the Czechoslovak party Presidium Apr. 12, the party issued a statement that, while not specifically mentioning Soviet troop reinforcements, warned against attempts to influence preparations for the planned Central Committee meeting Apr. 17. The statement said: "... Certain institutions are preparing meetings at which they want to adopt prior attitudes to the plenary session agenda. We cannot admit [that] such an important session should take place under external pressure which would create a tense situation." The statement reportedly was in response to worker and student plans for protest resolutions and demonstrations to prevent changes in the government's leadership, especially to prevent the removal of People's House Chairman Josef Smrkovsky from his posts.

The Defense Ministry announced Apr. 13 that Czechoslovakia would participate in new Warsaw Pact exercises with Hungary, Poland, the USSR and "other countries" Apr. 14-16. The maneuvers were to be directed by Soviet Marshal Pavel F. Batitsky, commander of Warsaw Pact air defense forces. (Czechoslovakia had participated in Soviet bloc maneuvers in late March.)

Just prior to these developments, Lubomir Strougal, chairman of the party's Bureau for the Czech Lands, had received Soviet Deputy Foreign Affairs Min. Vladimir Semenov in Prague Apr. 11 and, in the presence of the Soviet Amb. S. V. Chervonenko, they had discussed the political situation. Soviet party First Secy. Leonid Brezhnev the same day had received Vladimir Koucky, the Czechoslovak ambassador in Moscow, and had discussed with him the future development of relations between the 2 countries.

Husak Replaces Dubcek

Alexander Dubcek resigned as Czechoslovak Communist Party first secretary Apr. 17 after 15 months in office. Gustav Husak, Slovak party first secretary, was elected to succeed Dubcek. Husak was the 2d Slovak (Dubcek was the first) to assume the leadership since Czechoslovakia came under Communist rule in 1948. At the party Central Committee meeting at which the change in leaders was decided, the Central Committee also voted to reduce the membership of the party's ruling Presidium from 21 to 11 members. All of the Presidium members dropped, among them Josef Smrkovsky, deputy chairman of the Federal Assembly, were known progressives.

The changes in the party leadership were made at the Central Committee's meeting in Prague during the afternoon of Apr. 17, but the decision was not disclosed until an evening TV address by Pres. Svoboda. Svoboda, appealing for calm, said that Dubcek had asked "to be released from the post of first secretary." He added: "The name of Comrade Dubcek remains permanently linked in all our minds with the post-January [1968] policy of the Communist Party." Svoboda then announced that Husak, 56, had been elected to succeed Dubcek. Describing Husak as "honest, experienced and farsighted," Svoboda urged the public to give its support to the new party leader. (It was reported Apr. 18 that Svoboda had appointed Husak to replace Dubcek as chairman of the State Defense Council.)

Immediately after Svoboda's announcement, Husak addressed the nation on TV. He said that one of the main reasons for the changes in leadership and the creation of a new Presidium had been disunity "in the leading bodies of the Communist Party ... [and] of the state." Husak then pledged to continue the liberalization program. "The basis of our policy," he said, "remains the post-January policy [and] the process of democratization of our society, just as they were formulated and laid down in the November [1968] resolution of the Communist Party Central Committee." But Husak also warned against "extremists." He declared: "There are people who visualize freedom as boundless, without any limits and, I should say, freedom with anarchist features. Yet in every properly organized state, there must be certain rules of the game; in the first place compliance with law, preservation of social, party and civil discipline, and primarily emphasis on honest work. This is what we are concerned with." Concluding his address, Husak called for calm and order and for the "broadest participation of the people's masses, of every citizen, in the creation of our policy, in its implementation and in its control."

According to sources in Prague, the decision to replace Dubcek had been made at a meeting of Husak and other Czechoslovak party leaders Apr. 16. Husak reportedly had agreed to assume the first secretary's post if progressives would agree to support him at the Central Committee meeting. (Husak was elected by a vote of 177 to 5.) In turn, Husak was said to have agreed not to attempt to prove the existence of "counterrevolutionaries" prior to the August invasion. It was not known whether Dubcek attended the meeting with Husak, but in his speech to the Central Committee Apr. 17 Dubcek said: "After consultations and on the basis of the negotiations of the members of the Executive Committee and then also of the Presidium, I come before the plenum of the Central Committee with the request that I be released from the functions of first secretary of the party."

Husak had been born Jan. 10, 1913 in Bratislava, and he became a Communist in 1933. He studied at the faculty of law of Comenius University, Bratislava in 1933-7 and became a leader of the Slovak uprising against the Nazi occupation during World War II. Husak was a member of the Slovak party Central Committee, Presidium and Slovak National Council during 1945-50. Denounced as a "bourgeois nationalist" during Stalinist purges in 1951, Husak was sentenced to life imprisonment. He was released in 1960 and rehabilitated in 1963. Husak became a vice premier Apr. 8, 1968. He was rehabilitated as a Slovak Communist Party member and made first secretary of the Slovak party and member of the Czechoslovak party Central Committee and Presidium in Aug. 1968. Husak was elected a member of the Executive Committee of the Central Committee Presidium Nov. 16, 1968. He was relieved as vice premier Jan. 1, 1969 under federal reorganization of Czechoslovak government.

Husak Lectures Party

Husak's TV address late Apr. 17 was considered more temperate than his speech to the Central Committee after his election as first secretary. In the speech to the Central Committee Husak declared that the debates at the plenary meeting had confirmed great differences in the views of the members of the supreme party body. "This is a serious matter," Husak said of such differences. "We should all think it over. Today we shall not resolve the problem, yet we should look for a solution, an honest communist solution." Husak said:

The crisis situation is growing more acute. The recent events of the kind which took place during the night of Mar. 28-29 developed into actions bordering not only on the criminal; they disgraced us the world over, aggravated very much the international relations, and in some places they even assumed an obviously counterrevolutionary nature. And I am not afraid to use this expression.

It is particularly worth thinking about [that] some officers and members of the party and even members of this body [are] trying not to attach much importance to this. Several hooligans, they allege, have done something, but the entire society is being punished. I read about this and heard foreign radio talk of this. This information is also being disseminated in our country, via different channels. Were not the actions of people that night of an anti-Soviet nature? Is such a demonstration compatible with the honor of our peoples? I would like to remind you of one document. The organization of students of higher educational establishments in Prague, including all the Communists in these establishments, sent to the Presidium a letter of the following content: "The events of Mar. 28 were not only an expression of joy of our people in connection with sport successes, but they expressed the sentiments of our people ... evoked by August." In that way the organization of students of higher educational establishments explains directly the meaning of the demonstration. What it really was like could be confirmed by the [Federal] Ministry of the Interior and the Ministry of National Defense.

The 2d question is why many thousand people reason in this way. Let us take many of our magazines, for instance. I shall dwell on one of them, *viz.* the *Listy* literary magazine. Almost every issue on the eve of these events carried intensive anti-Soviet propaganda; many articles were devoted, for instance, to the self-immolation of Jan Zajic, etc. Or, for [another] instance, the *Zitrek* magazine regularly published anti-Soviet propaganda. And what did the other newspapers do? If such things are suggested to our people in this way, what result will it produce? Does this not show a deliberately organized affair? Can this be the work of just a few hooligans? We must call a spade a spade, without concealing anything from ourselves or from the public. I do not want to accuse anyone; however, if the malicious propaganda which had such an outcome [was] conducted long before August, let no one say that the guilty are a few hooligans who ought to have been arrested, and that's all there is to it. I am surprised at hearing people whom, by the way, I respect, speaking in this way....

You know what the situation in the party is, what its capacity for activity is, what the unity of the party is like and what effect this exerts on state power, on the economy, on party discipline, on labor morale, etc. The process of demoralization is going on and brings us to quite a dangerous line. The principles of this development were aptly reflected in last year's November resolution of the Central Committee. We have let various forces enter the political arena, forces which we generally qualify as anti-Socialist, for they are forces that are objectively directed against the Socialist system and are potentially striving to replace it with something else. They operate legally and terrorize Communists in some places. We receive letters about it.

Right-wing tendencies undermine the party's capacity for active functions and its unity. Here we frequently observe bonds with alien propaganda. Those who listen in on [Radio] Free Europe know that its broadcasts show the same language, the same kind of vocabulary and often the same terminology used by some of our publicists. What can this lead to if our Central Committee and central bodies take no measures? What can this lead to? It can lead to a civil war.

Every person who mixes with people knows that in the party masses among our people the realization is maturing that it is impossible to follow this road any longer.... [He also knows] that in some fundamental issues it is essential to introduce due order within the party and, within our society, to stop the activities of various subversive forces and tendencies and create conditions for fruitful, positive work in the party and in our entire society.

We do not seek to alter the political concept; we do not want to change the political line. But we must clearly change the approach to this line, to its implementation, to the organization of the effort to implement it. All these questions comprise political struggle. They are not a problem of the different views of these or those comrades. There have been diverse views inside the party [before]. In a certain sense there must [always] be a conflict of views, a clarification of views, because as the result of that we find the optimum point of departure. But it is quite a different thing when, after the discussion, the decision has been taken. It must be an unanimous decision [whether or not it was unanimously reached] and an effort must be made to carry it out. Otherwise there is no point in taking this decision, unless we wish to deceive ourselves or somebody else, unless we want only to play at decision-taking.

The case is similar with respect to all the different forces, however we might call them. I am not trying to attach labels. But we must not permit the aggravation of tensions and unrest in our society, which these forces are provoking, and deliberately at that. We must wage against that an organized political struggle both inside and outside the party. I mean a political struggle and none other, provided it does not go beyond the limitations of operating laws, provided this does not violate any law. But a struggle must be waged. And it must be waged, first of all, by the party leadership, by the membership of the Central Committee and other bodies.

Some of our comrades, for instance, furiously call for freedom. Does this mean that while some are for freedom, we, the others, are butchers of freedom? Does this mean that some carry the torch of freedom and democracy, while we are probably supposed to be a cluster of reactionaries who will trammel the press? However, I must say I don't know a single Western bourgeois democracy that would permit without consequences the goings on that we have had of late.

However, that is a divergence of great scope. The new approach in our work should be as follows: if we take a decision, [approve] a document, [adopt] the November resolution, we must organize a political struggle for their implementation and realize them....

Today, there are opposition trends, anti-Socialist trends, rightist trends, which hide behind the screen of patriotism, Czech and Slovak, hide behind the screen of Czechoslovak patriotism and spread anti-Sovietism by all legal means. Before the plenary meeting of the Central Committee, a comrade from Ostrava showed me an album of photographs from an exhibition arranged there. Each is provocatorily anti-Soviet in character. Meanwhile this exhibition was subsidized by the state. Today we discussed another such "document." You know what *The Black Book* is and you know the political harm it has done us. It was compiled by the Institute of History of the Czechoslovak Academy of Sciences. Its authors were paid emoluments to the extent of 30,000 crowns. The academy's money is not private money. Emoluments cannot be paid for what the party and government condemn. Anti-Sovietism in such circumstances is just the main weapon of the opposition forces and—I shall put it bluntly—of anti-party trends, even if they are to be found inside the party....

... If there is anyone who wants to think about the domestic safety of our state, then how can he permit and tolerate anti-Sovietism, spread hatred—moreover, by legal state means—on television, the radio and the press? Where can all this lead to? One comrade said here that anti-Sovietism had one meaning before August and another after August. Before August one should have thought about it, he said, but after August it has become a question of patriotism. We must explain such things. Anti-Sovietism is incompatible with the ideology of the Czechoslovak Communist Party and is a sharp contradiction to the state policy of our country!

We cannot tolerate it in [our] social life. We must explain this convincingly to the people. One may not turn ordinary citizens into one's enemies, but we cannot permit this venom to poison the minds of our people. If someone says here that in the post-August period we show a different approach to the main principles of Marxism-Leninism, and says so as a member of the Central Committee, then, you might excuse me, his Marxism-Leninism is somewhere on the other side....

One of the main causes of the present situation in the party was the absence of unity in the leadership. The absence of unity weakened the efficacy of the leadership, it allowed for, and tolerated, diverse, contradictory and absolutely opposite interpretation of decisions from top to bottom, and legalized this state of things. As the result these decisions were practically not obligatory to anyone.

If we in the party want to make headway, we should first of all introduce ideological unity in its very leadership, a unity of opinions and especially a unity of actions. We were told: Why do you talk of unification, when you have only 20 people in the leadership and you could not introduce proper order? How is it possible to achieve concord amidst such a multitude of trends? We were condescending and tolerant to the detriment of the party. In the course of the discussion let everyone express his views. Disorder begins when a decision is adopted without any benefit resulting from it.

Another cause was indifference in the instances when the principles of democratic centralism* were violated. We did not call to political responsibility the Central Committee member who interpreted the party line in the opposite sense, nor the Central Committee member who voted against the [Czechoslovakia-Soviet status-of-forces] treaty. People join the party

---

* Specifically, Marxist dogma that differences of opinion on a given policy may not outlast the taking of a decision on the policy. Its force is stronger than that of the doctrine that "the majority rules," which allows for the limited operation of dissent even after a decision has been reached.

voluntarily, and nobody is made forcibly to remain in the party. You should patiently work with people. However, in cases where persuasion does not help you should take measures which are directly contemplated by the party rules. It is necessary to call to responsibility the Communists who act against the party line. There is no other way out. In that manner we should discipline our party, we should know whether a Communist works for the party's benefit or against it.

Does a party decision make a Communist working on a newspaper or on the radio duty-bound to observe certain things? Is it logical to brandish the party card and work in the opposite direction? This kind of thing would not be tolerated by any society.

I know what some will say now: A new Novotny era is coming. Yet, people will judge us by our activities and our work. It is impossible to pursue a popular policy and be on good terms with everyone. We shall not count on cheap success. We should fight fearlessly for the solution of the problems on which we agree and for the fulfillment of the tasks set for us by the Central Committee.

This also refers to the leading role of the party in society. I shall cite an example of no small importance—the role of the Revolutionary Trade Union Movement. Members of the party, Communists, constitute a big percentage of leading representatives of trade union organs. Many Communists are working in trade unions honestly and selflessly. But do some of them show in general any feeling for the party? How do they understand the leading role of the party? Can the party, without the implementation of these principles in other organs, too, be responsible in economic organs for the whole [of economic] life, for all the questions? Our patience has gone so far that people in the apparatus are doing whatever they want. But this is complete rejection of the principles on which a Socialist state is being built. Thus, news came that students and factory workers would have a meeting in Prague, and this was without the knowledge of appropriate organs. What are they preparing? Some strikes. Definitely there are Communists among them. But let us find out: does it only concern them, what they are going to do with the republic at this moment, or does it concern the whole party and state organs? Will an end be put to their playing with the destiny of 14 million people? Everything has its limits, its capacity, and our patience must also have them. Otherwise all of us will be called to account, all of us will be justly blamed if we fail to prevent such actions of irresponsible elements.

This of course also refers to the mass media of which we have spoken. If the party does not ensure its decisive ideological influence on television, radio and the press, it will not be able to fulfill it role in this state.

It is the duty of the Communists in these spheres to help the party honestly. We shall not ask those who do not wish to. There is no other way. We must carry out staff and other measures. There is no other way out. They talk about the restriction of the press. But can a group of people hold in their hands a majority of the press which, in millions of copies, influences the public? And to whom is it responsible?

In this connection they are speaking about freedom. We regard the question of freedom and democracy from the class point of view. For people who in a crisis situation—which exists today and which we are living through now—abuse freedom and democracy against the laws of the state and socialism, there cannot be any freedom....

This also refers to the National Front. We know that outside the National Front no organization can act. But ... [just such a situation] has been lasting for months; we are flirting with this and ourselves violate the laws we have adopted.

Problems concerning the federation have been touched on here. We must see to it that the state should not become weaker in the conditions for a correct federative solution, but on the contrary we must see to it that it should function well in all spheres. We have a memory. They talk about the return to the old regime, to the pre-January conditions—I do not know to what other period, maybe up to the '50s. We know how people in [Radio] Free Europe are deftly playing on this.

From this rostrum a demand was voiced that we should guarantee the post-January policy. Who is going to reject the post-January policy here? We would find ourselves in the crisis situation again. Why are these things being constantly raised? And those who several years ago spoke absolutely different things are now posing as standard-bearers of freedom the like of which the world has never seen before. Some went abroad and from there want to teach the 14 million people democracy and independence. But what did they do 5 years ago, what were they writing at that time?

Who is hampering the realization of the post-January policy? The leadership of the party, the former leadership, Dubcek or me? Or is the implementation of the post-January policy hampered just by the forces which are constantly speaking of it, which organize various actions and strikes? Who jeopardizes it? Is it the leadership of the party which jeopardizes the policy for which it has opened scope and which it confirms in documents? This is idle demagogy.

Quite possibly we may have difficulties in the near future. It is said that there will be strikes. Possibly this is only panic, but it is a fact that here will be manifested a certain misunderstanding on the part of many people, many comrades. It is said that the post-January policy supposedly leans on 4 people. I admire the comrades about which this is said. However, if a policy leaned on 2 or 3 people then such a policy is worthless. It must rest on a much broader basis. There will be panic, and we shall have difficulties. But we shall not be afraid of these difficulties.

I want to say about myself, personally, that I shall not budge on questions of principle, I shall not budge a centimeter from the Marxist positions and from the basic questions that are decisive for the life of these peoples. We cannot beat a retreat either in the face of any hostile forces or in the face of right-wing elements. We shall accept the challenge to political struggle.

Progressives in Retreat

In what was regarded as an attempt to protect his position on the party Central Committee's Presidium before the Central

Committee meeting, Josef Smrkovsky admitted Apr. 15 to making an error in assessing the political situation in Czechoslovakia.

Smrkovsky, writing in the party newspaper *Rude pravo,* said he had been wrong in criticizing the party's left wing or conservatives as the greatest danger to Czechoslovakia. Rather, Smrkovsky asserted, "the anti-Soviet acts by right-wing [progressive] extremists at the end of March showed that my assessment ... was not correct. A sharp crisis exacerbated the situation, damaged the good name, international authority and interests of the state, and proved that the demands for more incisive measures against the right-wing were justified." In the rest of the article, Smrkovsky approved the adoption of measures to safeguard law and order, and argued that an extremist position would not solve the country's political and economic problems.

The Executive Committee of the party Presidium Apr. 16 exonerated 10 prominent conservatives accused of collaboration with the USSR. The committee said: There was no proof "of alleged treachery or some sort of collaboration brought against many comrades.... It was incorrect that the party and civic honor of a number of honest comrades, who are devoted to the party, should have been tarnished in this fashion." Among those cleared were Vasil Bilak and Alois Indra, secretaries of the Central Committee, and Drahomir Kolder, a Central Committee member. The 3 reportedly had been selected by Moscow to form a new government after the Aug. 1968 invasion. The others absolved were Frantisek Barbirek, Slovak trade minister; Jan Piller, a Presidium member; Oldrich Svestka, editor of the Central Committee's Czech lands bureau weekly *Tribuna;* ex-Premier Jozef Lenart; Antonin Kapek, an alernate member of the Presidium; Milos Jakes, chairman of the party Central Control & Auditing Commission; and Emil Rigo, an ex-Presidium member.

At its meeting Apr. 17, the Central Committee also reduced the membership of the Presidium from 21 to 11. Besides Dubcek, Husak and Svoboda, the other members elected were: Bilak, a member of the old Presidium; Peter Colotka, Federal Assembly chairman; Oldrich Cernik, Czechoslovak premier; Evzen Erban, National Front chairman; Piller; Stefan

Sadovsky, Slovak premier; Lubomir Strougal, chairman of the Central Committee's Czech lands bureau; and Karel Polacek, chairman of the Central Council of Trade Unions. The Central Committee also abolished the 8-man Executive Committee of the Presidium which had been established Nov. 17, 1968.

The Central Committee recommended Dubcek for the post of Federal Assembly chairman to replace Colotka. Colotka was recommended for the post of first deputy premier in the federal cabinet.

Another report on the Apr. 17 meeting, broadcast Apr. 18, said that Jiri Sekera, editor-in-chief of the Central Committee newspaper *Rude pravo,* had been "released from his post" in accordance with his request and that Miroslav Moc had been appointed to replace him.

At Prague celebrations Apr. 21 commemorating the 99th anniversary of Lenin's birth, Strougal delivered an address in which he stressed both stricter party control and loyalty to the USSR. Strougal's speech reportedly was interrupted with shouts of "Long live the Soviet Union."

At an extraordinary meeting, the presidium of the Czechoslovak Revolutionary Trade Union Movement (RTUM) decided Apr. 21 to approve the party Central Committee's Apr. 17 resolution and call on all member unions "not to allow the abuse of trade union premises and activities for inciting passions." "For every prudent-minded person," the resolution said, "what we are now in need of is clear: Is it to be strain, conflicts, crisis situations, the spreading of passivity and hopelessness—or is it to be unification of opinions and forces that will enable us, in our own interest, to convert our intentions into permanent values?"

An 8-member delegation of the RTUM's Central Council returned to Prague Apr. 29 from a 6-day official visit to the USSR. RTUM Central Council Chairman Karel Polacek, by then also a party Presidium member, described the trip on Radio Prague Apr. 29 "as a very useful and fruitful one."

While in Moscow, the delegation had conferred with Soviet party leader Leonid Brezhnev, who, *Prace* reported Apr. 29, "informed the Czechoslovak delegation about Communist construction in the USSR and Soviet party activities." Brezhnev had apparently underscored the lack of Soviet sympathy for further liberalization in Czechoslovakia. (Polacek said during the Radio Prague interview Apr. 29 that "it is no secret that some factories in Czechoslovakia devote 60% and even more of their production for the USSR.") The official communique of the meeting said that "the Czechoslovak trade unions recognize the leading role of the Czechoslovak Communist Party and will support the party Central Committee and its new leadership in the struggle for the development of Socialist achievements and against all anti-Socialist forces." The Czechoslovak delegation was reported to have agreed that it was the "duty" of the trade unions of both countries "to help in every possible way the further strengthening and improvement" of the Warsaw Treaty Organization for "collective defense of the Socialist countries."

FIRST PHASE OF HUSAK REGIME

Response to Dubcek's Ouster

According to Western press reports, Czechoslovaks expressed sadness at Dubcek's demotion, but there were no indications of mass demonstrations or strikes. The Czech Ministry of Education appealed to students Apr. 19 to avoid any disturbances. The warning came in response to a planned sit-in demonstration by Charles University students Apr. 21. The students had issued a statement that said: "In the selection of Husak we see not merely a personnel change but also a change of political course." Sit-in demonstrations did take place in Prague and at Ceske Budejovice College and Olomouc University Apr. 21, but they ended quietly by Apr. 24 in the absence of support from the workers.

The first union organization to indorse Husak's election was the presidium of the Slovak Council of Trade Unions Apr. 19. 2 days later, the presidium of the Central Council of Czechoslovak Trade Unions, representing more than 5½ million workers, issued a statement in support of Husak.

The *N.Y. Times* reported Apr. 21 that progressives viewed Husak's rise to first secretary with mixed feelings. They believed, it was reported, that Husak would institute new and tighter political restraints, but they acknowledged that Husak might be more effective in dealing with the USSR than Dubcek had been, particularly in obtaining Soviet troop withdrawals. One liberal was quoted as commenting: "Husak is so complex that no one is quite sure what he will do." An analysis of Husak in the London *Times* Apr. 19 described him as a center conservative and said that although he had stern views on discipline, he could not be regarded as a "stooge" of Moscow.

The Soviet Union warmly praised Husak's election. Party Gen. Secy. Leonid Brezhnev Apr. 18 sent Husak a telegram that declared: "You displayed courage, consistency and a high sense of Communist duty in the complex conditions of sharpened struggle against the threat to the Socialist gains of the Czechoslovak people." (Anatole Shub of the *Washington Post* reported Apr. 18 that the ouster of Dubcek and other progressives had been arranged by Soviet military leaders, especially Marshal Andrei A. Grechko, Soviet defense minister.)

Husak's election was praised Apr. 18 by Polish, East German and Bulgarian leaders, but in Yugoslavia newspapers expressed "shock" at the Prague developments. Rumania offered congratulations to Husak Apr. 19. In Italy, the Communist Party issued a statement denouncing Dubcek's ouster and calling for the "full restoration of Czechoslovak sovereignty and the end to all forms of interference."

At a news conference in Washington Apr. 18, Pres. Richard M. Nixon condemned the ouster of Dubcek. "The Soviet Union is aware of our disapproval of that action," Nixon said. "All Americans—in fact, all people in the free world—see this as perhaps the final chapter in the great tragedy of the Czechoslovak people under Communist rule." Nixon also warned that the USSR would "have to consider now, in terms of any future action, how that might affect their relations with the U.S. and with the Western world." (The Nixon Administration reportedly had warned the Soviet Union during the first week of April that any new repressive actions in Czechoslovakia could delay the opening of arms control talks.)

Speaking in Moscow Apr. 22 at a celebration of the 99th anniversary of Lenin's birth, Ivan V. Kapitonov, a secretary of the Soviet party Central Committee, defended the Czechoslovak invasion and praised the election of Husak as first secretary. Speaking as if the danger in Czechoslovakia were past, Kapitonov said: "History and life have shown that the cause of socialism is invincible, that any attempts of reaction to turn Czechoslovakia from the Socialist road are doomed to failure." Kapitonov's address was warmly applauded by representatives from 7 of the 8 member countries of Comecon; the only exception was the Rumanian delegation, which remained silent.

Repression of Progressives

Col. Emil Zatopek, former Olympic runner and one of the 70 signers of the "2,000 Words" manifesto, was suspended as an army athletics trainer, the news agency CTK reported Apr. 21. The report said that Zatopek had been dismissed "on suspicion of spreading untruthful reports and grossly slandering constitutional representatives of the republic and the Czechoslovak people's army."

Maj. Anton Poliacik, in charge of the passport section of the Czechoslovak Interior Ministry, defected to the West, it was reported Apr. 27. Poliacik reportedly possessed information on Russians holding Czechoslovak passports.

Alexander Dubcek Apr. 28 was elected chairman of the Federal Assembly. Dubcek, who had been recommended for the post by the party Central Committee, was elected by the assembly by a vote of 306-68 with 7 abstentions. In his acceptance speech, he emphasized the need for close relations with the USSR and other Socialist countries and for adherence to party policies.

Dubcek also declared again his support for Husak and pledged his best efforts toward the passage of pending legislation aimed at implementing the Apr. 5, 1968 action program in the light of the party Central Committee's Nov. 17, 1968 resolution.

In a TV address Apr. 30, Husak said that a new party congress and general elections to the Federal Assembly might take place "in the first half of next year." Husak cautioned, however, that the 2 actions, long desired by progressives, could occur only after "normalization and stabilization" had returned to Czechoslovakia. He said:

A concept and firm leadership ... [are] needed [for normalization and stabilization]. This concept is fundamentally given in party and state documents. I recall, for instance, the November resolution of the party Central Committee last year, the programs of the Czechoslovak government, of the Czech and Slovak governments and so on. It is necessary to translate them consistently and energetically into life and not to get diverted and pushed out of this path every day or every week.... Some people are speculating in vain that there is some kind of return to the 1950s or reversion to the old regime. No such thing is involved. Each state must in such crisis situations calm down the situation in the firmest possible manner. There is no other possible way. We want to attain in our state peace for our working people and at the same time assurance, assurance of their civil rights and civil status, certainty in living conditions and a prospect both in personal matters and in matters of the entire state of ours. This is a duty for every political leadership and a responsibility for each political leadership.... The citizen, the nation and the state must safeguard their freedom and must have it guaranteed. But the reverse side of freedom is discipline, conscious discipline; it includes certain rules of the game and order without which a modern, cultural and industrial society simply cannot exist.

The new leadership of the Communist Party and the leadership of our state do not want to come to the fore with promises to our citizens or with some cheap slogans. There was enough of this among our public....

The 2d sphere where we must clarify our relations is the safeguarding of our state, of our national development, of our Socialist society outwardly. Every one of us knows where Czechoslovakia is situated and knows what the Europe of today looks like. All our history has been, as it were, a struggle for the preservation of the national freedom of the Czech and Slovak nations, and this obligation for the political leadership and for us all is also valid today. In the last war, this freedom of our nations was again in peril; and we entered into a free state thanks to the help of the Soviet Union, thanks to the troops of the Soviet army, which liberated our entire territory....

After all, these relations on which the main guarantee of our state freedom and sovereignty has been built were in some way violated. This is why the leadership of the party and state lays great stress on the renewal, to the full extent, of fraternal and comradely relations with the Soviet Union and all the other Socialist states, in particular those with which we are allied by treaty.... Success ... [has again been] achieved in creating a good political atmosphere between Czechoslovakia and all allied states, especially the Soviet Union; our talks [a few days ago in Moscow] were cordial, amicable, frank, not in the way currently described in the communique, but literally; on both sides there is an effort to create a normal atmosphere. We discussed many questions which concern us, and I believe all fundamental decisive questions in which our people and our leadership are interested. Briefly, one may say that there is no question between us and the Socialist countries with which we are allied that we could not discuss and that we could not solve step by step.

We shall continue with these talks. A small country like ours needs allies and friends. This is the demand of our history and of the orientation on our Marxist teaching in the international sense, this is demanded by our concern and by our responsibility for the fate of our nations....

Stefan Sadovsky, premier of the Slovak Socialist Republic, was appointed first secretary of the Slovak party May 4 to succeed Husak. Peter Colotka, former chairman of the Federal Assembly, was named premier to succeed Sadovsky. The *N.Y. Times* reported May 14 that Husak had resisted Soviet pressure to install Vasil Bilak as first secretary of the Slovak party. Husak, however, had yielded to Soviet opposition to his choice, Viktor Pavlenda. The controversy, which reportedly took place when Husak attended a Soviet-bloc meeting in Moscow in late April, ended in the compromise appointment of Sadovsky.

Czech Interior Min. Josef Groesser announced Apr. 30 that legal action would be taken against an "underground group of conspirators operating in south Moravia." Groesser claimed that the group had a political program and "links with military circles" and was being supplied by arms factories in the area. He noted that thefts of weapons and ammunition had increased greatly during the past 6 months.

Groesser had appeared before the Czech National Council Apr. 29 to answer questions by deputies concerned over his allegedly ultraconservative tendencies and persecution-prone frame of mind. He told the Czech parliament of the existence of the "illegal" underground conspiracy and listed types and amounts of arms allegedly stolen from military depots and an ammunition factory in the Czech lands.

Groesser defended his verbal attacks in Trutnov Jan. 11 against ex-Vice Premier Ota Sik (under whom he once studied economics), ex-Foreign Min. Jiri Hajek and Charles University Prof. Vaclav Cerny. Groesser said that Hajek's attitude had raised questions about his loyalty. Dr. Sik had harmed the country by his Basel press conference Dec. 12, Groesser charged, and Dr. Cerny, regarded as the outstanding Czechoslovak expert on Romance literature, was allied with "forces striving for the elimination of the party's leading role and for a rightist reversal."

According to the June 1969 issue of the American magazine *East Europe:* "Observers took the issue of Dr. Cerny as an indication that the Czech Interior Ministry was collecting evidence for an eventual prosecution of prominent reformers. It would be up to the party leadership to decide whether the dossiers should be used as the basis of formal charges."

Groesser, questioned by deputies, said that police had uncovered all "offenders" in the Mar. 28-29 demonstrations "except those in Prague, where people gave them a chance to escape." He added that the Prague city police were in the process of "solving 12 cases, and 2 persons have been cited for criminal proceedings." The Czech Council ordered Groesser to stick to verified facts in his future public pronouncements.

CTK reported May 2 that police in Bohemia and Moravia had arrested 1,225 persons in raids on "criminal and anti-Socialist elements" Apr. 28-30. The police booked 524 persons and detained 141 persons on criminal charges, "mostly violence, theft, etc." Caches of stolen goods reportedly were recovered, including 24 cars, firearms and building materials.

In Prague, May Day celebrations were held in individual districts, rather than as an "all-Prague" parade. The usual celebrations reportedly had been called off to avert the possibility of anti-Soviet disturbances. CTK had appealed to citizens Apr. 24 to decorate their houses with Czechoslovak and red flags

May 1 and with Soviet flags May 9 to commemorate the anniversary of Czechoslovak liberation from Nazi occupation.

A large, pro-American demonstration took place in Plzen May 5, the 24th anniversary of the city's liberation by the U.S. Army. A reported 5,000 demonstrators, some chanting "U.S.A., U.S.A.," clashed with the police. *Rude pravo* reported May 13 that 60 persons had been arrested in Prague May 7-11 for "dishonoring" Soviet flags commemorating the World War II liberation anniversary.

The 24th anniversary of the defeat of Nazi Germany was celebrated May 9. In an article in *Rude pravo,* Husak said the Soviet liberation of the country in 1945 had set the line for its future political development. "We realized," he said, "that the free future of our country was based only on the most friendly relations with the Soviet Union.... [May 9] did not arrive for us as the start of a new way without preconditions." Husak said that the Czechoslovak party would not allow any excesses, and he denied there would be a return of Stalinist policies in Czechoslovakia.

The *Washington Post* reported May 16 that at a secret Federal Interior Ministry meeting May 12-13 ex-Interior Min. Josef Pavel, a progressive, had been criticized for the "destructive results" of his activity during 1968. (Pavel had implemented the program for dismantling the secret police.) At the same meeting, Lubomir Strougal, the conservative chief of the Czech-lands party bureau, had predicted that there would be "political, organizational and particularly cadre measures [personnel changes]" in the press and throughout the government. Sources in Prague reported similar measures under way in the Defense Ministry and armed forces.

A communique issued after a meeting in Moscow May 13 of Brezhnev and ex-Premier Jozef Lenart, a secretary of the Czechoslovak party, indicated Soviet dissatisfaction with the situation in Czechoslovakia. For the first time since Husak succeeded Dubcek as party first secretary, an official Soviet-Czechoslovak document mentioned "difficulties" and the need for "normalization" in Czechoslovakia.

Dubcek, speaking at a peace rally in Terezin, northern Bohemia May 18, appealed for national unity and improved relations with the Soviet Union. It was his first public appearance since his resignation as party first secretary.

In a speech May 19 at a meeting of federal and regional officials Premier Cernik warned:

The experiences of the past few months have confirmed the need for an emphatic restoration of the authority of the Socialist state and of all of its organs. Without this, it is impossible to stabilize the internal policy situation or to progress economically, in politics and in the advancement of the entire Socialist society. In our opinion the difficult tasks confronting us can only be coped with by united action. We are convinced that the efforts of the party to create broad unity in action of the people will be successful because the accomplishment of our tasks and the acceleration of the progressive development of our society is in the most proper interest of each citizen of our country. It will not be easy, however, to establish this unity. The state of our society still lacks much of the required degree of stability. The forces which do not want to be reconciled with the political course of the party and National Front have not yet ceased to count on the possible emergence of new political crises which could hamper our advance. We must also reckon with the fact that they will again attempt to weaken the advance of the party towards the assertion of its decisive ideological influence in the entire structure of our social life.

The spreading of anti-Sovietism hampers our resolute efforts to normalize relations with our allies. The decline in responsibility in the management of the economy produces deteriorating economic results. The process of the unification of the party's actions on the basis of the November resolution and of the conclusions of the April plenum of the party Central Committee frequently takes place at all levels of the party organization in bitter clashes with those people who verbally avow the Central Committee resolutions but who do not recognize them as binding documents in their practical activities....

In the first ministerial-level change since Husak replaced Dubcek as Czechoslovak Communist Party first secretary, Czechoslovak Prosecutor Gen. Milos Cerovsky was dismissed May 22 "at his [own] request" by Pres. Ludvik Svoboda. Cerovsky, appointed in Apr. 1968, was regarded as a moderate identified with the rehabilitation of Stalin-era victims. He had also been connected with efforts in 1968 to create an independent judicial system that would guarantee civil liberties. Slovak jurist Jan Fejes replaced Cerovsky May 23.

Fejes had been a prosecutor in some of the "Vatican spy" trials of 1950-1. Among those he prosecuted were 3 Roman Catholic bishops and a Greek Catholic prelate. Fejes apparently became a scapegoat in similar processes himself later on. Radio Prague said May 23 that he had been a victim of discrimination in the 1950s.

It was also reported May 22 that another moderate, Miroslav Galuska, culture minister in the Czech government, had submitted his resignation.

Regional party purges, which had begun in South Bohemia and North Moravia in May, spread to Central Bohemia May 22 when the Regional Party Committee ousted its secretary, Jaroslav Vitacek, and a member of its presidium, Frantisek Dvoracek. The committee also dismissed the editor-in-chief of the regional party journal, *Svoboda* of Prague. The news agency CTK May 23 reported that the dismissals resulted from internal "right-wing" and "anti-Soviet" tendencies.

Restrictions on the Press

The Prague government named a Federal Committee for Press & Information as the supreme organ of censorship shortly after the changeover in the Czechoslovak party leadership. Federal Min. Jaroslav Havelka was appointed chairman. The other members were: Jan Vigas, chief of Slovak Radio's political broadcasting, vice chairman; Jaroslav Havlin, director of the Czech Press & Information Bureau; Secy. Gen. Stanislav Malecek of the Czech Journalists' Union; CTK director Jindrich Suk; Czechoslovak TV director Josef Smidmajer; Andrej Sarvas, head of the Slovak Radio network; Jozef Vrabec, head of the Slovak TV network; Karel Hravel, Radio Czechoslovakia foreign broadcast director; Bohumil Travnicek, deputy editor of the Slovak party daily *Pravda* (Bratislava); Rudolf Rejhon and Jan Kovalcik.

After the new committee's first meeting, Dr. Havelka said over Radio Prague Apr. 22 that, in the "deep and serious crisis" in which the country found itself, state supervision of the mass communications media must "somehow be increased."

Havelka announced on TV Apr. 22 that additional measures would be taken to tighten control of the press. Havelka said: "If we are to emerge from the present crisis, the mass media must maintain the fundamental line of tactical and strategic aims of government policy." He added: "We need responsible editors and want the press to play an active role. But the state must also play an active role. We would like to provide more information and facts on internal and foreign policy." Havelka claimed that the new restrictions would be only temporary and that the controls would eventually pass to the Czech and Slovak press and information offices.

Havelka's TV announcement followed a meeting of the Communist Party Presidium that day. The meeting reportedly was devoted almost entirely to the subject of mass communications. During its meeting, the Presidium ordered an end to publication of the Central Committee journal *Politika* (it had been suspended Apr. 2) and replaced it with a new weekly, *Tvorba*. Jiri Hajek (no relation to the ex-foreign minister) was named editor-in-chief of the new journal. Hajek had been editor-in-chief until 1968 of *Plamen (The Flame),* a monthly of the Czechoslovak Writers' Union.

Havelka, ordered by the federal government Apr. 28 to elaborate more effective guiding principles to ensure "full conformity" with the country's policies at home and abroad, announced at a journalists' meeting in Ostrava that the committee would organize seminars for Czechoslovak journalists.

The Czech Journalists' Union's central committee, aware that further resistance was dangerous, adopted a resolution urging its membership's support of the Czechoslovak party Central Committee's Apr. 17 decisions and acceptance of preliminary censorship. It called for "voluntary discipline."

Meanwhile, 71 pro-Soviet Czech journalists had formed a new union, the Czech Union of Journalists, it was reported Apr. 24. The breakaway union reportedly had been proposed by Oldrich Svestka, editor of *Tribuna,* the Czech lands party bureau's weekly of the Czechoslovak party Central Committee. The journalists and publicists from Prague and other cities met in the capital Apr. 25 and announced their dissent from the "rightist actions of the representatives of the Czech journalists' union, especially from their [lack of a] ... self-critical attitude and their practical activity in rejection of party policy decisions."

(In the same city that day William N. Oatis, former head of the Associated Press bureau in Prague, and 2 of his Czechoslovak translators were exonerated by a special senate of the Prague Municipal Court of 18-year-old spy charges. The court said Apr. 25 that the charges against Oatis had been rigged to prevent AP from reporting Czechoslovak news. Oatis had been sentenced to 10 years' imprisonment July 4, 1951 but had been released May 16, 1953. The other defendants had been freed under a general amnesty act May 9, 1960.)

The Presidium of the party Central Committee adopted new measures May 6 to tighten controls over the press and mass media. Although the announcement of the Presidium's action did not specify what measures would be taken, it said they would assure "a fundamental change," and observers in Prague expressed fear that the announcement presaged a widescale purge.

CTK reported May 6 that the entire editorial board of *Nova svoboda,* the progressive-toned regional party committee newspaper in Ostrava, northern Moravia, had been dismissed. The board was accused of failing to engage "in the political struggle against rightist, anti-Socialist and anti-Soviet forces." Control over the newspaper was handed to a new 11-man council of "experienced party workers of merit," and Jaroslav Smetana, a known conservative, was appointed to replace Ladislav Bublik as editor. CTK also reported May 6 that a student weekly in Prague, *Studentske listy,* had been banned by the Czechoslovak Press & Information Office.

Rude pravo May 7 published a statement by the Academy of Sciences demanding an end to press censorship. The statement, which had been adopted by the academy Apr. 3, was accompanied by an apology by the newspaper's editor, Jiri Svoboda, for not having published it immediately after its adoption. (The newspaper instead had published an article by 4 staff members of the academy attacking the academy's leadership.) Svoboda said that the academy had demanded the publication of its statement and had asked *Rude pravo* in the future to present "the views and statements of legally elected representatives of the employes of the academy and not replace them by statements of self-styled groups."

The Soviet Czech-language newspaper *Zpravy* ceased publication May 9. *Zpravy* had been circulated in Czecholovakia by Soviet military and civilian personnel since the invasion. Responding to pressure from progressives, the government had announced in November that it had asked Moscow to suspend *Zpravy's* distribution. In its final edition, *Zpravy* declared: "The time has come to mention the fact that there was and is a counterrevolution directed by Western intelligence services and with entirely concrete representatives."

The Czech Press & Information Bureau May 15 banned 2 prominent progressive weeklies and suspended 3 other periodicals. It cancelled the registration of the Czechoslovak Writers' Union's weekly *Listy* and *Reporter,* the weekly news magazine of the Czech Union of Journalists, and suspended for 3 months *Plamen* (published by the Union of Czech Writers), *Svet v obrazech* (the weekly of the Czechoslovak Union of Journalists) and a youth monthly *My 69.* According to CTK, the 5 publications had violated laws forbidding deviations from the programs described in their license applications.

Both *Listy* and *Reporter* had been suspended for short periods in 1968 after the Soviet invasion for publishing anti-Soviet articles. Since November, *Reporter* had been the object of increasingly stringent censorship and Soviet propaganda attacks.

In another move to discipline the press, the Czechoslovak Central Trades Union Council's presidium May 15 criticized the domestic section of its daily, *Prace,* for printing "articles of a theoretical nature which neither helped to strengthen the Socialist social order nor contributed to the new trade union policy." The presidium replaced the editor and made new appointments to the editorial board. Jiri Vancura succeeded Ladislav Velensky as editor. The presidium also tightened control over its weekly, *Svet prace.* The editor, Jan Drda, received a formal warning to correct ideological "mistakes."

The South Bohemian Communist Party Regional Committee May 16 dismissed Jaroslav Sestak, the editor of its newspaper, *Jihoceska pravda,* in Ceske Budejovice. Antonin Bezdecek was named temporary editor. Sestak reportedly had failed to control the paper's political line.

Rude pravo May 17 published a statement entitled "A Word to Our Own Ranks." Signed by 130 pro-Soviet Czech journalists and publicists, it was addressed to workers in the public communications media. It attacked those who had disobeyed party directives and criticized the Dubcek party leadership for having tolerated their activities. The authors of the statement said formal agreement of the Czechoslovak Journalists' Union central committee with party decisions was not enough and that "honest self-criticism is the duty" of all. In their manifesto the supporters of Moscow charged that a large segment of the Czechoslovak media continued to arouse "anti-

Soviet passions" and that high public officials encouraged press attacks on pro-Soviet Communists. The signers of the appeal included Oldrich Svestka, Miroslav Moc and Jan Fojtik and others widely described as dogmatists.

The party Presidium May 20 officially indorsed the manifesto "A Word to Our Own Ranks." The *Washington Post* reported May 23, however, that only a small minority of the country's 4,500 journalists had signed the declaration. Although *Radio Prague* reported May 23 that the signatures were "voluntary," the *Post* said liberal writers believed that the party intended to make the manifesto a test of individual journalists' professional suitability and use it to require more active support for the new leadership in the press. According to the *Post,* some journalists already had left the profession for nonpolitical jobs.

The editorial staff of *Rude pravo,* Czechoslovakia's leading party daily, met May 21 and elected a new hard-line party cell, the *Washington Post* reported May 23. It was also reported that 8 members of the paper's cultural department had resigned and that the paper's circulation had dropped from a 1968 peak of nearly a million copies daily to about 350,000.

Economic Policy

Premier Cernik took part in the meeting of Communist Party and government leaders of the 8 nations of the Council for Mutual Economic Assistance (Comecon) in Moscow Apr. 23-26. (The only substantive decision reported was for the creation of a Comecon investment bank.) On his return to Prague Apr. 27, Cernik commented that the Comecon meeting had been "really extraordinary." He said he was convinced that the meeting had inaugurated a new stage in development of "mutual economic cooperation within the Socialist community."

The federal government, together with the Czech and Slovak governments, adopted new measures May 13 to curb inflation and stabilize the national economy. The immediate effects of the measures were wage-freeze regulations and retail price increases. According to CTK, the measures were taken to deal with (1) mounting inflationary pressures in 1968 caused by an exceptional growth of demand; (2) an excessive number of new construction projects exceeding the building industry's capacity; (3) a disproportionately large number of government grants and subsidies; (4) a "sudden" increase in wages; (5) an unsatisfactory export level. The government previously had introduced corrective measures, but these reportedly had proved inadequate.

The most important of the new measures involved the regulation of wages and wide-ranging price increases on transportation, services, food and consumer items. According to Jiri Typolt, chairman of the Federal Price Committee, the increases were expected to raise retail prices about 2.5% in 1969 and the cost of living 1.7%-3.1%.

Average wages had been scheduled to rise 5.4% and real wages 2.8% under an agreement concluded with the federal government by the workers Nov. 11, 1968. (The London *Times* reported May 14 that prices would be increased for canned meat by 41%, frozen food 34%, coffee 39%, sugar 11% and certain building and plumbing materials 53%.) Typolt assured workers that this agreement would be honored, but the raises already had been outmoded by the inflation. Other measures included a uniform retail turnover tax to end tax aids for unproductive industries and a new tax on farmers. Typolt said that the measures were partial and would be subject to review.

The Central Trades Union Council (CTUC) May 13 opposed the price increases and criticized the government for reneging on pledges to consult it about certain wage measures. The trade unions also demanded an effective price control system and quality control of products. Denouncing the new economic measures, Czechoslovak construction workers May 14 sent to Pres. Svoboda and Premier Cernik a resolution hinting at a work slowdown in the government's housing program if pay raises were not negotiated by the end of 1969.

(The presidium of the Slovak Union of Women had already issued a statement criticizing "the unbearable situation in supplies" and demanding that the government end food shortages. The women said that during May many Slovak shops had been depleted of bread, milk and meat supplies, and they blamed bad management.)

The CTUC told the workers that their raises had been assured for the rest of 1969, the trade union daily *Prace* reported May 17. At a special CTUC plenum May 21, a party presidium member, Karel Polacek, the workers' chief, stressed that the unions would go into their next contract talks with the view that the government should promise in writing to take the necessary steps to guarantee the economy. For their own part, Polacek continued, the unions would pledge to hold off on wage and bonus demands that threatened to intensify a wage-price spiral. He directed the workers' attention to slackening productivity, which he attributed largely to the general confusion attending the country's political vicissitudes of the past 2 years.

As part of its new anti-inflationary policy, the government June 10 introduced a drastic surcharge on the sale of used cars, raising free market prices 120%. The measure, according to a Radio Free Europe report June 10, was adopted because individuals had been selling used cars at prices higher than new cars.

Premier Cernik said in a speech in Brno June 29 that Czechoslovakia's economic problems were increasing and were forcing the government to adopt measures to "prevent further deterioration." The new measures he alluded to included: (1) a pending wage-price freeze; (2) the suspension of incentive bonuses and premiums for workers and (3) the curtailment of capital investment projects. Cernik ruled out currency reform, however, as not among the measures contemplated by the government to curb inflation. In the export trade sector, on which the Czechoslovak economy was heavily dependent, Cernik stressed the necessity of producing high-grade goods cheaply to compete in foreign markets. (The *Washington Post* reported July 5 that during the first 5 months of 1969 Czechoslovakia's overall exports had risen 1% although exports to Comecon nations were down 5%.)

At a plenary meeting of the Czech National Council July 7, Czech Premier Stanislav Razl announced additional measures to deal with the economic crisis. These measures included a factory employment tax to reduce chronic overemployment in industry and the creation of special work brigades to help harvest crops. Razl stressed the need for a "well-functioning harmonious state mechanism" and a more effective role for the state in the economy. (This was taken as a warning that economic decentralization, a characteristic of the middle 1960s, was at an end.) He added that the economic system of management would be "subordinated to set targets" within the framework of central economic planning. Razl disclosed that in the first quarter of 1969 average per capita income had risen 15.9% (25% less than anticipated).

The *Washington Post* had reported July 5 that an expected 5.8% increase in the Czechoslovak production level had not been reached; at best only a 2% increase had been realized. Both textile production and the output of construction materials—essential to overcome the housing shortage—had fallen. Wages for the first quarter of 1969, however, were 14.1% above the equivalent period in 1968. The *Post* said that purchasing power reportedly had risen at a dramatic rate and that Czechoslovaks were indulging in spending sprees in fear of all-out inflation.

Orthodoxy & Centralism Stressed

A plenary meeting of the Czechoslovak Communist Party Central Committee, held May 29-30 at Hradcany Castle in Prague, adopted new party guidelines which in effect marked a return to more orthodox forms of Marxism-Leninism and "democratic centralism." The meeting, the first since Gustav Husak succeeded Alexander Dubcek as first secretary Apr. 17, adopted, on the basis of a report by Husak to the plenum May 29, resolutions dealing with the implementation of political guidelines, party personnel changes, and foreign relations. The Central Committee's decisions were made public May 31 and June 1.

The first part of the Central Committee resolution on policy implementation set the general goals to be achieved by the party. These included (1) the restoration of party unity on the basis of Marxist-Leninist theory; (2) the restoration of party leadership in all areas of the society; (3) the implementation of effective solutions to combat the nation's "grave" economic problems; (4) the elimination of problems in relations with the Soviet Union and other Socialist countries.

The main thrust of the resolution, however, focused on strengthening the party, restoring its unity and reimposing the principle of "democratic centralism." The resolution said: "The Central Committee considers it an imperative condition for the party's ability to fulfill its role that in all party activity the Leninist norms of life and work be observed consistently, particularly democratic centralism.... [The party] cannot allow the principle of the obligatory nature of party decisions or the imperative demand for the observance of statutes to be denied in practice or denied in a programmatic way.... There can only be one party policy, and that is the one approved by the Central Committee."

The need for party discipline was reaffirmed by Husak May 31 in a speech at the CKD (Ceskoslovenska Kolben Danek Engineering) factory in Prague. (The address, nationally televised, constituted a report to the people on the Central Committee meeting.) He declared: "There has been enough freedom and democracy in our organizations and among our people; one might even say that there was an anarchical situation.... We must now stress all the more a disciplined approach to the fulfillment of decisions." Husak, who in his report to the Central Committee May 29 had specifically criticized cultural unions for forming opposition political platforms, warned students, intellectuals and cultural workers not to interfere in politics. He said: 'We shall distinguish very exactly between meritorious work in the fields of science, art and culture and their political abuse for antiparty or even anti-Socialist purposes."

(The party newspaper *Rude pravo* June 5 said that the coordinating committee of the Czech Creative Associations was illegal because of its "political activity outside the ... National Front and [its] variance with the stated program of the ... Front." [This assertion referred to a May 22 CCA coordinating committee report decrying the party's "general offensive against the mass communications media" and warning that "the day of the (party) monologue is returning."] Earlier, a Central Committee resolution of May 30 had warned that no organization, including the Union of University Students, would be permitted to exist outside the Front.)

The Central Committee's resolution on the strengthening of the party extended to the economic sphere. The resolution declared that the economy required "unified planned management, the strengthening of the role of the state and its central organs in economic management." (In his May 29 report, Husak stated that new measures for economic stabilization would include legal measures, such as a law on tax planning. He promised, however, that there would be "no return to the old bureaucratic and administrative methods of economic management.")

(Premier Cernik, speaking on TV with Husak May 31, indicated that the law on Socialist enterprises [aimed at turning individual enterprises into autonomous economic units] would again be postponed because of the controversy raised by the issue of workers' councils. The councils, which Cernik characterized as "basically an interference with existing power structures in Czechoslovakia," had been demanded by the trades unions to assure worker representation on factory management boards. Cernik said that the formation of new councils had been stopped pending their evaluation. The Czechoslovak Central Trades Union Council had demanded May 23 that the government prepare workers' council legislation soon.)

The Central Committee, in its resolution May 30, also announced plans for the party's 14th congress in 1970, to be followed by general parliamentary elections.

Central Committee Ousts Liberals

In line with its declared aim of strengthening the power and role of the party, the Central Committee expelled several known liberals from its own ranks. The expulsions were first disclosed by Husak May 31, when he announced that Frantisek Kriegel, a former chairman of the National Front and public health minister and for 38 years a party member, and Frantisek Vodslon, a deputy in the Federal Assembly, had been ousted because they had voted against the Oct. 15, 1968 Moscow protocol legalizing the presence of Soviet troops in Czechoslovakia. Husak also said that ex-Vice Premier Ota Sik, chief architect of the 1968 economic reform program, had been removed from the Central Committee. A Central Committee statement broadcast later May 31 said that Sik's activities abroad in Switzerland had deviated from the party's political line. The broadcast said: Sik had held political and ideological views that damaged national interests; Kriegel had been ousted from the party for his refusal to recant before the committee.

Kriegel, in a statement before his ouster (reported in full by the *Washington Post* June 5), had asked the Presidium of the Central Committee May 29 to explain why the 1968 protocol had not been subject to formal vote by the party's parliamentary caucus. Kriegel explained that he had voted against the protocol because it had been imposed "in the atmosphere of military occupation without the benefit of consultation with constitutional bodies and in contradiction to the feelings of the people of this country." Kriegel declared that ex-Premier Jozef Lenart, Otokar Simunek and Jiri Hendrych were among those responsible for the terror in the 1950s and that they and ex-Foreign Trade Min. Frantisek Krajcir also had to answer for the current Czechoslovak economic crisis. Kriegel urged that the entire Czechoslovak question be discussed at the world Communist conference opening in Moscow June 5. His defense statement was regarded as the most outspoken denunciation of the Soviet invasion by a leading Czechoslovak public figure. The Central Committee said that he had been ousted from the party for making it.

The public disclosure of Kriegel's statement to the Central Committee evoked strong criticism from official sources. An article in *Rude pravo* June 7 said that Kriegel had been given "ample opportunity to explain his conduct and present attitude and to make a self-critical assessment of his errors" but instead had used the "tribune of the Central Committee for an attack on the party and its policy of friendship with the Soviet Union and the Socialist countries." Kriegel's attitude, the article said, was that "of a man who does not care about the security and freedom of the people of this country." "More than 85%" of the Central Committee had voted to expel Kriegel from the party and the committee, *Rude pravo* said.

A Czechoslovak radio and TV broadcast June 12 warned that it was illegal to circulate copies of Kriegel's speech. The broadcast charged that Kriegel wished to maintain the "crisis in the party" and that his supporters were "acting at variance with the constitution and valid laws of this country."

Rude pravo reported June 12 that Kriegel's speech had been distributed and discussed June 6 at a workers' meeting in Kladno, an industrial city in Bohemia, and had been circulated anong members of the foundry workers union at the Klement Gottwald steel works in Ostrava. The newspaper accused the Ostrava workers of trying to organize "antiparty, antigovernment action hostile to the state." The party committee at the Ostrava plant reportedly suspended the leader of a group of union officials and workers who had visited Kriegel.

Leaders of the Czech Metalworkers' Union urged members June 14 to dissociate themselves from "seditious" pamphlets circulating in industrial plants.

Rude pravo confirmed June 16 that the Kriegel ouster and the decisions of the May 29-30 Central Committee meeting had brought a wave of critical and anonymous letters to the press. It denounced them as "anti-Socialist poison."

The Central Committee statement of May 30 also announced the dismissal of Josef Spacek "at his own request" as party secretary and as a member of the committee's Secretariat. Spacek, who had been removed as secretary of the South Moravian regional party committee in Brno May 26, was elected secretary of the National Front's Central Committee. Karel Neubert, a conservative, was elected to replace Spacek on the Secretariat. Vaclav Slavik also lost his post on the Secretariat. Conservatives, thus reportedly had won control in the body.

3 other Central Committee members, the historian Karel Kosik, the playwright Frantisek Pavlicek and the historian Karel Pavlistik, were expelled because, according to the broadcast, they had refused to dissociate themselves from an "antiparty" document, "2,000 Words." The party reprimanded but did not expel 3 other signers who had recanted: the ex-rector of Charles University Oldrich Stary, Jiri Gokar of the Architects' Union and Martin Vaculik (no relation of the manifesto's author), ex-first secretary of the Prague city party committee. An investigation of the manifesto's organizers and author, Ludvik Vaculik, was ordered.

The Central Committee May 31 announced the establishment of a commission to investigate the activities of government members who had stayed abroad after the invasion, among them Jiri Hajek, former foreign minister and a member of the committee. Although Pres. Svoboda May 26 had issued a decree granting amnesty until Sept. 15 to Czechoslovak citizens who left the country illegally after May 9, 1968, Milos Jakes, chairman of the party's Central Control & Auditing Commission, said May 31 that party members who had not returned by May 1 would have their memberships revoked; those who had been given "unauthorized consent" to extend their stay abroad would be suspended.

Husak said at the CKD factory in Prague May 31 that other expulsions would reach outside the party to eliminate "opportunistic tendencies" in trade unions and the press. In his May 29 report Husak had rejected the possibility of a purge or a "mass checkup on party members," and he promised that the party would not resort to instruments of fear but would use political arguments as its method of persuasion.

In a secret speech to the committee plenum (reported by the West German press agency DPA June 5), Interior Min. Jan Pelnar had advocated increased vigilance against "the activities of Western agents and Western journalists in Prague." Pelnar linked prominent Czechoslovaks to an alleged plan, code-named "Lyautey," said to have been concocted by foreign intelligence agents at the end of 1967 to (1) crush the party and state apparatus, (2) discredit the Interior Ministry, (3) discredit the CP leadership, (4) undermine Soviet confidence in Czechoslovakia and (5) mobilize emigres for hostile activities. Among those allegedly connected with the plan were Eduard Goldstuecker, ex-chairman of the Czechoslovak Writers Union; Ludek Pachman, the chess grand master; Ivan Svitak, a noted Marxist scholar; and Tad Szulc, the *N.Y. Times* correspondent expelled from Prague in 1968.

The West German weekly *Der Spiegel* of Hamburg reported July 14 that Pelnar had cited the existence since 1953 of "Operation Lyautey" as a British-led secret service activity cooperating with "anti-Socialist powers" in Czechoslovakia to subvert the Czechoslovak state. The operation was said to derive its name from Marshal-of-France Louis Hubert Lyautey (1854-1934), a famous colonial warrior. Lyautey, it was said, had once asked his gardener to have the road to the Lyautey chateau lined with stately trees. When the gardener protested that the process would take 50 years, the marshal is said to have replied: "Then we must certainly plant them today."

According to *Der Spiegel,* Pelnar charged that the ring-leaders of "Operation Lyautey" by Jan. 1968 were: Goldstuecker; Pachman; Emil Ludvik, who had been a secretary to the late Pres. Eduard Benes; Pavel Tigrid, editor of the Paris-based exile monthly *Svedectvi;* Svitak, ex-philosophy lecturer at Prague's Charles University and currently at Columbia University in New York; Benno G. Weigl, an exile in London, who had written under the pen-name Michael Rand on the subject of ex-Foreign Min. Jan Masaryk's death; Vilem Blazej, ex-general secretary of the Czechoslovak Social Democratic Party, currently in England; Cecil C. Parrott, ex-British ambassador to Prague; Deryck Viney, British Broadcasting Corp. correspondent in London; and Szulc, whom Pelnar described as an "experienced cadre specialist of the [U.S.] Central Intelligence Agency."

The entire presidium of the Prague city party committee, including its first secretary, Bohumil Simon, resigned June 2. The committee had met June 2 for an extraordinary session, attended by Husak, at which the presidium reportedly had voiced dissent at the newly adopted Central Committee decisions, particularly the expulsions. Simon, a strong Dubcek supporter, was replaced by Oldrich Matejka, a pro-Soviet member of the party's Czech Bureau and a secretary of the Prague committee.

The Central Committee announced June 1 that the Czechoslovak delegation to the Moscow summit conference of Communist parties would move that the question of the 1968 invasion be excluded from consideration. It said that it opposed any efforts to make Czechoslovakia a "subject of discussion" because the party did not have at its disposal a "complete analysis of the causes and results of the pre-January and post-January [1968] policy."

Husak's May 29 report to the committee had stressed that "the serious problems which arose in 1968 between us and our allies can only be solved by us in mutual agreement and confidence with our Warsaw Pact partners. The tendencies to internationalize the so-called Czechoslovak question, in whatever form they may occur, can only be assessed by the Central Committee as an effort which, irrespective of its motives, serves neither the vital needs of our party nor the international interests of the Communist movement." In his TV address May 31, Husak, who was scheduled to lead the delegation to Moscow, said that the "fraternal" Communist parties of the Warsaw Pact had watched events in the spring of 1968 "until they gradually lost their confidence that the leadership of our party was able to restore order by its own means." (Following a meeting with Polish United Workers' Party First Secy. Wladyslaw Gomulka in Warsaw May 24, Husak, for the first time, had indorsed the principle of "proletarian internationalism," thus reportedly implying the Prague government's approval of the invasion and the presence of Soviet troops in Czechoslovakia.)

Communist officials and miners in Ostrava, Northern Moravia were disclosed by *Rude pravo* June 5 to have demanded that the Prague leadership "reassess" and "adopt a correct international and Marxist attitude" toward the Presidium's declaration of Aug. 21, 1968, which had disavowed knowledge or approval of the invasion then under way.

The Czechoslovak party Presidium June 3 elected the pro-Soviet conservative Lubomir Strougal to the new post of deputy party first secretary. It was announced that Strougal would continue to direct the Central Committee's Czech affairs bureau, which he had headed since its creation in Nov. 1968.

Although the Presidium announcement gave no reason for the election, it came amid reports of growing contest for power between Strougal and Husak. In his capacity as Czech bureau chief—a post said to have political power independent of the Czechoslovak party—Strougal had been considered the driving force behind the expulsion of reformists in Bohemian and Moravian regional and local party organizations.

In addition to his responsibility for managing the Central Committee, the Presidium gave Husak "concrete responsibility" for the committee's defense, security and political organization departments. (The party leader, in his report to the Central Committee plenum May 29, had stressed the need to "strengthen, particularly politically, the army and security forces," which he said should "be more firmly guided by the party Central Committee.")

The Presidium June 3 also confirmed the creation May 30 of 3 new Central Committee departments and their respective heads: economy—Jozef Lenart; ideology and party policy in the mass media, schools, science and culture—Josef Kempny; agriculture—Jarolim Hettes. Other party appointments confirmed: Vasil Bilak, foreign affairs; Alois Indra, state administration and social organizations; Josef Penc, party work in industry, transport and communications. (The party Central Committee May 30 had approved the establishment of 2 commissions for the Czech affairs bureau: an economic commission headed by Vaclav Hula and a political and legal commission under Bureau Secy. Oldrich Prusa.)

More Progressives Ousted

Milos Jakes, chairman of the Czechoslovak Communist Party Central Control & Auditing Commission (the party investigative body), outlined measures for imposing the party's new conservative policy. He announced June 12 that 2,000 local and factory control and auditing commissions had been elected to "wage a decisive struggle for the implementation of party policy." Speaking at a nationwide conference of local commission chairmen in Prague, Jakes said the expulsion of "rightist-opportunist forces" from politics was a precondition for a transition to normality in Czechoslovakia. Stressing ideological conformity, Jakes warned commission chairmen not to overlook party officials who "declare that the resolutions of the Central Committee plenary meetings are not binding on them, that they disagree with them and that they will not fulfill them, that they go against their conscience."

In an apparent reference to solidarity agreements signed by students, workers and journalists after the 1968 Soviet invasion, Jakes said the party would forbid "worker-student or worker-intelligentsia fronts without the party, against the party and against its policy." Jakes also warned that party members who did not dissociate themselves from the coordinating committee of the Czech cultural unions would be "called to party responsibility." The control commission chairmen were urged to help local party bodies annul resolutions they had passed condemning the invasion and demanding the withdrawal of Soviet troops. Jakes said these resolutions were contrary to the "principles of proletarian internationalism."

In connection with the "2,000 Words" manifesto circulated in support of the Dubcek regime in 1968, Jakes said that signers must publicly dissociate themselves from the manifesto and withdraw their signatures. In cases "where there is no response to persuasion, action should be taken in the spirit of party rules," he said. Similar action would be applied to "certain Communist editors" and journalists who had an "unhealthy professional solidarity." Jakes said that the party would continue to rehabilitate Communists who, "because of their firm party standpoint on international relations, have been discriminated against in the recent past."

The Communist Party's Czech Affairs Bureau June 16 issued a communique denouncing reformists, who had "influenced a comparatively large section of the population in general and of Communists in particular." Even party ideological officials had been affected, the communique charged.

The bureau's political-legal department June 26 recommended faster action on a proposed press law imposing stricter censorship. It urged a swift "transition from preventive control of the press to effective ... control." (The suspension of Ludek Pachman, a writer and chess champion, who had denounced the party's conservative program at an unauthorized rally of foundry workers in Ostrava, was announced by the bureau June 26.)

Party Deputy First Secy. Lubomir Strougal announced a further campaign against progressives June 17. Strougal's announcement followed a statement issued by the party's Czech Affairs Bureau June 16 that it had become the party's task "to defeat the political platform of ... [the liberal] forces, to isolate their representatives, to split their centers of organization and to restrict their possibilities of influencing public opinion." Declaring that some party members had resorted to "obstructionist" tactics, Strougal remarked that "a serious destruction of valid Marxist-Leninist principles and values took place" during the 1968 liberalization period.

In June and July these resignations and appointments were reported:

- Bohuslav Chnoupek, a reportedly conservative journalist, was named director of Czechoslovak Radio June 19 to succeed Odon Zadovsky, acting director since January. It was announced that Zadovsky would return to his original post as the radio's Ostrava branch chief. Chnoupek, a former deputy minister of culture and information, was sworn in June 24.

- Slovak economist Eugen Loebl (according to a Radio Free Europe situation report June 25) resigned from the party June 19, reportedly because the party leadership refused to denounce the invasion of Czechoslovakia at the Moscow summit conference in June. CTK announced July 23 that the party had expelled Loebl because of activities abroad contrary to the party line. Loebl had been a former secretary general of the party and a deputy minister of foreign trade before his arrest and conviction as a traitor, spy and saboteur late in 1952. Loebl had been pardoned in 1956, exonerated in 1963 and had served as director of the Bratislava state bank until 1968.

- The Czechoslovak Academy of Sciences accepted the resignation of Ota Sik June 26 as director of the Economic Institute and chairman of the Scientific Council for the Economy. Sik, author of the 1967-8 economic reform program, was succeeded in both posts by Karl Kouba. As former chairman of the Academy's Czechoslovak Economic Association, Kouba reportedly had defended Sik's economic model when it was criticized by the Soviet Union in Sept. 1968.

- The Central Committee Presidium June 30 announced the appointment of Jan Fojtik, reportedly a conservative, as head of the Higher Party School, the ideological training school for party officials. The statement did not mention Fojtik's predecessor Milan Huebl, who had been suspended from his functions in June and reportedly was under investigation by a special party commission for "repeated critical comments" from within the party.

- Karel Kyncl, well-known journalist and TV editor, was suspended from the party and placed under investigation for criticizing the party's pro-Soviet policy, CTK reported July 9.

- Radio Prague announced July 10 that Czech Culture Min. Miroslav Galuska had been replaced at his own request. He was succeeded by Miroslav Bruzek, reportedly a hardliner who had been head of the Central Committee's cultural section.

• Josef Smidmajer was released Aug. 6 as central director of Czechoslovak Television. He was replaced by Jan Zelenka.

Party First Secy. Gustav Husak said at a national conference of regional and district leading party secretaries June 26 that he was pleased by the struggle waged by the provincial apparatus against "rightist-opportunist" tendencies. He said, however, that "cadre shifts" were still continuing in regional and district committees.

A new wave of regional purges was revealed July 1 in an announcement on Radio Prague that the entire presidium of the North Bohemian regional party committee had been forced to resign in Usti-nad-Labem that day. A plenary session of the committee annulled its previous resolutions concerning the invasion of Czechoslovakia, which were at variance with the party's current conservative policy. It also elected Antonin Krcek, a hard-liner, as leading secretary.

At plenary sessions in Brno June 20 and July 1, the regional party committee of Southern Moravia accepted the resignations of regional party committee Secy. Ladislav Manousek, of Vladimir Lenc, the Brno city party committee's leading secretary, and of Karel Slavik, the leading secretary of the Blansko district. The editor of the regional party daily *Rovnost,* Bohumil Marcak, was also dismissed.

Miroslav Kindl, editor of the North Moravian regional party daily *Pruboj,* was replaced July 1 by Jaroslav Duchek.

A Radio Free Europe situation report said Aug. 5 that a reshuffle of party posts in Slovakia was under way. It also reported that purges had affected nearly half the Czech districts.

The district committee of central Prague, whose membership included many intellectuals and Charles University faculty members, was accused by *Rude pravo* July 28 of using its information bulletin to "spread right-opportunist opinions" and to pressure the party Central Committee in the direction of anti-Sovietism and anarchy. *Rude pravo* indicated that a purge would follow.

(The Czech Affairs Bureau of the Czechoslovak party Central Committee named its chief, Lubomir Strougal, to head the Czech National Defense Council July 7. The council, a newly created addition to the federal Czechoslovak Defense Organization headed by Husak, was expected to strengthen and reorganize security in Bohemia and Moravia through a new system of local defense councils to be established alongside party regional committees. Strougal personally appointed the chairmen and members of the regional councils at the council's first meeting July 8. The Czech Affairs Bureau July 7 also appointed Strougal as commander of the Czech People's Militia, the party's paramilitary organization.)

Journalists Meet, Writers Reorganize

The Czech Journalists' Union June 9 elected a new presidium and reelected the union's chairman, Vladimir Kaspar. Jiri Rouml and Jiri Lederer, former staff members of the banned weekly *Reporter,* were dropped from the presidium. Kaspar delivered the principal speech, and the union then restated the "fundamental position" it had adopted Apr. 26; it provided for continuing loyalty to both the "action program" and the party Central Committee resolution Nov. 17, 1968.

Kaspar, who had supported the reform movement in 1968, explained that the charges against journalists were necessary to restore a dialogue with the party leadership. The union agreed to set up a commission to prepare a self-critical document acknowledging journalists' faults during the 1968 reform period, but it refused to accept responsibility for stirring up anti-Soviet feelings among the Czechoslovak people. (The party's Czech Affairs Bureau June 26 rebuked the union for its refusal.) Kaspar also rejected the May 17 manifesto, signed by pro-Soviet journalists, which accused journalists of instigating an anti-Soviet campaign.

Taking over as the union's new vice chairmen were Zdenek Fort, editor of *Zemedelske noviny,* considered a progressive; Jindrich Jirka, economic editor of *Rude pravo,* a moderate progressive and supporter of the progressive economic reforms; Bohumil Marcak, editor of the South Moravian regional party daily *Rovnost* (Brno), a moderate progressive; and Oldrich Vondrak, North Moravian bureau editor in Ostrava for *Lidova demokracie,* the People's Party daily.

The presidium's 7 other members, with the exception of Jan Vencovsky, employed in the press section of the party Central Committee secretariat, were professional journalists considered free of dogmatism. They were: Stanislav Malecek, chief secre-

tary of the union; Frantisek Kaucky, general secretary of the
Center of Czechoslovak Journalists; Jindrich Suk, director of
CTK, the official news agency; Vladimir Prikazsky, editor of
the Czechoslovak State Radio Network; Arnost Frydrych,
editor of the Czechoslovak State Television Network; Rene
Frauhauf, economic editor of *Rude pravo*.

Czechoslovak Party First Secy. Gustav Husak laid down
the party's law to the country's journalists at Prague's
Congress Palace July 2 at a special meeting to which 500 party
journalists were summoned by the party Presidium. The
Presidium June 30 had attributed to the communications
media—"including the party press"—the fault of having served
as sources of encouragement for a "marked increase" in subversive activities radiating from "foreign anti-Communist
centers since the beginning of ... [1968]."

Husak chided the journalists for failing to grasp the necessity of interpreting the concepts of freedom and democracy
from the working-class point of view. The journalists adopted,
495-1 (with 4 abstentions), a resolution drafted at the direction
of Central Committee Secy. Josef Kempny in charge of party
and ideological work in the media. It consisted of 6 guidelines:

● An order to "paralyze and isolate rightist-opportunist forces
in the mass communications media, oppose antiparty views and
maintain Marxist-Leninist positions."

● A command to "strengthen international Socialist conscious-
ness and propagate friendship with the Soviet troops temporarily" occupying the country.

● Instructions to make ready a campaign for the silver anniversary of the Slovak Uprising (Aug. 29, 1944) and of the
Battle of Dukla Pass (Sept. 8, 1944), another for the centennial
of Lenin's birth (Apr. 22, 1870) and one for the 25th anniversary of the Soviet liberation of Czechoslovakia and Prague
(May 9, 1945).

● An admonition to "follow basic party documents consistently" in working out "a concrete outline of ideological
preparations for the [coming] 14th [party] congress in all [news-
paper and magazine] bureaus."

● A warning to "strengthen party organizations in editorial
offices so that they may guarantee the implementation of party
policies."

● The demands that "Communists in the professional journalistic associations [the Czechoslovak, Czech and Slovak journalists' unions] display greater support for the Apr. [17] and May [30] 1969 Czechoslovak Communist Party Central Committee resolutions" and that "these institutions [the 3 unions] dissociate themselves from those individuals who have been in the forefront of right-wing opportunist endeavors."

The founding congress of the Czech Writers' Union June 10 elected what was described as a progressive 30-member Central Committee, and Jaroslav Seifert was elected as the new union's president. The Central Committee members included Ludvik Vaculik, author of the "2,000 Words" manifesto, Milan Jungmann, former editor of *Listy;* and Eduard Goldstuecker, ex-president of the old Czechoslovak Writers' Union.

The congress adopted a final resolution, which the press in Prague did not publish, on the problem of censorship and the methods used by the Czechoslovak Press & Information Bureau. The resolution appealed to the federal and Czech assemblies to investigate the legality of measures taken against the press, which were said to be "without parallel in the history of Czechoslovak policy concerning culture, both in extent and scope." The resolution also protested the banning of *Listy,* the journal of the former Czechoslovak Writers' Union.

The constituent congress of the Slovak Writers' Union, held June 11 in Bratislava, elected a central committee and chose Vojtech Mihalik, a noted Slovak poet and writer, as the union's chairman. Pavel Horov and Andrej Plavka were elected deputy chairmen.

Student & Worker Opposition

Prague Radio announced May 22 the resignation of Chairman Jan Trencansky of the Czech Union of Students. He had been elected to the post in April. Trencansky, in his letter of resignation, said that he disagreed with the members of the union's presidium and that their activities would cause the union's "liquidation." An article in *Rude pravo* May 22 warned that the Interior Ministry had the right to ban the student union for refusing to join the National Front, which incorporated all legal organizations and political parties. Josef Korcak, chairman of the Czech National Front, announced in a news conference the same day that the front would deal with the student organization, which represented 60,000 students in Bohemia and Moravia.

The Interior Ministry June 20 dissolved the Czech Union of Students for violating sections of the law on public order concerning voluntary organizations. A decree by the ministry justified the decision by citing speeches and published statements by union leaders and by citing other of the group's activities that were allegedly contrary to "important foreign policy interests" of the state, to the Socialist economic system and to the constitution. The ministry charged that the union had engaged in political activity reserved only for members of the National Front. The ministry noted that the union had refused to join the Front at its congress held Apr. 25-27 in Olomouc. (In an interview with the London *Times* June 23, Karel Kovanda, the union's acting president, conceded that financial advantages came with membership in the National Front, but he noted that accepting them "would make us supporters of the present leadership.")

A resolution reportedly passed by the Czech union rejected the ministry's action as the repressive decision of "a bureaucratic power center that temporarily has taken over power in Czechoslovakia." It declared that "activity of student organizations cannot be canceled by an administrative act and cannot be limited by repression of any sort." The student union promised to continue working for the reforms instituted by Alexander Dubcek.

Radio Prague reported June 24 that a preparatory committee for a new Student Union of the Czech Socialist Republic had been set up. The committee issued a statement describing itself as representing students in favor of joining the National Front, in which it would become politically active. The new committee said it would strive to "create the broadest possible scope in political, social and group-interest activities" and would continue to work with the trade unions.

In a display of worker-student solidarity, workers at the CKD factories in Prague threatened to strike after workers' delegates June 23 had informed Vlastimir Toman, head of the 900,000-man Metal Workers Union, that the ministry's ban on the Czech Union of Students had caused widespread discontent.

Although the strikes did not materialize, locomotive workers at the CKD plant participated in a 15-minute work stoppage.

Growing resentment over party domination of Czechoslovakia's trade unions was expressed in a resolution adopted by union officials of the SONP (United Steelworks National Enterprise) Kladno steelworks May 27. The resolution, which rejected "the differentiation of trade union functionaries according to political affiliations," in effect demanded equal status for Communists and non-Communists. *Rude pravo,* which had been conducting a campaign against activities of so-called "right-wing unionists," denounced the resolution June 16, charging that such a policy "would mean the party's giving up its influence in the trade unions."

The London *Times* reported June 24 that the works committees of Prague's 20 largest industrial plants had decided to begin July 1 to withhold membership dues from the central trade union organizations. The purpose of the action reportedly was to show disapproval of leaders who had failed to comply with a request to discuss trade union demands. The committees, however, agreed to continue to pay their union dues to the 900,000-member Czech Metal Workers Union.

In a statement issued from Kladno after a meeting June 6, the works committees of 8 mills and foundries had called on the union's central committee to take a stand on several "basic questions." These included (1) the official pressure against worker-student contacts; (2) a ban issued May 28 by the Czech Interior Ministry against the Society for Human Rights (an intellectuals' group formed after World War II, suppressed by the Communists after 1948 and revived in 1968 to protect personal freedoms within the law); (3) the postponement of the law of Socialist enterprises; (4) a strike and sit-down demonstration at a longshoremen's union hall by Prague shipbuilding workers preempting the hall May 28 against the Czechoslovak-Soviet Friendship Society, a pro-Moscow organization; and (5) the possibility of a conflict of interest in the tenure by Central Trades Union Council Chairman Karel Polacek of his high party post as a Presidium member. The statement also protested the suppression of the party's reform "action program" adopted in Apr. 1968 and the increased press restrictions as being incompatible with "the ethics of an advanced Socialist society." The statement warned trade union leaders that if the situation continued, workers would protest "in extreme cases by the most effective means at our disposal."

Rude pravo subsequently disclosed June 25 that payment of party dues had declined sharply in Czech areas. In some areas ⅓ of all party members reportedly were 3 months or more in arrears. *Rude pravo* said 17.48% of the local party organizations had not settled their arrears, as compared with 5.03% in 1967. In areas where party members were paying dues, the local organizations apparently had banked the money locally and collected the interest "as a sign of disagreement with policy." *Rude pravo* reported that the party's Czech Affairs Bureau had issued instructions for disciplinary proceedings against the party committees that had failed to forward their dues. According to party statutes, any member 3 or more months in arrears would be open to expulsion from the party.

Trade unions and workers drew criticism from both party First Sec. Gustav Husak and Premier Oldrich Cernik June 26. Husak announced that a concerted ideological effort to unify the party line would be carried down to local and factory organizations. He said "rightist-opportunist" forces had gained key positions in various works committees because of the weakened role of Communists in the trade unions in 1968.

Cernik denounced the "considerable drop in work discipline" among workers and criticized those "who think it is possible to work 4½ days a week and turn out goods of inferior quality and at the same time demand cheap products, low railroad and transit fares and plenty of foreign currency for traveling abroad."

In urging stricter labor legislation, Czech Premier Stanislav Razl July 7 accused the Czech labor force of idleness, slovenly work, lack of discipline and an attitude of laissez-faire.

At a meeting of the Central Council of the Revolutionary Trade Union Movement July 9, Husak announced a purge of "hostile elements" from trade unions, including the chairmen and members of works committees.

Workers at Czechoslovakia's largest steel mill in Ostrava posted a letter from chess champion Ludek Pachman that "rudely attacked" Husak, *Rude pravo* reported July 12. Pachman, who in late June had been suspended from the party, apparently had written the letter in response to an invitation to participate in a forum at the plant. The letter reportedly caused a 2-hour work stoppage while workers read and then voted indorsement of its contents. *Rude pravo* said action would be taken against the factory's union leadership for its "provocative attempt to affect the efforts of the party." (*Rude pravo* conceded July 24 that unrest among Ostrava workers had reached serious proportions and warned that hostile forces in the Klement Gottwald steelworks would be fought "consistently and more resolutely.")

A *Rude pravo* article reported by CTK Aug. 1 described right-wing opportunist activities at the No. 3 Works of the Klement Gottwald New Foundry in Ostrava, where allegedly anti-party and anti-Socialist elements had "set out on an entirely adventurous and anti-popular road" and where a selfless party official had been put under harsh surveillance by "all staff members," who did not excuse his slightest fault, while workers "daily crowded round the notice boards to read provocative leaflets and spend hours of working time in debate, with no one saying a word against it." In another report, the paper said that following criticism of "opportunist tendencies" in the Ostrava-Poruba party committee, many members had resigned from the local party organization. 7 members of the committee had been suspended from membership.

Rude pravo reported Aug. 1 that a "fanatical" provocation had taken place at the Avia-Letnany aircraft plant in Prague, where a visiting Soviet delegation had been prevented July 29 from entering the factory. Workers reportedly threw stones at the Moscow party delegation led by the Soviet party Politburo candidate member V. V. Grishin. *Rude pravo* gave prominence to a "condemnation of the provocation" by the factory's works committee and the Prague city party committee's presidium, which denounced this "irresponsible and antiparty conduct of political provocateurs." It was reported that the factory works committee had immediately investigated the affair and "ensured the exposure of the organizers." Prague's 9th District party committee had decided to take suitable measures against the culprits and had asked the Prague city party committee to make sure that Communists in the Prague Trade Union Council dealt with officials in the works trade union committee who had been involved in the "provocation."

2D PHASE OF HUSAK REGIME

Invasion Anniversary Riots

The first anniversary of the Soviet invasion was marked by protest demonstrations in Prague and other Czechoslovak cities Aug. 19-22. Disregarding government warnings, demonstrators conducted massive, orderly protests against the Soviet actions and the Husak regime. At least 5 persons were killed in Prague and Brno. Violence also occurred in Usti-nad-Labem, Liberec, Ostrava and Bratislava. The demonstrations, which were quelled by police and Czechoslovak army troops, culminated in tighter police controls and new emergency laws issued by the government Aug. 22.

The London *Times* had reported June 28 that a 10-point plan by students and workers had been circulating in Prague and had included the proposal that the anniversary be observed as a "day of shame" and mourning. Citizens were asked, in part: (1) to avoid using municipal transportation; (2) to boycott stores, restaurants, theaters, coffeehouses and movie houses; (3) to buy no newspapers; (4) to halt all work for 5 minutes at noon; (5) to decorate memorials; and (6) to halt all vehicles at noon.

Other leaflets circulated in July urged the population not to be tricked by fraudulent appeals for violence or insurrection and not to stage general strikes. Czechoslovaks were warned that Soviet agents would stage "provocations" as pretexts for further curtailment of freedoms or for a coup to bring additional pro-Soviet leaders to power. The Czech Metal Workers Union appealed to its 900,000 workers July 25 to avoid anti-Soviet acts on the anniversary.

Prague radio July 31 reported a statement issued by the Usti-nad-Labem regional prosecutor's office on the dissemination in the North Bohemian region of illegal pamphlets in which leading party and state representatives allegedly were attacked "in a rude manner" and in which citizens reportedly were incited to anti-party and anti-Socialist actions. The statement particularly warned factory and office workers at all levels to "oppose such attempts to incite people and to provoke crisis situations." Czech Deputy Interior Min. Jaroslav Kubik said in a broadcast that some leaflets were "very dangerous in their contents, because they call for rash acts and ... violent criminal acts." The public was largely unaware that the distribution of these leaflets was contrary to the law, Kubik said. He added that action was being taken against those who had been duplicating and distributing them. (Police Col. Kubik had alleged July 30 in the Czech Party Affairs Bureau's organ, *Tribuna,* that raiders had made several attacks on sentries at Czech armories and had taken "dozens of kilograms of explosives and a considerable number of weapons.")

Acknowledging the wide distribution of the leaflets, the Czechoslovak government—joined in the effort by Revolutionary Trade Union Movement and church officials—had appealed repeatedly for calm on the anniversary. The government instructed courts and prosecutors Aug. 14 "to procede immediately and with all severity" against persons who threatened public order. It announced that the army and the People's Militia would help the police maintain "calm, public order and security." The government warned plant managers that they would be held personally responsible for any disturbance or disruption of production.

The Soviets showed their concern by summoning Czechoslovak party First Sec. Gustav Husak and Pres. Ludvik Svoboda to the Crimea for consultations with Soviet leaders. Husak and Svoboda arrived at Simferopol Aug. 2. They were met by Soviet party leader Leonid Brezhnev, Pres. Nikolai Podgorny, other Soviet officials and Czechoslovak party Central Committee Secy. Alois Indra, vacationing in the area. The secrecy enveloping their visit prompted some observers in the West to surmise that the Soviets were applying pressure for a declaration of the invasion's validity. It also was thought that the Soviets wanted assurances that Czechoslovaks would not demonstrate their dissatisfaction publicly. The Soviet party organ *Pravda* Aug. 3 termed the invasion "absolutely correct and timely." Contrary to custom, neither country issued a communique on the Crimean talks at their close Aug. 10.

In a nationally televised address Aug. 17, Pres. Svoboda warned against alleged foreign subversion, which, he said, was inciting unrest. Svoboda denied that the USSR planned to annex Czechoslovakia.

In a speech instructing party functionaries on how to deal with anti-Soviet disturbances, Husak Aug. 19 rejected the portrayal of Czechoslovakia as a Soviet-occupied country. Czechoslovakia, he said, "is a fully sovereign, independent state, politically, economically and militarily." Speaking before 10,000 party members at the Julius Fucik Park of Recreation & Culture, Husak said that only the party's Central Committee would be able finally to assess the events of Aug. 1968. But he attributed the invasion and occupation to the failure of ex-party First Secy. Alexander Dubcek to strengthen Prague-Moscow relations, curb the news media and fight anti-Communist and rightist forces. Husak asserted that promises to Moscow had been broken and that the public had remained uninformed about high-level negotiations among Warsaw Treaty nations during the 1968 crisis—including an unpublicized bilateral discussion near Bratislava between Dubcek and Hungarian party First Secy. Janos Kadar Aug. 17, 1968. Husak added that Soviet leaders had warned Prague repeatedly that the situation in Czechoslovakia was deteriorating. Husak pledged that the government would defeat all subversive forces in the country, and he warned that any hostile demonstrations on the anniversary would be repressed. He promised that Czechoslovak authorities would "no longer" permit anti-Communist elements to "turn the state into a Wild West."

Only hours after Husak's warning, disorders erupted in Prague's half-mile-long Wenceslas Square Aug. 19. Shouting "Gestapo!" hundreds of students clashed with the police, who reportedly beat demonstrators with clubs. At 8 p.m., armored cars began to chase the demonstrators along the square and dispersed the estimated crowd of 1,000 with tear gas. Scores of demonstrators were detained.

A 9-hour demonstration Aug. 20 ended with police and army troops using armored cars and battling demonstrators with tear gas and water cannons. Some soldiers reportedly fired submachine guns over the heads of the demonstrators. The government announced Aug. 21 that 2 persons had been killed and more than 320 arrested during the demonstrations in Prague.

Czechoslovak army reinforcements moved into the center of Prague early Aug. 21 and took control of major intersections. Other units waited in readiness in suburban industrial plants, streetcar terminals and other installations. None of the Soviet occupation troops joined the Czechoslovak army units, although Soviet staff officers had been flown into Prague the night of Aug. 20. (A Soviet delegation headed by Gen. Aleksei Yepishev, political chief of the armed forces, returned to Moscow Aug. 21 after a 16-day visit to Czechoslovakia.)

At noon Aug. 21, a crowd estimated at 50,000 converged on Wenceslas Square chanting "Russians go home," "Long live Dubcek" and "Husak is a traitor." Chanting and car-horn blasting was permitted for 40 minutes before police and army units fired tear gas and moved in to clear the square. Shops and public transportation were boycotted during the day, while thousands stopped work for short intervals. At night the Czechoslovak army sent more than 100 tanks to disperse the crowd in Wenceslas Square.

CTK reported Aug. 21 that the country was quiet except for "attempts at riots" in Prague, Liberec and Brno. An estimated crowd of 5,000 students clashed with army troops and club-swinging police in Brno Aug. 22 following a wreathlaying ceremony for 3 persons killed in anti-Soviet demonstrations earlier in the week.

CTK reported Aug. 25 that 1,893 persons had been detained on political charges in Bohemia and Moravia, 1,239 of them in Prague, during the anniversary demonstrations. The Czechoslovak news agency said that disturbances had also occurred in Ostrava and Usti-nad-Labem; "isolated rallies of several hundred demonstrators" were reported in the Slovak capital of Bratislava.

The Prague city party committee had reported Aug. 22 that 66 foreigners had been arrested during the demonstrations Aug. 21. One of these was Thomas Engel, 23, an assistant accompanying U.S. Rep. Allard K. Lowenstein (D., N.Y.). Lowenstein said he had been tear-gassed 4 times during the demonstrations Aug. 21.

In an effort to restore law and order, the Federal Assembly Aug. 22 adopted emergency laws extending to Dec. 31; they broadened police powers and instituted summary court proceedings for political offenders. The laws, announced in an order signed by Pres. Svoboda, Premier Cernik and Federal Assembly Chairman Dubcek, included: (1) stiffer prison terms for disorderliness, defamation of other Socialist states and harming Czechoslovakia's interests abroad; (2) antistrike provisions, including fines or arrest for laxity at work; and (3) the expulsion of students and the firing of workers involved in protest demonstrations. Legal protections, such as pretrial hearings and access to evidence, were suspended. The new laws also allowed a 3-week detention of suspects "to ascertain if they are organizers of actions which disturb the public order."

Cernik said Aug. 23 that "anti-Socialist and counter-revolutionary elements" had organized protest riots in an attempt to overthrow the government. A Radio Prague broadcast the same day demanded that those responsible for the rioting "be removed from public life." The 2 statements hinted at more arrests and the removal of some government officials.

The Soviet party newspaper *Pravda* Aug. 20 expressed approval of the "firm hand" used by Czechoslovak leaders in dealing with the protests. *Pravda* did not mention the police action against the Prague demonstrators. In general, the Soviet press reported the anniversary briefly, using the CTK reports.

Communist China marked the anniversary with nationwide broadcasts Aug. 20. Peking attacked the USSR for "its suppression of the Czechoslovak people."

U.S. State Secy. William P. Rogers Aug. 20 termed the anniversary of the invasion a "grim reminder" of difficulties regarding peace talks with the Soviet Union. He described the Soviet actions since Aug. 20, 1968 as a "profound tragedy" for peace, security and justice.

(The Prague office of the *N.Y. Times* was ordered closed Aug. 21 and its correspondent Paul Hofmann expelled from the country. A Foreign Ministry statement said the action was not taken against Hofmann personally but against the *Times,* which had "intentionally distorted the situation [in Czechoslovakia] and in its editorials [had] launched flagrant attacks on the leading representatives of Czechoslovak political life."

(The *Washington Post* reported Aug. 27 that all Western newspapers had been banned in Czechoslovakia since Aug. 21.

(The Czechoslovak Foreign Ministry informed London *Times* correspondent Michael Hornsby Aug. 28 that his accreditation would not be renewed when it expired at the end of August. His expulsion, a ministry official said, resulted from his "gross distortion" of the situation in Czechoslovakia.)

The Czechoslovak government, party and press reported extensively Aug. 25-Sept. 1 on the demonstrations.

The Interior Ministry reported Aug. 25 that of 3,690 people arrested during the three days of rioting, 1,893 were still in custody.

In a report Sept. 1 to the defense and security committee of the House of the People (one of the Federal Assembly's 2 chambers), Deputy Interior Min. Frantisek Vasek disclosed official figures on the 3 days of demonstrations in Prague and Brno. Vasek said that 2,414 persons had been detained, including 2,003 under 25 years old. He also said that 416 of those arrested had served prior prison terms for criminal offenses. Vasek estimated that property damage in Prague and Brno had totaled 4.8 million crowns (officially about $666,667). Vasek said that 424 soldiers, police, members of the militia and firemen had been hurt, 48 of them seriously, but only 37 demonstrators had been injured. (The London *Times* had reported Aug. 26 that at least 70 civilians had been hospitalized in Prague, with one hospital alone treating 60 victims of police clubbings. Other Western press reports said that inquiries at 3 hospitals in Prague had revealed that 4 civilians had died, while 4 more reportedly were killed in Brno.)

Lt. Col. Jiri Hecko, an army political officer, complained in *Rude pravo* Aug. 25 that hospital medical staffs had neglected injured police and troops. The trade union newspaper *Prace* charged the same day that Prague's Vrsovice Hospital had refused out-patient treatment to injured policemen.

Rude pravo also reported Aug. 25 that prior to the demonstrations, Interior Ministry units had detained a group of young people in Nove Role, near Karlovy Vary, Western Bohemia, on charges that they had planned to "drag citizens into a demonstration on 21 August by means of demagogic slogans" and then attack a district police department building. In the same town, *Rude pravo* said, the police also had detained 4 young people possessing "a whole arsenal of weapons."

Svoboda, the daily party newspaper of Central Bohemia, reported Aug. 26 that 80% of the region's population had boycotted public transportation and shops Aug. 21. (According to CTK, the presidium of the Central Bohemian regional committee dismissed the entire editorial board of *Svoboda* Aug. 25.)

Rude pravo Aug. 25 accused 78 foreigners reported arrested during the disorders Aug. 19-21 of having "acted directly as liaison" between demonstration leaders. The Interior Ministry reported Aug. 25 that 19 Americans had been arrested. (In his Sept. 1 report, Vasek reported that 121 foreigners had been arrested and expelled.)

Husak Says Invaders Meant Well

Party First Secy. Gustav Husak, in a televised address marking the 25th anniversary of the Slovak uprising against the Nazis, defended the motives for the 1968 invasion of Czechoslovakia.

Speaking Aug. 29 at ceremonies in the central Slovak capital, Banska Bystrica, Husak said the invasion had been spurred by Czechoslovakia's allies' fears for "the development of socialism in Czechoslovakia" and for the Socialist camp as a whole. In his view, Husak said, the invasion had not been "a hostile act against the Czechoslovak people and the Czechoslovak state" but was motivated by the Warsaw allies' desire to "assist the Czechoslovak people, our working people." Husak stressed that Czechoslovakia was "a fully sovereign and independent state where domestic and foreign affairs are decided by the country's own party and state organs, with no one interfering in these basic questions." He said that Soviet troops stationed in Czechoslovakia were there as "friends and protectors" under a Czechoslovak-Soviet treaty. Husak reaffirmed Czechoslovakia's friendship for the USSR and said that the country owed much to "the struggle and sacrifices of the Soviet army and Soviet people."

As part of the anniversary activities, attended by Soviet, Polish, East German, Hungarian and Bulgarian representatives, Husak Aug. 27 received the Hero of Czechoslovakia award and the Order of Lenin, the USSR's 2d highest award. Federal Assembly Chairman Alexander Dubcek was among the 42 Slovak veterans honored during ceremonies Aug. 28.

Gen. Aleksei Yepishev, political chief of the Soviet armed forces, wrote in the Soviet Defense Ministry newspaper *Krasnaya Zvezda* Aug. 31 that the Czechoslovak army required more political indoctrination to make it a more reliable Soviet ally. Yepishev, who had returned to Moscow from Czechoslovakia Aug. 21, praised the ideological work done under Husak to correct the "negative consequences" of the Dubcek regime.

Dubcek & Smrkovsky Criticized

In an interview published in the party's Czech Affairs Bureau weekly *Tribuna* Aug. 27, Premier Oldrich Cernik charged that ex-Czechoslovak party First Secy. Dubcek had allowed a deteriorating situation to develop prior to the Warsaw Pact invasion of Czechoslovakia in 1968. The interview was circulated widely in the national press and media.

In an apparent attempt to dissociate himself from certain errors of the 1968 Dubcek regime, Cernik referred to the party Presidium's decision not to attend a Warsaw Treaty meeting in Warsaw July 14-15. Cernik said the Presidium had not been informed that a date had been set for the meeting, although Dubcek "was informed about it." He declared that had he known "the date of the meeting had been set and that the invitation was for a specific time," he would never have agreed with the Presidium's decision not to attend the meeting. He also charged Dubcek with failing to inform the Presidium about his private talks with Soviet representatives at the Cierna nad Tisou conference in July and August 1968.

Cernik asserted that Dubcek had failed to abide by a Presidium directive to condemn publicly the "2,000 Words" manifesto. (A Radio Free Europe report said Aug. 28, however, that Dubcek had explicitly condemned the manifesto in a speech at a party conference in Prague June 28, 1968. Dubcek was quoted as saying: "We in the Presidium have rejected the conclusions of ... '2,000 Words' because ... they could lead to the destruction of the existing social structure.... ")

Radio Prague Sept. 3 broadcast an interview with conservative Presidium member Vasil Bilak on the Dubcek liberalization program and its aftermath. The interview was published the same day in *Rude pravo* and in the weekly

Tribuna under the heading: "From Dresden to Bratislava."
Bilak, Presidium member and Central Committee secretary for
international affairs, described Dubcek as primarily responsible
for the "shortcomings and encroachments of 1968." Bilak said
Dubcek had "failed to resist the pressures of well-known forces
who most likely found his vacillation suitable." He called on
Dubcek to name the Presidium members and "dishonest people"
who had "misused and influenced" him. Bilak asserted that the
invasion could have been avoided had it not been for the leadership's "passive attitude," which promoted the growth and subversive activities of "rightist-opportunist, anti-Socialist and
counterrevolutionary forces."

Bilak described the Central Committee plenum July 18,
1968—at which it was voted unanimously to approve the party
Presidium's reply to the July 15 letter the 5 allies sent from
Warsaw—as irregular, since there was no vote against the
Presidium's request for bilateral talks with the Soviets before
further multilateral consultations. Tacitly conceding shortcomings on his own part, Bilak held that while some Central
Committee members had voted out of conviction, others had
done so for fear of becoming outcasts. Bilak confirmed that
Dubcek had not notified the Presidium about the July Warsaw
meeting. He also accused Dubcek of failing to properly inform
the party leadership about Czechoslovakia's talks with its allies
at the Dresden conference. (Dubcek had gone to Dresden Mar.
23, 1968 to meet with top party representatives from Bulgaria,
Hungary, Poland, East Germany and the USSR.)

Implying that Czechoslovakia had had ample warning of
an invasion unless it corrected its domestic situation, Bilak
described the concerns the allies had expressed at Dresden. He
said they had not objected to Antonin Novotny's ouster as
president Mar. 22, 1968 but had interpreted his dismissal
without prior consulation with the Central Committee as a
violation of cadre policy and an indication that the party was
losing control. Bilak claimed that the allies had also been concerned about the Czechoslovak leadership's tolerance of direct
attacks on the party and the Socialist system. He said they had
warned specifically against a Hungarian-style uprising from
"counterrevolutionary elements" in Prague.

At talks in Moscow May 3-5, 1968 Bilak said, Soviet leaders had warned Dubcek, Premier Cernik, National Assembly Chairman Josef Smrkovsky and Bilak, then Slovak party leader, that "on no account is it possible to permit a situation that sooner or later could result in a liquidation of Socialist achievements in the Czechoslovak Socialist Republic, and that it would no longer be merely Czechoslovakia's internal affair but rather an affair of world socialism in general." Bilak said the Soviet leaders had refused to lend gold to Czechoslovakia because they "did not want to contribute to the activities of anti-Socialist forces, to counterrevolution in Czechoslovakia."

Radio Prague Aug. 26 broadcast a demand by Frantisek Bedrna that Federal Assembly Chairman Dubcek and Federal Assembly Deputy Chairman Smrkovsky withdraw from public life. This was the first of a series of such demands by members reaching high into the party hierarchy. Bedrna, party chairman of an engineering plant at Pecky, 14 miles northwest of Kutna Hora, Central Bohemia, had rebuked the 2 leaders for preoccupation with self-interests and for "wanting to destroy our alliance with the USSR."

Dubcek and Smrkovsky, who had been dropped from the Czechoslovak party Presidium in April but had remained Central Committee members, were again called on to resign when Radio Prague Aug. 27 interviewed 2 of Smrkovsky's constituents in Kolin (Central Bohemia), district seat of Smrkovsky's parliamentary constituency. The 2 leaders were accused of dishonesty, distorting the 1968 reforms and conducting a "2-faced policy."

Vilem Novy, a pro-Soviet member of the Central Committee and former director of the party's ideological school in Prague, called for Dubcek's ouster Sept. 2. Speaking to South Bohemian regional party officials in Ceske Budejovice, Novy also opposed those who had tried to shift their own errors to Dubcek.

(The *Washington Post* reported Aug. 29 that Pres. Svoboda had personally blocked attempts by party hardliners to arrest and try reform-minded leaders. Svoboda reportedly had told the Presidium Aug. 21: "As long as I am president, there will be no political trials.")

The West German news agency DPA Oct. 18 published a
report on "eye-witness" accounts of Dubcek's reply Sept. 25 to
attacks at the party Central Committee's plenum. According to
the accounts, Dubcek rejected allegations that he had not
informed Czechoslovak leaders of negotiations with Warsaw
Pact states, especially with Soviet leaders. He said that the
party Presidium had been informed about the Dresden conference and that the Soviet ambassador in Prague had not told
him the date of the Warsaw summit conference in July 1968.
Dubcek asserted that his talks with Leonid I. Brezhnev at
Cierna July 29-Aug. 1, 1968 had been concerned with changes
in the Czechoslovak leadership, "especially in the party
Presidium[,] and [with] a postponement of the party congress."
Dubcek said he had "not wanted to make this known at the
time in Moscow's own interest, to avoid exposing the Soviets to
the charge that they were interfering in Czechoslovakia's internal affairs."

Dubcek, according to the accounts, claimed that
Brezhnev's Aug. 19, 1968 letter had not been a "final warning"
to the Czechoslovak regime but had been "one of the many
arriving every 2 to 3 days." Dubcek declared that Hungarian
party First Secy. Janos Kadar had not said anything about an
imminent invasion at their meeting at Komarno Aug. 17, 1968.
He added: "I considered the possibility of troops entering, but I
never believed it would happen."

He rejected allegations that there was evidence of counterrevolutionary activity or alleged subversive efforts by West
Germany and the U.S. in 1968. Dubcek demanded that all
Soviet letters to the Czechoslovak leaders be made public, at
least within the party, so that the truth could be shown. Dubcek
accused Czechoslovak party First Secy. Gustav Husak of not
allowing any dialogue within the party and of denying him the
chance to defend himself. Dubcek concluded: "You do not give
me the slightest chance of defending my political attitude. You
accuse me publicly but you seal my lips so that I cannot answer.
This is the kind of order which you have served up in the party
and in the country."

Dubcek's statements were answered by Bilak, who said
that Brezhnev had stated at a Warsaw Pact conference in
Moscow in May 1968: "We will not permit Czechoslovakia to
leave the Socialist camp even if thereby we have to set off the

3d world war." Dubcek, according to Bilak, had not attended the conference, because he said Dubcek had argued that "they will force us to keep the Soviet forces, which are taking part in maneuvers, in the country.... They will condemn us." Bilak said that when he had informed Dubcek Aug. 19, 1968 that the USSR would occupy the country and that he should go to Moscow immediately. Dubcek had replied: "One cannot negotiate with Brezhnev. It leads nowhere. The Russians are nervous, but I will not yield."

Government Revamped, Dubcek & Smrkovsky Out

At a plenary meeting of the party Central Committee, held Sept. 25-27 at Hradcany Castle in Prague, the committee ordered a long-predicted purge of reformists, including Dubcek and Smrkovsky, and issued its official version of the reasons behind the 1968 invasion. The actions were announced in resolutions made public Sept. 28. Premier Cernik's government resigned hours after the plenum ended early Sept. 27; a new and more conservative cabinet was announced Sept. 28.

In a report from the party Presidium to the Central Committee Sept. 25, party First Secy. Husak scored the prereformist Novotny leadership as "one-sided absolutism" but also criticized the 1968 party-reforming "action program" because it denied "the use of political and power instruments to implement the leading role of the party." He labeled Dubcek and Smrkovsky as men wanting to "play angels" and be on good terms with everyone up to mid-Apr. 1969. Husak attacked Smrkovsky's defense—his assertion that he sought a common language for all who favored "socialism." Husak called this policy "nonclass and *petit bourgeois.*"

Husak said that the consolidation of the party "in all spheres" was just beginning. The party's main task, Husak said, "remains the struggle against the anti-Socialist forces in our society, against right-wing opportunism inside the party."

The Central Committee Sept. 28 published a resolution approving Husak's report. The resolution reaffirmed the Central Committee's directive of May 30, 1969 (on the restoration of party unity and of its leading role, economic improvement and the resumption of Czechoslovakia's Soviet-bloc role) as the party's political guideline. At Husak's recommendation, the Central Committee "corrected" 3 party documents adopted before and after the invasion. It annulled:

(1) The July 18, 1968 Presidium resolution, refusing attendance at a Warsaw Pact meeting in Warsaw, as a "grave political mistake ... at variance with the interests of socialism in our country, and with internationalist traditions." (In connection with the new resolution, Husak had charged Sept. 25 that the 1968 leadership, and particularly Dubcek, had neglected "basic duties" in its negotiations with the Warsaw Treaty allies prior to the invasion. He had said: "If, in the negotiations with the CPSU [Soviet Communist Party] and with the other fraternal parties, caused by our internal development, they had proceeded from internationalist positions, with a political and statesmanlike responsibility, the allied troops would not have entered our territory.")

(2) The Presidium's resolution of Aug. 21, 1968, condemning the invasion, as "non-Marxist and fundamentally incorrect." (Referring to the invasion, the new resolution said: "Under no circumstances was it an act of aggression against the people, it was not a matter of occupation of Czechoslovak territory and of suppression of freedom and Socialist order in our state." Husak's report had depicted the invasion as coming after the allies had lost confidence in Dubcek and the party leadership to "stop the dangerous developments in Czechoslovakia." The Slovak party presidium Sept. 10 had withdrawn as "politically incorrect" its 1968 condemnation of the invasion and appeal to the invading troops to leave Czechoslovakia.)

(3) The documents and results of the extraordinary 14th Czechoslovak Communist Party Congress at the CKD Vysocany plant as a right-wing opportunist attempt to "seize the leadership of the whole party with the aim of ... severing the Czechoslovak Socialist Republic from the Socialist community and liquidating the Socialist achievements of the people." (The election of delegates in July 1968 to the party's forthcoming 14th Congress, which took place at the CKD factory, was also voided.)

In another resolution published Sept. 28, the Central Committee announced a broad purge of its ranks. This action was apparently in accordance with proposals submitted to the plenum Sept. 25 to discipline members "who abandoned the positions of Marxism-Leninism, discredited the party in an important period and who ... made no efforts to rid themselves of serious errors or to help the party in a difficult situation."

Dubcek was dropped from the Presidium, and the Central Committee ordered his removal as chairman of the Federal Assembly. According to press reports Sept. 28 and Oct. 18, Dubcek had refused to submit to "self-criticism" ·before the Central Committee. Dubcek reportedly said that his accusers shared responsibility for the policy currently assessed by the party as incorrect because they had voted for it.

(Party Deputy First Secy. Lubomir Strougal said Sept. 29 that Dubcek had given unclear answers to questions about the 1968 reform period and the role of "Socialist power." He said that Dubcek had failed "to understand the real meaning of the comradely endeavors of our Soviet comrades" and other Warsaw allies "as an effort to help solve matters which we did not see, and did not want to see.")

Dubcek was replaced on the 11-man Presidium by Josef Kempny, then 49, who was released as chairman of the Central Committee's ideological commission, co-opted to the Central Committee and assigned to the party's Czech Bureau.

Smrkovsky was dropped from the Central Committee. He also lost his posts as deputy chairman of the Federal Assembly and as chairman of the Assembly's House of the People.

Josef Havlin, chairman of the Czechoslovak press and information office, said Sept. 29 that Dubcek and Smrkovsky would remain in the assembly as deputies.

Others expelled from the Central Committee (*also denotes expulsion from the Federal Assembly): *Marie Mikova, former deputy chairman of the House of the People; Milan Huebl, former director of the party's ideological school; Zdenek Vokrouhlicky, former chairman of the Communist Youth Organization; *Zdenek Mlynar, a former party secretary; *Jiri Hajek, foreign minister in 1968; and Frantisek Vlasak, planning minister.

Expelled from the Central Committee and the party: Lt. Gen. Vaclav Prchlik, party security chief under Dubcek; Vaclav Slavik, former party Presidium member and Central Committee secretary; and Alfred Cerny, once a Brno regional party secretary in South Moravia.

Permitted to resign from the Central Committee "at their own request": Jiri Judl, Vladimir Kabrna, Josef Hauer, Antonin Hrotek, Zdenek Smolik, Jaroslav Belaj, Miluse Fischerova, Libuse Hrdinova, Ludmila Jankovcova, Bedrich Kralik, Ivan Malek of the Academy of Sciences, Academy Chairman Frantisek Sorm, Jirina Zelenkova, Josef Zuda, ex-Agriculture & Food Min. Josef Boruvka, Josef Svoboda, ex-Brno party First Secy. Josef Spacek, Bohumil Simon, the ex-Prague city party leader, and his predecessor Martin Vaculik. Included in this list were 5 other members of the Academy of

Sciences. The official press agency CTK reported Sept. 25 that
the academy's party cell had been disbanded.

14 of the 28 full Central Committee members dropped at
the plenum had been co-opted to the Central Committee Aug.
31, 1968 as a concession by the Soviets in return for the nullifi-
cation of the extraordinary 14th party congress held Aug. 22.
The plenum filled some of the resulting vacancies by promoting
6 candidates to full Central Committee membership and
drafting 7 others. The more conservative of the newcomers
included Miroslav Moc, editor of *Rude pravo;* Pavel Auersperg,
chief of the Central Committee department for international
affairs; Jan Fojtik, new rector of the Prague Party College;
and Bohuslav Chnoupek, earlier made director of Czechoslovak
Radio. Among those co-opted along with Kempny were
Frantisek Hamouz, Novotny's foreign trade expert and
COMECON representative; Dalibor Hanes and Dr. Sonia
Pennigerova, who were to be the new leaders in the Federal
Assembly; Jan Marko, federal foreign affairs minister; and the
new federal vice premier, Vaclav Hula.

6 moderates in Deputy First Secy. Lubomir Strougal's
Czech Affairs Bureau were dropped by the Central Committee,
but some were later reassigned. The plenum replaced Vaclav
Hula with Antonin Kapek as the bureau's secretary and Czech
Assembly Chairman Cestmir Cisar, Federal Premier Cernik,
Jaroslav Karhan, Vojtech Matejcek and Karel Simek with
conservatives Josef Kempny, Josef Korcak, Drahomir Kolder,
Oldrich Svestka and Kapek.

The Cernik cabinet had resigned Sept. 27. Pres. Svoboda,
who accepted the resignations, asked Cernik to form a new
government, and its composition was announced Sept. 28. The
new government's members:

Cernik—premier; Josef Kempny—vice premier; Peter
Colotka—vice premier; Frantisek Hamouz—vice premier and
minister of foreign trade; Vaclav Hula—vice premier and
minister of planning; Miroslav Hruskovic—vice premier and
minister chairman of the technology and investment development committee; Karol Laco—vice premier; Jan Marko—
minister of foreign affairs; Col. Gen. Martin Dzur—minister of
defense; Jan Pelnar—minister of the interior; Rudolf
Rohlicek—minister of finance; Michal Stancel—minister of
labor and social affairs; Ignac Rendek—minister-chairman of

the prices committee; Josef Krejci—minister-chairman of the industry committee; Koloman Boda—minister-chairman of the agriculture and food committee; Jaroslav Knizka—minister-chairman of the transport committee; Karel Hoffmann—minister-chairman of posts and telecommunications committee; Bohuslav Kucera—minister; Jan Pauly—minister; Lt. Gen. Vaclav Dvorak—secretary of state in the defense ministry; Col. Jan Majer—secretary of state in the interior ministry; Andrej Barcak—secretary of state in the foreign trade ministry; Vlasta Brablcova—secretary of state in the ministry of labor and social affairs. (Karel Kurka was appointed state secretary in the Foreign Affairs Ministry Oct. 20. Kurka had previously served as an ambassador to the UN and Rumania and as deputy foreign minister.)

The new members were Kempny, Colotka, Hula, Rohlicek, Rendek, Knizka, Hoffmann and Barcak. Hamouz, a previous vice premier, received the added post of foreign trade minister, while Hruskovic was elevated to the post of premier.

According to the *N.Y. Times* Sept. 28, Husak had been pressured to replace Cernik with a premier wholly committed to the pro-Soviet faction. Chairman Josef Havlin of the Czech Press & Information Bureau said Sept. 29 that Cernik had repented his past work with the reformers. Havlin said: "He was criticized as an honest man who saw his shortcomings and mistakes over the last year and on this basis the party Presidium decided to entrust him with the completion of a new government."

The Czechoslovak Federal Assembly revised its leadership Oct. 15, replacing its chairman, Alexander Dubcek, with conservative Dalibor Hanes, a professor at the Bratislava Law School. Hanes, then 55, a Slovak, had resigned his post as chairman of the House of Nations earlier in the day to accept the new post; Vojtech Mihalik, a Slovak writer, replaced him.

Josef Smrkovsky was replaced as chairman of the House of Peoples by Mrs. Sonia Pennigerova, a physician in Prague and a reputed "hard-line" party member. Smrkovsky's deputy, Mrs. Marie Mikova, was replaced by Josef Trojan. Dubcek, Smrkovsky and 6 others resigned as members of the Federal Assembly's presidium. Their replacements included Alois Indra and Vasil Bilak, secretaries of the Central Committee.

(The Federal Assembly Oct. 15 approved a delay in parliamentary elections until after Dec. 31, 1970, and the government then announced Dec. 2 that Federal Assembly elections would be postponed until 1971. It said that the 14th party congress would also be held in 1971.)

The Czech National Council's presidium named a new Czech Socialist Republic government Sept. 29 after Czech Premier Stanislav Razl, then 49, and his cabinet resigned. The presidium appointed Federal Vice Premier Josef Kempny to replace Razl as its leader. (Razl was recalled from his post on the Czechoslovak Defense Council Oct. 13. He was replaced thereon by Kempny.) Razl, a moderately progressive economist, became one of the 3 Czech vice premiers and replaced Drahomir Dvorak as national planning minister.

Among other replacements: Ex-Central Trade Union Council Secy. Emilian Hamernik succeeded Frantisek Toman as national labor and social welfare minister; Czech Vice Premier Antonin Cervinka, then 43, replaced Emanuel Bosak, then about 45, as youth and physical training minister; Jan Nemec, former left-wing Social Democrat and central secretary of the Czechoslovak-Soviet Friendship League, succeeded the progressive Socialist Vaclav Hrabal as national justice minister; Josef Simon, hitherto director of the Mlada Boleslav auto works, replaced Frantisek Cihak as national industry minister; and Stepan Hornik, an enterprise manager, succeeded Miloslav Kohoutek, an economist, as national trade minister.

The Czech legislature's presidium also dropped Min.-without-Portfolio Frantisek Jaska from this post and from his function as chairman of the Czech Prices Board. (The presidium had announced Sept. 25 that 5 of its members had resigned.)

Slovak Premier Stefan Sadovsky made 4 changes in his cabinet early in October after charging that 3 of the ministers had either performed unsatisfactorily from a professional standpoint or had failed to consolidate their departments politically. Sadovsky named Jozef Gajdosik, former state secretary of the federal Finance Ministry, as national finance minister to replace Karol Martinka; Vaclav Vacok as national industry minister to succeed Stanislav Luptak; ex-National Transport, Posts & Telecommunications Min. Stefan Sebesta, a rehabilitated "bourgeois Slovak nationalist," to replace Milan Hladky as national construction and technology minister; and Dr. Stefan Sutka to succeed Sebesta. Sutka, deputy minister under Sebesta, held both law and engineering degrees.

Cernik Outlines Program

In his first policy speech since forming his new government, Premier Cernik told the Federal Assembly Oct. 16 that the government intended to strengthen its role in all sectors of the economy and state administration. He said: "We shall increase the part played by the national economic plan and restore the authority of economic management at all levels. We shall consistently demand increased discipline in management systems with a principal orientation on the utilization of the large reserves which the Czechoslovak economy has."

Cernik stressed that the government would build up the army and security forces and "see to it that the press, radio and television assist actively in implementing the policy of the Socialist state." The emphasis on increased government control, he said, would also apply to education.

Cernik pledged that the country would strengthen its ties "of fraternity and alliance" with all Socialist states, "especially the Soviet Union." With regard to the invasion, Cernik asserted: "The government starts from the fact that the arrival of allied troops in Aug. 1968 was motivated by justified concern on the part of fraternal countries about the future of Socialist Czechoslovakia. It was therefore no aggression against [Czechoslovakia], nor an occupation of our country."

The assembly adopted a resolution approving Cernik's policies and evaluation of the economic and political situation in Czechoslovakia.

Soviet Links Strengthened, Invasion Justified

Following an 8-day visit by Prague leaders to the Soviet Union Oct. 20-27, the 2 countries Oct. 28 issued a joint communique announcing a strengthening of their economic, political and social relations.

The communique said the USSR would increase its trade with Czechoslovakia during 1970-5. "The Soviet Union," it said, "will increase above the planned quotas its deliveries of petroleum, cast iron, cotton and other important kinds of raw material ... as well as equipment Czechoslovakia greatly needs." Moscow also agreed to increase its deliveries of durable goods and "to render assistance in buying some of those commodities in the foreign market which are now in short supply in Czechoslovakia." There was no mention of a $500 million hard-currency loan that East European diplomats had claimed Prague was seeking.

The communique disclosed that an agreement had been reached on expanding cooperation in nuclear power engineering. The USSR agreed to supply equipment for the construction of atomic power stations in Czechoslovakia, and both countries were to cooperate in the manufacture of other equipment for the power stations and for computer facilities. Mutual cooperation in the fields of art, culture and the communications media was to be further developed.

Contrary to reports that the USSR would agree to a reduction of its forces in Czechoslovakia, the communique asserted that "interaction and friendship between the formations of the Czechoslovak people's army and Soviet troops temporarily stationed in [Czechoslovakia] will be deepened."

Regarding the events of 1968, the 2 sides agreed that "right[-ist] opportunistic forces" had weakened the country and "created the menace of a state-political coup." Accordingly, the communique continued, "the Czechoslovak delegation assesses the actions of the 5 fraternal Socialist countries in the crucial August days of 1968 as an act of internationalist solidarity, which helped to bar the road to the anti-Socialist counterrevolutionary forces." Indorsing the substance of the Brezhnev doctrine of "limited sovereignty" for Socialist states, the communique held that "each Communist party is responsible for its activities to the people of its country and bears international responsibility to the countries of the Socialist community and the international Communist and workers' movement."

The communique announced that a new treaty of friendship, cooperation and mutual assistance would be signed in May 1970 to mark the 25th anniversary of Czechoslovakia's liberation.

In a TV address Oct. 29, party First Secy. Gustav Husak, reporting on the visit to the USSR, admitted that there was opposition in Czechoslovakia to the presence of Soviet forces, but he appealed to Czechoslovaks to "make the Red Army soldiers feel at home." Husak said that the talks with Soviet leaders had demonstrated a "restored confidence" between the 2 nations.

The Soviet Union and Czechoslovakia Nov. 3 signed a 1970 trade agreement increasing their trade 6% to 2.2 billion rubles (officially more than $2.4 billion). Under the agreement, signed in Prague by Soviet Foreign Trade Min. Nikolai Patolichev and his Czechoslovak Foreign Trade Min. Frantisek Hamouz, the USSR would provide raw materials, fuel, machinery and equipment and other commodities in exchange for locomotives, machine tools, equipment and industrial installations and consumer products.

In an article in *Rude pravo* Nov. 4, Deputy Planning Min. Josef Hvorecky disclosed new measures to be taken in 1970 to strengthen the country's economy. These included (1) a decrease in Western imports; (2) an increase of 5.6% in the gross national product; (3) a rise of 2.6% in nominal wages; (4) a 4% investment growth (compared with 8.8% in 1968 and 7% in 1967); (5) a 5.8% increase in deliveries to trade, $2/3$ of the increase to be used in replenishing "exhausted stocks"; and (6) an increase of 6.4% in trade with Communist countries and 1.7% with non-Communist states.

In a speech before the Federal Assembly's Foreign Relations Committees Nov. 11, Foreign Min. Jan Marko reaffirmed that Czechoslovakia's security and sovereignty were intimately tied to the USSR and other Socialist states and that the 1968 invasion was "a sign of internationalist solidarity" and "an inevitable step—a positive one for Czechoslovakia." Marko further asserted that Czechoslovakia's policy with Western states was being implemented on the principles of peaceful coexistence and that Czechoslovakia would continue to develop relations with capitalist countries "according to the prerequisites for cooperation and according to the interest displayed by the country concerned." He said that a "certain grouping of political cal forces" that had taken place in West Germany could lead to a more flexible approach to fundamental problems, such as European security, but he added that Bonn's new chancellor,

Willy Brandt, had provided no "evidence of more essential changes in Bonn's foreign political line." In regard to the U.S., Marko criticized Washington's refusal to grant Czechoslovakia most-favored-nation treatment in foreign trade and its failure to return Czechoslovak gold (claimed to be worth close to $22.7 million) that had been in U.S. custody since after World War II. He added that Prague did not want to sever relations in the education and science fields "—with Canada and Japan, for instance."

Marko said Czechoslovakia would give "effective assistance" to developing nations in Asia, Latin America and Africa. He pledged Prague's continuing support to Arab states against Israel. On Communist China, Marko said the current anti-Soviet stand was not an "internal affair of China since it immensely damaged the cause of socialism and peace." He emphasized that Czechoslovakia was prepared to settle its relations with Peking and "favor[ed] some expansion" in economic cooperation.

Purges Continue

The Czechoslovak party Presidium announced Oct. 23 that it planned to recall the party cards of more than 1.6 million members. Sources said that the measure was designed to eliminate reformers from the party. The party regime had busied itself with purges for more than 6 months before making the decision.

Rude pravo had reported Sept. 25 that the Prague city party committee had expelled 17 members, including Bohumil Simon, the committee's former leading secretary. Others ousted included Venek Silhan (acting Czechoslovak party leader in late Aug. 1958 while Dubcek was held in Moscow); ex-Rector Milan Huebl of the Prague Higher Party School; Jaromir Litera, the city committee's ex-political secretary; the constitutional expert Bedrich Rattinger; and the journalists Karel Kyncl and Jiri Kanturek. 17 known conservatives became members of the committee Nov. 4. Some of them were "members of the working class whom the right-wing former leaders of the city committee despised and subjected to discrimination." The new members included Jiri Hajek, editor of the party weekly *Tvorba.*

In his final speech at the party Central Committee plenum, Party First Secy. Gustav Husak Sept. 27 had warned conservatives that the party "is not a slaughterhouse" for demoted reformers. He acknowledged that he himself had supported Dubcek's policies during and after the invasion, but when he met with Soviet leaders in Moscow in Oct. 1968 "my eyes opened a little for the first time."

Jiri Pelikan, former director of Czechoslovak Television, was expelled from the party Oct. 2, and 2 Czechoslovak officials at the UN, Alexander Zemanek and Jiri Nedela, and Karel Kral, an official of CTK accredited to the UN, were expelled the same day.

15 Members of the Slovak party Central Committee and its secretariat were ousted Oct. 3, including Samuel Faltan, a former Czechoslovak vice premier. 24 men were elected to the Slovak Central Committee, including Vasil Bilak, once its first secretary and a known conservative expelled from the Slovak hierarchy soon after the Soviet invasion.

4 prominent writers, Ludvik Pacovsky, Antonin Liehm, Pavel Kohout and Ludvik Vaculik, were expelled from the Czechoslovak party Oct. 9. Ludek Pachman, the chess grand master, had been expelled from the party Sept. 24.

Ex-Vice Premier Ota Sik, architect of the 1967-9 economic reform program, was expelled from the party Oct. 13. A CTK announcement said that Sik's activity abroad—he had been living in Switzerland since the invasion—"was incompatible with the principles and the policy of the party."

Col. Josef Pavel, ex-interior minister, was suspended from the party Oct. 16. Pavel had been one of the major leaders of the 1968 reform movement.

- CTK reported Oct. 15 that Jan Brod and Mrs. Sekaminova-Cakrtova had been expelled from the CP. Brod had signed the "2,000 Words" manifesto. Mrs. Cakrtova had been one of the few deputies to oppose the stationing of Soviet troops in Czechoslovakia.

Jan Prochazka, head of the Czechoslovak Writer's Union in 1968, was expelled from the party, it was reported Oct. 17. Prochazka reportedly was ousted for espousing "anti-party ideology."

(Zdenek Hejzlar, first secretary of the Czechoslovak legation in Vienna, was granted political asylum by the Austrian government, it was reported Oct. 15. Hejzlar had been director of Czechoslovak radio prior to the invasion.)

Col. Emil Zatopek, the former Olympic gold medal runner, was expelled from the Communist Party Oct. 24. An announcement in *Rude pravo* charged that Zatopek "does not understand the principal questions of the development of our Socialist state and the guarantee of its defense on the principles of Marxism-Leninism and proletarian internationalism." It claimed that Zatopek had "betrayed a number of internal measures of the Czechoslovak army contained in secret documents of the Ministry of National Defense." A supporter of the 1968 reform movement, Zatopek had been suspended as an army athletics trainer in April. Zatopek was dismissed from the army Dec. 5 on charges that he had "violated Czechoslovak legal norms to an extent which is incompatible with serving in the ... army." Zatopek until shortly before his dismissal had been working in Prague's sanitation department.

The Czechoslovak TV network announced Nov. 14 that the entire party-cell organization in its staff had been replaced.

7 journalists, including Jiri Hochman, a member of the editorial board of the former journal *Reporter,* were expelled from the party Nov. 14. They were accused of violating party statutes and of undermining relations between Socialist states.

Vaclav Kves, former head of the Czechoslovak-Soviet Friendship Society, was named head of the party staff college Nov. 18. Kves, regarded as an ultraconservative, replaced Jan Fojtik, 41, who had been appointed Nov. 3 as secretary of the party Central Committee.

Jindrich Suk, director general of the official news agency CTK since the 1968 invasion, was dismissed from his post Nov. 27. He was replaced by Otakar Svercina, a former CTK correspondent in Bonn, considered a "hard-line" Communist and outspoken supporter of Husak. CTK announced Nov. 28 that several newsmen in Central and North Bohemia had been dismissed from their jobs and that some had been expelled from the party.

Cestmir Cisar, chairman of the Czech National Council, resigned Nov. 26. Cisar, a leading supporter of the 1968 liberalization movement told the council: "I would like to confess to you that I have given my mind and my heart to the cause of the [Czechoslovak] federation. I profess my allegiance to what has been successful and to what needs to be corrected. I feel my share of responsibility for the shortcomings and mistakes, and I ask you to believe me that these have not occurred because of ill will." Evzen Erban, chairman of the Czechoslovak National Front, replaced Cisar as council chairman. Cisar remained a member. 9 progressive deputies were expelled and 53 others resigned from the council. Those expelled included ex-Czechoslovak Vice Premier Ota Sik and Eduard Goldstuecker, former president of the Czechoslovak Writers' Union. (62 members were elected to the council, including Czech Education Min. Jaromir Hrbek and Jiri Hajek and Josef Valenta, editors of the party's 2 ideological journals *Tvorba* and *Zivot strany.*)

Vlastimil Toman, head of the 900,000-man Metal Workers' Union, and Vlastimil Fisar, president of the Union of Scientific & Cultural Workers, were expelled from the Central Trades Union Council Nov. 26, along with 5 others. Another member of the council's presidium was expelled and 4 others resigned. In a speech to the council Nov. 26, Chairman Karel Polacek charged that during the 1968 reform period "right-wing forces wanted to turn the trade unions into a permanent opponent of the party."

Josef Smrkovsky, former chairman of the Federal Assembly's Chamber of People, and ex-Foreign Min. Jiri Hajek were expelled from the Czech Journalists' Union Nov. 18. No explanation was given for the expulsions.

Rude pravo reported Nov. 29 that Vladimir Skutina, an author and TV commentator, had been released from prison Nov. 11 and taken to a medical ward of a Prague hospital. Skutina's arrest at anniversary demonstrations of the 1968 invasion was never officially reported, and it was not known whether formal charges had been brought against him. Sources in Prague said that many others were being held as political prisoners at Pankrac Prison.

The weekly *Zivot strany* reported Dec. 5 that 335 members of local party committees in northern Moravia had been ousted from their positions because of "rightist opportunist tendencies." It said that in Bohemia 40 party chairmen had been replaced for allegedly supporting reformist leaders. (The Dec. 15 issue of *Newsweek* reported that more than 600,000 members had resigned from the Czechoslovak party, leaving membership at about one million.)

In an editorial in *Rude pravo* Dec. 13, editor-in-chief Miroslav Moc warned against large-scale purges of progressives. "This purge cannot be handled as a punitive expedition," Moc said. The editorial reportedly was the result of speculation that party First Secy. Husak was facing strong opposition from ultraconservatives in regard to the expulsion of liberals and moderates. In a radio broadcast Dec. 20, Husak said the Central Committee would rebuff extremists who opposed his more moderate policies.

Ex-party First Secy. Dubcek was appointed ambassador to Turkey Dec. 15. In a brief announcement, the official press agency CTK said that Pres. Svoboda had named him to replace Pavel Kanka "in connection with entrusting him [Kanka] with other tasks." Since October, Dubcek had been living in semi-isolation in his native Slovakia. His assignment was viewed as a defeat for conservatives who had wanted to bring disciplinary action against him.

Josef Smrkovsky and 10 other known liberals resigned from the Federal Assembly's Chamber of People Dec. 17. This was the last public office held by Smrkovsky. Among the other deputies who resigned were Mrs. Marie Mikova, his former deputy; Josef Boruvka, a former agriculture minister; Frantisek Sorm, a former president of the Academy of Sciences; the historian Josef Macek, a member of the academy; Martin Vaculik, former Prague city Communist Party secretary; and Oleg Homola, ex-secretary of the Czechoslovak-Soviet Friendship Society.

Sources in Prague reported Dec. 18 that 10 reformist members of the party Central Committee had resigned in protest against retrogressive policies. Among the 10 was Vladimir Kadlec, a former education minister. The size of the committee was reported to have shrunk from 180 members at the beginning of the year to 125 members.

In an interview in *Rude pravo* Dec. 18, Antonin Kapek, first secretary of the Prague city committee, said that 228 party members and administrators had been dismissed in December. A known ultraconservative, Kapek had replaced Oldrich Matejka as first secretary Dec. 16. 4 members of the Presidium of the Slovak National Council, Slovakia's legislature, resigned Dec. 22, while 2 others were relieved as deputies.

The party began to issue new membership cards Dec. 28 in an apparent attempt to insure the party of adherents loyal to the Prague leadership. At party meetings, members were told that they must submit to an investigation of their conduct and background during the past 2 years. Loyalty checks and the issuing of new cards were scheduled to be completed by May 25, 1970, the 25th anniversary of the formal restoration of Czechoslovakia after World War II.

In an editorial in *Rude pravo* Dec. 31, the party announced that it would begin the new year with a broad purge from its ranks of what it described as *"petit bourgeois."* It was the first time *"petit bourgeois"*—*i.e.,* centrists and moderates—had been named as primary targets of a wide-scale purge; previous purge campaigns had been mounted against "right-wing opportunists"—*i.e.,* progressives and liberals. The move was viewed as a sign that Husak was acceding to ultraconservative demands for a thorough "cleansing" of the party.

State Takes Control of Universities

Pres. Ludvik Svoboda Dec. 9 appointed 5 professors recommended by the government as rectors of Czechoslovakia's universities. The Federal Assembly Dec. 6 had approved a measure giving the state control over the country's higher learning institutes. Foreign observers looked on the state's new power as a victory for the conservative forces in the Czechoslovak Communist Party in their struggle of more than 25 months with outspokenly defiant students and progressive schoolmen.

The final power crisis of Antonin Novotny's regime had been precipitated by what was widely described as the party's brutal suppression of the Prague-Strahov dormitory students' demonstration of Oct. 31, 1967 over inadequate facilities. The students had been supported by many prominent schoolmen, including ex-Rector Oldrich Stary of Prague University and Prof. Eduard Goldstuecker.

After the post-Dubcek government in June 1969 had cut off annual state education subsidies of 7 million crowns, the students had lost much power in their role as Dubcek's most loyal and outspoken supporters. Their situation was not improved by the advent Aug. 27 of Dr. Jaromir Hrbek, 55, a neurologist, as the Czech education minister. The new minister's first address, at the beginning of the new school year Sept. 1, was an attack on liberal teachers, "particularly on some facilities and scientific institutions," whom he accused of being "initiators and organizers of revisionist, anticommunist and anti-Soviet actions." He called them "enemies of the party and the state" and promised to fire them—a step that the emergency legislation passed by the Federal Assembly Aug. 22 empowered him to take.

One of Hrbek's first acts as education minister was to circulate among the students a long questionnaire that encouraged them, among other things, to inform on liberal professors and progressive student colleagues. Hrbek, speaking at a convocation of Communist teachers in Prague Sept. 4, confirmed his determination to purge the schools of all unreliable elements. He announced plans to reorganize his ministry, to overhaul completely the provisions of the Apr. 5, 1968 party "action program" with respect to education—some parts of which he called "absolutely untenable"—and to "correct rehabilitations" so as to restore conservatives to their teaching posts.

Hundreds of students jeered Hrbek in a question-and-answer session in Prague Nov. 4 in the first reported encounter between a new pro-Soviet cabinet member and student supporters of the 1968 liberalization program.

Hrbek was the main speaker Nov. 17 at the official observance, at Charles University in Prague, of International Student Day, marking the 30th anniversary of the execution by the Nazis of Czechoslovak students in Prague's Ruzyne District. Hrbek asserted that the Communists—who then had supported the Hitler-Stalin pact—had been active in the students' resistance movement. (None of the 9 students executed, however, was a Communist Party member.) He condemned the

Nazi occupation in 1939 but lauded the Soviet invasion in 1968 as "necessary international assistance."

University students throughout Czechoslovakia held small demonstrations Nov. 17 to mark the 30th anniversary. Hundreds visited the grave of Jan Palach, the Prague University student who had burned himself to death in protest against the Soviet occupation. The party newspaper *Rude pravo* charged Nov. 17 that student leaders had caused "exaggerated nationalism and anti-Soviet trends" at universities, while the trade union newspaper *Prace* claimed that the student movement until shortly before then had been under the influence of "extreme rightist, anti-Communist and anti-Soviet forces" and was now "dominated by a chaos of opinions."

The Prague University philosophy faculty, which had been deeply involved in liberal activity in 1968, was closed by the government because, *Rude pravo* reported Nov. 8, its electrical system needed repair. Other sources had reported Nov. 12 that university authorities had suspended indefinitely all courses in sociology, pure philosophy and history. The move was viewed as an attempt to eliminate pockets of liberal thought.

Hrbek announced Nov. 18 that the Czechoslovak party's new version of the 1968 reform movement would be introduced into new textbooks. He also said that university chairs of Marxism-Leninism would be replaced by institutes.

Travel Restrictions

The Prague government announced Oct. 8 that effective at midnight exit visas were invalidated for private trips to Western countries. More than 100,000 visas for travel in the West became useless. Exit visas marked "tourism" were valid until Dec. 31, while visas marked "official journey" were valid until Dec. 1. Permission for persons to live abroad after Dec. 31 was cancelled. The new restrictions allowed private visits to immediate members of families who were legally living abroad. Travel to countries that had no diplomatic relations with Czechoslovakia—*e.g.,* West Germany, Spain or Portugal—was banned.

Col. Jan Majer, secretary of state in the Interior Ministry, said Oct. 9 that 50,000 Czechoslovaks were living abroad and "it is assumed that some 40% of them had their stay abroad legalized."

According to radio broadcasts, the restrictions were partially designed "to ensure better foreign exchange coverage of foreign trips." The curbs included new regulations on the issuance of travel documents. These gave officials virtually unrestricted authority to withhold a passport if they considered a planned trip to be in conflict with state security, internal order, public health or Socialist morals. The regulations also empowered authorities to hold up visas of citizens suspected of intentions to defect, of people planning visits to relatives who were abroad illegally and of citizens under investigation for tax arrears or nonpayment of alimony.

The government also restricted travel from the "capitalist" countries. It discontinued the issuance of weekend visas at the Austrian border and by its Vienna embassy and said that authorities henceforth would issue entry and transit visas only in exceptional cases at Czechoslovak borders.

The government announced Oct. 17 that the new travel restrictions to the West applied to Yugoslavia. Until the ban, Czechoslovak citizens had been allowed to visit Yugoslavia without an exit visa.

The official explanation for the restrictions was that Czechoslovakia was short of hard currency. Party leader Gustav Husak, however, explained Oct. 14 at the Skoda engineering plant in Plzen: "Tens of thousands of people are maintaining their apartments and jobs at home, but somehow legalize their stays abroad.... The question must be settled. The people must be given a firm deadline and the possibility to decide, until the end of the year, where their home is—whether here or in Austria. Foreigners lived here like lords, despising us and our society, especially in the border towns like Bratislava and Brno. We will no longer look on if [a foreigner] wants to speculate in our country and tries to make prostitutes out of our young girls."

(Trips by Czechoslovak citizens to the West had increased from 47,000 in 1963 to 450,000 in 1968 and to more than 500,000 in 1969. Trips to Czechoslovakia increased from fewer than

807,000 in 1963 to nearly 4.17 million in 1968 but declined to fewer than 2.9 million in 1969.)

Other Developments

The Czechoslovak Union of Film & Television Artists gave one of its highest awards Nov. 7 to a film that had been banned in October, *All Good Fellow Countrymen.* The movie, directed by Vojtech Jasny, portrayed life in a small Moravian village during the time of the collectivization of farms in the 1950s. The film earlier had received the Workers' Festival award, and it had been shown throughout the country. Sources in Prague said the award confirmed the refusal of the country's intellectuals to heed the government's political line.

TV officials denounced the union Nov. 10 for giving another of its awards to Vlastimil Vavra for his 4-part serialization on the death of former Foreign Min. Jan Masaryk in 1948. The officials said the serial, entitled *To the Assistance of the General Prosecutor's Office,* had "contributed towards the suggestive spreading of fabrications concerning the death of Masaryk" and to anti-Soviet and anti-Communist feelings.

Karel Pesta, head of the Investigations Department of the prosecutor-general's office, announced Dec. 11 that an investigation into Jan Masaryk's death suggested that he had fallen from a window while suffering from insomnia. Pesta said that the investigators "had definitely ruled out murder but had been unable to decide between suicide and accident." He added, however: "There is much evidence for the possibility of an unfortunate accident." Because the possibility of murder was excluded, the prosecutor-general's office said it would close the case and would not make a ruling on the cause of death.

(Masaryk had died 2 weeks after the Communist takeover in Czechoslovakia. The official version of his death was suicide. In Apr. 1968 a new investigation was initiated into the cause of Masaryk's death, based on charges he might have been murdered. After the Aug. 1968 invasion, reports indicated that the investigation had been suspended.)

(Some of Prague's newspapers had reported Feb. 19 on injuries early Feb. 18 to one Vaclav Kadlak as he traveled by car near Louny, northwestern Bohemia. Kadlak had given information in the press and on TV in 1968 on Masaryk's death. Kadlak said Masaryk had been murdered. Kadlak, also known in Czechoslovakia under the name of Maj. Chlumsky, was said to have been shot at while traveling to Prague with a briefcase containing documents on Masaryk's death that he had promised to produce in court. The trade union weekly *Svet prace* reported that Kadlak had been tried the week before for defaming the republic and some of its elder statesmen. Kadlak, at the trial, reportedly had retracted his story of a murder and reportedly had confessed to having lied. The trial then had been adjourned for 10 days to give the defendant an opportunity to submit certain documents to the court, the news weekly said.)

Sources in Prague reported Nov. 10 that the Polish play *Tango* had been closed after one performance. They said that the director and producer had been advised that the satirical play, which poked fun at conservatism and the foolishness of a working-class character, was deemed "liable to incite rebellion." It was also reported Nov. 10 that censors had refused to release a movie, *Larks on a String,* by director Jiri Menzl, whose *Closely Watched Trains* had won international recognition. The movie was said to be a parody about Socialist realists' concern for the joy of labor.

Rude pravo had reported Nov. 7 that Czech Culture Min. Miroslav Bruzek had denounced certain stands taken by writers, artists and creative unions "to questions of present political development in the country" as "incorrect and essentially incompatible with state policy." Bruzek warned artists Nov. 20 against what he called their "agitation" against the regime. Bruzek reaffirmed that scholarships and other state funds would be available only to artists who followed party policies, and he denied that government control over funds designated for cultural activities was illegal.

The Federal government announced Nov. 25 several measures to tighten worker discipline. Among these was a provision to allow the dismissal, without notice, of workers "who systematically violate labor discipline or whose job performance is inadequate." Another provision called for "fast and particularly effective punishment" of parasitism, negligence and corruption. (*Rude pravo* reported Nov. 26 that a daily average of 208,000 workers, or 4.72% of the labor force, had remained home as ill in October.)

The development and trends of the Czechoslovak economy in 1969 were reported by CTK Jan. 26-27, 1970. Measured against 1968 production, these major items were reported (1968 production increases in parentheses): National income increased 6.5% (8.4%); industrial production rose 5.2% (5.5%); construction work increased 5.8% (7.3%); gross agricultural output rose 0.9% (5.6%); monetary income of the population increased by 22.1 billion crowns (officially about $307 million). (In 1968 monetary income had risen by 20 billion crowns, or about $278 million.) The volume of retail trade rose 11.9%; sales of industrial goods increased by 16.2%; 83,400 new housing units were built (the plan had called for 105,000 new units); the cost of living increased by 3.6%; nominal wages rose 7.3%, real wages 3.6%; and the volume of foreign trade increased by 7.3%, with exports up 9.6% and imports 5.3%. Trade with Socialist countries rose 4.9%, and with capitalist countries 10.5% (total exports 14.2%, total imports 6.2%).

1970

During the first half of 1970, the struggle between the moderates and the ultras within the party centered around the fate of ex-Party First Secy. Alexander Dubcek. The gradual expulsion of Dubcek from all government and party positions was a victory for the ultras. Josef Smrkovsky, Dubcek's most loyal associate, was expelled from the party in late March, along with Zdenek Mlynar, principal author of the party "action program" of Apr. 5, 1968. Another protagonist of reform, Oldrich Cernik, had been deposed as federal premier at the end of January in a sweeping government and party reorganization.

Protests, especially by intellectuals, continued, though on a diminishing scale. Despite the progress of consolidation, the advocates of purge received an increasingly free hand. Whereas non-Communists suffered significantly less than party members, they were represented in large numbers among defectors who sought refuge in the West.

The Soviet Union received ultimate satisfaction as the Czechoslovak leaders officially indorsed its version of the 1968 intervention as necessitated by the ascendancy of "counter-revolutionaries" within the Czechoslovak party. Assured of Soviet backing, Czechoslovak party leader Gustav Husak attempted to check the ultras and slow down the purges from late June onwards. The calm that prevailed in August at the anniversary of the invasion strengthened his hand.

With Soviet assistance, the economic situation improved during 1970. By the end of the year repression had passed the climax as discouragement spread among the reform-minded Communists—much more so than among the bulk of the population. With the outbreak of popular discontent in neighboring Poland, which was successfully contained by concessions, it appeared that the Husak regime and Husak's Soviet backers had embarked on the policy of conciliating the still hostile masses of the people.

ASCENDANCY OF ULTRAS

Government Reorganized, Strougal Becomes Premier

In an interview in the Czechoslovak Communist Party newspaper *Rude pravo* Jan. 5, the 2d anniversary of Antonin Novotny's ouster as party leader, party First Secy. Gustav Husak pledged to further what he called the "positive aspects" of the 1968 liberalization movement. Rejecting conservative attempts for an all-out condemnation and purge of the concepts behind the reform movement and the persons involved, Husak said: "We shall develop everything possible which January [1968, the start of the liberalization] brought to the hopes of the people as the objective needs of our society.... We shall not allow things to reach a position where the entire party and organs are afraid of stating their opinions." Husak warned, however, that the party had to dissociate itself from "right-wing" reformists, asserting that "the party must break with those who compromised themselves too deeply and purposefully damaged the party and who are maintaining incorrect attitudes."

The Communist Party Central Committee accepted the resignation of Oldrich Cernik as premier of Czechoslovakia Jan. 28 and named the conservative Lubomir Strougal to succeed him. (Soviet Premier Aleksei N. Kosygin sent a congratulatory message to Strougal Jan. 30.) The committee, at its plenary meeting Jan. 28-30, also accepted the resignations of other government and party leaders and heard a 7,000-word speech in which Husak pledged the party's support to avoid show trials in its purges against former progressive leaders.

Cernik, who had been appointed premier Apr. 4, 1968 and who had been considered a major leader of the 1968 democratization movement, also resigned from the committee's Presidium. But he remained a member of the committee and was named minister-chairman of the Board for Technical & Investment Development in the cabinet, replacing Miroslav Hruskovic. During the last month of summer in 1969, Cernik had criticized Dubcek for permitting a deteriorating situation to develop prior to the Aug. 1968 invasion and reportedly had repented his involvement with the reformers. He took these actions in what appeared to be an attempt to dissociate himself from "errors" and to maintain his position. Analysts viewed his dismissal not only as an effort by conservatives to eliminate reformers in the government but also to blame current economic ills on the 1968 movement.

Strougal, who took over the federal cabinet at 45, had risen rapidly to power in 1969. A former interior minister under the deposed Pres. Antonin Novotny, Strougal had been elected June 3, 1969 to the new post of party deputy first secretary; a native of South Bohemia, he had been named chief of the party's Czech Affairs Bureau Nov. 16, 1968 and was appointed to head the Czech National Defense Council July 7, 1969. At the Central Committee meeting Sept. 25-27, 1969, Strougal had assailed Dubcek for not properly understanding Soviet-Czechoslovak relations. He remained a Presidium member but relinquished his 2 other posts and his membership on the Central Committee Secretariat on becoming premier.

The Central Committee Jan. 28 accepted the resignation of Dubcek from the committee. Dubcek had arrived in Ankara Jan. 26 to begin his new post as ambassador to Turkey. The committee accepted the resignations of 2 other members from its 11-man Presidium—Stefan Sadovsky, outgoing Slovak party first secretary, and Karel Polacek, chairman of the Central Council of Trades Unions. 3 new members were named—Antonin Kapek, first secretary of the Prague city party committee; Josef Korcak, chairman of the Czech National Front; and Jozef Lenart, a former premier replaced by Cernik in Apr. 1968. Alois Indra, an ultraconservative and a member of the committee's Secretariat, Dalibor Hanes, chairman of the Federal Assembly, and Vice Premier Vaclav Hula, also federal minister of planning, were named alternate members of the Presidium. Lenart also was named first secretary of the Slovak party to replace Sadovsky. Jan Piller, a Presidium member and known conservative, replaced Polacek in the trade union post. Miroslav Moc, editor-in-chief of *Rude pravo,* was named a member of the Secretariat.

5 ministers in the cabinet resigned their posts—Vice Premier Josef Kempny, who also resigned as premier of the Czech government; Jan Pelnar as federal interior minister; Frantisek Hamouz as foreign trade minister; Koloman Boda, minister-chairman of the Board for Agriculture & Nutrition; and Josef Krejci, minister-chairman of the Industrial Board. Josef Korcak was named federal vice premier to replace Kempny, and he also succeeded him as Czech premier. Radko Kaska succeeded Pelnar, and Andrej Barcak replaced Hamouz, who remained a vice premier. Bohuslav Vecera replaced Boda and Jindrich Zahradnik replaced Krejci. Kempny was named to succeed Strougal as Czech Bureau chief and as a member of the Secretariat. Jan Fojtik, a secretary of the Central Committee, was named a member of the Secretariat. 6 state secretaries in separate ministries also resigned.

Pavel Auersperg, spokesman for the Central Committee, said Jan. 29 that institutionally there was no office of deputy first secretary of the Central Committee and that, therefore, that designation no longer applied either to Lubomir Strougal or to Josef Kempny, who succeeded Strougal as secretary of the Central Committee and chairman of the Czech Affairs Bureau. But the statement on the meeting of the Central Committee Presidium of June 3, 1969, when a distribution of offices was carried out, said that "Strougal is in charge of the work of the Bureau of the Central Committee and deputizes for the first secretary of the Central Committee." With Strougal's appointment to the premiership, however, this function apparently was tacitly abolished.

In his address at the Central Committee meeting Jan. 29, Husak asserted that "the much needed calm for creative work and for solving the urgent problems facing us has been reestablished throughout the country." He also said:

We have achieved ... positive and encouraging results through our political struggle against the anti-Socialist and rightist forces in the party and in society. Without exaggeration it may be said that over this period we have won a major political battle in our fight against the subversive groups, which involved the party and society in crisis situations so that they could fish in troubled waters to achieve their aims. These forces sought to demoralize the party from within and to denigrate the positive results of 25 years of work done by the party and the people. They cast slurs on the main ideals of socialism and pushed the society towards political chaos and anarchy. There were signs that under certain conditions this situation might have ended in a civil war. These forces brought on an aggravation of the economic difficulties facing us, an economic crisis and inflation. They tried to break our allied ties with the Soviet Union and other friendly Socialist states.

We can state today that these forces in our country have been defeated politically and are barred from open legal political activities. It goes without saying that this is a great political success, a prerequisite for further normal constructive activity by the party, public organizations and state bodies. Of course, this is not to say that these forces have disappeared or that they are not acting in other ways. They are still spreading panic and a feeling of depression, and they seek to retain their positions in the party.

This defeat of the right-wing anti-Socialist grouping is the chief result of work done by the party and all honest people in the past 9 months. It provides the conditions for creative work to solve the major problems facing us.

Western propaganda, along with the emigre deserters, are constantly spreading rumors about impending political trials, attacks on intellectuals, etc. in the country. They are spreading uncertainty and trying to make people believe that some ultraconservative forces are operating in the country, pressurizing you and me and seeking to introduce a police regime or one of terror. The Central Committee knows very well that neither in the party leadership nor in the Central Committee are there forces which would want a return to the '50s [and] to violations of law. As a political party, we primarily want to use political methods. We shall apply administrative measures only when the laws have clearly been violated. But we must constantly remember that hostile propaganda is acting against us, acting from outside; that inside the country, too, there are people who share similar views. Therefore, our propaganda, our daily political activity, our political work must be on the offensive. We must now, especially in this 25th year since the liberation of our state, restore in the people's mind all the positive things that have been achieved over these 25 years....

The Presidium of the party supports the trend to unify the youth movement and establish a single mass voluntary youth organization that would be a vehicle for exercising the Party's influence on the young generation....

... [As for] Czechoslovakia's federal arrangement, its main principles had completely justified themselves and were quite sound. The federal arrangement created the necessary conditions for strengthening ties between Czechs and Slovaks. At the same time it was necessary to bring to the fore, from a political point of view, those features that helped unite our peoples and strengthen the state of Czechoslovakia.

Experience has shown that to some extent it was necessary to consolidate the federal center and the federal agencies so that it would be possible not only to come to agreement on basic issues, but also to take decisions. We want the Czechoslovak state to be strong and united. The Czechoslovak Communist Party is the main uniting force. It is a united party, guided by a united Central Committee with a single program and [unified common] goals.

On foreign policy, we have consistently pursued the policy launched by the Central Committee in Apr. 1969. Today, we can say that all the misunderstandings which existed between the Czechoslovak Communist Party and the Communist Party of the Soviet Union and other fraternal parties have been eliminated, as well as the misunderstanding between the Czechoslovak Socialist Republic and the fraternal countries. An atmosphere of trust and friendship has been established.

This is clearly seen from the visit of our party and state delegation to the Soviet Union, the results of the stay and from the joint Czechsolovak-Soviet statement. This is also seen from the meetings with representatives of other fraternal parties. We can say that the Czechoslovak Communist Party is no longer isolated from the world Communist movement, that it is definitely a component in the international Communist and working-class movement, that today our state has restored, in their fullness, our ties and fraternal relations with the Socialist countries.

We call 1970 the year of Czechoslovakia's consolidation. And we should provide for Czechoslovakia's citizens a lasting and sure foundation for their life and work, and offer them future prospects. It is true that in some areas, for instance in the economy, it is impossible to solve these problems completely in 1970. Yet, here, too, it is possible to achieve some very substantial results. We must do this so that in 1971 it will be possible to call a party congress, and then have general elections.

The main instrument in this process of consolidation this year is our party and all its organizations. We want to achieve unity, to clean the party's ranks, to restore the party's fighting capacity and efficacy, to restore to the party a leading role in society. And this basic purpose is to be served, among other things, by the exchange of party cards.

[At] the plenary meeting has been submitted a draft letter from the Central Committee to all Communists and a draft of organizational [and] political directives which will form the basis for the exchange of party cards.

The directives say that we should not lose upright people, but that there is no place in the party for enemies.

The exchange of party cards calls for thoughtful action, patience and self-lessness from those responsible for carrying out this campaign. Only then will it produce proper results.

... Party bodies and organizations should devote much more attention to economic problems. With all the existing difficulties, Czechoslovakia's economy is advanced and healthy. With a sound guidance and organization, it is capable of yielding much more. Even if we do not solve some problems in a year or 2, there are opportunities for achieving greater results. For us, economic problems are another party program. It is necessary to fight ruthlessly against manifestations of irresponsbility in economy, against profiteering, shirking, lack of discipline, embezzlement of public property.

An overwhelming majority of people work honestly and want to work honestly and live honestly. And these people find themselves unfavorably placed as compared with all kinds of shady characters and profiteers. We must set‑our bearings on the overwhelming majority, consisting of upright people; we should properly appreciate them, offer them as a model and give them support, and provide for them the necessary conditions for work. It is necessary to boost in the country the role of state and economic agencies and the role of the trade unions.

In the coming work we are counting, in everything, on the support of the working class. The working class has played a historic part in our Socialist development, and it fought in difficult conditions for the triumph of the Socialist ideas. It was the main guiding force in Feb. 1948. And in tackling our political and economic problems we shall continue to count on the support of the working class.

We are also appealing to our cooperative [*i.e.*, collective] farmers and to the workers of state farms and calling upon them to fulfil the plan targets and to increase the output of meat, eggs and other foodstuffs.

... This year it will be necessary to complete the process of consolidation of society, to strengthen the party and to rally the bulk of workers, farmers and intellectuals around its positive program of [Socialist] construction.... We have enough forces to solve these basic problems. We are looking with hope and optimism at 1970, though we know that there are difficult problems to be tackled, a good deal of work and effort....

Josef Havlin, chairman of the Czechoslovak Press & Information Office, said Jan. 31 that the party would begin to solve the country's economic problems since the dangers of "counterrevolutionaries" had been removed. Reporting on the 3-day meeting, Havlin said the committee wanted a full investigation of Dubcek's activities from Jan. 1968, when he ascended to power, until Apr. 1969, when Husak replaced him as first secretary. Havlin also reported that since Apr. 1969, 70 to 80 progressive members of the Central Committee had been expelled. He said its current membership was 148 persons.

Cernik Resigns from Government

Ex-Premier Oldrich Cernik June 23 resigned his federal cabinet post as minister-chairman of the Board for Technical & Investment Development. The official Czechoslovak news agency CTK reported that Cernik did so at his own request. He was succeeded as minister-chairman by Ladislav Supka.

Cernik severed all public ties July 8 by resigning, along with 4 others, as a deputy of the Federal Assembly's Chamber of People. It had been reported July 6 that Cernik had been suspended from membership in the Czechoslovak Communist Party.

Federalization Modified

The federal parliament Dec. 20 approved a group of constitutional amendments that returned to central government control many of the functions exercised by the Czech and Slovak regional governments under the 2-year-old federal regime.

The amendments, previously approved by the Czech and Slovak national councils, were submitted to the federal parliament Dec. 20 by Premier Strougal. Strougal described them as necessary "to strengthen the position of the entire state apparatus" and to perfect "mutual relations both between the federal organs and the organs of the republics." Strougal asserted that the division of authority among the different levels of government had made it difficult to assess responsbility for some programs.

Under the amendments, the regional ministries created by the federal reforms instituted Jan. 1, 1969 would continue to exist, but the federal government was empowered to overrule their decisions dealing with air, sea and land transportation, communications, fuel and power and metallurgy.

Struggle over Dubcek's Fate

At a 2-day meeting of the Slovak Communist Party Central Committee in Bratislava Feb. 5-6, a resolution was introduced demanding the ouster of ex-Czechoslovak party First Secy. Alexander Dubcek—Slovak party leader before Jan. 5, 1968—from the Slovak party.

The resolution, which was published in the Slovak party's weekly journal and which reportedly was a result of a meeting of 400 Communists from Slovakia in Dec. 1969, said: "We must proceed to an assessment not only of the over-all situation ... but also of the part played by individuals and draw conclusions from their anti-Socialist [and] anti-Soviet activities.... We therefore ask that Comrade Dubcek be expelled from the party." The resolution also urged that the word "temporary" be removed from any future references to the presence of Soviet troops in Czechoslovakia, and it thanked Soviet and other Socialist leaders for preventing "an open conflict and civil war in Czechoslovakia in 1968."

The Czechoslovak party newspaper *Rude pravo* Feb. 3 printed a 10,000-word document stating that responsibility for the current Czechoslovak crises rested with "the former party leadership's revisionist wing." It said the "revisionist wing" was guilty during 1968 of "permitting the party to lose its position in society and to fail in its obligations to fraternal Communist parties." Dubcek, who was identified only once, was described as "the main obstacle in the way of the process of consolidation." The document also listed 47 persons who it claimed had aided anti-Socialist elements in the press, radio and TV.

Jozef Lenart, first secretary of the Slovak Communist Party, opposed a resolution before the Slovak Central Committee to expel Dubcek from the party. In a speech reported by the *Washington Post* Feb. 18, Lenart said the resolution was "at variance with the party line."

Dubcek was reported Mar. 21 to have been suspended from Czechoslovak party membership. Writing in *Rude pravo,* the party newspaper, editor Miroslav Moc said that Dubcek had been suspended "pending completion of a party investigation" into his conduct as first secretary during 1968-9. Dubeck was currently ambassador to Turkey.

The suspension was decided on Mar. 6 at a meeting of the Communist Party Presidium at which a number of other prominent members were expelled. These included: Josef Smrkovsky, ex-chairman of the National Assembly; Cestmir Cisar, former head of the Czech National Council; Josef Spacek and Zdenek Mlynar, party ideologists under Dubcek; Jiri Sekera, former *Rude pravo* editor; Zdenek Vokrouhlicky, former youth leader and head of the International Union of Students; the theater director Frantisek Pavlicek; and Karel Kaplan of the Academy of Science's Historical Institute.

Dubcek was released Apr. 28 as a member of the Slovak National Council. *Rude pravo* criticized him that day for having received a delegation from one of the "Dubcek clubs," formed after the Soviet invasion, which the paper claimed were antiparty organizations.

Dubcek. flew from Ankara to Budapest May 30 and traveled by road to Bratislava to visit his mother, who was seriously ill. An official at the Czechoslovak embassy in Ankara, where Dubcek was ambassador, said that Dubcek was expected back, but the London *Times* reported May 31 that he had been ordered to Prague to face a party tribunal.

Mirsolav Moc accused Dubcek in *Rude pravo* May 31 of having received money from the pre-1968 regime of Antonin Novotny. Dubcek was said to have been "in the narrow circle of the chosen ones in receipt of the notorious envelopes containing high financial appreciation of his work." Moc had charged Dubcek May 23 with "hypocrisy, insincerity and narrow-mindedness" in connection with a July 19, 1968 interview in which French Communist Party First Secy. Waldeck Rochet urged him to temper the liberalization program and freedoms of the press. (Notes on the conversation had been published May 18 by *L'Humanite,* the French Communist Party newspaper, in an effort to refute allegations by Roger Garaudy, former party spokesman, that French party leaders had supplied the current Czechoslovak regime with a stenographic recording of the interview for use against Dubcek. Garaudy was expelled May 20 from the French party.)

The Soviet party newspaper *Pravda* attacked Dubcek by name June 3. The attack was made in an article welcoming measures by the current Czech leadership to remove "all revisionist and right-wing opportunist elements" from the party and state machinery.

Dubcek was expelled from the Czechoslovak Communist Party June 26 by vote of its Central Committee. The same meeting recalled him from his post as deputy of the Federal Assembly's Chamber of the People and confirmed his recall as ambassador to Turkey June 24. These actions followed a May 25 session of the party Presidium in which Dubcek's ouster had been approved by a vote of 7-4. Opposing the ouster were party First Secy. Gustav Husak, Pres. Ludvik Svoboda, Slovak Premier Peter Colotka and Czech National Council Chairman Evzen Erban. Joining the majority were Federal Premier Strougal and Alois Indra and Vasil Bilak, Czechoslovak party secretaries. Dubcek's expulsion was regarded as a victory for conservatives who favored political trials to punish those involved in the 1968 reform movement.

(Dubcek had been reported June 24 to be undergoing medical treatment at a Prague hospital as a result of a nervous breakdown following prolonged questioning by a party commission.)

Widespread comment followed the news of Dubcek's expulsion from the party and ouster as ambassador. Most of it was critical of the party, but some of it was in defense of the party's course.

Luigi Longo, general secretary of the Italian Communist Party, deplored Dubcek's ouster. Speaking in Rome June 26, he said that the "serious political crisis" in Czechoslovakia could not "in any way be resolved positively" by such decisions.

The party daily *Pravda* June 27 reported Dubcek's ouster as part of routine administrative shifts in the Czechoslovak party.

Misoslav Moc, editor of *Rude pravo* and member of the Secretariat of the party Central Committee, was reported June 29 to have listed the charges leading to Dubcek's expulsion as follows: "responsibility for ideological and organizational disruption, for a '2-faced' policy, ideological capitulation, lack of principles, lack of firmness that ... caused heavy damage to the national economy, responsibility for the violation of international and allied relations with the USSR and ... for capitulation to counterrevolutionary and anticommunist forces." Dubcek also was charged with failing to fulfill the duties of his office as ambassador to Turkey.

Radio Prague July 4 accused the Voice of America and Radio Free Europe of trying to make it appear that Dubcek "would be tried as a common criminal and, perhaps, even physically liquidated." The commentator said that the June Central Committee meeting "reaffirmed once again that there will be no political trials in Czechoslovakia, and that applies to Alexander Dubcek as well."

Speaking at a Pan-Slavic friendship rally outside Bratislava July 5, Czechoslovak Party First Secy. Husak delivered his first personal attack on his predecessor. He denied that there had been disagreement between himself and other high-ranking party leaders about Dubcek's expulsion from the party. (Husak said that the last Central Committee session had decided on Dubcek's expulsion because "he led our party into a state of disintegration which it had not known since 1945; he led our society, public organizations, the trade unions and youth to such a degree of disruption, he led our economy into such a wave of inflation, into such a disorganization that we found ourselves on the brink of economic bankruptcy; and in our international relations the links with the Soviet Union and with the other allied states were disrupted and Czechoslovakia stood isolated." Although Husak declared it right that "a man in such a high post ... be made to bear the political responsibility for his actions," he did not specify whether this would require further steps against Dubcek.

Husak said the Western press had tried to "weave legends around renegades, around emigres, around deserters and around other people ... to whom Alexander Dubcek, too, belonged." Husak specifically denied "nonsensical fabrications" about "how I was outvoted by the conservatives" at the Presidium session in which Dubcek's expulsion was approved. He declared that "on fundamental questions' there were "no differences between my opinions [and those of] Comrades Svoboda, Strougal, Bilak, Lenart and other comrades in the leadership."

The Federal Assembly July 8 unanimously confirmed the recall of Dubcek from his post as deputy.

The Czechoslovak party daily *Rude pravo* and the Slovak party daily *Pravda* July 16 carried a long denunciation expressly intended to debunk the "Dubcek legend." The party daily contended that the choice of Dubcek to succeed Antonin Novotny as Czechoslovak party leader was a mistake. Whereas the times called for a "steeled Marxist, ideologically firm and principled, and a good organizer," the article said Dubcek filled the bill "only weakly," was egoistical and indecisive and, through his dealings with "right-wing opportunists," exposed himself as "an unprincipled, compromising and cowardly party member."

Rude pravo confirmed earlier reports that Dubcek had steadfastly refused to indulge in "self-criticism." It said: "The new party leadership gave [him] a full opportunity to understand his mistakes and, as far as possible, to find his way out of the renegade mud. Dubcek did not take this path in his appearances before the party organs.... It was he who expelled himself from our ranks."

(The *N. Y. Times* reported Apr. 11, 1971 that Dubcek, "in poor health," was maintaining mechanical saws at a lumber mill near Bratislava. The American magazine *Life* May 14, 1971 reprinted photos, taken by a German photographer, that showed Dubcek waiting for and riding in a Bratislava streetcar and apparently gardening in the yard of a residence. The accompanying captions asserted that Dubcek lived with his wife and 3 grown sons at the edge of the city and worked from 6:30 a.m. to 3 p.m. as a city parks department garage manager for 2,300 crowns [officially $319] a month. Speaking to Western newsmen in Prague May 11, 1970, Husak had denied Western press reports that Dubcek was a garage manager for the city's parks department. Dubcek, he had said, was "living freely, working and has enough money.")

Climax of Purges

The Czechoslovak Communist Party announced Jan. 7 that it had begun "proceedings" against these former leaders during the democratization period: ex-Czechoslovak Interior Min. Jozef ˙Pavel, the former chairman of the Union of Czechoslovak Writers Eduard Goldstuecker and Milan Huebl, former head of the Party Staff College. The charges against the 3 were not disclosed.

Col. Pavel was reported Mar. 13 to have been expelled from the Communist Party. Pavel had initiated curbs on the power of the secret police. During Aug. 1968, according to *Rude pravo,* he had ordered "a watch to be kept on Soviet troop movements and took measures to isolate the Socialist embassies in Prague."

The Czech Interior Ministry announced Jan. 12 that it had uncovered a "Trotskyite" plot aimed at "overthrowing the existing political system." The announcement said that unidentified plotters had distributed "antistate printed matter" and had "found abroad the necessary aid and support in the form of instructions for work against the republic, supplies of Trotskyite and other hostile literature."

10 student members of an extreme left-wing group labeled as "Trotskyites" were arrested in Slovakia Jan. 16 on the first anniversary of Jan Palach's self-immolation. (The anniversary passed without a major demonstration.) A government announcement said that the students, identified as 9 Czechoslovaks and a West Berlin girl, had collected clandestine political, military and economic information for a spy center in Austria. (Police had arrested 1,740 persons in Bohemia and Moravia Jan. 15 in a crackdown of alleged "criminal elements.")

The government said Jan. 17 that the plot it had uncovered Jan. 12 had been concocted not only to overthrow the Czechoslovak government but also governments "in other Socialist countries, in particular the Soviet Union." An article in *Rude pravo* claimed that the alleged conspirators were members of a "revolutionary Socialist party" who were instrumental in "strikes, acts of sabotage and fires of which there was an unusually large number in 1968 and 1969."

The CTK news agency announced Jan. 27 a wide reorganization of its staff. Director Gen. Otakar Svercina said that the new management would be more in line with the party leadership.

Jozef Lenart was confirmed Feb. 5 as first secretary of the Slovak Communist Party, replacing Stefan Sadovsky. In an address before the Slovak party Central Committee, Lenart rejected the concept of the party containing 2 extreme wings, with the best people in the center; but he warned against "conservatism and dogmatism," which, he said, was used sometimes as a line of least resistance. Lenart also rejected the idea of a "general amnesty"; he repeatedly stressed the need to distinguish between honest Communists who had made mistakes and "adventurists" and arrant "initiators."

In other Feb. 5 developments, Jozef Zrak resigned from the Slovak party presidium and Central Committee, and Viktor Pavlenda resigned as a member and secretary of the presidium and Central Committee. Other unidentified members and alternate members also resigned from the Central Committee. Jan Pirc, secretary general of the East Slovak regional party committee, and Bohumil Travnicek, editor-in-chief of the Slovak party journal *Pravda,* were elected members of the secretariat.

According to the Yugoslav press agency Tanyug Feb. 10, a total of 18 members of the Slovak Central Committee had resigned at its Feb. 5-6 meeting in Bratislava. Together with earlier resignations and ousters, the new resignations reduced the committee's membership by ¼.

Jan Janik, leading secretary of the Bratislava city party committee, was quoted by the Bratislava *Pravda* May 21 as saying that the committee, after interviewing its members during an exchange of party cards, had decided to oust "some officials of the party, [some] persons employed in the mass information media and others who proved to be advocates and propagators of right-wing opportunist and other incorrect views and of incorrect party working methods." Janik mentioned the names of Andrej Sarvas, former director in Slovakia of the Czechoslovak Radio; Jozef Zrak (as ex-secretary of the city party committee); Julius Turcek, an ex-secretary of the Slovak party Central Committee; and R. Ruzickova-Stefdlova, the editor of *Pravda.*

The Czechoslovak Communist Party had announced Feb. 3 that it had begun a drive to carry out loyalty checks on its reported 1½ million members. A letter sent to lower units said each member would be asked his position during the 1968 liberalization movement and whether he accepted the official justification of the invasion. It also said that members must adhere to Communist beliefs with total conviction and submit to party discipline with "selflessness and inner enthusiasm."

According to *Rude pravo* Mar. 10, the first interviews in connection with the exchange of party membership cards at the primary organizational level, which had begun the previous week, showed that the Feb. 3 letter of the party Central Committee had not yet reached those levels. *Rude pravo* had said Mar. 9 that party members at lower levels, who often were close friends, were showing "false solidarity" against the directive.

Marie Mikova, deputy chairman of the Federal Assembly during the waning months of the Dubcek period, was reported to have been expelled from the party Mar. 20.

CTK reported Mar. 24 that the district party organization at Kladno near Prague had been dissolved when members failed to vote on expulsion of "rightist elements." The agency noted that this was "one of the first known cases where a whole party organization has been dissolved."

The Prague newspaper *Vecerni Praha* reported the party's expulsion of Bohumil Simon Mar. 25 and of Vanek Silhan Mar. 26. Both had been members of the Prague city organization and were accused, along with Martin Vaculik, of having been instrumental in the calling of the underground party congress held Aug. 22, 1968, the day following the Soviet invasion.

Bratislava *Pravda,* the Slovak Communist Party newspaper, reported Apr. 3 that Jiri Hajek, foreign minister at the time of the 1968 invasion, had been expelled from the party. Also expelled were: Martin Vaculik; Frantisek Sorm, ex-president of the Academy of Sciences; Oldrich Stary, ex-rector of Charles University; Karel Kosik, ex-professor of Marxism-Leninism at Charles University, and ex-Planning Min. Frantisek Vlasak.

Radio Prague Mar. 21 announced the expulsion from the party of many of the leading reformers of the Dubcek era, including the former Presidium members Josef Smrkovsky, Josef Spacek and Zdenek Mlynar, ex-Central Committee Secy. Cestmir Cisar, ex-editor-in-chief Jiri Sekera of *Rude pravo,* ex-Czechoslovak Youth League Chairman Zdenek Vokrouhlicky, and the cultural figures Frantisek Pavlicek and Karel Kaplan. The expulsions were ordered by the Czechoslovak party Central Committee Mar. 21 in line with an earlier decision (Mar. 6) by the Central Committee's Presidium.

(Cisar was reported Apr. 22 to be under treatment in a Prague clinic for a nervous breakdown. Smrkovsky was reported June 4 to be under treatment at a Prague hospital for cancer of the hip.)

Milos Jakes, chairman of the Party Control & Auditing Commission, made several references to the progress of the exchange of party cards: in an interview in *Rude pravo* Apr. 14, in a radio interview Apr. 16 and again Apr. 17 on the occasion of the district party meeting in Jicin, northeastern Bohemia. He said that more than 120,000 of the 1½ million party members had already been interviewed. These were chiefly officials of the Central Committee, of the Czechoslovak regional committees and district committees of the party and officials of social organizations.

Jakes said that it had become the turn of the basic organizations, and thus of the rank and file party members. Referring to the experiences of the first stage, Jakes said that the fears that too many people might leave the party had proved unsubstantiated, that the contrary had proven true.

Jakes criticized a much-too-liberal approach to the interviews. "Should this attitude also persist in the future," he said, "it will be difficult to achieve the [desired] goal ... *i.e.,* to purge the party of all those who do not fit into it, to activate and

cement its ranks and to restore its working class character."
According to Jakes, there were 2 kinds of shortcomings: (1)
party members had insufficient knowledge of party policy and
of the way in which the interviews had been set up; (2) members
of the interview commissions were too liberal and tolerant in
making their judgment of some of the activities of party members, excused wrong acts and all too often suggested further
investigation, instead of adopting a clear and unequivocal
standpoint. Many of these commissions, Jakes said, let themselves be maneuvered into a situation in which they had to
prove that the interviewed party member had made the mistake
and had expressed rightist-opportunist views, instead of
making the member talk openly and self-critically about his
attitudes in the past and proving where he stood and what he
intended to do in the future.

Jakes criticized the fact that the main subject of these
interviews was the past and that little attention was paid to the
future, particularly with regard to the members' attitudes
toward the economic policy of the party.

An extensive purge took place Apr. 19 in the presidium of
the Socialist Academy, the central institute for adult education.
Removed from the presidium were ex-Czech Education Min.
Vilibald Bezdicek, the philosopher Ladislav Tondl,
Academician Ivan Malek, and the university professors
Bedrich Weiner, Frantisek Kavka and Gustav Bares. Among
those co-opted to the plenum of the central committee in their
place were Cestmir Amort, deputy director of the
Czechoslovak-Soviet Institute; Ivo Hruza of the Higher School
of Politics; and O. Sucharda, director of the State Publishing
House of Technical Literature. Vladimir Ruml, director of the
Institute of Marxism-Leninism attached to the party Central
Committee, was elected deputy chairman of the academy.

According to a report in *Rude pravo* May 8 there was also
a purge in the Czechoslovak Sociological Association. The
association's committee decided at a meeting May 7 that it
needed a critical evaluation of its work so far. Because of
certain allegedly serious shortcomings, the committee concluded that its composition also had to be changed. The
resigned chairman, Josef Solar, and other members—only some
of whom had been named by the report—included the sociol-
ogist Prof. Josef Kral, 87, a pupil of Tomas Masaryk's and his

successor at the philosophical faculty of Charles University, Prague, and Profs. Josef L. Fischer and Milos Kalab. To replace the outgoing committee members, Profs. Karel Galla, Antonin Hodek and Vladimir Cech, the lecturer Karel Rychtarik, Frantisek Charvat and others were co-opted.

The federal Chamber of the People May 27 dismissed the president and 6 judges of the Czechoslovak Supreme Court for failure to counter anti-Socialist and anti-Soviet opinions. CTK said May 27 that Otomar Bocek, the court's president, had "engaged himself politically in an incorrect manner during 1968." Dismissed along with Bocek were Judges Otakar Adamec, Milena Hoferova, Julius Lehocky, Frantisek Paldus, Josef Silin and Lubomir Valeta. (Also dismissed, on the same charges, were Chamber Deputies Zdenek Gudrich and Leopold Hofman.) Vojtech Prichystal was elected as the new president of the Supreme Court.

At the 7th plenum of the Czech Trade Union Council Feb. 26, Chairman Rudolf Pacovsky had reported that "the trade union situation in Prague remains very unfavorable." CTK, the official news agency, had that day cited Pacovsky as saying that 17 officials of the Trade Union Council and 117 functionaries of the Association of Trade Unions had been dismissed for "right-wing opportunist tendencies" since the 5th plenum.

Pacovsky himself was dismissed as chairman of the Czech Trade Union Council May 21 along with the entire presidium and secretariat of that body. He was replaced by Josef Hlavicka, a veteran trade union official. Among those elected to the new secretariat were Jan Kriz, Vladimir Marik and Marie Ruzickova.

Commenting on the extent of the purge June 10, Jan Piller, chairman of the Central Council of Czechoslovak Trade Unions, said: "To date, 37 members and alternate members have left the Central Council, 181 members have left the Central Committees of Czech unions, 24 have left the Slovak unions, 47 members and alternate members have left the Czech Trade Union Council, and three members and alternate members have left the Slovak Trade Union Council.... By the middle of May this year, ... 503 members left the district trade union councils in the Czech Lands and 52 in Slovakia."

A resolution of the Central Council June 13 ordered trade unions to complete the purge of "the bearers of rightist opportunist tendencies" in higher organs by June 30 and in plant and enterprise committees by Sept. 30.

Vasil Bilak, a Czechoslovak party Central Committee secretary, declared it necessary at the Slovak party Central Committee plenum July 9 "to purge all National Front organizations of right opportunists and anti-Socialists." He singled out the intelligentsia as the chief font and source of the 1968 reform period. Bilak conceded that "in many places after the checks there will not be any Communists; many party organizations will not know how to implement the party's leading role, ... [and] it will be necessary to explain these problems very seriously and to tell them which correct methods to apply." "In this context," he said, "the principle must be stated that everybody who works in a responsible place must, regardless of party membership, proceed from Marxist positions.

"The [Czechoslovak party] was subverted from within," Bilak added. "This is no secret. If it was split not from outside but from within, who then caused it to split? Where are these rightist opportunists? Was it just Smrkovsky, Kriegel, Spacek, Mlynar and other [reform-minded] exponents? If we allow that there was counterrevolution here—and there indeed was—then we must say who began to establish the anti-Socialist theories and form ideological groupings. Either the antiparty theories were formed in factories and in villages or in certain institutions, academies, universities, offices, and so forth. I am convinced that this grouping took place among a section of the intelligentsia. With all due respect to it, this is where the grouping took place. And this is why assessment of this activity on the basis of principled Marxist-Leninist policy cannot be understood as persecution but as a serious purge of the party from people who do not belong in it [and] nothing else."

It was reported unofficially from Prague Aug. 17, that Jaroslav Sedivy, a leading Czechoslovak Communist historian, had been arrested by security police in his flat in the early hours of Aug. 3.

Informed sources also reported the expulsion from the Czechoslovak Communist Party of one of its oldest members, Pavel Reimann, 68, a party member since 1920, a member of the party's Political Bureau in the 1930s and a former official of the Comintern.

The senate of the regional court in Brno Aug. 19 sentenced 5 persons as members of an illegal "Kajman" of youths for conspiring to—and deliberating the conditions to—commit the criminal act of undermining the republic. The 5 defendants received prison sentences of from 6 months to 3 years.

According to the court the "Kajman" group had been founded in Breclav, South Moravia, toward the end of 1969. Its aim allegedly was: to duplicate and distribute leaflets of an inciting nature on May Day of 1970; to find out the addresses of public security corps members, army officers, members of the people's militias and Communist Party functionaries; to procure arms by assaulting public security patrols; and to ascertain people's militia arms depots. The group was also accused of planning "destructive" actions against Soviet forces stationed in Czechoslovakia and of planning to damage public buildings.

(The London *Sunday Times* Mar. 1 had published a report on the political purges of the 1950s. The report had been prepared by the Czechoslovak party before the Soviet invasion of 1968. The document, written under the direction of Jan Piller, from 1968 to 1971 a member of the party Presidium, was to have served as a basis for the rehabilitation of purge victims. During the purges, 178 persons had been executed and thousands arrested, among them Husak, who spent 9 years in prison. The report stressed the physical and psychological violence of the period and the flimsy evidence on which many of the arrests had been made.

Dissent & Its Repression

Journalists, intellectuals, students, educators and other cultural figures faced further corrective action by party conservatives firmly in power in 1970. The program extended in at least one instance to religion. Relations between Prague and the Vatican further deteriorated.

Among the first to feel official displeasure were writers. Pavel Kohout, a leading author and playwright, was denied an exit visa to attend a literary meeting in Switzerland Jan. 6. The previous day, Kohout, a Jew, had been denounced in the Slovak party newspaper *Pravda* as one of the "advocates of Israeli aggression" and linked with an alleged "Zionist world conspiracy" because of his support for Israel in 1967. Kohout had been expelled from the party Oct. 9, 1969.

Sources in Prague reported Feb. 2 that Jiri Lederer, a leading journalist during the 1968 liberalization period, had been arrested Jan. 29 on charges of being connected with an alleged antistate emigrant center. Authorities had charged earlier that the center was directed from a capitalist nation and was financed by U.S. intelligence. (The London *Times* reported Apr. 3 that Lederer had been released from jail. Lederer had been accused of a connection with a Paris-based Polish emigre organization.)

The regional court in Ostrava, North Moravia Feb. 17 sentenced Ota Filip, editor of the Profile Publishing House, to 18 months' imprisonment for "undermining the republic." A Bratislava broadcast that day said that Filip had since 1968 "expressed himself in a derogatory way about our ties of alliance with the Soviet Union and about state representatives."

Czech Culture Min. Miroslav Bruzek announced Mar. 12 that the government had seized the publishing house and recreation centers of the Czech Writers' Union. Speaking at a meeting of Prague artists and cultural workers that day, Bruzek asserted that the leaders of the creative unions "still adhere to wrong positions" and that his ministry would "transfer the Czech writers' publishing house to the literary fund managed by the ministry so that state funds could be granted ... those writers who support the current policy." The move had been foreshadowed Feb. 23, when Bruzek, speaking at a meeting of Ostrava journalists on the need to restore state direction of cultural policy, had added: "I say openly that we shall be able to do without the leadership of the Union of Artists and creative unions."

DPA, the unofficial West German news agency, reported Mar. 23 that Bruzek had ordered the Czechoslovak Writers Union "to discontinue at once its relations with foreign countries and not to enter into new ones." The report said that these relations would be handled in future by the Culture Ministry.

(DPA also revealed the dismissal of Svetoslav Stur as chairman of the Slovak Journalists Union. As chief editor of Bratislava radio, Stur reportedly was accused of having allowed "anti-Communist propagandists from West Germany" to use the Bratislava studios and of having failed to forbid his editors to cooperate with Western radio stations.)

The writer Jan Prochazka, however, struck back at his accusers and publicized his protest against the mounting attacks on him. His complaint was directed against an Apr. 21 Czechoslovak TV program entitled "Testimony from the Seine." In this program, Prochazka was seen conversing with a person hinted at as Pavel Tigrid, the editor of the Czech-language periodical *Svedectvi* of Paris, an emigre publication. Prochazka was accused of having been in contact with a representative of the Czechoslovak emigres. Parts of this program were quoted in *Rude pravo* Apr. 23.

Prochazka sent his protest to *Rude pravo* and all the other Prague newspapers and to more than 100 Czechoslovak and foreign writers. He said the conversation reproduced was one he had had with Prof. Vaclav Cerny in the latter's apartment in 1968; that it had been recorded by a listening device and then tendentiously distorted and adjusted; and that even under Dubcek the secret police had not abandoned their illegal methods. (Prochazka thus refuted by implication the current leadership's repeated assertion that under Dubcek the power positions of the "Socialist" state had been gradually eroded.)

Ludvik Vaculik, the author of the "2,000 Words" manifesto, joined Prochazka's protest by a letter addressed to the general prosecutor. Vaculik said that he was living in a gangsterlike environment in which the writ of the law does not run and in which everyone has to look after himself.

Prochazka's letter was mentioned in *Zemedelske noviny* of Apr. 30, 1970 and Vaculik's letter by the CTK press agency. Neither CTK nor *Zemedelske noviny* reproduced the text of the letter, however.

(Prochazka died in Prague Feb. 20, 1971 after a long illness.)

An internal circular of the Czech Writers Union announced June 8 the reception of a letter from the Federal Interior Ministry saying that "the Czechoslovak Writers Union has ceased to exist legally and factually, and the [Czech

Writers] Union must liquidate its assets without delay." The union argued in a letter to both the federal and the Czech interior ministries June 18 that it could cease to exist only in the manner prescribed by the union's statutes. These authorized dissolution only by a vote of ¾ of the membership.

Stanislav Neumann, who had received a Klement Gottwald Prize for poetry in the 1950s, committed suicide Sept. 18 because of disillusionment with government policies. Neumann left a note that read: "I decided to kill myself because I see more and more that the ideals for which I entered the party and for which my closest friends were executed on May 2, 1945 [at the Terezin concentration camp] are not being realized but have been trampled upon in political practice."

The Czechoslovak National Front, representing all legal political and cultural organizations, expelled the Movie & Television Artists' Union Jan. 7 for its alleged "contrary attitudes." A statement issued by the Front charged the union's leadership with being "unwilling to come to terms with the deformities of the post-January period," and it claimed that "right-wingers" in the union were still "attempting to boycott the culture and art of the Soviet Union and Socialist countries." The Front also criticized the Radio & Theater Artists' Union and added that the unions of painters, architects and composers would be scrutinized.

The Prague City Theatres' management announced Feb. 2 that it had cancelled the performances of 3 plays because they produced "undesirable reactions by the audience, which have reduced to vulgarity the apparent topicality of these productions and thereby reduced their artistic effectiveness." The 3 plays were Edward Albee's *A Delicate Balance;* Moliere's *Amphitryon;* and Oldrich Danek's *I Shall Return to Prague.*

Divadelni noviny, the official journal of the Theatrical Writers Union, was suspended because its criticism was deemed a threat to state interests. The final issue of the journal had accused *Rude pravo,* the Communist Party newspaper, of publishing "biased judgments and distortions whereby the party was trying to attribute sinister motives to every theatrical work and to present ... a completely false image of Czech theater life."

Czech Culture Min. Bruzek said Mar. 19 that there were "still a number of negative phenomena causing us anxiety in culture. ... There are still echoes of ideological and political doubting and hostile tendencies on the pages of cultural periodicals, as is evidenced by the [reaction to] the banning of *Divadelni noviny* and [by] the abuse of the stage for political gestures and provocation, counting on cheap success with a certain part of the audience."

Alois Polednak, former director of the Czechoslovak film industry, was charged Sept. 1 with subversion. A Czechoslovak government spokesman gave no explanation of the charge against Polednak, who had been arrested Aug. 14.

Czech Education Min. Jaromir Hrbek was revealed Feb. 7 to have issued a directive to university presidents banning all "uncontrolled contacts" between universities and scientific institutions in the West and those under his jurisdiction. The directive stated that contacts had to be stipulated in plans developed by the ministry; all other contacts had to be approved first by the university president and then "submitted for final approval to the approval committee of the ministry."

21 professors and lecturers were dismissed from the philosophy department of Charles University in Prague at the end of February. The dismissals followed a speech Feb. 25 in which Hrbek charged that "the most aggressive anti-Socialist, anti-party and anti-Soviet elements are still operating among the students, particularly at universities." He added: "The lamentable heritage of 1968 and of the first half of 1969 must be corrected ... at all levels of education." Hrbek said that students of working class origin would be given priority for university admission.

The London *Times* said Mar. 11 that an equally strong political campaign was being waged in the primary schools; teachers in northern Bohemia had been asked to complete a loyalty questionnaire asking such things as their reaction to the invasion of 1968 "in view of information now available" and their attitude toward the Soviet Army. Disciplinary action had been reported against a headmaster in east Prague after his students responded to a question about their favorite statesman by naming Alexander Dubcek and saying that they condemned the Soviet invasion of 1968.

Disturbances occurred Mar. 4 in the village of Zazriva, Slovakia following the arrest of Albin Senaj, a Roman Catholic priest, for what authorities described as "several criminal offenses." The villagers injured one policeman. A Prague broadcast Mar. 16 criticized the way Western news agencies had covered the incident and said Senaj had been anti-Semitic and pro-Nazi.

Bratislava *Pravda* accused the Roman and Greek Catholic clergy Mar. 28 of having tried to bring about "radical changes" in church-state relations during the reform movement of 1968. The Roman Catholic clergy was said to have tried to "create a broad base for the appearance of political Catholicism" through the organization Dielo Koncilovej Obnovy (Work of Council Revival). The paper noted that the group had never received official permission to function. *Pravda* accused the Greek Catholic clergy of having "unleashed in East Slovakia religious hatred against the Orthodox Church, its clergy and followers, spreading at the same time various anti-Socialist and anti-Soviet moods and committing various criminal acts not only in the sphere of religious freedom but also in that of coexistence of citizens." The paper stressed the need for all churches and religious societies "to realize their religious education in compliance with the laws of a Socialist state and social norms." (Ladislav Abraham, a secretary of the Slovak party Central Committee, had said Mar. 24 that religious belief was not incompatible with membership in the Communist Party.)

The Associated Press reported July 27 that a bronze tablet had been removed the previous weekend from the grave of Jan Palach, who had burned himself to death in protest against the Soviet occupation. The report said that residents in the neighborhood of Olsany Cemetery had accused police of removing the grave marker and that in previous months authorities had removed Prague and Bratislava memorials to victims of Soviet gunfire during the 1968 invasion.

Czech Interior Ministry police had taken 18,152 people in for questioning between Jan. 12 and 15 in Prague, elsewhere in Bohemia and throughout Moravia, detained 1,470 of them, arrested 118 and searched 2,052 apartments, houses and places of work in an effort to prevent public demonstrations Jan. 16, the anniversary of Palach's self-immolation. Many persons reportedly visited Palach's grave on Prague's outskirts and left flowers and lighted candles to commemorate his 3 days' agony before dying.

Defectors

38 Czechoslovak tourists in a group of 68 sought political asylum in Sweden and Denmark Jan. 4. In late Dec. 1969, 74 of 96 persons in another group had sought asylum in Sweden. 49 Czechoslovak tourists who had arrived in Stockholm before Christmas were granted political asylum in Sweden Jan. 20.

Dusan Havlicek, former head of the press department of the Czechoslovak Communist Party Central Committee, was granted asylum in Switzerland Jan. 8. He had become a correspondent for the CTK press agency in Geneva in Feb. 1969. In November he had been ordered to return to Prague but had refused.

The Czechoslovak government announced Jan. 27 that Ota Sik, architect of the 1968 economic reform program, had asked for asylum in Switzerland. He had been living there since 1968. The Interior Ministry announced Feb. 24 that Sik and 3 other Czechoslovak exiles—Jiri Pelikan, Ivan Svitak and Otakar Rambousek—had been deprived of Czechoslovak citizenship.

Jiri Mladek, Czechoslovakia's 3d-ranking diplomat at the UN, was reported Feb. 18 to have sought asylum in the U.S. Mladek, who also asked for asylum for his wife and son, was said to have been reprimanded by the Czechoslovak Mission at the UN for his failure to show enthusiasm for government policies. It was reported Feb. 20 that Mladek had been granted permanent residence status.

Slava Volny, an exile and former radio announcer, was reported Mar. 12 to have been deprived of his Czechoslovak citizenship for "alien activities towards our state" in the services of Radio Free Europe.

Rude pravo had announced Mar. 5 that the state planned to confiscate 5,505 apartments belonging to citizens who had remained abroad after Aug. 1968.

Czechoslovak diplomats abroad had been warned that they might face disciplinary action for "opportunism or counter-revolutionary activity," according to a *N.Y. Times* report Mar. 13. The warning was made in a letter of that date attributed to Pavel Auersperg, head of the foreign affairs division of the

Communist Party Central Committee. The letter accused Czechoslovak diplomats of allowing "anti-Socialist conceptions" to reach "unbelievable proportions" in some embassies in 1968.

Czechoslovak Amb.-to-Denmark Anton Vasek asked for asylum for himself and his family June 26 in Copenhagen following orders to return home.

A spokesman for the U.S. State Department said in Washington June 30 that Antonin Nenko, scientific affairs officer at the Czechoslovak embassy, had requested political asylum for himself and his family. Nenko's request was reportedly made after orders to return home.

Karel Sachar, head of the Czechoslovak commercial mission in Ecuador, disappeared with his wife and 2 sons July 7 and was reported to have sought political asylum in the U.S. Sachar had terminated all his functions at the mission June 30.

Kristina Hanzalova, Miss Czechoslovakia of 1969, sought political asylum Aug. 2 in Nuremberg, West Germany.

Vaclav Albert, first secretary of the Czechoslovak embassy in Kenya was said Aug. 24 to be in London, after resigning his post Aug. 21.

Vaclav Cihac, 2d secretary at the Czechoslovak embassy in The Hague, was provisionally granted political asylum in the Netherlands Aug. 26.

Ladislav Bartos, a Czechoslovak consular official in Sydney, was granted resident status in Australia Sept. 2. Bartos, due to return to Czechoslovakia on leave Sept. 1, had represented Koospol, the Czechoslovak foreign trade corporation, dealing in foodstuffs.

Pavol Majling, the Czechoslovak ambassador to Greece, shot himself in the mouth Nov. 3 in Athens and was taken to a local hospital. The embassy said Majling shot himself during a "crisis of honor," but failed to give further details.

Pavel Verner, an official of a Czechoslovak uranium plant, hijacked a company airplane May 5, forcing the pilot to land in Horching, Austria. The pilot, Pavel Bidermann, was taken to the hospital after being stabbed with a penknife by Verner. A passenger whom Verner had knocked unconscious with a shoe said he wanted to return to Czechoslovakia. Verner was sentenced Sept. 3 by a court in Linz, Austria, to a year in prison for hijacking.

4 men and 4 women hijacked a Czechoslovak airliner to West Germany and forced it to land in Nuremberg June 8. They were convicted of coercion Sept. 16 in Munich. The 8 received prison terms ranging from 8 months to 2½ years, but it was reported that they would not be extradited to Czechoslovakia afterwards. The sentences of 5 were suspended.

3 men hijacked a Czechoslovak airliner on a domestic flight from Prague to Bratislava and forced it to land in Vienna Aug. 8. The men, all Czechoslovaks, requested political asylum.

Arthur London, deputy foreign minister under Antonin Novotny, was deprived of his Czechoslovak citizenship Aug. 28. (Released from 3½ years' imprisonment in 1956 after sentencing in the Slansky trial, London was afterwards fully rehabilitated and had been decorated by Pres. Svoboda in May 1968. In that year London published *The Confession,* a book describing the methods by which the Slansky trial had been prepared.) London had lived in France since 1956. In depriving London of his citizenship, the Czechoslovak Interior Ministry said that his book had "caused damage to the important interests" of Czechoslovakia and that London had helped "deepen anti-Soviet and anti-Socialist tendencies." London rejected his denaturalization, saying Aug. 30 that he considered "this arbitrary decision as contrary to Socialist legality and Socialist morality." The Italian Communist Party weekly *Rinascita* Sept. 3 deplored the action as "a sort of blind automatism, an absurd mechanism of revenge." *Rinascita* said of the methods employed by the Novotny regime that "the prestige of socialism and the interests of a Socialist country are damaged by resorting to those methods, not by denouncing them."

Czechoslovak refugees in Western countries were being advised that their presence abroad was illegal and they would have to pay for their legal defense costs, according to a *N.Y. Times* report Dec. 15. Letters sent from "legal advisory centers" in Prague were informing refugees that, under section 109 of the Czechoslovak penal code, they "can be tried *in absentia* and may be sentenced to prison for terms of 6 months to 5 years, to corrective measures and to confiscation of property." In the letters, signed by individual lawyers, recipients were told that "since you have not chosen a defense counsel, I have been nominated to represent you." It was suggested the refugees appeal for legalization of their stay abroad. The refugees were advised that unless they made a "down payment" in foreign currency within 5 days for defense costs the amount would be collected from their "nearest relatives" in Czechoslovakia. (An estimated 70,000 refugees were affected by the action.) A spokesman for the Australian Foreign Office said in Canberra Dec. 15 that his government had expressed concern to Prague over reports that refugees were being asked for as much as $150 in defense costs.

According to an article published Sept. 30 in the periodical *Narodni vybory* (a survey of local government news), there were 50,000 emigres in the West who had fled or remained outside of Czechoslovakia after the Soviet-led invasion of 1968. Of these, 36.6% were classified as intellectuals and 35.8% as workers. 54.1% of the exiles ranged from 15 to 30 years of age and 30.8% were from 30 to 45 years old, according to the article's author, Jaroslav Zizka, press spokesman of the Czech Interior Ministry.

PROGRESS OF CONSOLIDATION

Hard Line Modified

In what was considered a warning against overzealous attempts to deal with ex-reformers, party First Secy. Gustav Husak told the Central Committee June 25 that it was "incorrect to put all those with whom the party has parted into the same group as the outright enemies of socialism and the organizers of disruption."

The acid test of the Husak regime's stability was considered the 2d anniversary of the 1968 Soviet invasion, and observers held that the regime passed it handily. Heavy police patrols and other security measures helped ensure the failure Aug. 21 of a passive resistance campaign planned to mark the event.

The resistance appeal, reported Aug. 4 to have been circulated by hand in Prague, had called for a boycott of shops, theaters and newspapers, together with a voluntary 7 p.m. curfew. The appeal had read in part: "They can forbid us to do something, but they cannot prevent us from not doing something. They can forbid us to go into the streets, but they cannot prevent us from not going into the streets." The only incident known to have occurred Aug. 21 was the detention by police of 3 young East Germans and 2 Italians who arranged flowers and candles at the grave of Jan Palach. Shortly after midnight Aug. 20, the East Germans had been prevented by police from laying flowers at the statue of King Wenceslas in the main Prague square.

Entry into the country was temporarily denied Aug. 14 to "all persons born but not domiciled in Czechoslovakia" as well as to foreign journalists, students, lawyers and clergymen. By Aug. 16, Czechoslovak border officials had turned back more than 400 prospective visitors, and the ban was extended Aug. 20 to include vacationing members of the West German armed forces.

Soviet and Czechoslovak military units conducted joint exercises Aug. 10-17. The official news agency CTK revealed Aug. 24 that 6,217 persons had been detained and a number of rifles seized during the days preceding the invasion anniversary. The agency referred to those detained as "hidden manipulators ... who wanted to disrupt the quiet lives of our citizens." The British weekly *Economist* reported Sept. 5 that more than 800 of those detained were charged later with offenses ranging from murder to petty theft.

Husak Aug. 28 praised the "high degree of political consolidation" in the country and declared that Czechoslovakia had "overcome the critical period." Speaking at Nizna in Central Slovakia, Husak said that in the period since his election as first secretary, "temporary and necessary measures" had rapidly "eliminated ... the crisis in which our society and state were involved." He added: "However, we carried them out by political methods, guided by the principles of Socialist humanism. There are many examples in the world where, in a situation like ours, there was bloodshed and various victims. We tried to avoid, and we did avoid, such a procedure, such methods and such grave consequences." "After bridging this crisis period," Husak said, "we now wish to move over to the normal type of life, to normal forms of Socialist democracy."

Recalling the 26th anniversary of the Slovak National Rising, Husak said that Warsaw Pact leaders, at their August conference in Moscow, had discussed ways in which "states with different social systems might ... cooperate." He welcomed a recently-signed treaty between the USSR and West Germany and said "there is also good will on our side to contribute to the solution of the problems still existing between our country and the [German] Federal Republic."

The Communist party weekly *Tribuna* Sept. 10 accused opponents of the 1968 reform era of political failure, hypocrisy and greed. Oldrich Svestka, the paper's editor and a conservative member of the party Presidium under Dubcek's leadership, wrote that political mistakes by hard-liners in the previous 20 years had led to Dubcek's rise. Svestka maintained: "At stake was their fate, or, more accurately, their livelihood, the jobs they held [and therefore their standard of living], which they in more than one case identified with the fate of the party, with the fate of our friendship with the Soviet Union and other Socialist countries."

Party First Secy. Husak indicated Sept. 10 that the party was making an effort to improve its standing with intellectuals. He said at a gathering of miners in Ostrava that "the time has come for very active political work" with "all sections of our intelligentsia" to ensure "that no artificial wall is created here." Because "such an advanced economy as the Czechoslovak cannot be run and expanded without the technical intelligentsia, ... the attitude to all who are outside the party and also to those who have left the party must be comradely, must be humane, and must be honest."

In his speech, Husak emphasized the need for reconciliation between the leadership and the population. He declared that "the millions of our working people who are not or will not be members of the party are also honest working people and equal members of our society." This statement recalled his pronouncement—"He who is not against us is our potential ally"—at the Jan. 1970 party Central Committee plenum. (It was patterned on Hungarian party First Secy. Janos Kadar's reconciliation appeal: "He who is not against us is with us.") Husak tried to reassure the public by discussing "rumors" that permanent purges would be carried out and stated that the Central Committee had "no such plans." He cited "foreign bourgeois propaganda" as the source of these rumors; actually such demands had been made in his own party.

Premier Lubomir Strougal, speaking Oct. 10 at a meeting of ironworkers in the North Moravian foundry town of Vitkovice, referred to the intelligentsia as "the most dynamically developing part of the economically active population." He said that during the past 2 years this group had "succumbed least to the disrupting views," and he was confident they "will realize where their place really is." Strougal added: "We want to gain for our program the largest possible number of honest members of the intelligentsia, people devoted to socialism, and to ensure their utilization as workers and experts to the utmost."

At a Nov. 5 ceremony in Prague commemorating the 53d anniversary of the Bolshevik revolution, Vasil Bilak, a prominent conservative member of the party Presidium, interpreted the 1968 reform movement. He said:

We cannot blame the working people for what happened or accuse them of anti-socialism and anti-Sovietism. They became the victims of those who sought to prepare a coup in Socialist Czechoslovakia....

A counterrevolution is not prepared in villages and small towns but in a center from which villages and small towns can be influenced and controlled. A counterrevolution—this is neither a nation nor a people, but a small group of reactionaries who in their endeavor to gain support proclaim their reactionary and conservative aims as a people's cause and the nation's cause. Today many of those who held responsible high positions are lamenting and crying that they did not know where the political coup was being prepared. However, they were so blinded by their false popularity—organized for them by anti-Socialist forces—that they were more fearful of losing their personal popularity and fame than they were about the party and Socialist cause. Thus they found themselves being dragged along by the counterrevolution, even becoming its symbols. This is why these people have no place in our party and cannot hold high positions in this state.

Today, when we are evaluating our whole development in 1968, we again realize that those who let developments in our country get out of hand and who ceased to defend the gains of the Socialist revolution in Czechoslovakia have a heavy responsibility to the party, people and international Communist movement. In this way the counterrevolution created a free range for exerting its influence. Thus, the situation came to a head, with the result that in mid-Aug. 1968 Czechoslovakia stood on the threshold of a bloody counterrevolution and civil war. This is why the assistance of 5 fraternal countries on 20 August 1968 was an act of international solidarity which barred the way to counterrevolutionary forces and saved us from a fratricidal fight and from the physical liquidation of many honest builders of socialism.

Purges Slowed

Czechoslovak radio stations announced Sept. 8 that Bohuslav Chnoupek, hitherto director of the Czechoslovak broadcasting system, had been appointed Czechoslovak ambassador in Moscow. He replaced Vladimir Koucky, who had occupied the post since May 1968. Chnoupek was replaced as broadcasting system director by Jan Risko. Western observers interpreted Risko's appointment as Husak's victory over the ultras, who had been particularly active in Czechoslovak broadcasting under Chnoupek.

The London *Times* reported Sept. 9 that 75 former professors and teachers at the Czechoslovak Communist Party College in Prague had been expelled from the party.

Zdenek Zuska was elected mayor of Prague at the 35th plenary meeting of the Prague National Committee Sept. 10, replacing Ludvik Cerny, reportedly relieved of the post at his own request. Deputy Mayor Bohumil Havlicek and National

Committee Secy. Miroslav Borkovec were also relieved of their posts.

The process of screening party members, begun in February, was described Sept. 22 by Czech Premier Josef Korcak as drawing to a close. Speaking at a party rally in Jihlava, Moravia, Korcak announced: "The cleansing of the party has been fundamentally completed and, on average, one out of every 5 members has left." The expulsions caused a reduction of membership by 300,000, the London *Times* estimated Sept. 23.

Rude pravo Sept. 11 had published steps necessary to validate the new membership cards. The announcement said: "Many party organizations have already held festive meetings at which the new party membership cards were handed to Communists. In order that their party document is completely in order, they must also fulfill the duty of reporting with the new membership card to the party organization in their place of residence. Through this measure, street organizations and the party organizations in the villages gain knowledge about the members of works organizations living in their district. Communists have the same duty whenever they change their place of residence."

Urging party members to work actively in their village organization or place of residence, the paper added: "It is naturally not possible to overburden people with functions, and to load on to one individual more obligations than he would be capable of managing. But it is our wish that no party member should stand on the sidelines, that he should work actively and that his capacities and experiences are fully utilized. A Communist must be a Communist everywhere. He must not only work, but he must also live in such a way that it is obvious that this is a Communist, a person worthy to be called such."

Rude pravo declared Sept. 29 that the exchange had "proceeded in a severe struggle with right-wing opportunist elements, which suffered a crushing defeat."

Czechoslovak Radio had reported Sept. 19 that the presidium of the Slovak Academy of Sciences had recalled the heads of all its scientific boards and institutions until new chairmen and vice-chairmen were installed Oct. 1. According to the *N.Y. Times* Oct. 3, educational and scientific units in Czechoslovakia faced the dissolution or recall of 107 union units, apparently because the unions had failed to purge reformist elements.

The Czech Trade Union Council Oct. 15 accepted the resignations of 11 of its members and all of its alternate members and relieved 4 other members of their posts. Jan Kriz, a member of the secretariat, said that regional councils were being changed to become "a more normal element of the integral trade union structure."

The party biweekly *Zivot strany* Oct. 25 published a guide for party control commissions by Milos Jakes, party Central Control & Auditing Commission chairman. With regard to the question of the party cleanup, on which a difference of opinion had arisen between the moderates and the ultraconservatives, Jakes took a middle course. According to him, there would not be another purge campaign, but the party would "continually cleanse its ranks of those who do not belong in it." Jakes modified the party approach toward ousted members. He pointed out that 80% of those who had forfeited their party cards had merely been stricken off the roster, *i.e.,* their membership had been canceled but they had not been expelled. Cancellation did not constitute a form of party punishment according to party statutes, and a return of membership to those affected would not be barred. Jakes implied that only 20% had been expelled.

Jan Simek, leading regional party secretary in western Bohemia (Plzen), who had opposed the moderation of the purges in September, adopted a milder line in a speech broadcast over Radio Plzen Nov. 17. Simek accepted the official theses that the purge had been completed and that the party has entered the new stage of economic consolidation and ideological struggle, designed to win over the broad public. He noted with apparent regret that many members had had to leave the party because of errors committed by the directing bodies rather than because of their own failures.

Other important officials also indorsed the policy of relative moderation. Antonin Kapek, Presidium member and leading municipal party secretary in Prague, hitherto considered a staunch hardliner, asserted that the exchange of party cards has been completed, that extraordinary measures have been discontinued and that "no one has the right to lay down a policy of continued screening, permanent purge or the like."

The news agency CTK had announced Oct. 24 that the Slovak Writers Union had accepted the resignation of 5 members of its committee on the previous day.

The Czechoslovak government Oct. 27 removed Gen. Otakar Rytir as liaison officer to the Soviet forces stationed in the country and announced his election as chairman of the Union for Cooperation With the Army (Svazarm), a group organizing voluntary military training for young civilians. Rytir and Josef Groesser, dismissed as the Czech republic's interior minister Oct. 23, were reported by the London *Times* Oct. 30 to have been associated with the activities of a conservative opposition group said to include at least 2 federal cabinet ministers and a prominent member of the Federal Assembly. Evidence of the group's existence was reportedly discovered in the personal effects of a Bohemian party official killed in a car accident in September. The man's safe was said to contain a list of those willing to serve in a new government and a draft letter to Soviet officials accusing party First Secy. Husak of insufficient vigor in opposing reformists.

The London *Times* said Oct. 30 that a liberal manifesto circulating in Prague accused the current leadership of "bureaucratic socialism" and of endangering the country through economic and cultural repression. The manifesto reportedly declared: "If it is not to destroy itself, it [the current leadership] must gradually move over to the formulation of a pseudo-positive program, and cannot endlessly continue in permanent mass purges and personnel changes."

An article by Jaroslav Vavrinec, entitled "We Like to Suspect One Another," was published in the Slovak party daily *Pravda* Nov. 4. According to the author, suspicion was rampant in Czechoslovakia: "The workers blame the party when they earn less than they expected; those who were not cleared in connection with the party card exchange believe that the commission—and thus the party—acted in bad faith. Where there should be cooperation for the common good, there is instead suspicion."

Pavol Kiraly, former chairman of the Supreme Court of the Slovak Republic, was appointed Slovak justice minister Dec. 3. Kiraly replaced Felix Vasecka.

The Czechoslovak Communist Party Central Committee ended a 2-day plenary session Dec. 11 by accepting a final report from the Presidium on the earlier concluded exchange of membership cards and by passing a resolution on party unity. Delivering a report on the card exchange Dec. 10, party First Secy. Husak revealed that since the beginning of the exchange in February, a total of 326,817 members had been either expelled or had their memberships canceled. Since Jan. 1968, some 475,731 members had left the party involuntarily. The current membership was 1,200,000. (According to a *N. Y. Times* report Dec. 22, about 220,000 unclaimed cards were being held by local branches, and the party's real membership was less than a million.) Speaking of tasks still faced by the party, Husak distinguished between the right wing, which he described as the main danger, and "opportunism," a condition "where people are inactive, where they don't want to commit themselves to anything new which is linked with any risk, where everyone tries ... only to keep his peace, to keep out of difficulties." Husak said that "the further stage of consolidation which we are facing cannot mean a return to the methods of work which were used in the party and in society before 1968." (The state economic development plan for 1971 was approved at the meeting.)

The Central Committee Dec. 11 expelled from party membership ex-Czechoslovak Premier Oldrich Cernik, whose membership had been suspended in July. Although no official reason was given for the expulsion, it was generally attributed to Cernik's close association with the reform policies of Alexander Dubcek.

Oldrich Svestka was named to the Secretariat of the Central Committee Dec. 11, replacing Frantisek Penc, whose new position was not disclosed.

CTK reported Oct. 29 that the federal Culture Ministry had established a Literary Council with the power to advise state-owned printing houses on which books to publish. The agency said the council was being set up with the aim of "unifying and activating Czech writers."

Foreign Relations

Kenneth Ames, a correspondent of the British weekly *Economist* (London), was ordered to leave Czechoslovakia by Jan. 8. He was told that he had not met the conditions for residency and had displayed "negative attitudes." Eric Bourne of the American daily *Christian Science Monitor* (Boston) was refused renewal of his visa Jan. 8 for similar reasons.

Rude pravo charged Jan. 20 and 21 that the British secret service had been engaged in espionage during the first half of 1968. The newspaper said that 2 former British ambassadors in Prague, Sir Cecil Parrott and Sir William Barker, had worked with the secret service. The newspaper also charged that Cyril Jonsen, British press attache in 1968, had been involved with the service in "smuggling out various manuscripts attacking socialism and publishing them." Describing the secret service as "one of the most aggressive tools of foreign policy," *Rude pravo* claimed that it had been "directly engaged in influencing the Czechoslovak developments in the first half of 1968."

Soviet Foreign Min. Andrei A. Gromyko paid a 6-day visit to Czechoslovakia Mar. 17-22. While there he initialed a new treaty of friendship between his country and Czechoslovakia. The *Washington Post* Mar. 17 quoted Czechoslovak officials as saying that the current treaty, due to expire in 1983, would be "brought up to date to conform with our mutual cooperation in all fields." Czechoslovak Foreign Min. Jan Marko also initialed the treaty.

Pres. Ludvik Svoboda paid a 4-day visit to Mongolia Mar. 26-29 and conferred with Chief of State Zhamsarangin Sambu. A communique issued at the end of the visit said the 2 had discussed European security and the situation in Indochina. It asserted that "the political course of the leaders of the Chinese People's Republic contradicts the interests of the struggle of Socialist countries and merely plays into the hands of the forces of world imperialism and reaction."

The new 20-year Czechoslovak-Soviet friendship treaty, to enter into force when instruments of ratification had been exchanged, was signed May 6 in Prague. Signing for the Soviet Union were Soviet Party Gen. Secy. Leonid I. Brezhnev and Premier Aleksei N. Kosygin; for Czechoslovakia, Czechoslovak party First Secy. Gustav Husak and Premier Lubomir Strougal.

After reaffirming the obligations of the 2 countries under the 1955 Warsaw Treaty, the UN Charter and within the framework of the Council for Mutual Economic Assistance (COMECON), the preamble of the 14-article agreement declared that the "support, the strengthening and the protection of Socialist acquisitions, which were achieved through heroic efforts and sacrifice-filled toil by the people of the 2 countries, are the joint international duty of the Socialist countries."

Article 10, which committed Czechoslovakia to possible military support of the USSR outside Europe, stated that "each signatory party pledges to consider any armed attack against the other party, by any state or group of states, as an attack directed against itself and to supply it without delay all necessary aid, including military aid." Article 6 noted the invalidity of the 1938 Munich agreement. Article 9 expressed the 2 countries' belief that one of the principal conditions for European security was the "immutability of state borders in Europe formed after the 2d World War" and pledged both powers to ensure "the inviolability of the borders of the member states" of the Warsaw Treaty.

The Soviet delegation returned to Moscow May 7 after participating in ceremonies marking the 25th anniversary of the liberation of Czechoslovakia by the Soviet army.

The treaty was ratified June 1 at ceremonies in Moscow and Prague. Attending ceremonies at the Presidium of the Supreme Soviet in Moscow were Pres. Nikolai V. Podgorny and Premier Kosygin. In Prague, where the Federal Assembly had approved the treaty May 28, ceremonies were attended by Pres. Svoboda, party First Secy. Husak, Premier Strougal and Soviet Amb.-to-Czechoslovakia Stepan V. Chervonenko.

Strougal said Sept. 8 in Prague that Czechoslovakia was "taking pertinent steps through government channels" for "the adjustment of ... relations between West Germany and our Socialist republic." Strougal did not specify which steps had been taken.

Czechoslovakia and the Soviet Union in Moscow Sept. 29 signed an agreement on coordinating economic development plans for 1971-75. The volume of trade envisioned between the 2 countries was approximately $14.8 billion, a 43% increase over the figure for the previous 5-year period. Agreements on cooperation in extracting oil in the USSR and the delivery of natural gas to Czechoslovakia were part of the trade document, as were provisions for the construction of nuclear power stations and prefabricated housing plants in Czechoslovakia.

24 tourists on a hiking trip—3 West German and the others American—were taken into custody by Czechoslovak officials Aug. 8 when they strayed across the border near the West German town of Furth Im Wald. The party was released by Aug. 10.

The U.S. embassy in Prague announced Aug. 14 that Czechoslovak secret police had arrested Fred H. Eidlin, age given as 27, of Rochester, N.Y. on spy charges. An embassy spokesman said that Czechoslovak authorities had informed embassy officials Aug. 6 that Eidlin had been seized Aug. 3. He had been held incommunicado since his arrest. The spokesman said that U.S. officials were "particularly concerned at the failure of the Czechoslovak government to grant [consular] access." He said that granting access, despite the lack of a consular convention between Czechoslovakia and the U.S., was standard international practice. The U.S. State Department also voiced concern Aug. 14 over the denial of access to Eidlin and said that it had no reason to believe he was involved in intelligence activities. Eidlin, a former employe of Radio Free Europe, was touring Europe prior to enrolling at Toronto University for doctoral study.

Eidlin was convicted in Prague Dec. 18 and sentenced to 4 years in prison. Judge Miloslav Topinka ruled that Radio Free Europe, for which Eidlin had worked as a policy assistant in Munich from Apr. 1968 to Nov. 1969, was conducting subversive activites against Czechoslovakia and that Eidlin had been a foreign agent during his employment there. Eidlin was also convicted of having arranged a meeting between RFE employes and 2 Czechoslovak students in 1969 but was acquitted of charges that he tried to recruit the students for RFE.

Economic Policies

Speaking at the plenary meeting of the party Central Committee Jan. 28, Federal Planning Min. Vaclav Hula urged stronger centralized control by the federal government over the Czech and Slovak Planning Ministries. The Central Committee Jan. 30 adopted a resolution on the basic problems of the party's economic policy.

According to the CTK press agency, the resolution emphasized that the Czechoslovak economy had been developing at a fast rate since 1948. At the same time, however, serious shortcomings could be observed in economic development.

It was charged in the resolution that the post-January leadership of the party had stopped exerting an influence on economic development and that the resolutions on economic matters made by the Central Committee in 1967 were not being carried out: Right-wing forces had launched an outright offensive on the system of planned management of the Socialist national economy. The actions of the right revisionist and anti-Socialist forces in 1968 and at the beginning of 1969 had inflicted a great deal of harm on the Czechoslovak economy, had aggravated existing imbalances and had affected its efficiency. They had undermined the party's leading role and the system of Socialist economic management and had tried to weaken Czechoslovakia's economic relations with countries in the Socialist community. The Central Committee's new leadership, at its plenary meetings in May and Sept. 1969, was said to have taken the first steps aimed to stop this reverse trend and inflation tendencies.

The 1970 plan and other measures envisaged ways to solve basic problems in the national economy, the resolution noted. The aim of these measures was to stop inflation, to "consolidate the positive results already obtained from the 2d half of 1969 and to create the necessary conditions for further economic development," *Rude pravo* reported Feb. 1. The 1970 economic plan set targets that were deemed "realistic, though difficult." The Central Committee considered their attainment to be a necessary prerequisite for the general consolidation of Czechoslovak society.

The resolution mapped out the basic trends for improving planning and economic management and laid down measures for boosting the party's leading role and "positive work" to be done by party organizations and all Communists. The plenary meeting gave government organs until mid-1970 to draft the directives for economic development for the 5-year period 1971-5 and until Dec. 31 to draft the new 5-year plan.

The Czechoslovak government Mar. 19 introduced 4 additional Saturday work days during 1970 because, according to CTK, "winter calamities and consequent breaks in electric power supplies and transport" had diminished the prospect of "fulfilling the planned targets for the current year."

In a Prague TV interview Mar. 13, Premier Lubomir Strougal said that "in the near future" comprehensive measures would be announced to "rationalize the work of our economic, state and entire management apparatus." He warned further: "There are very grave shortcomings in management in all sectors of production; there are grave shortcomings in working morale, in labor discipline and in the observation of working hours in some places. ... Naturally we must deal today with the problem of manpower ... because we cannot condone some people very often fluctuating, going from one factory to another and getting paid better in the new place of work." Strougal spoke also of the need to strengthen the role of the state plan: "We know that there has been no central plan in the past 2 years ..., that investments in terms of incomplete projects at the beginning of 1970 are roughly 25% higher than I should say would be tolerable for the economy of this country."

In a speech to the Federal Assembly May 29, Strougal reviewed the domestic situation for the first 4 months of 1970, outlined the draft 1971-5 economic plan and announced reforms designed to strengthen state control. He said that the government had "devoted its main attention to economic problems," chiefly those of strengthening the role of the state plan and management. After reporting on growth rates, Strougal said that primary emphasis had been given to the completion of unfinished housing projects. He said that the government would enforce a ban imposed on new projects.

In foreign trade, Strougal said, the plan aimed at increasing trade with the Socialist countries, although "imports are not *de facto* controlled and ... the Foreign Trade Ministry, and particularly the foreign trade organizations, are still not capable of satisfactorily managing and controlling this sphere." Czechoslovakia's aim of eliminating "short-term debts with capitalist states at the beginning of 1971" and with Socialist states "within the next 2 or 3 years" could be realized only "if we start to produce and deliver whatever those countries need and require," Strougal said.

During the next 5-year plan, "approximately ⅓ of the contemplated industrial investments" would be devoted to fuel and power. Demand for hospitals, transport, schools, cultural facilities and tourism "simply cannot be met in 5 years," Strougal declared, although these were "politically most sensitive problems." Planned national income growth was 5% a year; average wage growth 2.6% to 2.8%. The number of persons employed in management administration would be reduced by at least 10% from the 1969 total.

Asserting there was a need for reform to increase government controls, Strougal said: "Changes are demanded in many legal regulations.... We must do this first of all in the economic sector where mass violation of the law still occurs." In the area of public prosecution, he said, there had been "an aversion toward prosecuting offenses against the internal and external interests of the Socialist state. They were prosecuted incorrectly, and there was a clear tendency to treat offenses of a clearly political character as minor offenses of a general criminal nature and even not to prosecute such criminal activities at all." As regards judicial rehabilitation, he continued, "there were endeavors toward wholesale quashing of old verdicts, even when the offenses were really committed." Criminal offenses were ⅕ higher than in 1967, and juvenile delinquency was rising in Prague, he said.

"Far-ranging work aimed at raising political, professional and technical preparedness is going on in the security corps," Strougal reported, and "bourgeois propaganda" about "show trials" could not "divert us from the basic purpose of our policy." The Czechoslovak foreign service was "eliminating all the ballast that has not served the interests of our republic," Strougal said. "Only those who are convinced of the correctness of the given political line and who are resolved consistently to implement it can work in this sector."

CTK announced the results of the 1970 economic development plan Jan. 28, 1971. Measured as increases over the figures for 1969, these major items were reported: Industrial production 7.7% (consumer goods 8%, producer goods 7.5%), retail trade turnover 2.2%, exports to Socialist countries 17%, exports to capitalist countries 10%, gross agricultural output 1.3%. (A Radio Free Europe research report Jan. 14, 1971 said that livestock production had increased 5.7% while crop production decreased 3.3%.) Coal output totaled 28,183,000 tons; pig iron 7,548,000 tons; crude steel 11,480,000 tons. The state built 107,700 apartments and 18,465 tractors were produced.

A Radio Prague report Jan. 31, 1971 said that although real wages had risen only 1% in comparison with increases of 13.5% in 1968 and 1969, the previous increases had been "unhealthy" and had been accomplished by running down reserves and taking imports on credit.

1971

By late May 1971 "normalization" was pronounced an accomplished fact of Czechoslovak life. This assessment was made by party First Secy. Gustav Husak at the 14th Communist Party Congress, which took place 33 months after the Soviet-led invasion. Soviet party Gen. Secy. Leonid Brezhnev concurred in Husak's finding. All domestic opposition had been silenced, exiles seemed discouraged, and Western analysts were pessimistic about the country's prospects for any early democratization. It was announced early in June that the party congress had restored the ex-party leader Antonin Novotny to full party membership, and events appeared to have come full circle from the "Prague Spring" of 1968.

Husak's foes continued to erode the federalization advocated by Husak as Slovak party leader. Separate national citizenship for Czechs and Slovaks was abolished and single citizenship reinstituted throughout the federal republic. The material condition of the people improved as a result of extensive imports of consumer goods from other countries of the Soviet bloc. Prices of a few consumer items were reduced and Western visitors reported about well-stocked stores in Prague. At the same time, restored central control over production and distribution left little latitude for further economic experimentation.

Czechoslovakia followed the examples of the Soviet Union and Poland in initiating the normalization of its relations with West Germany. Legal problems concerning the annulment of the 1938 Munich treaty, however, prevented an agreement about the establishment of dipolomatic links. In all issues of foreign policy, Czechoslovakia followed closely the Soviet leadership, and its relations with most Western countries remained strained.

NORMALIZATION COMPLETED

Ultras Reassert Themselves

In a document approved in Dec. 1970 and released Jan. 14, 1971, the Czechoslovak party Central Committee asserted that "thousands of the party's rank and file" had invited Soviet-led Warsaw Treaty troops into the country in Aug. 1968. It also charged the reformers Ota Sik, Eduard Goldstuecker, Frantisek Kriegel (still in Czechoslovakia) and others of Jewish origin with having provoked the invasion by their allegedly reactionary role in the liberalization period. In a nod to party moderates, the Central Committee also declared that the "conceit, subjectivism, megalomania and suspiciousness" of ex-First Secy. Antonin Novotny had been responsible for the reform period of 1968. The Central Committee also criticized Vladimir Koucky, currently ambassador to Belgium, as well as reform leader Alexander Dubcek.

The British weekly *Economist* of London asserted Jan. 23 that the release of the month-old resolution showed up "the mid-December meeting of the Central Committee ... [as] a test of ... [Husak's] ability to hold his ground." The *Economist* reported that Central Committee Secy. Vasil Bilak had "produc[ed] a list of 40 people ... alleged to have signed a document asking for Soviet intervention" in Czechoslovakia in 1968 at the Central Committee's mid-Jan. 1971 meeting. Bilak thus caught "Husak, whose signature was conspicuously missing, off balance."

The Soviet Defense Ministry organ *Krasnaya Zvezda* had reported Jan. 22 on how 3 Soviet officers, who in Aug. 1968 had entered Czechoslovakia at the head of invading units, had reacted to the document adopted by the December plenum of the Czechoslovak party Central Committee. The reactions were printed under the heading "Fidelity to international duty." A Lt. Col. Kovalev, for instance, wrote: "We found ourselves at that time in a very complex situation, but we were convinced that before long the time would come when every honest citizen of Czechoslovakia would thank us from the bottom of his heart for our fraternal aid. Now we are reading words of thanks in a party document. We are proud of having participated in a noble international mission."

A Czechoslovak government delegation led by First Secy. Husak made a one-day visit to Moscow Jan. 25 for talks with Soviet officials. A communique issued after the meeting said that the report published Jan. 14 by the Czechoslovak Central Committee on political developments in the country since 1968 "had encountered widespread approval and support from members of the Communist Party and from the working masses."

Zagreb radio Jan. 25 broadcast a dispatch from its correspondent in Moscow on Husak's and Premier Lubomir Strougal's visit there. He said that it was assumed there that the Czechoslovak document on the lessons of the developments after the 13th Czechoslovak Party Congress in 1966 had been "one of the most important reasons for the meeting.... The impression one gains is that the document was required both by the Czechoslovak and the Soviet parties, because the Soviet party congress is close at hand, on Mar. 30 and the Czechoslovak document will be referred to at it.... Another impression is that [the visit] and the Czechoslovak document are intended ... [to remind] those who, for a few days [in mid-Dec. 1970], dramatically took power into their own hands in certain Polish towns ... that this path leads to circumstances similar to the 1968 Czechoslovak ones and hence to the same consequences."

Alois Indra, a secretary of the Czechoslovak party Central Committee and regarded as a conservative, was elected to the party's Presidium Feb. 4. Indra replaced Jan Piller, chairman of the Central Council of Trade Unions, who resigned for undisclosed reasons.

The Soviet Communist Party newspaper *Pravda* warned Feb. 19, in an article on the World Conference of Jewish Communities on Soviet Jewry to be held in Brussels, that anyone believing in Zionism would "automatically become an agent of international Zionism and hence an enemy of the Soviet people." The article, written by Vladimir Bolshakov, charged prominent associates of ex-Czechoslovak party First Secy. Alexander Dubcek with having been "Zionists" who "tried to seize leading posts in all the mass information media

of Czechoslovakia so as to carry out a frantic propaganda
campaign against the Socialist system."

Precongress Developments

The Czechoslovak Communist Party Central Committee
voted Feb. 4 to convene the 14th party congress May 25.
Gustav Husak Apr. 17 denied rumors that his party was
planning to have the authorities take a number of its opponents
into preventive internment during the forthcoming party
congress. Husak was referring to a report in the London *Times*
Apr. 6.

Western news agencies in Prague May 24 received a protest letter containing the charge that delegates in Prague for
the 14th party congress had not been democratically chosen and
that they could not represent Czechoslovak Communists or the
public at large. (Elections had been held throughout
Czechoslovakia in June and July 1968 to choose delegates for
the congress, but those elections and the clandestine congress at
which many of the elected delegates assembled in Prague Aug.
22-23, 1968 were later declared invalid by the party under
Soviet duress.)

Reuters, the independent British agency, reported that the
letter had not been signed but contained the assertion that it
had been written "in the name of ½ million Czech and Slovak
Communists who were either expelled from the party or
stricken from the party's rolls after Apr. 1969," when Husak
succeeded Dubcek as first party secretary.

Party Congress: Husak Thanks Brezhnev

The 14th Czechoslovak Communist Party Congress was
held May 25-29 in Prague. At the congress, First Secy. Husak
thanked the country's invaders and the Soviet party leader
Leonid I. Brezhnev agreed that the normalization process had
been effected. The party delegates approved changes brought
about by the Soviet-led invasion, adopted draft directives for
the 1971-5 economic development plan and elected new party
officials. (The secret party gathering at Vysocany, on the
outskirts of Prague, held a day after the 1968 invasion, had also
been known as the 14th congress.)

The congress was attended by 1,195 delegates and 1,500 guests and foreign Communist party leaders, including Janos Kadar of Hungary, Todor Zhivkov of Bulgaria, Edward Gierek of Poland, Erich Honecker of East Germany and Brezhnev.

The Spanish party, which had opposed the 1968 invasion, did not send a delegate. The London *Times* said May 26 that the British party delegate was not attending because the Czechoslovak party had refused to approve in advance the delivery of his speech terming the 1968 invasion "a grave mistake and a violation of the commonly agreed-on principles of the international Communist movement concerning relations between ... Communist countries." *Le Monde* of Paris reported May 30 that the congress had refused to hear a condemnation of the invasion by the Italian party representative. (An appeal to the visiting Communist delegations to condemn the invasion was reported May 11 to have been issued in Paris by 5 members of the pre-1968 Czechoslovak government. Those signing the document were Eduard Goldstuecker, Zdenek Hejzlar, Jiri Pelikan, Josef Pokstefl and Ota Sik.)

In his 3-hour opening remarks May 25, Husak said that "the advance of counterrevolutionary forces has been repelled [and] the Socialist system defended." The Warsaw Pact invasion had prevented "a defeat which would have had far-reaching consequences," he asserted. Husak turned toward Brezhnev and said: "In the name of the whole of our party and the overwhelming majority of our working people, we express our sincere thanks, to the Soviet party, government and people and especially to you, Comrade Brezhnev."

Husak assured the congress that the crisis before and after the invasion had been solved, and he announced that the party purges had been completed. "It was necessary to execute important cadre changes and to get rid of all those who betrayed Marxist-Leninist principles," Husak said. "The congress closes a difficult and complicated period.... The aim of cleansing the party ... has been fulfilled."

Husak set forth the current party line that thousands of Czechoslovaks had invited the invasion to avert a bloody civil war incited by the liberalizing policies of the "Prague Spring." "Our allies understood the fears of the Czechoslovak Communists and workers who appealed for help," Husak declared. "I want to thank our Socialist allies for their brotherly help which they rendered to us. This avoided a civil war and a counterrevolution.... This act of international solidarity saved the lives of thousands of people."

The leaders of the other 4 invading powers, Hungary, Poland, Bulgaria and East Germany, sat near Brezhnev as Husak spoke.

Husak divided the blame for the early crisis evenly between Antonin Novotny and Alexander Dubcek. He accused Novotny, who had held power from 1953 to 1968, of direct responsibility for the mistakes of the Stalin era, of dogmatism and of allowing right-wing and anti-Socialist forces to attain positions of power. Novotny, Husak said, had failed to "struggle against right-wing opportunism in the party and to draw the lesson of the Hungarian counterrevolution to protect the party against the methods of ideological diversion used by the imperialsts as their main weapon against the Socialist countries."

Husak repeated charges that Dubcek, currently employed in a minor manager's post in Slovakia, was weak and 2-faced, had yielded to anti-Socialist pressure and had done great and lasting harm. Husak said that Dubcek, Oldrich Cernik, Josef Smrkovsky, Frantisek Kriegel and others had "paralysed all the main elements of our Socialist political system."

With respect to the economy, Husak said that in the coming 5-year period the state would build "at least 500,000 apartments" and 700,000 cars, and that there would be a 33%-to-36% increase in industrial production, a 38% rise in construction and a 14% increase in agricultural output. Declaring that the party had learned the necessity of giving economic incentives to the workers, he promised that individual real income would rise by about 5% annually over the next 5 years.

Brezhnev, addressing the congress May 26, said Czechoslovakia had achieved a "triumph over the enemies of socialism." He added: "Nobody will ever be successful in taking Czechoslovakia out of the Socialist camp. Nobody ever will be successful in breaking our friendship and fraternity." Husak and Svoboda had shown that they were "real patriots and true internationalists." Brezhnev praised Husak both for his role in the Slovak national uprising against the Nazis in World War II and for his work as party leader since Apr. 1969. He held that the Husak leadership had done the job the Soviet leaders wanted: "You have won the battle. You have defeated the right-revisionists."

Brezhnev, renewing his earlier appeal for East-West discussions on European security, criticized Western efforts to separate the question of Berlin's future from that of a mutual reduction of forces in Europe and a European security conference. He said: "We see attempts to sabotage progress in achieving European security and we are aware of who stands behind it. In order to boycott the constructive initiatives of the Socialist countries, a new concept has been invented, according to which European problems can be solved only all together in a single complex."

(Speaking at an auto factory in Prague May 27, Brezhnev raised the prospect of political trials. He said: "Under the cover of demogogy, right-wing revisionists [in power in 1968] broke the democratic laws of Socialist Czechoslovakia" and "stripped the defenders of socialism of their basic rights as guaranteed by law." In a reference to Dubcek's policies, Brezhnev derided "2-faced politicians who spoke so much about humane socialism.")

Premier Lubomir Strougal reported May 26 on the draft directives for the economic development plan. He said the volume of investment during 1971-5 would increase 35% to 37% and that national income would rise 28% and foreign trade 38%.

Hungarian Party First Secy. Janos Kadar, also speaking May 26, diverged somewhat from the general line that "rightist-revisionists" in Czechoslovakia had created a mortal danger to the party and had raised the specter of civil war there in 1968. Kadar said: "Outside imperialists" had constituted the only real threat to Czechoslovak communism in 1968. "Even at that time [the spring and summer of 1968] we were certain that if the imperialists had no chance to interfere from the outside, the Communists, the working class, and the followers of socialism in Czechoslovakia would succeed in making order in their own ranks."

At the final session of the congress May 29, the delegates adopted 3 changes in the party's statutes: congresses were to be convened every 5 years instead of every 4, a 2-year period of candidate membership was restored prior to admission into the

party, and the party leader's title was changed from first
secretary to general secretary.

Gustav Husak was reelected and named general secretary
May 29, and a Central Committee of 115 members was chosen,
replacing a body of 132 members. Missing from the new
Central Committee were Frantisek Barbirek and Jan Piller,
conservatives believed to have supported the Dubcek government immediately following the 1968 invasion. The committee
elected the following 11-member Presidium: Husak, Pres.
Svoboda, Vasil Bilak, Peter Colotka, Karel Hoffmann
(replacing Evzan Erban), Alois Indra, Antonin Kapek, Josef
Kempny, Josef Korcak, Jozef Lenart and Lubomir Strougal.

Prague newspapers published the final resolution of the
14th congress May 31. The document said: "The grave crisis in
the party and society has been overcome" but "right-wing
opportunism and revisionism" were still the "main danger we
must fight against"; "the completion of the defeat of the
rightists in the ideological sphere is, at the present stage, an
especially important task." The resolution pledged continued
opposition to "all expressions of *petit burgeois* thinking, the
survival of religious thinking, nationalism, anti-Sovietism and
all forms of bourgeois ideology."

The Western press reported June 3 that Antonin Novotny
had been readmitted to party membership as a result of a compromise reached at the congress. The reports said that Novotny
was being restored to membership in return for agreement on
the part of conservative forces not to demand strict punishment
for Alexander Dubcek.

Slovak Party Congress

The Slovak Communist Party held a 3-day congress in
Bratislava May 13-15. At the conclusion of the congress, the
Central Committee elected these 11 persons to its presidium:
Ladislav Abraham, Peter Colotka, Herbert Durkovic, Jan
Tanik, Ondrej Klokoc, Jozef Lenart, Elena Litvajova, Ludovit
Pezlar, Gejza Slapka, Vaclav Vacok and Miroslav Valek. The
names of Litvajova and Slapka were new. In reporting the
election May 15, the Yugoslav news agency Tanyug said that
all the old presidium members had been reelected "except a
prominent Slovak writer and revolutionary, Ladislav

Novomesky, who [had] suffered a heart attack a few months ago." The list of presidium members did not include Gustav Husak and Vasil Bilak, Slovaks prominent in the Czechoslovak party.

The congress reelected Jozef Lenart as first secretary and ordered Egyd Pepich ousted as Slovak interior minister. Pepich had been in power when Alexander Dubcek was party leader in Slovakia.

Gustav Husak had told the delegates May 14 to beware of Western attempts to "create panic" with stories of unrest in Czechoslovakia. Such forces, he said, had created "a great sensation around" Karel Gott, a pop singer on tour in West Germany, who had requested an extension of his visa despite the "glory" and "money" given him in Czechoslovakia.

Interparty Relations

The 8th East German Socialist Unity (Communist) Party congress, held June 15-19 in East Berlin, was attended by 94 delegations from 83 countries. The foreign Communist party leaders Leonid I. Brezhnev of the USSR, Edward Gierek of Poland, Gustav Husak of Czechoslovakia, Janos Kadar of Hungary, and Todor Zhivkov of Bulgaria were among those present.

In deference to the Soviet doctrine of limited sovereignty, the final resolution of the congress said that East Germany would incorporate itself "more and more firmly in the community of Socialist states through an all-round deepening of the alliance with the Soviet Union and the other fraternal states." The resolution backed the 1968 invasion of Czechoslovakia and stated that East Germany would "see to it that socialism in Europe is not affected either by military pressure or by hidden counterrevolution."

The Soviet view of proletarian internationalism had already been supported by Husak Apr. 1 at the 24th Soviet Party Congress in Moscow. There the Czechoslovak party leader first thanked the Soviet Union for "responding to the appeal for help" which led to the occupation of his country by Warsaw Pact forces in 1968. (Husak himself had not signéd such an appeal.) Husak said that if "opportunist and revisionist forces" had succeeded in Czechoslovakia, it "would have

threatened the positions of socialism in Europe and ... changed
the results of the 2d World War."

Trend Toward Centralization

In 1971 there was a swing in Czechoslovakia back toward
central control—in politics as well as in economics. The British
weekly *Economist* reported Jan. 9 that the Czechoslovak
government had announced further constitutional changes
restoring control over economic planning and agriculture to
Prague and abolishing separate citizenship for the 2 halves of
the country. The federal government also received the power to
overrule the 2 national governments "if it sees fit."

Following legislation to strengthen the central government, Pres. Ludvik Svoboda had appointed 8 new federal officials Jan. 3. Named federal deputy premiers were Jindrich
Zahradnik, ex-chairman of the federal industrial board, and
Jan Gregor, ex-Slovak industry minister. Stefan Sutka was
relieved of the post of Slovak transport, post and telecommunications minister to become federal transport minister;
Josef Simon, ex-Czech state industry minister, became federal
minister of metallurgy and engineering. Jaromir Matusek was
named federal minister of fuel and power, and Drahomir
Kolder became chairman of the federal control committee.
Neither Matusek nor Kolder had previous government
experience. Vaclav Hula, a federal deputy premier, was
appointed to head the state planning committee with Karol
Martinka, a minister without portfolio, as his deputy.

Jaroslav Knizka, the federal transport minister, was
recalled from his post and named permanent representative at
UN agencies in Geneva. Jan Pauly, minister without portfolio,
was recalled at his own request.

2 Czech state ministries were abolished and Antonin
Cervinka, Czech deputy premier, was recalled from his post.
Stefan Sadovsky, former Slovak deputy premier, was reported
Jan. 3 to have been dismissed in Dec. 1970.

Wage/Price Freeze Averts Crisis

Czechoslovakia had averted an economic crisis in 1970 by
imposing an absolute freeze on wages and on wholesale and

retail prices, the country's financial authorities reported in 1971. Not everyone cooperated in this effort, however. Bratislava radio reported Mar. 1 that the Czech Price Office had uncovered wholesale pricing irregularities in 70 of the 100 enterprises that it had investigated in Bohemia. According to the radio, the errant firms had used incorrect methods in fixing the prices of new products.

Price reductions on some home appliances and synthetic materials were announced by the government Apr. 29. CTK explained that the reductions, in some cases as high as 30%, had been made possible by "a favorable report on the development of the national economy and the domestic market situation."

Other Developments

A number of unrelated events on the federal level were also reported:

Gen. Alexander Mucha, 53, deputy minister of defense, was killed in an auto accident Jan. 31 when the car in which he was riding was hit by a Prague streetcar.

The official news agency CTK reported May 24 that Karel Hoffmann had been relieved as Czechoslovak minister of telecommunications in view of his election as chairman of the Central Council of the Czechoslovak Revolutionary Trade Union Movement. The new federal minister of telecommunications was Vlastimil Chalupa.

The London *Times* reported July 6 that the Czechoslovak Federal Assembly had passed a law providing for general elections. The law established procedures for elections to both houses of the Federal Assembly and to the Czech and Slovak National Councils, the state legislatures. It also provided for general elections every 5 years, instead of every 4, to parallel the timing of Communist Party congresses. (The *Times* said that elections had been due in 1970 but that the Federal Assembly had extended its term of office for another year.) Commenting on the measure July 10, the Czechoslovak news agency CTK declared that the 7-year delay since the last elections had been caused by those in power before the Soviet invasion of 1968.

The Czech National Council Feb. 11 appointed Jaroslav Prokopec as Czech Republic minister of health, replacing Vladislav Vlcek. The council also named Vaclav Svoboda as minister of agriculture and Antonin Pospisil as minister without portfolio.

Jaromir Hrbek, minister of education in the Czech regional government, was relieved of his functions July 8 by the Czech National Council "at his own request," it was reported by CTK. Hrbek was replaced by his deputy minister, Josef Havlin.

The Czechoslovak National Front, representing all legal political organizations in the country, elected as its chairman Jan. 27 Czechoslovak party First Secy. Gustav Husak, bypassing former chairman Evzen Erban, member of the party's Presidium and one of Husak's supporters. In announcing Husak's election, the official Czechoslovak news agency CTK did not give reasons for the change in leadership. Tomas Travnicek was elected acting deputy chairman, and Miloslav Vacik was chosen central secretary.

In his speech to the conference earlier Jan. 27, Husak denied rumors "spread by our enemies" of a purge against the intelligentsia. He distinguished between the technical intelligentsia, of which "the majority" was on "the side of the working class," and the humanist intelligentsia, where party policy was "finding growing support," although many in this group had "wavered politically 3 years ago." (The National Front's presidium had expelled the Union of Czech Scientists Jan. 26 on the grounds that it represented only 10% of the scientists in Bohemia and Moravia, according to a *Le Monde* report. The union was also said to have pursued policies contrary to the interests of socialism.)

Jan Piller, dismissed in February from the federal party Central Committee Presidium, was relieved Mar. 10 as chairman of the Central Trade Union Council, one of the most influential groupings in the Czechoslovak National Front. Piller's duties were assumed by Karel Hoffmann, hitherto the federal minister of telecommunications.

Radio Prague announced Jan. 5 that authorities planned to unveil a 13-foot-high "memorial to the Soviet liberators"— bearing the inscription "1945 and 1968"—in the South Bohemian community of Suchdol-nad-Luznici near the Austrian border.

The East Slovak regional court in Kosice May 7 handed down sentences of 4½ to 9½ years' imprisonment for 6 men convicted of shaving the hair off a woman as a Soviet sympathizer Aug. 23, 1968. The victim was identified in court as a Soviet citizen and the men were characterized as unemployed ex-convicts.

Prague Repudiates Shakedown

The Czechoslovak leadership, disclaiming any knowledge of the attempt begun late in 1970 to extort money from exiles for so-called legal defense purposes, reported in mid-February that the practice had been stopped. Events leading to this announcement left many observers unconvinced of the regime's ignorance.

Zdenek Hrazdira, chairman of the Czech Lawyers Association, said Jan. 7 that demands for money had been made of Czechoslovak emigrants in the West only to pay lawyers appointed to defend the emigrants on charges of leaving the country illegally. (Conviction carried the penalties of confiscation of property and from 6 months' to 5 years' imprisonment if the accused later returned to Czechoslovakia.) Hrazdira declared that lawyers in Czechoslovakia were not subsidized by the state and that the law required every accused to be defended. "Lawyers throughout the world expect to be paid," he added.

Party First Secy. Gustav Husak declared in a speech Feb. 16 that although neither he nor Premier Lubomir Strougal had known about the practice at first, "the whole matter has been stopped." Husak commented that the practice "was not very reasonable because, if somebody runs to the West, one would not think he would pay for legal representation."

Trade & Diplomacy

Czechoslovakia and Bulgaria concluded a 1971-5 trade agreement in Sofia Jan. 10. The agreement, signed for Czechoslovakia by Foreign Trade Min. Andrej Barcak and for Bulgaria by Foreign Trade Min. Luchezar Avramov, envisioned that the volume of trade between the 2 states would double compared with the previous 5-year period.

Bolivia Apr. 2 signed a contract with the Czechoslovak firm Skoda for the installation of an antimony foundry at Vinto.

During a trip to eastern Europe, Chilean Foreign Min. Clodomiro Almeyda visited Czechoslovakia, where he and Czechoslovak Foreign Trade Min. Barcak June 8 signed a protocol on economic and technical cooperation between the 2 countries.

Following preliminary talks on normalization held by West German and Czechoslovak officials in 1970, discussions at a higher level were begun Mar. 31 and Apr. 1 and continued May 13-14 in Prague. The talks, which were scheduled to continue, were conducted for Czechoslovakia by Deputy Foreign Min. Milan Klusak and for West Germany by Paul Frank, a state secretary in the Foreign Ministry. The 2 May 19 signed a trade protocol completing a commercial accord reached in Dec. 1970.

According to the British weekly *Economist* of Apr. 3, the principal roadblock to eventual diplomatic rapprochement lay in the validity of the famous Munich *Diktat* of Sept. 1938, which the Czechoslovaks soon afterwards denounced as invalid from the very outset, together with all its consequences. The Czechoslovaks' position since early in World War II was to ignore the agreement as something forced on them and that they had never ratified. The *Economist* pointed out, however, that other governments (France, Great Britain, Italy and Germany) did sign the agreement.

"The German position is that, although the Munich Agreement was admittedly unjust, it cannot merely be wiped from the slates of international law," the magazine's East European correspondent wrote. The German "view is that it was abrogated in Mar. 1939, when Hitler's troops went on to occupy Bohemia and Moravia" besides the Sudetenland of northern and western Bohemia and and Czechoslovak Silesia. "The Germans' argument is that the nationality act passed by the Nazi government in Nov. 1938, which turned the Sudetens into German citizens (and which is recognized under the present German constitution), could never have had any legal validity if the Munich agreement was invalid from the start. This would open up the possibility of legal action by the present

Czech[oslovak] government against Sudeten Germans for acts committed during the war," the article said.

Tsung Kowen, Communist China's new ambassador to Czechoslovakia, presented his credentials to Pres. Ludvik Svoboda in Prague June 2. The ambassadorial position had been officially vacant since June 1969, but Tsung's predecessor, Chung Shi-tung, was believed to have left his post a few years earlier, during the Cultural Revolution.

Expulsions & Jailings

The press department of the Czechoslovak Foreign Ministry Jan. 13 withdrew the accreditation of Allan Levy, a freelance U.S. journalist, for allegedly misusing his stay for anti-Czechoslovak activity and breaking "laws and regulations." Levy was asked to leave the country within 48 hours and did so. Levy's specific offense was that he allegedly wrote lies about Czechoslovakia in an unpublished manuscript.

Canadian businessman Erich Knapp was expelled Jan. 31 on charges of possessing "distorted and hostile" political information about the country.

Velimir Budimir, a Prague correspondent for the Yugoslav news agency Tanyug, was expelled from Czechoslovakia Feb. 2. Budimir was accused of nonobjective reporting and of allowing his articles to be used in the Western press.

Frederick H. Eidlin, a U.S. citizen sentenced in Dec. 1970 to 4 years in prison for subversion, was released by the Czechoslovak government Feb. 24 and expelled from the country.

George Ipser, a Czechoslovak-born U.S. citizen from Chicago, was sentenced near Prague Apr. 6 to 2 years' imprisonment for criticizing Pres. Svoboda and calling the country a Soviet colony. A U.S. embassy spokesman said Ipser had apparently made the offending remarks in a private home.

Authorities expelled 7 persons in early May, CTK reported May 11. The first, a West German named Helmuth Groewald, was charged with having acted as a commercial agent for several foreign firms—"contrary to Czechoslovak regulations"—and deported May 10. The Czechoslovak Interior Ministry announced May 11 that 2 West German and 4 American students had been expelled from the country for pulling down flags in Prague during the Czechoslovak liberation anniversary celebrations earlier in May.

Espionage Abroad

Nicholas Anthony Prager, 42, an electrical engineer and former sergeant in the Royal Air Force (RAF), was found guilty June 23 by a jury in Leeds, England on 2 charges of spying for Czechoslovakia. He was sentenced to 12 years' imprisonment on each charge but was to serve the terms concurrently.

Prager was convicted of making a sketch of secret RAF equipment—a radar jamming device—and of passing it, along with photos and documents, to Czechoslovak intelligence in 1961. He had pleaded innocent. During the trial, which began June 14, it was disclosed that Prager's Czech-born wife—who had disappeared June 12—had had affairs with a Czechoslovak intelligence officer and an RAF technician.

The defendant had last worked as a computer expert for a British firm that was building a steel plant in Czechoslovakia.

DISSENT & REPRESSION

Visits to Palach's Grave Increase

Prague residents visited the grave of Jan Palach Jan. 16, the 2d anniversary of Palach's suicidal gesture in protest against the Soviet invasion of Czechoslovakia.

The *N. Y. Times'* Prague correspondent reported, in a story that appeared Aug. 3, that the grave at Olsany Cemetery had become "the last token of resistance" to the Soviet occupation and that visits to it had grown frequent (the correspondent counted 7 within 20 minutes "on a recent weekday afternoon"). Most of the visitors were Czechoslovaks, he said, but there was an occasional tourist. "More than 200 [flower] pots are needed to hold the daily offerings," he wrote.

Trials & Sentences

Vladimir Skutina, former TV commentator and a prominent member of the reform movement of 1968, was sentenced Feb. 18 to 2 years in prison on charges of having written 2 unpublished pamphlets slandering Czechoslovakia and the USSR. (Skutina, believed to have been held in jail since his arrest in Aug. 1970, was reported Feb. 10 to have been expelled from the Czech Union of Journalists.) Skutina received an additional 26-month term July 1 from a court at Hradec Kralove in East Bohemia. According to *Le Monde* July 3, Skutina was tried a 2d time for his participation in public discussions at factories in the region in 1968-9 and for publishing articles in the foreign press.

Alois Polednak, former head of the Czechoslovak film industry, was sentenced July 9 in the Prague city court along with 5 other persons, including foreign nationals, to 2 years in jail for "undermining the republic" and "endangering official secrets" between 1968 and the time of his arrest in 1970. Foreign journalists and diplomats were barred from the trial. Sentenced with Polednak were Jaroslav Sedivy, historian and ex-member of the Institute of International Politics &

Economics in Prague (18 months), and Edita Cerenska, ex-secretary of the Federal Assembly (one year). 3 other persons were given long terms for espionage as well as for undermining the republic. These were: Vaclav Cerenska, Edita's husband and a retired army colonel (7 years); Milada Kubiasova, an interpreter at the French embassy (10 years); and Hubert Stein, an interpreter at the Dutch embassy (12 years). The proceedings of the trial were not published. (It had been reported Jan. 26 that Sedivy, also charged with subversion and maintaining illegal contacts with the West, had been released from prison without a trial.)

A group of 15 Czechoslovak intellectuals charged with "subverting the republic" were sentenced in Prague Mar. 19 to prison terms ranging from 12 months to 2½ years. Peter Uhl, the principal defendant, was sentenced to 4 years' imprisonment. 2 other defendants were given suspended sentences and one was acquitted. The 19 accused—one of them a girl—had been charged with membership in an organization called the Revolutionary Socialist Party and with preparing and distributing leaflets based on the writings of Leon Trotsky and Milovan Djilas, the former Yugoslav vice president. The group was also said to have opposed "consolidation of the political and economic conditions" in Czechoslovakia by joining demonstrations on the first anniversary of the Soviet invasion.

According to the Mar. 13 issue of the British weekly *Economist,* "when the tribunal told the first defendant, Jan Frolik, that he was being tried for his acts and not for his opinions, he ... countered: 'Our acts are dictated by our opinions and our opinions are translated into acts. It is an entirety and you cannot separate one from the other.'"

Courtroom proceedings had been interrupted Mar. 1-5 while the judges examined a motion from Uhl that they disqualify themselves if they had ever sentenced political prisoners unjustly and while authorities acted on a request by one of the defendants, a West German, for a copy of the indictment in her own language. Western newsmen were barred from the trial, and several foreign reporters in the court Mar. 19 were detained briefly by security police.

The sentencing judge confirmed Mar. 23 that Frantisek Stilip, the prosecuting attorney, had urged stricter penalties for at least 13 of the defendants. The Communist party newspaper *Rude pravo* said Mar. 23 that the trial was not political but (as the Czech Justice Ministry had said Mar. 9) dealt with offenses of a criminal nature and that the government was entitled to prosecute "an illegal anti-state organization grouped into secret conspiratorial cells." (A document reported by *Le Monde* of Paris Mar. 17 and signed by a number of French intellectuals, including Simone de Beauvoir, Marguerite Duras and Jean-Paul Sartre, declared that the accused had been working for "the arrival of an authentic socialism.")

Vaclav Prchlik, formerly a lieutenant general and head of the party Central Committee's military department, was sentenced to 3 years in prison Mar. 26 for having criticized, at a press conference, Soviet domination of the Warsaw Treaty Organization in July 1968. Prchlik had been accused of "frustrating and jeopardizing the activity of state agencies." Following his ouster from the Communist Party and the Central Committee in 1969, Prchlik had been employed in Prague as a laborer. The Czechoslovak Supreme Court June 2 reduced Prchlik's sentence to 22 months. The court ruled that an intent to harm in Prchlik's remarks had not been proved.

Journalists Disciplined

CTK reported Feb. 9 that the Secretariat of the Union of Czech Journalists had expelled from the union additional members involved in the developments of 1968. Those ousted included Jiri Dinstbier, Vera Stovickova, Jiri Hanak, Ludvik Vaculik, Vladimir Skutina, Stanislav Hastaba, Zdenek Fort and a group of former journalists whose expulsion was proposed by the Ostrava regional committee of the Union of Czech Journalists.

The Czech Journalists' Union announced Feb. 19 that it would blacklist an estimated 70 of its 170 free-lance members.

Bohemian Police Round Up Hundreds

The Czechoslovak news agency CTK said May 3 that police during the preceding few days had detained 522 persons for questioning and had arrested 91 others in the central Bohemian region, which included Prague. 79 of those arrested were charged with illegally taking "national property"— building materials in 35 of the instances. CTK said that police in the Ustinad-Labem area of North Bohemia in the previous 15 days had searched nearly 2,500 restaurants and 2,000 flats and other buildings, had found 129 "wanted persons" there and had detected 608 crimes and more than 3,500 minor offenses. According to the news agency, "the action" in the Prague area, "received positively by the whole population of the Central Bohemian Region, will be repeated."

INDEX

CZECHOSLOVAKIA: Crisis in World Communism

Contents:

- Antonin Novotny's Pro-Soviet Regime Under Pressure from Liberal Forces
- Alexander Dubcek Replaces Novotny as Communist Party Leader, and Ludvik Svoboda Succeeds Him as President of Czechoslovakia
- Dubcek Regime Starts Program of Liberalized Communism
- Czechoslovak Leaders Resist Demands of Warsaw Pact Allies that Democratization Be Reversed
- Czechoslovak Leaders Confront Leaders of USSR and 4 Other Warsaw Pact Allies in Cierna and Bratislava
- The 'Warsaw 5' Reportedly Consent to Continuation of Democratization in Czechoslovakia
- Rumania and Yugoslavia Support Czechoslovak Liberalization
- Led by USSR, 5 Warsaw Pact Nations Invade Czechoslovakia to End Experiment with Liberalized Communism
- USSR Announces that It Acted on Request of Czechoslovak Leaders, Who Sought Aid Against 'Counterrevolution'
- Czechoslovak Leaders Seized and Flown to Moscow, Where They Sign, Under Pressure, a Pact Calling for Swift 'Normalization'
- Invading Powers Subjected to Worldwide Criticism
- Civil Resistance to Invasion Fails
- USSR Asserts that World Socialism Has Right to Intervene if Socialism Is in Danger in Any Socialist Country
- Democratization Program Abandoned Under Soviet Pressure
- Dubcek and Supporters Replaced by Pro-Soviet Officials

FACTS ON FILE, 119 W. 57th St., NEW YORK, N.Y. 10019

INTERIM HISTORY

The Bridge Between Today's News and Tomorrow's History

DATE DUE